THE EVERYMAN
LIBRARY

*The Everyman Library was founded by J. M. Dent
in 1906. He chose the name Everyman because he wanted
to make available the best books ever written in every
field to the greatest number of people at the cheapest possible
price. He began with Boswell's 'Life of Johnson';
his one-thousandth title was Aristotle's 'Metaphysics',
by which time sales exceeded forty million.*

*Today Everyman paperbacks remain true to
J. M. Dent's aims and high standards, with a wide range
of titles at affordable prices in editions which address
the needs of today's readers. Each new text is reset to give
a clear, elegant page and to incorporate the latest thinking
and scholarship. Each book carries the pilgrim logo,
the character in 'Everyman', a medieval morality play,
a proud link between Everyman
past and present.*

Juan Ruiz

THE BOOK OF
GOOD LOVE

Translated by
ELIZABETH DRAYSON MACDONALD
New Hall, University of Cambridge

Consultant Editor for this volume
MELVEENA MCKENDRICK
University of Cambridge

EVERYMAN
J. M. DENT · LONDON
CHARLES E. TUTTLE
VERMONT

J. M. Dent
Orion Publishing Group
Orion House, 5 Upper St Martin's Lane,
London WC2H 9EA
and
Charles E. Tuttle Co. Inc.
28 South Main Street
Rutland, Vermont 05701, USA

Typeset in Sabon by SetSystems Limited, Saffron Walden
Printed in Great Britain by
The Guernsey Press Co. Ltd, Guernsey, C.I.

British Library Cataloguing-in-Publication Data
is available upon request.

ISBN 0 460 87762 3

This translation is dedicated
to the memory of

COLIN SMITH

dear friend and guide
who first opened my eyes to the medieval world

CONTENTS

NOTE ON THE AUTHOR AND TRANSLATOR

The identity of the author of the *Book of Good Love* is a medieval mystery yet to be solved. What we know of him is still only supposition, the essence of which can be deduced from the text itself. We learn from the poem that its author was called Juan Ruiz, and that he was the Archpriest of Hita, a town in the plateau of Castile, though he may have come originally from Alcalá de Henares. He lived in the late thirteenth and first half of the fourteenth centuries, and was probably dead by 1351, or was certainly no longer the Archpriest of Hita, since documentary records show that this office belonged to one Pedro Fernández at that time. Various attempts have been made to identify Juan Ruiz, a task made more difficult because the name itself was common, an equivalent perhaps to John Brown. No fewer than sixteen Castilian clergy named Juan Ruiz have been found in the papal register for the years 1305–42. In 1972 Professor Emilio Sáez and his colleague José Trenchs* found references in the Vatican archives to a man called Juan Ruiz de Cisneros, the illegitimate son of a nobleman from Palencia, born in 1295 or 1296, who had an ecclesiastical career and died in 1351 or 1352. The dates fitted, but as in the case of other Juan Ruizs of that time, there was nothing to indicate that he was the Archpriest of Hita, nor that he wrote the *Book of Good Love*. The most exciting recent discovery, though ultimately inconclusive, was made by Francisco J. Hernández in 1984. In a cartulary or register-book from Toledo cathedral appears a ruling delivered by an ecclesiastical court, dated about 1330. The first of the eight witnesses listed at the end of the document is 'the venerable Juan Ruiz, Archpriest of Hita'. Although so far no independent written record of his authorship of the *Book of Good Love* exists, the

---

* Sáez, Emilio, y José Trenchs, 'Juan Ruiz de Cisneros (1295/1296–1351/1352), autor del *Buen Amor*' in *Actas del I Congreso Internacional sobre el Arcipreste de Hita*, ed. Manuel Criado de Val (Barcelona, 1973), pages 365–8.

presence of both name and title in a historical document must strongly suggest that what the book tells us about its author's name and profession is true.

ELIZABETH DRAYSON MACDONALD is a Fellow of New Hall and Affiliated Lecturer and Supervisor in the Department of Spanish and Portuguese at the University of Cambridge as well as a freelance translator.

CHRONOLOGY OF JUAN RUIZ'S LIFE

Year   *Age*   *Life*

1295/6   Birth of Juan Ruiz de Cisneros

CHRONOLOGY OF HIS TIMES

Year	Historical Events	Literary Context
1285	Montpellier University founded, as well as Gloucester Hall, Oxford	
1292	Marco Polo visits Indonesia as ambassador for the Mongols	
1295	Ferdinand IV becomes king of Castile	
1296	Giotto, *Life of St Francis* begun	
1297	Edward I of England confirms the Magna Carta	
1298	Barcelona Cathedral begun	
1300	Foundation of the University of Lérida	
1303	León Cathedral completed; Rome University founded	
1304		Birth of Francesco Petrarca (Petrarch)
1306	Robert the Bruce crowned King of Scotland	
1312	Alfonso IX accedes to the Castilian throne	Dante, *Inferno*
1313		Birth of Giovanni Boccaccio, poet and writer
1320		Birth of John Wycliffe, ecclesiastical reformer and translator of the Bible

Year   Age   Life

1330   34/35   Gayoso manuscript gives this date for the completion of
                 the *Book of Good Love*. The 'venerable Juan Ruiz,
                 Archpriest of Hita' is named as one of eight witnesses in a
                 church document of this year

1343   47/48   Salamanca manuscript gives this as the completion date
                 for the *Book of Good Love*, and states that the Archpriest
                 wrote it while in prison at the order of Cardinal Albornoz

Year	Historical Events	Literary Context
1325	Founding of Tenochtitlán city, Mexico	
1327	Death of Meister Eckhart, philosopher	
c. 1327	Birth of the Flemish artist Hubert van Eyck	
c. 1330		Birth of William Langland, English poet
1333	Gibraltar taken by the Arabs	
1337	Beginning of the Hundred Years War; Gil de Albornoz becomes Archbishop of Toledo	
1340	Alfonso IX of Castile defeats the Muslims at the Battle of Salado	
c. 1340		Birth of Geoffrey Chaucer
1342	Letters from Pope Boniface XII to the Archbishops of Seville, Compostela and Toledo, ordering them to admonish clergy who did not accept celibacy; Synod of Toledo, and distribution of letters on the subject of priests' celibacy to archpresbyterships	
1343	Peter IV of Aragon annexes the Balearic Islands	
1346	Founding of Valladolid University	
1348	The Black Death reaches Spain	Boccaccio starts Il Decamerone (The Decameron)

Year   Age   Life

1351   55/56   Pedro Fernández was Archpriest of Hita
1351/2   55/57   Death of Juan Ruiz de Cisneros

Year	Historical Events	Literary Context
1350	Alfonso IX dies of the Plague; accession of Peter the Cruel, followed by the start of Trastamaran opposition and propaganda; the English defeat the Spanish fleet off Winchelsea; Gil de Albornoz ceases to be Archbishop of Toledo	

INTRODUCTION

The Archpriest's Life and Work

As the brief preceding biography of the Archpriest of Hita reveals, virtually nothing concrete is known about the writer's life as an individual, nor do we know whether he wrote any other works. We can surmise that he was born at the end of the thirteenth century and probably died around 1351 or 1352. There is convincing evidence of his presence in Toledo as Archpriest in the year 1330, a date of significance because it appears in one of the three extant manuscripts of the *Book of Good Love*. None of the manuscripts is complete, though each contains a large proportion of the text. They are known as S (Salamanca), G (Gayoso) and T (Toledo), and it is the G manuscript which tells us that the work was finished in 1330. The S manuscript bears the date of 1343 and contains sections which appear not to have been included in the G and T versions, supporting the critical view that the Archpriest extended and revised the original 1330 version. The S text has additional interest in terms of the Archpriest's life, as the colophon states that the book was written while its author was imprisoned at the order of Cardinal Gil de Albornoz, Archbishop of Toledo from 1337 to 1351. At the start and end of his poem, Juan Ruiz refers to his suffering in prison, which some have interpreted as a metaphorical prison of the flesh. However, his assertion in stanza 1683 that his suffering is undeserved does not square with the characteristic Catholic idea of suffering as a just desert for sin. If the Archpriest was indeed imprisoned, the real reasons for it are as yet shrouded in mystery, even though hypothetical explanations have been given. One suggestion is that the content of his book was too immoral and rebellious to be tolerated. Another possibility could be that his potential support and sympathy for clerical concubinage was viewed unfavourably by Cardinal Gil, who issued the letters denouncing that common practice.

While we lack the defining detail of Juan Ruiz's life, we can form an idea of the kind of job he had and of the area covered by his archpresbytership. In the Christian Church, 'archpriest' was originally the title given to the chief of priests in a diocese, and the office appears as early as the fourth century as that of the priest presiding over the presbyters of the diocese and assisting the bishop in matters of public worship. By the Middle Ages the office of archpriest merged with that of rural dean and was strictly subordinate to the jurisdiction of the archdeacon. It was the highest rank of secular priest and the office-holder would have had a perpetual living with cure of souls or spiritual charge of parishioners, as well as jurisdiction over them, although not over any individual church. To exercise this jurisdiction he would need to know something of canon law and should in theory have been a university graduate, though the latter was not always the case.

In the fourteenth century Hita was a rural archpriest's diocese, dependent on Guadalajara, with responsibility for twenty-one dioceses. The archpriest would have had to visit all his parishes and attend an annual synod meeting held in Toledo on the second Sunday after Easter. He would also have had to publish all the synodial constitutions of his archbishop. Hita today is a desolate ghost of what it once must have been, with just a few dilapidated houses and a boarded-up church overlooking a vast empty plain. At the time when Juan Ruiz was writing, it was an important town in a strategically important area, thronged with people, many of whom were Jews and Mozarabs, the name given to Spanish Christians who had adopted Muslim clothes and spoke Arabic. There were important monasteries close by (Sopetrán, Bonaval, Talamanca) and castles (Hita itself, Atienza, Beleña de Sorbe). It would have been prestigious to hold the position of archpriest in such a town.

We can imagine Juan Ruiz in what must have been quite extensive travel, probably on foot, gathering useful material for his book from the many people with whom he must have had contact. His task was essentially a secular one and he was a highly educated man of the world, clearly widely read, as can be deduced from his parody of a number of literary texts and genres. There is nothing to suggest that he wrote any significant work other than the *Book of Good Love*, though in the text he mentions certain songs and poems which he composed which have either been lost, or were never included in the corpus of the work. He had no need to write more. As he tells his listeners and readers, he was one in a thousand poets, whose range and depth of expression exceeds in one work what is achieved by some writers in many. His book must have been extremely popular and widely read in the first hundred years after it was written, because fragments of a fourteenth-century Portuguese translation still exist, as well as various fragments of what were probably minstrels' copies. It is quite possible that Chaucer knew the work and was influenced by it, while within Spain the Archpriest of Talavera quotes from it in his fifteenth-century work *El Corbacho*, the Marquis of Santillana refers to it and lines from it also appear in a sixteenth-century text.

The question of who the audience or readership of the *Book of Good Love* might have been is an interesting one. Though it seems highly likely that parts of the book were circulated orally by minstrels, much of the text is clearly aimed at an educated audience and sometimes at a specifically clerical one. It may have been read by individuals or, more feasibly, read aloud to small groups of people. It could have had musical accompaniment to the songs, or musical interludes, and must have been performed in public, allowing rich and varied interpretations of the text through gesture and facial expression. In the same way that the book offers multiple interpretations of its meaning, it offers multiple possibilities of dissemination, at varying levels.

Relationship to Literary Groups and Movements

The placing of a work of literature within a specific literary group or movement can be of value in assessing its degree of conformity to contemporary norms, or conversely in establishing its originality or uniqueness within a particular literary framework. Literary movements and groups were perhaps not so intensely defined in the Middle Ages as they are in the twentieth century, partly because they were not self-conscious and partly because the whole process of diffusion was slower and generally affected European literature as a whole rather than the literature of a single country.

Spain was of special interest in this respect because it felt the influence of literary developments from north of the Pyrenees, while simultaneously benefiting from the richness of Moorish and Jewish artistic and literary cultures. Even a superficial reading of the *Book of Good Love* in this light shows evidence of a strong Christian Catholic didacticism mingled with the savour of Moorish Spain as expressed in specific vocabulary or in the author's familiarity with Moorish music and instruments. However, with characteristic intractability, the *Book of Good Love* has resisted categorization within any individual or typical literary movement, group or genre. It is entirely unique in European literature and this remarkable singularity is one of its greatest sources of fascination.

For some scholars the anthological nature of the *Book of Good Love* pointed to a model from Hispano-Arabic literature and it has even been seen as a supreme example of *mudéjar* art. The Spanish critic Américo Castro felt that the complexity and flexibility of its structure, its metrical diversity, the erotic autobiography and the movement between fiction and reality all derive from Hispano-Arabic models. He identified particular similarities with *The Dove's Neck-Ring* by Ibn Hazm (994–1064), yet there is no reason to believe that the Archpriest knew the work, or that he could read Classical Arabic, although he uses some Vulgar Arabic in his text.

The Hispanist María Rosa Lida de Malkiel identified a Hebrew source in the Hispano-Hebraic *maqamat* and a specific text called the *Book of Delights* by Yosef ben Meir ibn Sabarra (born *c.* 1140), but the Archpriest seems even less likely to have known Hebrew than Arabic. It is possibly more logical to search for European models in a work whose individual segments draw strongly upon Western Latin sources. There are a number of Latin works which use an apparently autobiographical narrative to present love intrigue, the most well-known being Ovid's *Pamphilus de amore*, which Juan Ruiz parodies in the adventure with Endrina. The most likely candidate used as a model has been identified as an elegiac comedy, *De vetula*, attributed to Richard de Fournival. It was widely known in medieval Europe and coincides with the *Book of Good Love* in its erotic autobiography, the use of a prose prologue and doctrinal excurses. However, there are significant differences. In the case of *De vetula* the autobiography is not that of the author but pretends to be that of Ovid, nor does the Latin text contain songs, stories and other tales.

These possible models, and others such as Machaut's *Voir-Dit*, fail to convince. Consistent with his very personal reworking of known sources, to be discussed in more detail in relation to form and content, it seems highly likely that the Archpriest selected the best from the literary models known to him and interpreted them in a completely new way.

Historical and Literary Background

At the beginning of the 1300s Spain was about to embark upon its sixth century of coexistence with an alien religion and culture in the form of Islam. In 711 Muslims from North Africa overran most of the Hispanic peninsula and it was not until 1492, when the Christians captured Muslim Granada after centuries of frontier warfare, that their reconquest of Spain reached its conclusion. The intermingling of Christian, Moorish and Jewish cultures and lifestyles over a period of seven hundred years bequeathed upon Spain a uniqueness within Europe and left a cultural and political heritage whose influence is still apparent today.

Although the Christian reconquest did not end until 1492, most of its objectives had been achieved by the late thirteenth century. The *Book of Good Love* was written a little later, in the reign of Alfonso XI (1312–50). At this time Castile was enjoying a vast expansion of its maritime trade and had also begun to exploit the Flanders wool market. Under Alfonso's rule Castile began an economic recovery which was nipped in the bud by the spread of the Black Death to Spain in 1348 and by civil war. Alfonso was only one year old when he inherited the throne of Castile and until he came of age his reign was blighted by the struggles of the nobility to gain power for themselves. Eventually the king managed to reassert the central authority of the monarchy in a way pleasing to both the Church and the common people. He continued the task of reconquest by winning the Battle of Salado in 1340, after which invasion from the south was never a problem again. Alfonso XI died of the plague during a siege on Gibraltar in 1350. The latter part of his reign had inspired vigour and confidence, which sadly gave way to the fear and misery of the reign of his son, Pedro I, whose disastrous war with his half-brother Enrique de Trastámara further weakened a country stricken by Black Death.

Change was not confined to the political and social life of Spain. There were also changes afoot in the literary environment of fourteenth-century Castile. In the first half of the previous century the dominant literary vehicle had been *cuaderna vía*, a verse form which has four stanzas of fourteen-line syllables, a central caesura and full rhyme. The common background to most of this verse lay in the monasteries of Old Castile and its subjects were religious and didactic. Two opposing tendencies of social conflict and intellectual expansion in late thirteenth- and early fourteenth-century Castile led to something of a collapse of *cuaderna vía* in its initial form. The accession of two child kings in Fernando IV in 1295 and Alfonso XI in 1312, depopulation and economic stagnation led to social, political and economic strife. This was to a large extent counterbalanced by intellectual developments in the founding of new universities and schools and the expansion of Church activities. The Church's insistence on education was assisted by two technological innovations, the introduction of paper and the use of spectacles. By the end of the thirteenth century, paper was being widely used instead of much more expensive parchment or vellum and this meant that books were accessible to far more people. Additionally, spectacles to correct failing sight were in common use by the middle of the fourteenth century, a development which did much to further the spread of literacy.

As a result, new *cuaderna vía* poems were composed which left aside religious and moral themes for social ones. The descriptive narrative tendency of thirteenth-century poetry gave way in the fourteenth century to criticism of society and mores. Religious didacticism evolved into a literature of denunciation of the kind we might call 'committed' writing today.

Form and Content
Form and content depend on each other in varying proportion, according to the specific aims of a literary text. In the *Book of Good Love*, the Archpriest draws on a wide range of literary sources and metrical variations to give form to his meaning. Critical attention has focused on this variety and diversity of form in extremely divergent ways. Some critics view the work as a poetic miscellany, an inorganic and disjointed anthology whose coherence lies in its themes and content rather than its structure. L. Arturo Castellanos[1] has argued for exactly the opposite view of an almost parenthetic structure for the work, while Lida de Malkiel[2] sees substantial structural unity provided by the author's personality and Gonzalo Sobejano[3] finds a unifying coherence in the textual movement from human to divine, from vitalism to spirituality.

While critical opinion on general structure is as prismatic as the text itself, the form of specific sections and episodes can clearly be seen to originate in many of the common sources drawn on by medieval writers within the European tradition. These sources are of both popular and learned derivation. The opening invocation to God in *cuaderna vía* precedes a prose prologue based on the learned sermon or *divisio intra*. This was nearly always in Latin, although there is one surviving four-teenth-century example in the vernacular. It was addressed to highly educated clerics and aimed to instruct through the exegesis of a Biblical text. In this case Juan Ruiz parodies his source, for his stated intention of warning against the folly of worldly love is ultimately subverted by his mischievous hint that the book will also provide instruction for lovers. In direct contrast with this learned parody, the Archpriest also uses a technique common in popular sermons, the *exemplum* or fable with a moral, set within the overall narrative framework and forming part of a character-istic debate, thereby combining these two major medieval genres. Most of these tales come from the Aesopic animal-fable tradition so widespread in medieval Europe. Sometimes there is only a minimal link between the tale and the narrative, which suggests that the Archpriest enjoyed developing the stories for their sheer entertainment value over and above their moral purpose.

The first major episode in the *Book of Good Love*, the love affair with Endrina, is based very closely on a twelfth-century elegiac comedy called the *Pamphilus*, which explains Ovidian ideas on love and then shows how to use them. Once again the Archpriest reveals his inventiveness in creating a vividly Castilian setting in his adaptation. The protagonist's success in this love affair is preceded by some advice on courtship given by both Love and Venus, based largely on Ovid's *Ars amatoria*, again well-known in the Middle Ages, though modified to an extent in this text by the precepts of courtly love. The second major episode in the *Book of Good Love*, the mock epic battle between Carnal and Lent, is a uniquely Spanish version of the Carnival and Lent poems which flourished in Europe at the time. In much the same anti-clerical spirit the Archpriest exploits Goliardic motifs in the welcome given to Love and Carnal by various ranks and orders of clergy, and this idea is amplified in the final song of the Talavera clergy, an imitation of a Goliardic piece called the *Consultatio sacerdotum* attributed to Walter Map (1140?–

1209?), Archdeacon of Oxford. Juan Ruiz had much in common with the Goliards, that wandering band of students and scholars who behaved riotously and wrote satirical poems lampooning the clergy, most of which were attributed to their imaginary bishop, Golias.

In the rest of the poem, the *cuaderna vía* verse form is interspersed with a variety of lyrics in different metres. The amusing and scurrilous story of the Archpriest's failed love affair with Cruz the baker's wife is written in what the author describes as *troba cazurra*, *cazurros* being the lowest type of minstrel. Further on, the lyrics and the *cuaderna vía* stanzas describing the protagonist's adventures with the mountain girls are a parody of the *pastourelle*, which generally represented the attempted seduction of a lovely shepherdess by a knight. Juan Ruiz's version subverts all the features of the traditional genre and imports the wild-woman folklore of the Middle Ages. In complete opposition are the religious lyrics, mostly dedicated to the Virgin, drawing on the long-standing Marian tradition of the Joys. There are no other comparable refrain-based lyric forms in Castilian religious poetry prior to the fifteenth century and it is quite possible that the Archpriest was an innovator here as in so much else. One of the aims stated in his prologue is to instruct in the art of rhyme and metre, an aim more than fulfilled throughout the text in the extraordinary metrical range and variety of rhyme used.

This brief survey demonstrates great variation of forms used in the *Book of Good Love* in terms of the types of sources used as well as in poetics, encompassing the erudite, the popular and the folkloric and containing something for every level of reader or listener, from the illiterate to the educated cleric. In the light of this it is illuminating to consider how those forms relate to content and how the Archpriest manipulates poetic expression to fulfil his literary intentions.

Any discussion of content and meaning in the *Book of Good Love* must take account of the nature of 'good love' itself. When the Archpriest used this term to describe his book, was he referring to the love of God or to the love of a woman? Much in the text leads us to believe in the sincerity of the author's love for God. The religious lyrics which appear at the beginning, mid-point and end of the manuscripts, the earnest examination of the nature of confession during the battle between Lent and Carnal and the heartfelt attack on death after the demise of Trotaconventos convince us of his authentic Catholic dedication. However, the love of woman is clearly a tantalizing and powerful force which the Archpriest allegedly warns against, but never wholeheartedly denounces. His exhortations to understand his book correctly make the reader or listener wonder whether the 'correct' reading would be to see the text as an art of love, as its protagonist moves from utter failure in affairs of the heart to the fulfilment of his aims in his liaisons with Endrina and the nun Garoza, a success achieved largely through applying the advice of Love and Venus. As modern readers, we need to see this ambiguity over love in terms of two major aims of medieval literature, didacticism and entertainment. There are undoubtedly didactic features in the *Book of Good Love*. The attack on the power of money, the section on the seven deadly sins, the description of the arms of the Christian were part and parcel of the priest's repertoire, conventional features of Catholic doctrine which might substantiate a treatise on the folly of worldly love. Yet the author's indomitable humour prevails in his tendency to favour entertainment value over instruction, to hint ambiguously at the pleasure of sexual love in the guise of delivering a learned sermon on moral folly. While the purposes of didacticism and entertainment are mutually supporting, what these two features point up are the conflicts which create much of the work's dynamic tension. These are the conflicts between divine love and secular love, between the priest and the poet/lover, between the two sides of the Archpriest's own nature and between the doctrine of the Catholic Church and the reality of fourteenth-century Castile.

In these terms, form matches content in so far as content and meaning express these conflicts. The treatise is the appropriate didactic vehicle to construct the Arms of the Christian. The *exemplum* is the quintessential form for medieval entertainment, even if under the guise of moralizing. Yet in his prose prologue the Archpriest expresses a third purpose, beyond those of instruction and amusement, which is a literary purpose. He tells his readers and listeners that he will show them how to compose verse – the master will instruct the uninitiated. Over twenty years ago Anthony Zahareas was the first to remark on the abundance and quality of Juan Ruiz's personal comments on his art. These comments are placed at strategically important, emphatic places in the text, often within the context of statements encouraging us to understand his work correctly. Viewed together with the remarkable and original reworkings of literary sources discussed above, there is a good case to be made for a primary artistic and poetic intention in the writing of the *Book of Good Love*. Certainly the Archpriest's elaboration of conventional themes and techniques far transcends anything which had gone before in medieval Spain. His unique poetic consciousness imposes a creative pattern on the diversity and contradiction in his experience in a surprisingly modern way, and one which has ensured the lasting artistic value of this great work.

The Translations

In 1833 Henry Wadsworth Longfellow published a review of Tomás Sánchez's 1790 edition of the *Book of Good Love*, which included his own lyrical translation of stanzas 1606–17. Since then there have been only four previous English-language translations of the *Book of Good Love* in its entirety, all published in the USA and all of very high quality. The first was made in 1933 by Elisha Kent Kane and published at his own expense, although it was reprinted by the University of North Carolina Press in 1968. Kane's translation is in rhyming verse, accompanied by ribald, comic illustrations drawn by the translator. He claimed he was translating for 'humanity and not solely for the erudite', and his classic Translator's Preface contains a humorous attack on pedantry and scholarly ambiguity. Yet his admiration for the Spanish poem was unquestioned. He quotes Cejador, who described the *Book of Good Love* as the 'most powerful book ever written in the Spanish language'. Kane looked upon the work as absolutely lacking in any plan or formal unity, but focused on the personal quality of the text. As a result, his lively translation conveys the spirit if not the letter of the original, though inevitably adherence to rhyme means that accuracy of meaning must be relinquished on many occasions.

The next translation, published by the State University of New York Press, appeared in 1970 and was the work of Rigo Mignani and Mario A. di Cesare. It was an unadorned prose rendering whose aims were clarity, simplicity and fidelity to the original. In total contrast to Kane, both translators felt that any attempt to use rhyme or verse would defeat these intentions. The literalness of the translation extends to proverbs, which are rendered directly rather than equivalently because there were deemed to be no equivalents with the flavour or relevance of the originals. At times fidelity is achieved at the cost of obscurity in English language, but the translation reads well and fluidly and captures the essential tone of the original.

Raymond S. Willis published his edition of the *Book of Good Love* with an introduction and parallel English paraphrase in 1972 using Princeton University Press. This prose rendering retains the division into stanzas, but uses no rhyme. Willis stated in the introduction that the English version was designed exclusively as an aid to understanding the Spanish and not as a literary text in its own right. Rather than creating a translation of the Spanish, he describes the English as a 'facing glossary of equivalent English terms arranged in syntactical structures' (page lxvi) paralleling the original. The edition and paraphrase are highly scholarly and rigorously literal, often resulting in extremely stilted English.

The last of the four translations appeared in 1978 with the title of *Book of True Love*, with the translation and introduction by Saralyn R. Daly and a parallel text edited by Anthony Zahareas, published by Pennsylvania State University Press. The translation is in rhyming verse, based on a draft made by Hubert Creekmore in the mid-1950s. Its aims are to be faithful to Juan Ruiz's meaning, wit, ambiguity and hilarity. The English has a heptameter for *cuaderna vía*, and has a minimum of two rhymes per stanza. There is an attempt to approximate devices of medieval rhetoric, especially wordplay and oral-formulaic devices. In this case English proverbs are used to replace Spanish ones. The introduction claims that translation is interpretation, but emphasizes that the translator's role is not to replace but to invite a return to the original. The reinventiveness and creativity of this version must be admired, though once again the constraints of rhyme frequently lead to significant departures from the original meaning.

The fundamental aim of the present translation is to provide students and general readers with a modern, direct translation of the text. The search for a balance between accuracy in terms of language and spirit and accessibility for the reader of the twenty-first century has been arduous. The decision to translate into free verse was in part an acknowledgement of the impossibility of metrical cognation and in part a belief that free verse preserves the rhythms of poetic and oral discourse to a degree and in general gives virtual linear equivalence. The other major consideration in this translation was the role of the *Book of Good Love* as a performance text. While the work in its overall form must have been read by private individuals, it would also have been read aloud to small groups. John Walsh at the University of California, Berkeley, suggests there were public readings or recitals of the work, including the alternation of spoken and sung segments, possibly accompanied by an instrument. Clearly the performance context bears greatly upon its English translation. Naturalness and fluidity are essential if the text is to be spoken or sung and this has been a prime consideration in presenting a text which reflects the rhythms of speech.

A work whose translation needs to span a space of nearly seven hundred years and at the same time attempts to capture the tone, nuance and register of a masterpiece of profound complexity in both language and ideas inevitably presents many linguistic challenges. One of the most resistant to easy resolution was the translation of names. In general where a name has a direct English equivalent this has been used, as in the case of Love and Lent. Don Carnal has stayed as Carnal because there is sufficient equivalence in meaning in English to validate its use and minimize translation loss. Endrina, Garoza and Trotaconventos, the three major female characters, were less yielding in their direct English equivalents, namely Sloe, Bride and Convent-Trotter, which seemed to lend a comicality and stereotyping in English that was not significant in the original. They also lose the sonorous assonantal rhythms of the Spanish versions. As a result it seemed best to opt for exoticism, retain them as they are and have recourse to a note on meaning.

The use of *don* and *doña* in the Spanish, for example *Don Amor, Doña Cuaresma*, has previously been translated as either Lord or Sir, or Lady or Dame respectively. There appears to be no linguistic reason for the elevation of status, since Lord or Lady would tend to be *Su Señoría*. *Don* is not usually translated when it precedes a first name, and is rendered as Esquire when used in a full title in correspondence. Again there might be a case for leaving the original as it is, but in this translation it has been omitted, according to the precepts of modern translation practice.

A further question in need of satisfactory response was how to render the Latin quotations used in the original text. Was it preferable for the modern reader to have an English translation alone, thereby losing any differentiation in the target text between the two languages in the source text, or was it more loyal and accurate to retain the Latin and translate it within the text? All four previous translations opted for a sole English rendering. The decision in this translation to retain the Latin and provide an English translation immediately after was made out of respect for authorial intention. Presumably the Archpriest used Latin to achieve a specific effect, to create an air of erudition or for the purpose of euphemistic humour. If not, he would have chosen to write in the vernacular, for Spain had a flourishing tradition of vernacular Bibles from the thirteenth century onwards. The use of Latin is especially appropriate for a written text and in performance it would be viable to recite the Latin and repeat it in its English translation. The Latin has been retained as it appears in the S manuscript, with only very minor modifications.

Lastly, the difficulties arising from debatable meanings are magnified in a medieval text. The author is not available for consultation and understanding is hampered by the lapse of time and the loss or absence of documentary guidance. Decisions of this kind have been made as best they can within the constraints of the manuscript and are based on contextual and semantic clues and, failing these, on a translator's experience and intuition. Some of these obscurities are indicated in the notes.

References

1. Castellanos, Luis Arturo, 'La estructura del *Libro de buen amor*', in *Actas del I Congreso Internacional sobre el Arcipreste de Hita*, ed. M. Criado de Val (Barcelona, 1973), pages 30–7.
2. See 'Ruiz and His Critics', page 440.
3. Sobejano, Gonzalo, 'Consecuencia y diversidad en el *Libro de buen amor*' in *Actas del I Congreso Internacional sobre el Arcipreste de Hita*, ed. M. Criado de Val (Barcelona, 1973), pages 7–17.

NOTE ON THE TEXT

The *Book of Good Love* is preserved in the three extant manuscripts, known as S, G and T. Various other fragments of the work exist which indicate its wide diffusion. The S manuscript is the most complete of the three and is so called because it originally came from Salamanca, where it belonged to the Colegio Mayor de San Bartolomé. It was then transferred to the National Library in Madrid and is currently in Salamanca once more, in the library of the University of Salamanca. The G manuscript is known as Gayoso, after its owner, Benito Martínez Gayoso, and is now housed in the library of the Spanish Academy. The T manuscript belonged to Toledo cathedral and is in the National Library in Madrid.

The text used for this translation is substantially the Salamanca manuscript as printed in the critical edition of the *Book of Good Love* by Manuel Criado de Val and Eric W. Naylor, published by the Consejo Superior de Investigaciones Científicas in Madrid in 1972. This is because it is certainly the most complete of the three, and the scribe's date of 1343 for the text itself indicates that it was the latest of the extant versions. In the few places where there are lacunae in the S manuscript, I have used the G manuscript printed in the same edition.

THE BOOK OF GOOD LOVE

Esta es oraçion quel açipreste iizo a dios quando començo este libro suyo.

1   Señor dios, que a los jodios, pueblo de perdiçion
       sacaste de cabtiuo del poder de fa[ron];
       a daniel sacaste del poço de babilon,
       ¡saca a mi coytado desta mala presion!

2   Senõr, tu diste graçia a ester la Reyna,
       antel el rrey asuero ouo tu graçia digna;
       señor, da me tu graçia e tu merçed Ayna,
       ¡sacame desta lazeria, desta presion!

3   Señor, tu que sacaste al profecta del lago,
       de poder de gentiles sacaste a santiago,
       a santa marina libreste del vientre del drago,
       libra A mi, dios mio, desta presion do ya[go].

4   Señor, tu que libreste A santa-susaña
       del falso testimonio de la falsa conpaña,
       libra me, mi dios, desta coyta tan maña,
       dame tu misericordia, tira de mi tu s[aña].

5   A jonas el profecta del vientre de la ballena,
       en que moro tres dias dentro en la mar ll[ena],
       sacastelo tu sano, asy commo de casa buena,
       ¡mexias, tu me salua sin culpa e sin pena!

6   Señor, a los tres niños de muerte los libraste,
       del forno del grand fuego syn lision;
       de las ondas del mar a sant pedro tomeste;
       ¡Señor, de aquesta coyta saca al tu açipre[ste]!

7   Avn tu, que dixiste a los tus seruidores
       que con ellos serias ante Reys dezidores,

JESUS OF NAZARETH, KING OF THE JEWS

The Archpriest offered this prayer to God as he began his book.

1 Lord God, who saved the Jews, that outlawed race,
   from captivity and from Pharaoh's power,
   who saved Daniel from the lion's den in Babylon,
   save me from my suffering in this terrible prison!

2 Lord, you gave grace to Queen Esther,
   finding her worthy before King Ahasuerus;
   Lord, give me your grace and mercy now,
   release me from this torment and this prison!

3 Lord, who saved the prophet from the lion's den,
   and saved Saint James from the Gentiles' possession,
   who freed Saint Marina from the dragon's belly,
   free me, my God, from this prison where I lie.

4 Lord, who freed Saint Susanna
   from the false witness of false friends,
   release me, dear God, from this great anguish,
   show me your mercy and take away your wrath.

5 The prophet Jonah was captive in the whale's belly
   for three days, in the vastness of the sea.
   You set him free, safe and sound, as if from home –
   Messiah, save me, free from blame and sorrow!

6 Lord, who freed three sons from death,
   saved unscathed from the fiery furnace,
   who lifted Saint Peter from the waves of the sea,
   Lord, free your archpriest from this suffering!

7 You spoke to your servants too, saying
   you would be with them when they spoke with kings,

> E les diras palabras que fabrasen mejores;
> ¡Señor, tu sey comigo, guardame de trayd[ores]!

8   El nonbre profetizado fue grande hemanuel,
     fijo de dios muy alto, saluador de ys[rael];
     en la salutaçio[n] el angel grabiel
     te fizo çierta desto, tu fueste cierta del.

9   Por esta profeçia e por la salutaçion,
     por el nonbre tan alto, hemanuel saluaçion,
     Señora, da me tu graçia E dame consolaçion,
     ganame del tu fijo graçia E bendiçion.

10   Dame graçia, señora de todos los señores,
     tira de mi tu saña, tira de mi Rencores,
     ffaz que todo se torne sobre los mescladores,
     ¡Ayuda me, gloriosa madre de pecado[res]!

'Intellectum tibi dabo et Instruam te In via hac qua gradieris, firmabo super te occulos meos.'
El profecta dauid, por spiritu santo fablando, a cada vno de nos dize en el psalmo triçesimo primo del verso dezeno, que es el que primero suso escreui. en el qual verso entiendo yo tres cosas, las quales dizen algunos doctores philosophos que son en el alma E propia mente suyas. Son estas: entendimiento, voluntad E memoria las quales, digo, si buenas son, que traen al Alma conssolaçion, e aluengan la vida al cuerpo, E dan le onrra con pro e buena fam[a]. Ca, por el buen entendimiento, entiende onbre bien E sabe dello el mal.

E por ende, vna de las petiçiones que demando dauid a dios po[r] que sopiese la su ley fue esta: *'Da michi intellectum e cetera.'*

Ca el ome, entendiendo el bien, avra de dios temor, el qual es comienco de toda sabidoria; de que dize el dicho profecta: *'yniçium sapiençie timor domini.'*

Ca luego es el buen entendimiento en los que temen A dios.

E por ende sigue la Razon el dicho dauid en otro logar en que dize: *'jntellectus bonus omibus façientibus eum, e cetera.'*

Otrosi dize salamon en el libro de la sapiençia: *'qui timet dominun façiet bona.'* E esto se entiende en la primera rrason

would give them the right words to say.
Lord, be with me too, protect me from betrayers!

(A number of stanzas which start the prayer to the Virgin
are missing in all manuscripts.)

8   The name foretold was great Emmanuel,
     Son of God on high, saviour of Israel,
     as spoken in greeting by the angel Gabriel
     to show you certainty, Mary, as you were certain of him.

9   In the name of this prophecy and greeting,
     by His name on high, Emmanuel, salvation,
     My Lady, give me your grace and consolation,
     win me your Son's grace and blessing.

10   Give me grace, Lady above all lords,
     take away your anger and wrath,
     and lay it upon the slanderers:
     help me, O glorious one, Mother of sinners!

'Intellectum tibi dabo et Instruam te In via hac qua gradieris,
firmabo super te occulos meos' (I will give thee understanding, and
instruct thee in the path that thou shouldst follow: my eyes shall be
fixed upon thee).

These words were spoken to every one of us by the prophet
David, when inspired by the Holy Spirit in verse ten of the thirty-
first psalm of the Vulgate Bible, as written above. This verse
suggests three things to me, which certain wise philosophers claim
are properties of the soul: understanding, will and memory. When
these are sound, they can bring great consolation to the soul,
lengthen the life of the body and bring honour, advantage and good
repute, because with good understanding, man can distinguish
good from evil.

For this reason, one of the requests David made of God, to
enable him to know His laws, was: 'Da michi intellectum e cetera'
(Give me understanding, et cetera).

If a man understands what is good, he will fear God, who is the
source of all wisdom. As the prophet says: 'yniçium sapiençie timor
domini' (The fear of the Lord is the beginning of wisdom).

Thus, those who fear God have good understanding.

David pursues this line of thought elsewhere when he says:

del verso que yo començe, en lo que dize: '*Intellectum tibi dabo.*'

E desque esta jnformada E jnstruyda el Alma, que se ha de saluar en el cuerpo linpio, e pienssa e ama e desea omne el buen amor de dios e sus mandamientos.

E esto atal dize el dicho profeta: '*E meditabor in mandatis tuis que dilexi.*'

E otrosi desecha E aborresçe el alma el pecado del amor loco deste mundo.

E desto dize el salmista: '*qui diligitis dominum, odite malum, e cetera.*'

E por ende se sigue luego la segu[n]da rrazon del verso que dize: '*E instruan te.*'

E desque el Alma, con el buen entendimiento e buena voluntad, con buena rremenbrança escoge E ama el buen Amor, que es el de dios, E ponelo en la çela de la memoria por que se acuerde dello, e trae al cuerpo a fazer buenas obras, por las quales se salua el ome.

E desto dize sant Ioan apostol, en el Apocalipsi, de los buenos que mueren bien obrando: '*beati mortui qui in domino moriuntur, opera enim illorum secuntur illos.*'

E dize otrosi el profeta: '*tu redis vnicuique justa opera sua.*' E desto concluye la terçera rrazon del verso primero que dize: '*jn via hac qua gradieris, firmabo super te occulos meos.*'

E por ende deuemos tener sin dubda que obras sienpre estan en la buena memoria, que con buen entendimiento E buena voluntad escoje el alma E ama el Amor de dios por se saluar por ellas. Ca dios, por las buenas obras que faze omne en la carrera de saluaçion en que anda, firma sus ojos sobre el.

E esta es la sentençia del verso que enpieça primero: 'breue'. Como quier que a las vegadas se acuerde pecado e lo quiera e lo obre, este desacuerdo non viene del buen entendimiento, nin tal querer non viene de la buena voluntad, nin de la buena obra non viene tal obra. Ante viene de la fraqueza de la natura humana que es en el omne, que se non puede escapar de pecado. Ca dize Caton: '*Nemo sine crimine viuit.*'

E dize lo job: '*quis potest fazere mundum de jmudo conçeptum semine?*'

quasi dicat: '*ninguno saluo dios.*' E viene otrosi de la mengua del buen entendimiento, que lo non ha estonçe, por que ome piensa vanidades de pecado.

E deste tal penssamiento dize el salmista: '*Cogitaciones hominum vane sunt.*'

'*jntellectus bonus omibus façientibus eum e cetera.*' (All those who do His commandments have good understanding, et cetera).

Moreover, in the Book of Wisdom* Solomon says: '*qui timet dominun façiet bona*' (He who fears the Lord doeth good), which is borne out in the first part of the verse I quoted, where it says '*Intellectum tibi dabo*' (I will give thee understanding).

And since the soul is informed and instructed to live in a pure body, man thinks of, longs for and desires the good love of God and his commandments.

The aforesaid prophet also says: '*E meditabor in mandatis tuis que dilexi*' (And I will practise Thy commandments, which I have loved).

The soul casts aside and abhors the sin of foolish worldly love.

As the psalmist says: '*qui diligitis dominum, odite malum, e cetera*' (He who loves the Lord shall abhor evil, et cetera).

Hence the second part of the verse, which says: '*E instruan te*' (And I shall instruct thee).

Thus, the soul, with perfect understanding and good will, clearly remembers these words, and chooses and holds fast to good love, which is the love of God, and keeps it in the secret storehouse of its memory so that man might remember it, and guide the body to good works, through which man is saved.

In the Apocalypse, Saint John the Apostle speaks of the good who die doing good: '*beati mortui qui in domino moriuntur, opera enim illorum secuntur illos*' (Blessed are the dead that die in the Lord, for their good works shall follow after them).

And the prophet also says: '*tu redis unicuique justa opera sua*' (Thou will render to every man according to his works). This concludes the third part of the first verse, which says: '*in via hac qua gradieris, firmabo super te occulos meos*' (In the path that thou shouldst follow, my eyes shall be fixed upon thee).

So we must understand that such works always remain in a good memory, and that with perfect understanding and good will, the soul chooses and loves the love of God and gains salvation through good works. For God's eyes are indeed upon man as he does good deeds on the path to salvation.

And this is the meaning of the first line of the verse. Because at times when sin is brought to mind, desired and committed, this discord does not come from good understanding, nor such desire from good will, nor such a deed from good works. It comes rather from the weakness of human nature within man, who cannot

e dice otrosi a los tales, mucho disolutos E de mal entendimiento: '*Nolite fieri sicut equs E mulus jn quibus non est jntellectus.*'

E avn digo que viene de la pobledad de la memoria, que non esta instructa del buen entendimiento, ansi que non puede amar el bien nin acordarse dello para lo obrar.

E viene otrosi esto por rrazon que la natura vmana, que mas aparejada E jnclinada es al mal que al bien, e a pecado que a bien; esto dize el decreto.

E estas son algunas de las rrazones, por que son fechos los libros de la ley E del derecho e de castigos E constunbres E de otras çiençias.

otrosi fueron la pintura E la escriptura e las ymagenes primera mente falladas, por rrazon que la memoria del ome desleznadera es; esto dize el decreto. ca tener todas las cosas en la memoria E non olvidar algo, mas es de la diuinidat que de la vmanidad; esto dize el decreto.

E por esto es mas apropiada a la memoria del alma, que es spiritu de dios criado E perfecto, E biue sienpre en dios.

otrosi dize dauid: '*Anima mea illius viuet, querite dominum e viuet Anima vestra.*' E non es apropiada al cuerpo vmano, que dura poco tienpo,

et dize job: '*breues dies hominis sunt.*'

E otrosi dize: '*homo natus de muliere, breues dies hominis sunt.*' E dize sobre esto dauid: '*Anni nostri sicut aranea meditabuntur e cetera.*'

onde yo, de mi poquilla çiençia E de mucha E grand rrudeza, entiendo quantos bienes fazen perder el alma e al cuerpo, E los males muchos que les aparejan e traen el amor loco del pecado del mundo, escogiendo E Amando con buena voluntad saluaçion E gloria del parayso para mi anima, fiz esta chica escriptura en memoria de bien.

E conpuse este nuevo libro en que son escriptas algunas maneras, e maestrias, e sotilezas engañosas del loco Amor del mundo, que vsan algunos para pecar.

las quales leyendolas E oyendolas ome o muger de buen enten-demiento, que se quiera saluar, descogera E obrar lo ha.

E podra dezir con el salmista: '*veni veritatis E cetera.*'

Otrosi los de poco entendimiento non se perderan; ca leyendo E coydando el mal que fazen o tienen en la voluntad de fazer, e los porfiosos de sus malas maestrias, e descobrimiento publicado de

escape from sin. For Cato says: '*Nemo sine crimine viluit*' (No one lives without fault). And Job says: '*quis potest fazere mundum de imudo conçeptum semine?*' *Quasi dicat ninguno saluo dios!* (Who can bring the pure from the impure, as if to say: 'No one except God'). So sin arises from diminished understanding, in which state man thinks only of the vanities of sin.

As the psalmist says: '*Cogitaciones hominum vane sun*' (The Lord knows the thoughts of man, that they are vanity).

And he also speaks to very dissolute people with impaired understanding: '*Nolite fieri sicut equs E mulus, in quibus non est intellectus*' (Be not like the horse and the mule, who do not have understanding).

And I myself believe that sin arises from defective memory, which has not been taught by perfect understanding, so that it is neither able to love goodness nor recall it in order to do good.

And this happens because human nature is more suited and inclined to evil than to good, to sin than to purity. This is stated in the Decretals.*

And these are some of the reasons for the compilation of books on law and rights, punishments and customs and other subjects.

Painting, writing and sculptures were created fundamentally because the memory of man is fallible, as the Decretals state. For to remember everything and forget nothing is more divine than human, as the Decretals claim.

For this reason it is more relevant to the soul's memory, which is the spirit created by God in perfection, and always abiding in God.

As David says: '*Anima mea illius vivet, querite dominum e vivet Anima vestra*' (My soul lives for Him: seek the Lord and your soul shall live). It is not appropriate to the human body, which endures so short a time.

Job says: '*breues dies hominis sunt*' (The days of man are short) and elsewhere: '*homo natus de muliere, breues dies hominis sunt.*' (Man born of woman is of few days). David has more to add: '*Anni nostri sicut aranea meditabuntur e cetera*' (Our years are like a spider's web, et cetera).

So, though I have little knowledge and great lack of sophistication, I do understand how the depraved love of sin causes the soul and body to lose so many good things, and brings many ills, and I willingly choose and love the salvation and glory of paradise

sus muchas engañosas maneras, que vsan para pecar E engañar las mugeres, acordaran la memoria E non despreçiaran su fama; ca mucho es cruel quien su fama menospreçia; el derecho lo dize. E querran mas amar a si mesmos que al pecado; que la ordenada caridad de si mesmo comiença: el decreto lo dize. E desecharan E aborresçeran las maneras E maestrias malas del loco Amor, que faze perder las almas E caer en saña de dios, apocando la vida E dando mala fama e deshonrra E muchos daños a los cuerpos. en pero por que es vmanal cosa el pecar, si algunos, lo que non los conssejo, quisieren vsar del loco amor, aqui fallaran algunas maneras para ello.

E ansi este mi libro a todo omne o muger, al cuerdo E al non cuerdo, al que entendiere el bien e escogiere saluaçion, E obrare bien Amando a dios, otrosi al que quisiere el ammor loco, en la carrera que andudiere, puede cada vno bien dezir: '*jntellectum tibi dabo e cetera.*'

E rruego E conssejo a quien lo oyere E lo oyere que guarde bien las tres cosas del Alma; lo primero que quiera bien entender E bien juzgar la mi entençion, por que lo fiz, E la sentençia de lo que y dize, E non al son feo de las palabras. E segud derecho las palabras siruen a la jntençion E non la jntençion a las palabras.

E dios sabe que la mi jntençion non fue de lo fazer por dar manera de pecar, ni por mal dezir, mas fue por Reduçir a toda persona A memoria buena de bien obrar, e dar ensienpro de buenas constunbres e castigos de saluaçion.

E por que sean todos aperçebidos e se puedan mejor guardar de tantas maestrias, como algunos vsan por el loco amor.

Ca dize sant gregorio que menos firien al onbre los dardos que ante son vistos, E mejor nos podemos guardar de lo que ante hemos visto.

E conposelo otrosi a dar algunos leçion e muestra de metrificar E rrimar E de trobar; Ca trobas E notas e rrimas e ditados e uersos, que fiz conplida mente, Segund que esta çiençia Requiere.

E por que toda buena obra es comienço E fundamento dios e la fe catholica, e dize lo la primera decretal de las crementinas que comiença: 'fidey catholiçe fundamento'. e do este non es cimiento non se puede fazer obra firme nin firme hedifiçio:

Segud dize el apostol.

Por ende començe mi libro en el nonbre de dios, e tome el verso primero del salmo, que es de la santa trinidad E de la fe catholica,

for my soul, so I have written this modest piece of scripture in remembrance of goodness.

I composed this new book in which some of the techniques, skills and deceiving subtleties of the foolish love of this world are described, which some folk use to sin.

If any man or woman of good understanding reads or hears them and wishes to be saved, he or she must make a choice and act upon it.

Then they may join the psalmist in saying: '*veni veritatis E cetera*' (I have chosen the way of truth, et cetera).

But those of little understanding shall not be lost because when they read about the evil they do, or intend to do, and learn of the evil deeds of persistent sinners, and find their many deceitful ways of sinning and tricking women are under public scrutiny, they will arouse their memory and will not despise reputation, for it is wicked to do so, as the Law states. And they will want to love themselves more than they love sin, since the requisite universal love starts from within, as the Decretals say. And they will cast aside and abhor the evil ways and wiles of foolish love, through which the soul is lost, invoking God's wrath, shortening life and bringing disrepute, dishonour and many physical ills.

However, because it is human to sin, if some people want to indulge in the excesses of worldly love, which I do not advise, they will find various ways to do so described here.

May my book be for all men and women, wise and foolish, who understand goodness and choose salvation, charitable deeds and love of God. So that they can truly say to those who long for mad worldly love on the path they have chosen: '*intellectum tibi dabo e cetera*' (I shall give thee understanding, et cetera).

I beg and advise whoever may hear or read this to cultivate the three attributes of the soul: firstly, to be able to understand and judge my intention correctly, as well as the reason for writing the book, and its meaning, and not to be misled by the deceiving sound of the words. The rules say that the words are subservient to purpose and not the purpose to the words.

And God knows that my purpose was not to write it to suggest ways of sinning, nor to speak evil, but to guide everyone to the clear recollection of how to do good and set a good example in their habits and penances on the road to salvation.

And also to make them aware, so that they can protect them-

que es 'qui cuque vul', el vesso que dize: 'ita deus pater, deus filius
e cetera.'

AQUI DIZE DE COMO EL AÇIPRESTE RROGO A DIOS QUE LE DIESE GRAÇIA QUE PODIESE FAZER ESTE LIBRO

11   Dyos padre, dios fijo, dios spiritu santo,
el que nasçio de la virgen, esfuerçe nos de tanto
que sienpre lo loemos en prosa E en canto;
sea de nuestras almas cobertura E manto.

12   El que fizo el çielo la tierra E el mar,
el me done su graçia e me quiera alunbrar,
que pueda de cantares vn librete Rimar,
que los que lo oyeren puedan solaz tomar.

13   Tu, señor dios mio, quel omne crieste,
enforma e ayuda a mi el tu acipreste,
que pueda fazer vn libro de buen amor aqueste,
que los cuerpos alegre e a las almas preste.

14   Sy queredes, senores, oyr vn buen solaz,
escuchad el rromance, sosegad vos en paz,
non vos dire mentira en quanto en el yaz,
Ca por todo el mundo se vsa E se faz.

15   E por que mejor de todos sea escuchado,
fablar vos he por tobras e cuento rrimado;

selves better from the many wiles used by some in the madness of worldly love.

Saint Gregory says that arrows already seen injure less, and so we can protect ourselves better from a harm already perceived.

I also wrote the book as an example and guide to metrification, rhyme and artistic composition, and I have composed lyrics, music and rhyme, poetry and metrics with great skill, as this discipline demands.

God and the Catholic faith are the source and essence of any good work, as Pope Clement V's Decretals tell us, which begin: '*fidey catholiçe fundamento*' (The foundation of the Catholic faith), and where this is not the foundation, no solid work nor stable building can be made, as the Apostle says.

On account of this, I began my book in the name of God, taking the first verse of the psalm '*qui cuque vult*' (Whosoever wishes), which is about the Holy Trinity and the Catholic faith, and the verse which says: '*ita deus pater, deus filius e cetera*' (God the Father, God the Son, et cetera).

HOW THE ARCHPRIEST ASKED GOD FOR THE GRACE TO WRITE THIS BOOK

11   God the Father, God the Son and God the Holy Ghost,
        may He born of the Virgin give us the strength
        to praise Him always in verse and song;
        may He be the cover and mantle of our souls.

12   May He who made heaven, land and sea
        give me His grace and shine His light on me,
        for me to write a small book of rhyming poetry
        that will give pleasure to all who hear it.

13   You, my Lord God, who created man,
        instruct and help me, your archpriest,
        to write this book of good love
        to gladden the body and sustain the soul.

14   Now, sirs, if you would like to listen
        to some good entertainment, relax at your ease
        and hear this story. I shall tell no lies in it,
        but speak only of the ways of the world.

15   And to make it sound more pleasant to the ear,
        I will tell the tale in rhyming verse.

es vn dezir fermoso e saber sin pecado,
rrazon mas plazentera, ffablar mas apostado.

16   Non tengades que es libro neçio de devaneo,
nin creades que es chufa algo que en el leo;
Ca segund buen dinero yaze en vil correo
ansi en feo libro esta saber non feo.

17   El axenuz de fuera mas negro es que caldera,
es de dentro muy blanco mas que la peña vera;
blanca farina esta so negra cobertera,
açucar negro e blanco osta en vil caña vera.

18   Sobre la espina esta la noble Rosa flor,
en fea letra esta saber de grand dotor;
como so mala capa yaze buen beuedor
ansi so el mal tabardo esta buen amor.

19   E por que de todo bien es comienço e Rayz
la virgen santa maria, por ende yo joan rroyz,
açipreste de fita, della primero fiz
cantar de los sus gozos siete que ansi diz:

GOZOS DE SANTA MARIA
20   Santa maria
luz del dia,
tu me guia
toda via.

21   gana me graçia E bendiçion
e de jhesu consolaçion,
que pueda con deuoçion
Cantar de tu alegria.

22   El primero gozo ques lea
en çibdad de galilea,
nazarec creo que sea,
oviste mensajerya,

23   Del angel que a ty vino,
grabiel santo E digno;
troxo te mensaz diuino;
dixote: 'ave maria.'

It is a fine story, learned, free from sin,
a pleasing discourse in elegant language.

16 Do not think it a book of foolish extravagance,
nor that what I am teaching you are just jokes and fun;
a poor leather purse can hold great wealth,
a plain-looking book can hold complex wisdom.

17 The fennel seed is blacker than a cauldron
but inside it is whiter than ermine;
white flour is contained in a black outer husk,
sweet white sugar comes from the humble sugar-cane.

18 The noble rose rises above the thorn,
and bad handwriting belies a sage's wisdom;
beneath a tattered cloak can be found a good drinker,
and under a lowly tabard, good love lies.

19 And because the Virgin Mary is the source
and root of all good, I, Juan Ruiz,
Archpriest of Hita, first wrote this song
of her seven Joys, which goes like this:

THE JOYS OF THE VIRGIN MARY

20 Oh Mary!
light of day,
guide me now
and always.

21 Win me grace and blessing,
consolation from Jesus,
that I might devotedly
sing of your joy.

22 The first Joy we read of
was in a city in Galilee
named Nazareth.
A message came to you

23 brought by an angel.
The worthy, holy Gabriel
gave you a message divine,
saying: 'Hail, Mary.'

24   Tu, desque el mandado oyste,
       omil mente rresçebiste,
       luego virgen conçebiste,
       al fijo que dios en ti enbia.

25   En belem acaesçio
       el Segundo, quando nasçio
       e sin dolor aparesçio
       de ti virgen el mexia.

26   El terçero cuenta las leyes
       quando venieron los Reyes,
       e adoraron al que veys
       En tu braco do yazia.

27   ofreçiol mira gaspar,
       melchior fue ençienso dar,
       oro ofrecio baltasar,
       Al que dios e omne seya.

28   Alegria quarta e buena
       fue quando la madalena
       te dixo, goço sin pena,
       quel tu fijo veuia.

29   El quinto plazer oviste
       quando al tu fijo viste
       Sobir al çielo, E diste
       graçias a dios o subia.

30   Madre, el tu gozo sesto
       quando en los discipulos presto
       fue spiritu santo puesto
       En tu santa conpania.

31   Del Septeno, madre santa,
       la iglesia toda canta;
       sobiste con gloria tanta
       al çielo e quanto y avia.

32   Reynas con tu fijo quisto,
       nuestro señor jhesu xpisto;
       por ti sea de nos visto
       En la gloria syn fallia.

24   When you heard the commandment,
      you humbly received it,
      and in virginity conceived
      the Son God sent to you.

25   In Bethlehem came
      the second Joy, where
      the Messiah was born of you,
      Holy Virgin, without pain.

26   The Scriptures speak of the third Joy,
      when the three kings came
      to adore the One you
      held in your arms.

27   Gaspar offered him myrrh,
      and Melchior gave incense,
      Balthasar brought gold
      to He who was both God and man.

28   The fourth great Joy
      came when Mary Magdalene
      brought news of untroubled joy
      to say your Son still lived.

29   The fifth Joy you felt
      when you saw your Son
      ascend to Heaven, and you
      gave thanks to God, with Him on high.

30   Mother, your sixth Joy
      was when the disciples
      received the Holy Spirit
      in your holy presence.

31   The whole church sings of the
      seventh Joy, Holy Mother,
      when you ascended to Heaven
      in supreme glory.

32   You reign with your beloved Son,
      our Lord Jesus Christ,
      whom we see through you
      in never-ending glory.

GOZOS DE SSANTA MARIA

33 Tu, virgen, del çielo Reyna,
e del mundo melezina,
quieras me oyr muy digna,
que de tus gozos ayna,
escriua yo prosa digna
por te seruir.

34 Dezir de tu alegria,
rrogando te toda via,
yo pecador,
que a la grand culpa mia,
non pares mientes maria,
mas al loor.

35 Tu siete gozos oviste:
el primero quando rresçebiste
salutaçion,
del angel quando oyste:
'aue maria' conçebiste
dios saluaçion.

36 El Segundo fue conplido
quando fue de ti nasçido,
e syn dolor
de los angeles seruido,
ffue luego conosçido
por saluador.

37 ffue el tu gozo terçero
quando vino el luzero
a demostrar
el camino verdadero,
a los rreyes conpañero
ffue en guiar

38 ffue tu quarta alegria
quando te dixo: 'ave maria'
el grabiel,
que el tu fijo veuia
e por señal te dezia
que viera a el.

39 El quinto fue de grand dulçor,
quando al tu fijo Señor

THE JOYS OF THE VIRGIN MARY

33   Virgin, Queen of Heaven,
       healing balm of the world,
       hear me if it is your pleasure,
       that I might write of your Joys
       in worthy verse, to serve you.

34   I must speak of your Joy,
       still begging you,
       sinner that I am,
       to overlook my faults,
       Oh, Mary,
       and only heed my praise.

35   Seven Joys were yours.
       The first, when you were
       greeted
       by the angel, saying:
       'Hail, Mary,' then you conceived
       God, salvation.

36   The second Joy came
       when he was born of you,
       without pain,
       with angels in waiting,
       acknowledged at once
       as the Saviour.

37   The third Joy was
       when the evening star came
       to show
       the Kings the true path
       as their companion
       and guide.

38   Mary, your fourth Joy was
       when the angel
       Gabriel
       told you your Son lived
       and gave a sign
       that you would see Him.

39   The fifth Joy was very sweet,
       when you saw your Son, the Lord

        viste sobir
        al çielo a su padre mayor,
        e tu fincaste con amor
        de a el yr.

40   Este sesto non es de dubdar,
        los discipulos vino alunbrar
        con espanto,
        tu estauas en ese lugar,
        del çielo viste y entrar
        spiritu santo.

41   el septeno non ha par,
        quando por ti quiso enbiar
        dios tu padre,
        al çielo te fizo pujar,
        con el te fizo assentar
        commo a madre.

42   Señora, oy al pecador,
        que tu fijo el saluador
        por nos diçio
        del çielo, en ti morador
        el que pariste, blanca flor,
        e por nos murio.

43   Por nos otros pecadores non aborescas,
        pues por nos ser merescas
        madre de dios,
        antel con nusco parescas,
        nuestras almas le ofrescas,
        Ruegal por nos.

AQUI FABLA DE COMO TODO OME, ENTRE LOS SUS
CUYDADOS, SE DEUE ALEGRAR, E DE LA DISPUTACION
QUE LOS GRIEGOS E LOS ROMANOS EN VNO OVIERON

44   Palabras son de sabio e dixo lo caton,
        que omne a sus coydados que tiene en coraçon
        entre-ponga plazeres e alegre la rrazon,
        que la mucha tristeza mucho coydado pon.

45   E por que de buen seso non puede omne Reyr,
        abre algunas bulrras aqui a enxerir;

ascend
to Heaven, to His Majestic Father,
leaving you with the desire
to follow Him.

40   The sixth Joy cannot be doubted,
the disciples were enlightened in
their fear,
and you were there
to witness the descent of
the Holy Spirit.

41   The seventh Joy is peerless.
When God wished to send
for you
you rose up to Heaven
and sat beside Him
as a Mother.

42   My Lady, hear the sinner,
for whom your Son, the Saviour
came down
from Heaven, and now abides in you.
You gave birth, white flower, to Him
who died for us.

43   Do not abhor us sinners,
since for our sake you are the worthy
mother of God;
intercede for us before Him,
offer Him our souls
and pray to Him for us.

HOW ALL MEN SHOULD LIGHTEN THEIR CARES WITH LAUGHTER, AND THE STORY OF THE DISPUTE BETWEEN THE GREEKS AND THE ROMANS

44   These are the words of the sage Cato,
who said that man should mingle pleasures
and happy talk with his cares,
for great sadness leads to great sin.

45   Because no man can laugh at serious matters,
I have included some comic tales.

cada que las oyerdes non querades comedir
Saluo en la manera del trobar E del dezir.

46 Entiende bien mis dichos e piensa la sentençia,
non me contesca con-tigo commo al doctor de greçia
con nel rribaldo Romano e con su poca sabiençia,
quando demando Roma a greçia la çiençia.

47 ansy fue que rromanos las leyes non avien,
fueron las demandar a griegos que las tienen;
rrespondieron los griegos que non las meresçien,
nin las podrian en-tender pues que tan poco sabien.

48 pero si las querien para por ellas vsar,
que ante les convenia con sus sabios disputar,
por ver si las entienden e meresçian leuar;
esta rrespuesta fermosa dauan por se escusar.

49 Respondieron rromanos que les plazia de grado;
para la disputaçion pusieron pleito firmado,
mas por que non entedrien el lenguage non vsado,
que disputasen por señas, por señas de letrado.

50 Pusieron dia sabido todos por contender;
ffueron rromanos en coyta, non sabian que se fazer.
por que non eran letrados, nin podrian entender
a los griegos doctores nin al su mucho saber.

51 Estando en su coyta, dixo vn cibdadano
que tomasen vn rribaldo, vn vellaco Romano,
Segund le dios le demostrase fazer señas con la mano
que tales las feziese; fueles conssejo sano.

52 ffueron a vn vellaco, muy grand E muy ardid;
dixieron le: 'nos avemos con griegos nuestra conbit
para disputar por señas, lo que tu quisieres pit
E nos dar telo hemos; escusa nos desta lid.'

53 vistieron lo muy bien paños de grand valia,
commo si fuese doctor en la filosofia;
subio en alta cathreda, dixo con bauoquia:
'doy mays vengan los griegos con toda su porfia.'

54 vino ay vn griego doctor muy esmerado,
escogido de griegos, entre todos loado;

Do not reflect upon them when you hear them,
except in the way they are composed.

46   Understand what I say and consider its meaning.
I want no repeats of what happened to the learned Greek
and the uncouth Roman ruffian with his scant knowledge,
when Rome asked Greece for learning.

47   It happened that the Romans had no laws,
and asked the Greeks to give them some.
The Greeks answered that the Romans were unworthy
and would not understand them because of their ignorance.

48   If they wanted to use the laws themselves,
they would first have to hold a debate with the Greek sages
to see whether they understood them and deserved them.
They said this pretty piece by way of a deterrent.

49   The Romans replied that they would gladly do so,
and made a firm agreement over the debate,
but since they did not understand Greek, they requested
that they should debate using learned signs.

50   They fixed a date for the debate.
The Romans were worried and did not know what to do,
because they were uneducated and could not understand
the Greek doctors with their great knowledge.

51   Amid their concern, one citizen suggested
they should employ a ruffian, a Roman thug;
God would show him how to use sign language
like the Greeks did. It was good advice.

52   They approached a thug, burly and bold,
and said: 'We have challenged the Greeks
to a debate using sign language. Ask anything
you want of us, but get us out of this contest.'

53   They dressed him well in expensive clothes,
as if he were a doctor of philosophy.
He mounted a tall dais and said in his foolishness:
'Now let the Greeks come with all their challenges.'

54   A Greek arrived, an elegant doctor,
chosen among Greeks, praised by all;

sobio en otra cathreda, todo el pueblo juntado.
E començo sus señas, commo era tratado.

55   leuantose el griego, sosegado, de vagar,
   E mostro solo vn dedo que esta çerca del pulgar;
   luego se assento en ese mismo lugar.
   leuantose el rribaldo, brauo, de mal pagar.

56   Mostro luego tres dedos contra el griego tendidos,
   el polgar con otros dos que con el son contenidos,
   en manera de arpom los otros dos encogidos;
   assentose el neçio, Catando sus vestidos.

57   leuantose el griego, tendio la palma llana,
   E assentose luego con su memoria sana.
   leuantose el vellaco, con fantasia vana,
   mostro puño çerrado, de porfia avia gana.

58   A Todos los de greçia dixo el sabia griego:
   'meresçen los rromanos las leyes, yo non gelas niego.'
   leuantaron se todos con paz e con sosiego;
   grand onrra ovo rroma por vn vil andariego.

59   Preguntaron al griego sabio que fue lo que dixiera
   por señas al rromano, e que le rrespondiera.
   diz: 'yo dixe que es vn dios; El rromano dixo que era
   vno e tres personas, e tal señal feziera.

60   yo dixe que era todo a la su voluntad;
   rrespondio que en su poder tenie el mundo, E diz verdat.
   desque vi que entendien e crey en la trinidad,
   entendien que meresçien de leyes çertenidad.'

61   Preguntaron al vellaco qual fuera su antojo,
   diz: 'dixo me que con su dedo que me quebrantaria el ojo;
   desto ove grand pesar e tome grand enojo,
   E Respondile con saña, con yra e con cordojo,

62   que yo le quebrantaria, ante todas las gentes,
   con dos dedos los ojos, con el pulgar los dientes.
   dixo me luego, apos esto, que le parase mientes,
   que me daria grand palmada en los oydos Retinientes.

63   yo le Respondi que le daria vna tal puñada,
   que en tienpo de su vida nunca la vies vengada.

he mounted another dais, with everyone around,
and began the sign language as they had agreed.

55 The Greek stood up calmly, with tranquillity,
and showed only his first finger,
then he sat down in the same place.
The ruffian arose, puffed up and belligerent.

56 He showed the Greek three raised fingers,
his thumb and the two adjoining,
holding the other two bent like a harpoon.
The idiot sat down, preening himself.

57 The Greek stood up and showed the flat palm of his hand,
then sat down again with a quiet conscience.
The ruffian arose with a flourish
and showed his fist, spoiling for a fight.

58 The wise Greek told his countrymen:
'The Romans do deserve the laws, I cannot deny.'
Everyone stood up quietly and calmly.
Rome gained great honour through a worthless vagabond.

59 They asked the Greek what the Roman had said
in sign language and what his answer had been.
He replied: 'I said there was one God – the Roman
said He was three persons in one, using this sign.

60 I said everything was God's will and he replied
that He held the world in His power, and that was right.
When I saw that they understood and believed in the Trinity,
I realized that they truly deserved the Laws.'

61 The ruffian was asked how he had understood it:
'He told me he would poke my eye out with his finger;
it upset me, and I got very angry,
and replied with rage, ire and ill humour,

62 that in front of all these people, I would poke out his eyes
with two fingers, and break his teeth with my thumb.
Then he told me to pay attention,
and that he would box my ears thoroughly.

63 I answered that I would give him such a punch
that he would never be avenged in his lifetime.

desque vio que la pelea tenie mal aparejada,
dexose de amenazar do non gelo preçian nada.'

64   Por esto dize la pastraña de la vieja ardida:
'non ha mala palabra si non es a mal tenida.'
veras que bien es dicha, si bien fuese entendida;
entiende bien my dicho e avras dueña garrida.

65   la bulrra que oyeres non la tengas en vil,
la manera del libro entiendela sotil;
que saber bien e mal dezir encobierto e doñeguil,
tu non fallaras vno de trobadores mill.

66   ffallaras muchas garças, non fallaras vn veuo;
rre-mendar bien non sabe todo alfayate nuevo.
a trobar con locura non creas que me muevo,
lo que buen amor dize con rrazon telo prueuo.

67   En general a todos ffabla la escriptura:
los cuerdos con buen sesso entendran la cordura,
los mançebos liuianos guardense de locura;
escoja lo mejor el de buena ventura.

68   las del buen amor sson Razones encubiertas;
trabaja do fallares las sus señales çiertas.
ssi la rrazon entiendes o en el sesso açiertas,
non diras mal del libro que agora rrefiertas.

69   Do coydares que miente dize mayor verdat;
en las coplas pyntadas yaze la falssedat.
dicha buena o mala por puntos la juzgat,
las coplas con los puntos load o denostat.

70   de todos jnstrumentos yo libro so pariente;
bien o mal, qual puntares, tal te dira çierta mente.
qual tu dezir quisieres y faz punto y tente;
ssy me puntar sopieres ssienpre me avras en miente.

AQUI DIZE DE COMO SEGUND NATURA LOS OMES E LAS
OTRAS ANIMALIAS QUIEREN AVER CONPANIA CON LAS
FENBRAS

71   Commo dize aristotiles, cosa es verdadera,
el mundo por dos cosas trabaja: por la primera
por aver mantenençia; la otra cosa era
por aver juntamiento con fenbra plazentera.

When he saw that the fight was ill-matched,
he stopped making threats where it wasn't appreciated.'

64 The wise old woman's proverb goes:
'No evil word is spoken, if it is not thought to be evil.'
You will see that something is well said if well understood.
Understand my book correctly and you'll have a lovely lady.

65 Do not look on the humour as worthless.
Understand the subtle teaching of the book,
good and bad knowledge, elegant and cryptic language;
you will soon find I'm one in a thousand poets.

66 You'll find a lot of herons, but not a single egg.
Not every new tailor knows how to mend properly.
Don't think I am moved to write through mad passion.
I will prove to you that what good love says is true.

67 In general, my book speaks to everyone, like Scripture.
The wise with good understanding will grasp its wisdom,
but frivolous lads should beware of foolishness.
The luckiest one chooses most wisely.

68 The words of good love are secret words.
Try hard to find the clearest signs.
If you follow the argument or hit on the meaning,
speak no ill of the book you criticize now.

69 Where you fear it is false, it speaks the deepest truth:
the deceptions of rhetoric are ugly indeed.
Judge it good or bad depending on each case,
praise or denounce the music of my verses.

70 I, the book, am ancestor of all instruments,
I can tell how well or badly you pluck my strings.
You will find in me whatever you choose to find –
if you know how to play me, I shall stay in your mind.

HOW MEN AND OTHER ANIMALS NATURALLY DESIRE FEMALE COMPANY

71 As Aristotle says, and this is true,
the whole world strives for two things in life,
firstly, to have enough to eat, and the other thing
is to mate with an attractive female.

72 Sy lo dixiese de mio seria de culpar;
    dizelo grand filosofo, non so yo de Rebtar.
    de lo que dize el sabio non deuemos dubdar,
    que por obra se prueva el sabio e su fablar.

73 que diz verdat el sabio clara mente se prueua:
    omnes, aves, animalias, toda bestia de cueva
    quieren Segund natura conpañia sienpre Nueva,
    E quanto mas el omne que a toda cosa se mueva.

74 Digo muy mas del omne que de toda creatura;
    todos a tienpo çierto se juntan con natura,
    el omne de mal sseso todo tienpo syn mesura,
    cada que puede e quiere fazer esta locura.

75 El ffuego ssienpre quiere estar en la çeniza,
    commo quier que mas arde quanto mas se atiza;
    el omne quando peca bien vee que desliza,
    mas non se parte ende Ca natura lo enriza.

76 E yo como ssoy omne commo otro pecador,
    ove de las mugeres a las vezes grand amor;
    prouar omne las cosas non es por ende peor,
    e saber bien e mal e vsar lo mejor.

DE COMO EL ARCIPRESTE FFUE ENAMORADO
77 Assy fue que vn tienpo vna dueña me prisso,
    de su amor non fuy en ese tienpo rrepiso,
    ssienpre avia della buena fabla e buen rriso,
    Nunca al fizo por mi nin creo que fazer quiso.

78 Era dueña en todo e de dueñas señora;
    non podia estar solo con ella vna ora;
    mucho de omne se guardam ally do ella mora,
    mas mucho que non guardan los jodios la tora.

79 ssabe toda nobleza de oro e de seda,
    conplida de muchos byenes anda manssa e leda,
    es de buenas construnbres sossegada e queda,
    non se podria vençer por pintada moneda.

80 Enbiele esta cantiga, que es de yuso puesta,
    con la mi mensajera que tenia enpuesta;

72   If this were my idea alone, I might be blamed,
      but these are the words of a great philosopher, so don't
                                                   chastise me;
      we should not doubt the words of a sage,
      since facts back up the wise man and his words.

73   It is quite clear to see that he spoke the truth:
      men, birds, animals, all wild beasts in cave and burrow
      constantly seek out new companions,
      and man more than any living thing.

74   I insist, man above all creatures – all others mate
      by natural instinct in the right season.
      Misguided man does it unrestrainedly, all the time,
      whenever he is willing and able to indulge in this folly.

75   Fire always longs to be among the ashes,
      since it burns more fiercely the more it is poked.
      When man sins he well knows he is slipping,
      but does not turn away, because Nature impels him.

76   And I, being man and sinner, like any other,
      have at times been greatly in love with women.
      It is not always wrong to try out everything
      and learn good and bad, then make use of the best.

HOW THE ARCHPRIEST FELL IN LOVE

77   Once it happened that I fell in love with a lady,
      and was not at all repentant at that time.
      She always made lively conversation, smiled a lot,
      but that was all she did for me, and all she wanted to do.

78   She was ladylike in every way, a lady above all others,
      but I couldn't even get one hour alone with her.
      There were more people guarding her at her house
      than there are Jews guarding the Torah.

79   She was skilled at working with gold and silk fabrics,
      accomplished in all ways, calm and happy;
      well-mannered, quiet and relaxed,
      the shine of money would not corrupt her at all.

80   I sent her this song, written below,*
      using my messenger woman, who was in the know,

dize verdat la fabla que la dueña conpuesta,
si non quiere el mandado, non da buena rrepuesta.

81   dixo la duena cuerda a la mi mensajera:
        'yo veo otras muchas creer a ti, parlera,
        E fallanse ende mal; castigo en su manera,
        bien commo la rrapossa en agena mollera.

ENXIEPLO DE COMO EL LEON ESTAUA DOLIENTE E LAS
OTRAS ANIMALIAS LO VENIAN A VER

82   Diz que yazie doliente el leon de dolor,
        todas las animalias vinieron ver su señor;
        tomo plazer con ellas e sentiose mejor;
        alegraron se todas mucho por su amor.

83   Por le fazer plazer E mas le alegrar,
        conbidaronle todas quel darian A yantar.
        dixieron que mandase quales quisiese matar:
        mando matar al toro, que podria abastar.

84   ffizo partidor al lobo e mando que a todos diese,
        el aparto lo menudo para el leon que comiese,
        E para si la canal, la mejor que omne viese.
        al leon dixo el lobo que la mesa bendixiese:

85   "Señor," diz, "tu estas flaco, esta vianda liuiana
        comme la tu, señor, que te sera buena e sana;
        para mi E a los otros, la canal que es vana."
        el leon fue sañudo, que de comer avia gana.

86   alço el leon la mano por la mesa santiguar,
        dio grand golpe en la cabeça al lobo por lo castigar;
        el cuero con la oreja del caxco le fue arrancar.
        el leon a la rraposa mando la vianda dar.

87   la gulpeja con el miedo e commo es artera,
        toda la canal del toro al leon dio entera,
        para si e los otros todo lo menudo era;
        marauillose el leon de tan buena egualadera.

88   El leon dixo: "comadre ¿quien vos mostro ha fazer partiçion
        tan buena, tan aguisada, tan derecha con rrazon?"
        ella dixo: "en la cabeça del lobo tome yo esta liçion,
        en el lobo castigue que feziese o que non."

but the saying is true: 'A discreet woman
will not reply to advantage if she doesn't want the message.'

81   The wise lady said to my messenger:
'I have seen many believe what you say, chatterbox,
and end up in trouble. This was a lesson to me
like the one the fox learnt because of the wolf's head.

THE FABLE OF THE SICK LION AND THE OTHER ANIMALS WHO CAME TO SEE HIM

82   One day the lion was lying suffering in great pain.
All the animals came to see their lord.
He took pleasure in their company and felt much better.
They were all happy because he was fond of them.

83   To please and cheer him even more
they invited him to eat with them,
and asked him to tell them what they should kill.
He ordered them to kill the bull, ample to feed everyone.

84   He made the wolf divide the food to share among them all.
The wolf gave the smallest portion to the lion
and kept the whole body for himself.
The lion asked the wolf to bless the meal table.

85   "My lord," he said, "you are weak, eat these innards,
sir, they will do you a lot of good.
The empty carcass will do for me and the others."
The lion was angry, for he was very hungry.

86   The lion raised his paw to make the sign of the cross
and dealt the wolf a great blow on the head as punishment.
The blow tore off his scalp and ear.
Then the lion ordered the vixen to dole out the meat.

87   The vixen was frightened and very cunning,
she gave the lion the whole bull carcass.
A small amount was left for her and the others.
The lion marvelled at such fair sharing out.

88   He said: "Old mother fox, who showed you
how to share out so well, so justly, so correctly?"
She replied: "I learnt my lesson from the wolf's head,
I learnt from the wolf what to do and what not to do."

89   Por ende yo te digo, vieja e non mi amiga,
        que jamas a mi non vengas nin me digas tal enemiga.
        sy non yo te mostrare commo el leon castiga,
        que el cuerdo E la ouerda en mal ageno castiga.'

90   E segund diz jhesu xpisto, non ay cossa escondida
        que a cabo de tienpo non sea bien sabida;
        ffue la mi poridat luego a la plaça salida,
        la dueña muy guardada ffue luego de mi partida.

91   Nunca desde esa ora yo mas la pude ver;
        enbio me mandar que punase en fazer
        algun triste ditado, que podiese ella saber,
        que cantase con tristeza, pues la non podia aver.

92   Por conplir su mandado de aquesta mi Señor,
        ffize cantar tan triste commo este triste amor;
        cantavalo la dueña creo que con dolor,
        mas que yo podria sser dello trobador.

93   Diz el prouerbio viejo: 'quien matar quisier su can,
        achaque le leuanta por que non le de del pan.'
        los que quieren partir nos como fecho lo han,
        mesclaron me con ella e dixieronle del plan.

94   Que me loaua della commo de buena caça,
        E que profaçaua della commo si fuese caraça.
        diz la dueña sañuda: 'non ay paño syn rraça,
        nin el leal amigo non es en toda plaça.'

95   Commo dize la fabla: 'quando a otro sometem
        qual palabra te dizen, tal coraçon te meten.'
        posieron le grand ssaña, desto se entremeten.
        diz la dueña: 'los novios non dan quanto prometen.'

96   Commo la buena dueña era mucho letrada,
        sotil, entendida, cuerda, bien messurada,
        dixo a la mi vieja, que le avia enbiada,
        esta fabla conpuesta, de ysopete sacada.

97   Diz: 'quando quier casar omne con dueña mucho onrrada,
        promete E manda mucho; desque la ha cobrada,
        de quanto le prometio, o le da poco o nada,
        ffaze commo la tierra quando estaua finchada:

89 So, I'm telling you, old lady, you are no friend of mine,
don't ever come to me with such badness,
or I'll show you how the lion punishes,
for the wise man and woman learn from others' mistakes.'

90 As Jesus Christ said, nothing is hidden
that shall not be revealed in time,
so my secret was made public
and the well-guarded lady was parted from me.

91 I could not see her from that time on,
but she sent a message for me to try to write
some sad little poem for her to learn,
to be sung with great sorrow, as I couldn't have her.

92 To carry out her wishes I wrote a song,
as sad as my sad, sad love;
the lady would sing it mournfully, I think,
since she was the real poet, rather than me.

93 The old proverb says: 'Anyone who wants to kill their dog,
will find some pretext for not feeding it.'
Those who wanted to separate us, which they did,
spoke badly of me to her and certainly told her

94 that I boasted of her as easy prey,
and defamed her as if she were a whore.
She spoke in anger: 'No cloth is without a flaw,
and a loyal friend cannot be found everywhere.'

95 As the story goes: 'When people put someone down,
anything they say will turn your heart against that person.'
They went out of their way to rouse her anger,
and she said: 'Suitors do not give what they promise.'

96 As the good lady was very well educated,
subtle and understanding, wise and moderate,
I sent my old woman to call, and my lady told her
this elegant fable taken from Aesop.

97 She said: 'When a man wants to marry a very honourable
lady,
he makes all kinds of promises. As soon as he wins her,
he gives little or nothing of what he has promised,
like the earth when it was pregnant:

ENSIENPLO DE QUANDO LA TIERRA BRAMAUA

98 Ansy ffue que la tierra commenço a bramar.
    estaua tan fynchada que queria quebrar;
    a quantos la oyen podie mal espantar;
    commo duena en parto començose de coytar.

99 la gente que tan grandes bramidos oya,
    coydauan que era preñada, atanto se dolia,
    penssauan que grand sierpe o grand bestia pariria,
    que a todo el mundo conbrie e estragaria.

100 quando ella bramaua pensauan de foyr,
     E desque vino el dia que ovo de parir,
     pario vn mur topo; escarnio fue de rreyr,
     ssus bramuras e espantos en burla fueron salir.

101 E bien ansi acaesçio a muchos e a tu Amo;
     prometen mucho trigo e dan poca paja tamo.
     çiegan muchos con el viento, van se perder con mal Ramo;
     vete, dil que me non quiera, que nol quiero nil amo.'

102 omne que mucho fabla, faze menos a vezes,
     pone muy grant espanto, chica cosa es dos nuezes;
     las cosas mucho caras, alguna ora son rrafezes,
     las viles e las rrefezes son caras a las de vezes.

103 Tommo por chica cosa aborrençia e grand saña,
     arredrose de mi, fizo me el juego mañana;
     aquel es enganado quien coyda que engaña,
     desto fize troba de tristeza tam mañana.

104 ffiz luego esta cantigas de verdadera salua,
     mande que gelas diesen de noche o al alua.
     non las quiso tomar. dixe yo: 'muy mal va;
     al tienpo se encoje mejor la yerua malua.'

DE COMO TODAS LAS COSSAS DEL MUNDO SSON VANIDAT SINON AMAR A DIOS

105 Commo dize salamo, e dize la verdat,
     que las cosas del mundo todas son vanidat,
     todas son pasaderas, van se con la hedat,
     ssaluo amor de dios, todas sson lyuiandat.

THE FABLE OF THE EARTH THAT GROANED

98   It happened that the earth began to groan.
It was swollen up fit to burst,
and filled whoever heard it with terror.
It began to complain, like a woman in labour.

99   The people heard this terrible groaning,
and thought the earth must be pregnant, to be in such pain.
They thought it would give birth to a mighty serpent or
monster
which would devour everyone in one gulp.

100   When the earth groaned, people began to flee,
but as soon as the day came for it to give birth,
it produced a mole – what a joke it was.
All the groaning and fear ended in laughter.

101   This has happened to many, including your master.
They promise a lot of corn and give a little straw and chaff.
Many are blinded by their wind, they come to a bad end.
Go away, tell him not to love me, as I do not love him.'

102   A man who talks a lot often does little,
he fills you with fear, but two little nuts don't amount to
much;
sometimes things which are very costly have no value
and worthless, vile things are sometimes very dear.

103   She conceived great hatred and anger over very little,
she distanced herself from me and deceived me.
The deceived is the one who thinks he deceives.
I composed some verse of deepest sadness about this.

104   Then I wrote these songs of true justification,
and sent them to be given her at night-time or at dawn.
She would not have them and I thought: 'No luck,
the mallow plant is best picked when the time is right.'

HOW ALL WORLDLY THINGS ARE VANITY, EXCEPT FOR LOVING GOD

105   As Solomon said, and he spoke the truth,
all worldly things are vanity,
all are fleeting and pass in time,
all is frivolous except the love of God.

106 E yo, desque vi la dueña partida E mudada,
dixe: 'querer do non me quieren ffaria vna nada,
rresponder do non me llaman es vanidad prouada.'
parti me de su pleito pues de mi es rredrada.

107 Sabe dios que aquesta dueña e quantas yo vy,
sienpre quise guardalas e sienpre las serui,
ssy seruir non las pude nunca las deserui;
de dueña mesurada sienpre bien escreui.

108 Mucho seria villano e torpe Pajez
sy de la muger noble dixiese cosa rrefez,
ca en muger loçana, fermosa e cortes,
todo bien del mundo e todo plazer es.

109 ssy dios, quando formo el omne, entendiera
que era mala cosa la muger, non la diera
al omne por conpañera, nin del non la feziera;
ssy para bien non fuera, tan noble non saliera.

110 ssy omne a la muger non la quisiesse bien,
non ternia tantos presos el amor quantos tien;
por santo nin santa que seya, non se quien
non cobdiçie conpaña, sy solo se mantiem.

111 vna fabla lo dize que vos digo agora,
que vna ave sola nin bien canta nin bien llora;
el mastel syn la vela non puede estar toda ora,
nin las verças non se crian tan bien sin la noria.

112 E yo commo estaua solo, syn conpañia,
codiciava tener lo que otro para sy tenia;
puse el ojo en otra non santa, mas sentia;
yo cruyziaua por ella, otro la avie val-dia.

113 E por que yo non podia con ella ansi fablar,
puse por mi menssajero, coydando Recabdar,
a vn mi conpanero. Sopome el clauo echar;
el comio la vianda e a mi fazie Rumiar.

114 ffiz con el grand pessar esta troba caçura;
la dueña que la oyere por ello non me aburra,
Ca devrien me dezir neçio e mas que bestia burra,
sy de tan grand escarnio yo non trobase burla.

106 When I saw my lady was inaccessible and changed,
     I said: 'It would be foolish to love where I am not loved,
     to answer when I am not called is proven vanity.'
     I ended the relationship, as she had turned away from me.

107 God knows I always wanted to protect and serve
     this lady and all the others I ever saw.
     If I could not serve them, I never did them disservice.
     I have always written well of virtuous, restrained women.

108 It would be very base and low
     if I spoke badly of a noble lady,
     because a lively, beautiful and courteous woman
     holds all the pleasure and goodness in the world.

109 If when God made man he had intended
     woman to be a bad thing, he would never have given
     her to man as his companion, nor formed her from him.
     If she were not made for good, she would not be so noble.

110 If man were not so fond of woman,
     love would not hold so many people captive.
     However saintly a person may be, I don't know anyone
     who does not long for company if they live alone.

111 I can tell you a story about this now, on the theme of
     'a solitary bird neither weeps nor sings well'.
     A mast cannot always be without a sail
     and vegetables do not grow so well without a waterwheel.

112 And as I was alone, with no company,
     I longed to have what others possessed.
     I set my sights upon another, not saintly, but foolish.
     I suffered archly for her, worse than crucifixion,* but
                                          another won her easily.

113 Because I could not speak to her directly
     I asked a friend of mine to act as a messenger,
     thinking of success. But he knew how to drive home
     the nails of deceit. He ate the meat while I chewed the cud.

114 In grief, I wrote this satirical minstrel's song.*
     If a lady hears it, she must not dislike me for it,
     as I would be a fool and more stupid than a donkey
     if I could not see the funny side of such a trick.

DE LO QUE CONTESÇIO AL ARÇIPRESTE CON FERRAND
GARÇIA SU MENSSAJERO

115   Mys ojos non veran luz
       Pues perdido he a cruz.

116   Cruz cruzada panadera
       tome por entendera,
       tome senda por carrera
       Commo andaluz.

117   Coydando que la avria,
       dixielo a fferrand garçia
       que troxiese la pletesia
       E fuese pleytes e duz.

118   dixo me quel plazia de grado
       e fizo se de la cruz priuado;
       a mi dio rrumiar saluado
       El comio el pan mas duz.

119   Prometiol por mi conssejo
       trigo que tenia Anejo,
       E presentol vn conejo,
       El traydor falso marfuz.

120   Dios confonda menssajero
       tan presto e tan ligero,
       non medre dios tal conejero
       que la caça ansy aduz.

121   quando la cruz veya, yo sienpre me omillava,
       santiguava me a ella do quier que la fallaua;
       el conpaño de çerca en la cruz adoraua;
       del mal de la cruzada yo non me rreguardaua.

122   Del escolar goloso conpañero de cucaña,
       fize esta otra troba, non vos sea estraña,
       Ca de Ante nin despues non falle en españa
       quien ansy me feziese de escarnio magadaña.

WHAT HAPPENED TO THE ARCHPRIEST AND HIS
MESSENGER, FERRAND GARCÍA

115 My eyes shall see no light
     since I have lost my Cross.

116 Cross crusaded, Cross the baker girl,*
     I took her for my lover,
     mistook a pathway for a highway
     like the Andalusian Moor.*

117 Thinking I should have her soon
     I asked Ferrand García
     to put my case before her,
     as negotiator and guide.

118 He said it would give him pleasure,
     but soon became her favourite;
     he gave me the bran to chew
     while he ate the tasty bread.

119 On my advice he promised her
     some corn I had stored up,
     and gave her a fine rabbit,*
     the false, deceiving traitor.

120 May God confound a messenger
     so ready and so agile!
     God will not favour a rabbit-hunter
     who catches his prey like that.

121 When I saw Cross I always knelt in greeting,
     crossed myself whenever I met her.
     My companion worshipped the Cross at close hand,
     I had no defence against the evil crusade.

122 I wrote this new poem, which I hope will not shock you,
     about the greedy student, an opportunist like the cuckoo,
     for neither before nor after did I find a person in all Spain
     who ever made a bigger scarecrow dummy of me.

AQUI FABLA DE LA CONSTELAÇION E DE LA PLANETA, EN
QUE LOS OMNES NASÇEN, E DEL JUYZIO DE LOS ÇINCO
SSABIOS NATURALES DIERON EN EL NASÇEMIENTO DEL
FIJO DEL REY ALCAREZ

123   Los antiguos astrologos dizen en la çiençia
    de la astrologia vna buena sabiençia:
    quel omne quando nasçe, luego en su naçençia,
    el signo en que nasçe le juzgan por sentençia.

124   Esto diz tholomeo e dizelo platon,
    otros muchos maestros en este acuerdo son:
    qual es el asçendente e la costellaçion
    del que naçe, tal es su fado e su don.

125   Muchos ay que trabajan sienpre por clerezia,
    deprende grandes tienpos, espienden grant quantia,
    en cabo saben poco, que su fado les guia,
    non pueden desmentir a la astrologia.

126   otros entran en ordem por saluar las sus almas,
    otros toman esfuerço en querer vsar armas,
    otros siruen Señores con las manos anbas,
    pero muchos de aquestos dan en tierra de palmas.

127   Non acaban en orden nin son mas cavalleros,
    nin han merçed de Senores nin han de sus dineros;
    por que puede ser esto, creo ser verdaderos,
    Segund natural curso, los dichos estrelleros.

128   Por que creas el curso destos signos atales,
    dezir te vn juyzio de çinco naturales,
    que judgaron vn niño por sus çiertas senales;
    dieron juyzios fuertes de acabados males.

129   Era vn Rey de moros, alcaraz nonbre avia;
    nasçiole vn fijo bello, mas de aquel non tenia,
    enbio por sus sabios, dellos saber querria
    el signo e la planeta del fijo quel nasçia.

130   Entre los estrelleros quel vinieron a ver,
    vinieron çinco dellos de mas conplida saber;
    desque vieron el punto en que ovo de nasçer,
    dixo el vn maestro: 'apedreado ha de ser.'

ON THE SUBJECT OF THE CONSTELLATIONS AND PLANETS
UNDER WHICH MEN ARE BORN, AND THE DIFFERENT
OPINIONS OF THE FIVE LEARNED SAGES REGARDING THE
BIRTH OF KING ALCARAZ'S SON

123   The ancient sages learned in the science
of astrology had an interesting saying:
the destiny of man can be judged at his birth
by the ascending star at that moment.

124   This was said by both Ptolemy and Plato.
Many other learned men are in agreement.
A man's destiny and aptitudes are shown
in the ascendant star and constellation of his birth.

125   Many work hard for ecclesiastical knowledge,
spend many years learning and a great deal of money
yet at the end they know little, for their destiny guides them,
and astrology cannot be denied.

126   Others enter an order to save their souls,
some try to master arms,
yet others serve their masters with both hands,
but many fall hands down on the ground.

127   They don't end up in the Order, nor are they knights,
they get no thanks from their masters, nor any of their
money.
The reason for this, and I believe it is true,
lies in the laws of nature, as told by the astrologers.

128   To encourage you to believe the signs,
I will tell you the judgement made by five men of science,
who gave their verdict on a boy from clear indications,
boldly foretelling the direst evils.

129   There was a Moorish king whose name was Alcaraz,
to whom a fine son was born, his only one.
Sending for his sages, he wished to know
the sign and planet of the new-born child.

130   Among the astrologers who came to see him
were five of the greatest experts.
When they saw the moment at which the boy was born
one of the wise men said: 'He will be stoned to death.'

131   Judgo el otro e dixo: 'este ha de ser quemado.'
      el terçero dize: 'el niño ha de despeñado.'
      el quarto dixo: 'el jnfante ha de ser colgado.'
      dixo el quinto maestro: 'morra en agua afogado.'

132   quando oyo el Rey juyzios desacordados
      mando que los maestros fuesen muy bien guardados,
      fizo los tener presos en logares apartados,
      dio todos sus juyzios por mitrosos prouados.

133   desque fue el infante a buena hedat llegado,
      pidio al rrey su padre que le fuese otorgado
      de yr a correr monte, caçar algun venado.
      rrespondiole el rrey que le plazia de grado.

134   Cataron dia claro para yr a caçar;
      desque fueron en el monte ovose a leuantar
      vn rrevatado nublo, començo de agranizar,
      e a poca de ora començo de apedrear.

135   Acordose su Ayo de commo lo judgaron
      los sabios naturales que su signo cataron;
      diz: 'vayamos nos, Señor, que los que a vos fadaron
      non sean verdaderos en lo que adevinaron.'

136   Penssaron mucho Ayna todos de se acojer,
      mas commo es verdat e non puede fallesçer
      en lo que dios ordena en commo ha de ser,
      segund natural curso, non se puede estorçer,

137   ffaciendo la grand piedra el infante aguijo,
      pasando por la puente vn grand rrayo le dio,
      fforado se la puente, por alli se despeño,
      en vn arbol del rrio de sus faldas se colgo.

138   Estando ansy colgado, ado todos lo vieron,
      afogose en el agua, acorrer non lo podieron;
      los çinco fados dichos todos bien se conplieron,
      los sabios naturales verdaderos salieron.

139   desque vido el Rey conplido su pessar,
      mando los estrelleros de la presion soltar,
      fizo les mucho bien e mandoles vsar
      de su astrologia en que non avie que dubdar.

131   The second said: 'He will be burnt.'
The third declared: 'The child will fall from the rocks,'
the fourth said: 'The infant will be hanged,'
and the fifth master spoke: 'He will drown in water.'

132   When the king heard all these different opinions,
he ordered the sages to be put under guard
and held them prisoner in separate places.
He took all their words as proven lies.

133   As soon as the young prince reached a suitable age,
he asked his father the king if he could go
into the mountains to hunt for deer.
The king replied that he could do so with pleasure.

134   They waited for a fine day to go hunting,
but as soon as they reached the mountain,
a cloud suddenly appeared and it began to sleet.
In a short time huge hailstones fell.

135   The boy's tutor remembered the words
of the five wise scientists who examined his sign.
'My lord,' he said, 'let's go back, so that the words
of your fortune-tellers do not come true.'

136   Everyone began to leave,
but since what God ordains must be,
for it is true and cannot fail,
the laws of nature must be obeyed.

137   Because it was hailing so heavily, the prince spurred on
his horse, but as he crossed the bridge a great bolt of lightning
struck – the bridge collapsed, he was thrown down
and left hanging by his clothes from a tree by the river.

138   Hanging there where all could see him,
he drowned in the water, as no one could help him.
The five destinies foretold had been fulfilled;
the wise men of science had spoken the truth.

139   When the king saw his long-feared grief fulfilled,
he ordered the astrologers' release from jail.
He did many good things for them and ordered them to use
their astrology, which he no longer doubted.

140 Yo creo los estrologos uerdad natural mente,
pero dios que crio natura e açidente,
puede los demudar e fazer otra mente,
segund la fe catholica yo desto creyente.

141 En creer lo de natura non es mal estança,
e creer muy mas en dios con firme esperança;
por que creas mis dichos e non tomes dubdança
prueuo telo breue mente con esta semejança.

142 Cyerto es que el rrey en su Regno ha poder
de dar fueros e leyes e derechos fazer;
desto manda fazer libros e quadernos conponer,
para quien faze el yerro que pena deue aver.

143 Acaesçe que alguno ffaze grand trayçion
ansi que por el fuero deue morir con rraçon,
pero por los priuados, que en su ayuda son,
si piden merçed al Rey dale conplido perdon.

144 O sy, por aventura, aqueste que lo erro,
al rrey, en algund tienpo a tanto le seruio,
que piedat e seruiçio mucho al rrey mouio,
por que del yerro fecho conplido perdon le dio.

145 E ansy commo por fuero avia de morir,
el fazedor del fuero non lo quiere conssentyr,
dyspensa contra el fuero e dexalo beuir;
quien puede fazer leyes puede contra ellas yr.

146 otrosy puede el papa sus decretales far,
en que a sus subditos manda çierta pena dar;
pero puede muy bien contra ellas dispenssar,
por graçia o por seruiçio toda la pena soltar.

147 veemos cada dia pasar esto de fecho,
pero por todo eso las leyes y el derecho
E el fuero escripto non es por ende desfecho.
anti es çierta çiençia e de mucho prouecho.

148 bien ansy nuestro señor dios, quando el çielo crio,
puso en el sus signos E planetas ordeno,
sus poderios çiertos E juyzios otorgo,
pero mayor poder rretuvo en sy que les non dio.

140   I naturally believe that astrologers speak the truth,
but God, who created nature and chance,
may alter them and do otherwise.
I believe in this, according to the Catholic faith.

141   To believe in Nature's laws is not a sin,
any more than to believe in God with firmest hope.
I will make this brief comparison
so that you might believe my words and have no doubt.

142   It is a certain fact that a king has power in his own kingdom
to lay down laws and statutes and establish rights.
He may order books to be written, volumes composed,
to establish the penalty for those that err.

143   Sometimes people become great traitors
and they must die for it, according to the statute,
but the favoured, who receive the king's help,
are pardoned completely if they ask him for mercy.

144   Or if by chance the errant person
once did the king a service which
greatly moved him in its loyalty,
then he will fully pardon the error.

145   So even if the statute decrees death,
the maker of the statute will not allow it.
He goes against the law and lets the man live.
He who makes laws can also go against them.

146   The Pope may establish his decretals in the same way,
in which the subjects are given a specific punishment,
but he may give dispensation against those decretals
and grant exemption from punishment through grace or
                                      service.

147   We see this happening every day,
but for all that, laws and rights
and written statutes are not cast aside.
This is a certain fact and of very great benefit.

148   In the same way, when our Lord created heaven,
He ordained the signs of the zodiac and the planets,
and bestowed their powers and specific interpretations –
but He kept more power than He gave.

149   Anssy que por ayuno e lymosna e oracion
      E por seruir a dios con mucha contriçion,
      non ha poder mal signo nin su costellaçion;
      el poderio de dios tuelle la tribulacion.

150   Non son por todo aquesto los estrelleros mintrosos,
      que judgam Segund natura, por sus cuentos fermosos;
      ellos e la çiençia son çiertos e non dubdosos,
      mas non puedem contra dios yr nin son poderosos.

151   Non sse astrologia nin so ende maestro,
      nin se astralabio mas que buey de cabestro,
      mas por que cada dia veo pasar esto,
      por aqueso lo digo, otrossy veo aquesto:

152   Muchos nasçen en venus que lo mas de su vida
      es amar las mugeres, nunca seles olvida;
      trabajan E afanan mucho syn medida,
      E los mas non rrecabdan la cosa mas querida.

153   En este signo atal creo que yo nasçi;
      sienpre pune en seruir dueñas que conosçi,
      el bien que me feçieron non lo desagradesçi,
      a muchas serui mucho, que nada non acabesçi.

154   Commo quier que he provado mi signo ser atal,
      en seruir a las duenas punar e non en al;
      pero avn que omne non goste la pera del peral,
      en estar a la sonbra es plazer comunal.

155   muchas noblezas ha en el que a las dueñas sirue;
      loçano, fablador, En ser franco se abiue;
      en seruir a las dueñas el bueno non se esquiue,
      que si mucho trabaja, en mucho plazer byue.

156   El amor faz sotil al omne que es rrudo,
      ffazele fabrar fermoso al que antes es mudo,
      al omne que es couarde fazelo muy atrevudo,
      al perezoso fazer ser presto e agudo.

157   Al mançebo mantiene mucho en mançebez
      e al viejo faz perder mucho la vejez,
      ffaze blanco e fermoso del negro como pez,
      lo que non vale vna nuez amor le da grand prez.

149 So through fasting, alms and prayer,
and by serving God with a contrite heart,
an evil sign or constellation has no power,
for the power of God takes away tribulation.

150 For all this, the astrologers tell no lies, for they judge
according to Nature in their clever calculations.
They and their science are authentic, not dubious,
but they can have no power against God.

151 I have no knowledge of astrology, am not an expert,
I know no more about the astrolabe than an ox in a halter,
but I see this happening every day,
which is why I speak of it. I also see this:

152 many are born under the sign of Venus and most of their lives
are spent loving women, it is constantly in mind.
They work and strive without restraint,
and the majority do not obtain what they most desire.

153 I believe I was born under this sign,
as I have always striven to serve the ladies I knew.
I am not ungrateful for the good they did me,
I did great service to many and never achieved a thing.

154 Although I have proved my sign to be what it is,
I have tried hard to serve women and nothing else;
yet although I may not eat the pear from the pear-tree,
it is pleasant for everyone to stand in its shade.

155 The man who serves woman has many good qualities,
he strives to be vigorous, forthcoming, generous;
the good man does not flinch from serving women,
for with hard work, he will live a life of great pleasure.

156 Love makes the ignorant man wise,
makes the dumb speak with eloquence,
love makes the coward bold
and the lazy quick and sharp.

157 It keeps the young man youthful,
and the old man's age falls away,
skin as dark as pitch becomes white and handsome,
love gives great value to the worthless.

158 El que es enamorado, por muy feo que sea,
    otrosi su amiga maguer que sea muy fea,
    el vno E el otro non ha cosa que vea
    que tan bien le paresca nin que tanto desea.

159 El bauieca, el torpe, el neçio, El poble
    a su amiga bueno paresçe E rrico onbre,
    mas noble que los otros; por ende todo onbre
    como vn amor pierde luego otro cobre.

160 Ca puesto que su signo sea de tal natura
    commo es este mio, dize vna escriptura
    que buen es-fuerço vençe a la mala ventura,
    E a toda pera dura grand tienpo la madura.

161 vna tacha le fallo al amor poderoso,
    la qual a vos, dueñas, yo descobrir non oso;
    mas, por que non me tengades por dezidor medroso,
    es esta: que el amor sienpre fabla mentiroso.

162 Ca, Segund vos he dicho en la otra consseja,
    lo que en si es torpe con amor bien semeja,
    tiene por noble cosa lo que non vale vna arveja;
    lo que semeja non es, oya bien tu oreja.

163 Sy las mancanas sienpre oviesen tal sabor
    de dentro, qual de fuera dan vista e color,
    non avrie de las plantas fructa de tal valor;
    mas ante pudren que otra, pero dan buen olor.

164 bien atal es el amor que da palabra llena,
    toda cosa que dize paresçe mucho buena;
    non es todo cantar quanto rruydo suena;
    por vos descobrir esto, dueña, non aya pena.

165 diz por las verdades sse pierden los Amigos,
    E por las non dezir se fazen des-amigos;
    anssy entendet sano los proverbios antiguos
    E nunca vos creades loores de enemigos.

DE COMO EL ACIPRESTE FUE ENAMORADO E DEL ENXIENPLO DEL LADRON E DEL MASTYN

166 Como dize el sabio, cosa dura e fuerte
    es dexar la costunbre el fado e la suerte;

158   If a man is in love, however ugly he may be,
and however lacking in beauty is his lady friend,
neither one of them will have seen anything
which looks better or more desirable.

159   The fool, the dim-witted, the idiot and the pauper
seem fine rich men to the women who love them
and nobler than the rest; therefore any man
who loses a lover will soon acquire another.

160   Since his birthsign is of that nature,
like mine, there is a saying which goes:
'Great effort will conquer bad luck',
and 'a hard pear will eventually ripen.'

161   I find one fault in all-powerful love,
which I dare not reveal to you ladies.
But just in case you think I am frightened to speak,
I'll tell you – love always speaks falsely.

162   Because, as I said in my previous advice,
what is crude in itself seems good in the eyes of love;
the worthless vetch is held to be noble,
appearances deceive, so listen carefully.

163   If apples always tasted as good on the inside
as their colour and appearance promised,
no other plant would bear fruit of such worth;
yet they rot sooner than others, though they smell sweet.

164   Love is the same, which promises everything,
everything it says to us seems good;
but all noise is not singing.
There is no sin in revealing this, madam.

165   It is said that speaking the truth loses friends,
and in not doing so enemies are made.
So interpret the ancient proverbs wisely
and never believe the praise of enemies.

HOW THE ARCHPRIEST FELL IN LOVE, AND THE FABLE OF THE THIEF AND THE MASTIFF

166   As the wise man says, it is a hard and serious thing
to cast aside habit, fate and luck.

la costunbre es otra que natura cierta mente,
apenas non se pierde fasta que viene la muerte.

167   E por que es constunbre de macebos vsada,
querer sienpre tener alguna enamorada,
por aver solaz bueno del amor con amada,
tome amiga nueva, vna dueña ençerrada.

168   duena de buen lynaje e de mucha nobleza,
todo saber de dueña sabe con sotileza,
cuerda E de buen seso non sabe de villeza,
muchas dueñas e otras de buen saber las veza.

169   De talla muy apuesta E de gesto amorosa,
loçana, doñeguil, plazentera, fermosa,
cortes e mesurada, falaguera, donosa,
graçiosa e donable amor en toda cosa.

170   Por amor desta dueña ffiz trobas e cantares,
ssenbre avena loca Ribera de henares;
verdat es lo que dizen los antiguos rretraheres;
quien en el arenal sienbra non trilla pegujares.

171   Coydando la yo aver entre las benditas
davale de mis donas, non paños e non çintas,
non cuentas nin sartal, nin sortijas, nin mitas,
con ello estas cantigas que son de yuso escriptas.

172   Non quiso Reçeuirlo, bien fuxo de avoleza,
ffizo de mi bauieca, diz: 'non muestra pereza
los omnes en dar poco por tomar grand rriqueza;
leuadlo E dezidle que mal mercar non es franqueza.

173   Non perdere yo a dios nin al su parayso
por pecado del mundo que es sonbra de aliso;
non soy yo tan ssyn sesso, sy algo he priso;
quien toma dar deue, dizelo sabio enviso.'

174   anssy contençio a mi con la dueña de prestar
commo conteçio al ladron que entraua a furtar,
que fallo vn grand mastyn, començole de ladrar,
el ladron, por furtar algo, començole a falagar.

175   lanço medio pan al perro, que traya en la mano,
dentro yuan las çaraças, varrunto lo el alano.

Habit is second nature, for sure,
and is rarely abandoned until death.

167 And because it is the common habit of young men
to long constantly for a loved one,
to enjoy the pleasure of love with their lover,
I found a new love, a lady under lock and key.

168 A lady of high birth and great nobility,
with subtle knowledge of women's skills,
sensible and wise, devoid of all meanness,
who taught many women what they should know.

169 Her figure was elegant, her face inspired love,
she was lively, graceful, pleasing, beautiful,
polite and moderate, affectionate, generous,
witty and light-hearted, love in every way.

170 For love of this lady I wrote poems and songs,
I sowed wild oats on the banks of the Henares.*
What the old proverbs say is true:
'Whoever sows in the sand does not till his own plot.'

171 Thinking I would have her in my pious flock,
I gave of my own gifts, not fine cloth or girdles,
nor beads, nor rings, nor gloves,
I gave her the songs written here below.*

172 She would not have them, she shunned baseness,
she made a fool of me, saying: 'Men are not slow
to give little in order to gain great riches; take them away
and tell him that underselling is not generosity.

173 I will not lose God nor paradise
for the sin of the world, which is like the alder's shade;
I am not so foolish, for if I take something,
then the taker must give, as the sage says.'

174 The same thing happened with this excellent lady
as it did in the tale of the robber who broke in to steal
and found a huge mastiff. It started to bark,
so the robber cajoled it, to enable him to thieve.

175 He threw a small piece of bread to the dog,
spiked with glass. The dog sniffed it well

diz: 'non quiero mal bocado, non serie para mi sano;
por el pan de vna noche non perdere quanto gano.

176　Por poca vianda que esta noche çenaria,
non perdere los manjares nin el pan de cada dia;
ssy yo tu mal pan comiese con ello me afogaria,
tu furtarias lo que guardo E yo grand trayçion faria.

177　Al señor que me crio non fare tal falsedat.
que tu furtes su thesoro que dexo en mi fealdat;
tu leuarys el algo yo faria grand maldat,
vete de aqui, ladron, non quiero tu poridad.'

178　Començo de ladrar mucho, el mastyn era masillero,
tanto siguio al ladron que fuyo de aquel çillero,
asy conteçio a mi E al mi buen mensajero
con aquesta dueña cuerda e con la otra primero.

179　ffueron dares valdios de que ove mansilla.
dixo: 'vno coyda el vayo e E otro el que lo ensilla.'
rredreme de la dueña E crey la fabrilla
que diz: 'por lo perdido non estes mano en mexilla.'

180　Ca, segund vos he dicho, de tal ventura seo,
que si lo faz mi signo o ssy mi mal asseo,
nunca puedo acabar lo medio que deseo;
por esto a las vegadas con el amor peleo.

DE COMO EL AMOR VINO AL ARÇIPRESTE, E DE LA PELEA QUE CON EL OVO EL DICHO ARÇIPRESTE

181　Dyre vos vna pelea que vna noche me vino,
pensando en mi ventura sañudo e non con vino:
vn omne grande, fermoso, mesurado, a mi vino;
yo le pregunte quien era, dixo: 'amor, tu vezino.'

182　Con saña que tenia fuylo a denostar,
dixel: 'si amor eres, non puedes aqui estar;
eres mentiroso, falso en muchos enartar;
saluar non puedes vno, puedes çient mill matar.

183　Con engaños E lyjonjas E sotiles mentiras,
enpoçonas las lenguas, en-eruolas tus viras,

and said: 'I don't want bad food, it would make me ill;
I will not lose everything for one night's bread,

176 nor for the little meat I would dine on tonight
will I lose my daily food and bread;
if I ate your evil bread, it would choke me,
then you would steal what I guard and I would betray it.

177 I will not deceive the man who brought me up,
and let you steal the treasure he has entrusted to me.
If you take anything I will cause such trouble,
get out of here, thief, I don't want your friendship.'

178 He started to bark loudly – he was a carnivorous dog;
he chased the robber till he fled from that store room.
This is what happened to my messenger and me
with this wise lady and with the previous one.

179 They were worthless offerings and caused me sorrow.
I said: 'The bay horse thinks one thing, the one who saddles
him thinks another.' I left the lady, believing the saying
which goes: 'Don't be downcast at your loss and hold your
head in your hands.'

180 Because, as I have said, it is my fortune,
whether because of my birthsign or my poor appearance,
never to achieve half of what I desire and
for this reason I quarrel with Love at times.

THE GOD OF LOVE VISITS THE ARCHPRIEST AND THEY HAVE A QUARREL

181 I shall tell you of the battle I had one night,
when thinking of my luck, feeling angry and stone-cold
sober.
A tall, handsome man with an air of composure visited me.
I asked who he was and he replied: 'Your neighbour, Love.'

182 I felt so angry, I was going to insult him, and said:
'If you are Love, then you can't stay here, you are lying,
false and deceive too many people; you can't save a single
person, but you can kill a hundred thousand.

183 With your deception and flattery and subtle lies
you poison tongues, your arrows are poisoned too.

al que mejor te syrue, a el fieres quando tiras,
partes lo del amiga al omne que ayras.

184 Traes enloquecidos a muchos con tu saber,
fazes los perder el sueño, el comer y el beuer;
ffazes a muchos omes tanto se atreuer
en ti fasta que el cuerpo e el alma van perder.

185 Non tienes Regla çierta nin tienes en ti tiento,
a las vegadas prendes con grand arrevatamiento,
a vezes poco a poco con maestrias çiento;
de quanto yo te digo, tu sabes que non miento.

186 Desque los omnes prendes non das por ellos nada,
traes los de oy en cras en vida muy penada,
fazes al que te cree lazar en tu mesnada,
E por plazer poquillo andar luenga jornada.

187 Eres tan enconado que, do fieres de golpe,
non lo sana mengia, enplasto nin xarope,
non se ffuerte nin rrecio que se contigo tope,
que nol debatas luego, por mucho que se enforce.

188 de commo enflaquezes las gentes e las dapñas,
muchos libros ay desto, de commo las engañas
con tus muchos doñeos e con tus malas mañaz;
sienpre tiras la fuerça, dizenlo en fazañas.

ENSSIENPRO DEL GARÇON QUE QUERIA CASSAR CON TRES
MUGERES

189 Era vn garçon loco, mançebo bien valiente,
non queria cassar se con vna sola mente,
sy non con tres mugeres, tal era su talente;
porfiaron en cabo con el toda la gente.

190 Su padre e su madre e su hermano mayor,
afyncaron le mucho que ya por su amor
con dos que se cassase, primero con la menor,
E dende a vn mes conplido, casase con la mayor.

191 ffizo su cassamiento con aquesta condiçion.
el primer mes ya pasado dixieron le tal Razon,
que al otro su hermano con vna e con mas non,
quisiese que le casasen a ley e a bendiçion.

You fire at and wound the one who serves you best,
you part the man who angers you from his love.

184   Your kind of knowledge drives people crazy,
      you make them lose sleep and their appetite,
      you tempt men to dare anything for you,
      until they lose both body and soul.

185   You have no fixed rules nor any restraint.
      At times you imprison with great violence,
      at times little by little, with a hundred different wiles,
      and you know I'm speaking the truth.

186   Once you seize a man, you don't give a toss;
      he is forced to wait, to live a life of misery.
      All who believe in you suffer in your retinue;
      they have a long day's march, but very little pleasure.

187   You are so malevolent that where you suddenly wound
      no medicine will heal, nor plaster nor syrup.
      I know no man, however strong, who comes up against you
      and is not brought down, however hard he resists.

188   You harm people, make them grow thin,
      as many books say; you deceive them
      with your false praise and evil tricks;
      you always sap their strength, as old tales tell.

THE FABLE OF THE YOUTH WHO WANTED TO MARRY
THREE WOMEN

189   There was a reckless youth, a valiant lad,
      who was not content to marry one woman,
      but three – such was his desire.
      Everyone argued long and loud with him.

190   His mother and father and elder brother
      pleaded with him, for the love he bore them,
      to take on just two, the younger first
      and then, after a month, the elder.

191   His wedding took place on this condition.
      After the first month had passed, they told him
      that his brother wanted to marry one wife
      by law and with a Church blessing.

192   Respondio el cassado que esto non feçiesen,
       que el tenia muger en que anbos a dos oviesen
       casamiento abondo e desto le dixiesen;
       de casarlo con otra non se entremetiesen.

193   Aqueste omne bueno, padre de aqueste neçio,
       tenia vn molyno de grand muela de preçio;
       ante que fuese casado el garçon atan Reçio,
       andando mucho la muela teniala con el pie quedo.

194   aquesta fuerca grande e aquesta valentia,
       ante que fuese casado, lygero la fazia;
       el vn mes ya pasado que casado avia,
       quiso prouar commo ante e vino ally vn dia.

195   prouo tener la muela commo avia vsado,
       leuanto le las piernas, echolo por mal cabo;
       leuantose el neçio, maldixole con mal fado,
       diz; "¡ay! molyno Rezio, avn te vea casado."

196   a la muger primera el tanto la amo
       que a la otra donzella nunca mas la tomo,
       non prouo mas tener la muela, sol non lo asomo;
       ansy tu deuaneo al garçon loco domo.

197   Eres padre del fuego, pariente de la llama,
       mas arde e mas se quema qual quier que te mas ama.
       amor, quien te mas sygue quemas le cuerpo e alma,
       destruyes lo del todo, commo el fuego a la rrama.

198   los que te non prouaron en buen dya nasçieron,
       folgaron sin cuydado, nunca entristeçieron,
       desque A ti fallaron todo su bien perdieron,
       fueles commo a las Ranas, quando el Rey pidieron.

ENXIENPLO DE LAS RANAS EN COMO DEMANDAUAN REY
A DON JUPITER

199   las rranas en vn lago cantauan E jugauan,
       cosa non les nuzia, bien solteras andauan;
       creyeron al diablo, que del mal se pagavan,
       pidyeron Rey a don jupiter, mucho gelo Rogauan.

200   Enbioles don jupiter vna viga de lagar,
       la mayor quel pudo; Cayo en ese lugar.

192   The newly-wed replied that they should not proceed,
as he had wife enough for two
in great abundance, and to tell his brother so,
that he was not to marry another.

193   The good father of this young fool
owned a mill with a powerful millstone.
Before he was married the lad was so strong
that he could stop the working millstone with his foot.

194   Such was his strength and valour
that he did this easily before his marriage,
but just a month after his wedding
he tried to do the same one day.

195   He tried to halt the millstone as he used to do,
but his legs flew up and he had a bad fall.
The fool got up and cursed it with ill grace,
"Right, mighty mill, I'll see you married yet."

196   He loved the first woman so very much
that he never took the second.
He didn't try to halt the millstone, nor even gave it a thought,
so your foolish extravagances tamed the reckless youth.

197   You are the father of fire, kinsman of flame,
whoever loves you most burns and is burnt the most.
Love, you burn the body and soul of your closest followers,
you completely destroy them, like a branch in the flames.

198   Those who had never known you were born on a lucky day,
they could rest easy, they were never sad,
but when they found you, they lost all their good fortune
like the frogs who asked for a king.

THE FABLE OF THE FROGS WHO ASKED JUPITER FOR A
KING

199   The frogs were singing and playing in the lake;
nothing harmed them, they were quite free.
They believed in the devil and were inclined to evil.
They asked Jupiter often to give them a king.

200   Jupiter sent them the beam from a wine press,
the largest he could find landed among them.

el grand golpe del fuste, fizo las rranas callar;
mas vieron que non era Rey para las castigar.

201 Suben ssobre la viga quantas podian sobyr;
dixieron: "non es este rrey para lo nos seruir."
pidieron Rey a don jupiter como lo solyan pedir;
don jupiter con saña ovolas de oyr.

202 Enbioles por su Rey çigueña mansillera,
çercava todo el lago, ansy faz la rribera,
andando pico abierta, como era ventenera,
de dos en dos las rranas comia bien lygera.

203 Querellando a don jupiter, dieron boces las rranas:
"señor, señor, acorre nos tu que matas E sanas;
el rrey que tu nos diste, por nuestras bozes vanas,
danos muy malas tardes e peores las mañanas.

204 Su vientre nos ssotierra, su pico nos estraga,
de dos en dos nos come, nos abarca e nos astraga;
sseñor, tu nos deffiende; Señor tu ya nos paga:
danos la tu ayuda, tira de nos tu plaga."

205 Respondioles don jupiter: "tenedlo que pidistes;
el rrey tan demandado, por quantas bozes distes,
vengue vuestra locura, Ca en poco touistes
ser libres e syn premia; rreñid pues lo quesistes."

206 quien tiene lo quel cunple con ello sea pagado,
quien puede ser suyo non sea en-ajenado,
el que non toviere premia non quiera ser apremiado,
lybertat e ssoltura non es por oro conplado.

207 byen anssy acaesçe a todos tus contrallos;
do son de sy Señores tornan se tus vasallos;
tu, despues, nunca pienssas synon por astragallos,
en cuerpos e en almas asy todos tragallos

208 Querellan se de ti, mas non les vales nada,
que tan presos los tienes en tu cadena doblada,
que non pueden partir se de tu vida penada;
rresponde a quien te llama, ¡vete de mi posada!

The great crash the wood made silenced the frogs,
but they soon realised this king could not chastise them.

201 As many as were able climbed out on to the beam.
They said: "This king will not serve us."
So they asked Jupiter once more, in the usual way,
and he had to listen, although he was angry.

202 He sent them a carnivorous crane as their king,
who stalked around the lake and the banks too,
with his beak open wide. He was very greedy,
and made a light meal of the frogs, two by two.

203 The frogs cried out, rebuking Jupiter:
"Lord, lord, run to help us, you who kill and heal.
The king you sent us at our vain cries
is giving us bad evenings and worse mornings.

204 His belly buries us, his beak devours us,
he's eating us two by two, grabbing and devouring.
Lord, defend us, Lord, give us satisfaction,
help us, help us, take away your scourge."

205 Jupiter replied: "You have what you asked for,
the much-requested king, whom you cried out for.
I have conquered your foolishness, for you thought
freedom, lack of oppression, was nothing – so complain all
you like."

206 A person who has what is fitting should be content with it,
those who are masters of themselves shall not be in another's
power, those without oppression do not want to be
oppressed.
Freedom and no restraints are not bought with gold.

207 The same happens to all who oppose you – though
masters of themselves, they soon become your vassals.
You think of nothing else but devouring them
body and soul, everything is swallowed up.

208 They complain of you, but it does them no good;
you keep them prisoner with a double chain,
and they cannot escape your life of torment.
Answer those who call you, get out of my house!

209   Non quiero tu conpaña, ¡vete de aqui, varon!
       das al cuerpo lazeria, trabajo syn Razon,
       de dia E de noche eres fino ladron;
       quando omne esta Seguro, furtas le el coraçon.

210   En punto que lo furtas luego lo en-ajenas;
       das le a quien non le ama, tormentas le con penas;
       anda el coraçon syn cuerpo en tus cadenas,
       penssando e sospirando por las cosas ajenas.

211   ffazes lo Andar bolando como la golondrina,
       rrebuelves lo amenudo, tu mal non adeuina,
       oras coyda en su saña, oras en merjelina,
       de diuerssas maneras tu quexa lo espina.

212   En vn punto lo pones a jornadas tresientas,
       anda todo el mundo quando tu lo rretientas,
       dexas le solo e triste con muchas soberuientas
       a quien nol quiere nil ama ssyenpre gela mientas.

213   Varon ¿que as con-migo? ¿qual fue aquel mal debdo
       que tanto me persygues? vienes me manso e quedo,
       nunca me aperçibes de tu ojo nin del dedo,
       das me en el coraçon, triste fazes del ledo.

214   Non te puedo prender, ¡tanta es tu maestria!
       E maguer te presiese, crey que te non matarya.
       tu cada que a mi prendes, ¡tanta es tu orgullya!
       syn piedat me matas de noche e de dia.

215   Responde, ¿que te fiz? ¿por que me non diste dicha
       en quantas que ame, nin de la dueña bendicha?
       de quanto me prometie luego era des-dicha;
       en fuerte punto te vy, la ora fue mal dicha.

216   quanto mas aqui estas, tanto mas me assaño;
       mas fallo que te diga, veyendo quanto dapño
       syenpre de ti me vino con tu sotil engaño;
       andas vrdiendo sienpre, cobierto so mal paño.

AQUI FABLA DEL PECADO DE LA COBDIÇIA
217   Contigo syenpre trahes los mortales pecados;
       con mucha cobdiçia los omnes enganados,

209　　I do not want your company, leave now, at once!
　　　You make the body suffer, make it labour for no good reason,
　　　you are a cunning thief by night and day.
　　　When a man feels safe, you steal his heart.

210　　As soon as you steal it, you put it in another's power,
　　　you give it to one who scorns it, you torment it with
　　　　　　　　　　　　　　　　　　　　　　　　suffering.
　　　The disembodied heart lies within your chains,
　　　thinking of, sighing for what belongs to others.

211　　You make the heart fly like a swallow and often
　　　stir it up, though it never guesses your wickedry.
　　　Sometimes it thinks of Susanna, sometimes of Marceline.
　　　Your goading pain pricks like a spine in many ways.

212　　In a trice it can soar three hundred miles away,
　　　it covers the globe when you are tempting it;
　　　you leave it sad and lonely, greatly shocked,
　　　you always give it to someone who does not love or want it.

213　　What do you want with me? What is my evil debt
　　　which makes you pursue me like this? You come here
　　　quiet and gentle, with no warning wink or secret sign,
　　　to wound my heart and turn joy to sorrow.

214　　I cannot catch you, you are too clever,
　　　and if I could, I don't think I would kill you.
　　　Each time you seize me, in all your pride,
　　　it is you who slays me without mercy, night and day.

215　　Tell me, what have I done to you, why deny me happiness
　　　with all those I love, not even with the devout lady?
　　　All your promises turned to misfortune.
　　　It dawned a cursed, evil day when I met you.

216　　The longer you stay, the more angry I get,
　　　the more I condemn you for all the harm
　　　your clever trickery brings me.
　　　Your poor attire conceals the schemes you always weave.

THE SIN OF COVETOUSNESS

217　　The mortal sins are always your companions.
　　　Your own great covetousness beguiles and tricks,

ffazes les cobdiçiar e mucho ser denodados,
passar los mandamientos que de dios fueron dados.

218   de todos los pecados es rrayz la cobdiçia,
      esta es tu fija mayor, tu mayordoma anbicia,
      esta es tu alferez E tu casa offiçia,
      esta destruye el mundo, sostienta la justiçia.

219   la sorberuia E ira que non falla do quepa,
      avarizia e loxuria que arden mas que estepa,
      gula, envidia, açidia, ques pegan commo lepra,
      de la cobdiçia nasçen, es della rrays e çepa.

220   En ti fazen morada, aleuoso traydor,
      con palabras muy dulçes, con gesto engañador;
      prometen e mandan mucho los omnes con ammor,
      por conplir lo que mandan cobdiçian lo peor.

221   Cobdiçian los averes que ellos non ganaron,
      por conplyr las promesas que con amor mandaron;
      muchos por tal cobdiçia lo ajeno furtaron,
      por que penan sus almas e los cuerpos lasraron.

222   murieron por los furtos de muerte sopitaña,
      arrastrados E enforcados de manera estraña;
      en todo eres cuquero e de mala picaña,
      quien tu cobdiçia tiene, el pecado lo engaña.

223   Por cobdiçia feciste a troya destroyr,
      por la mançana escripta, que se non deuiera escreuir,
      quando la dio a venus paris, por le jnduzir,
      que troxo a elena que cobdiçiaua seruir.

224   Por tu mala cobdiçia los de egipto morieron,
      los cuerpos enfamaron, las animas perdieron;
      fueron e son ayrados de dios los que te creyeron,
      de mucho que cobdiçiaron poca parte ovieron.

225   Por la cobdiçia pierde el omne el bien que tiene,
      coyda aver mas mucho de quanto le conviene,
      non han lo que cobdiçian, lo suyo non mantienen;
      lo que contescio al perro a estos tal les viene.

making men covetous and bent upon their sins,
ignoring the commandments God gave them.

218   Covetousness, your elder daughter,
is the root of all sins; ambition, your stewardess,
she is your standard-bearer and runs your house.
She destroys the world, corrupts justice.

219   Pride and anger cannot be contained,
avarice and lechery burn better than kindling,
greed, envy, sloth, all cling like leprosy,
all are born of covetousness, their root and stock.

220   They all lodge with you, you lying traitor,
with gentle words, deceiving gestures;
men in love promise much and offer more,
but to fulfil their promises they covet the worst.

221   They covet what they have not earned
to fulfil the promises made in love.
Many are led to thievery, for which their souls
are punished and their bodies suffer.

222   They have died a sudden death for theft,
been dragged along and cruelly hung;
in all you are the evil trickster, ever deceiving,
sin deceives those filled with your coveting.

223   You destroyed Troy itself by covetousness,
the graven apple bearing words which never
should have been written, when Paris gave it to Venus
to persuade her to bring him Helen, whom he longed to
                                                    serve.

224   Evil covetousness slayed the Egyptians,
shamed their bodies, lost their souls.
Those who believed you incurred God's anger, still do;
their great coveting brought them very little.

225   Through covetousness man loses the good thing he has,
he longs for far more than he really needs.
He does not get what he covets, nor looks after what he has.
The tale of the dog and his meat illustrates the point.

ENSIENPLO DEL ALANO QUE LLEUAUA LA PIEÇA DE
CARNE EN LA BOCA

226   alano carniçero en vn Rio andava,
        vna pieça de carne en la boca passaua,
        con la sonbra del agua dos tantol semejaua;
        cobdiçiola abarcar, cayesele la que leuaua.

227   Por la sonbra mentirosa E por su coydar vano
        la carne que tenia perdiola el alano,
        non ovo lo que quiso, nol fue cobdiçiar sano,
        coydo ganar E perdio lo que tenia en su mano.

228   Cada dia contesçe al cobdiçiosso atal,
        coyda ganar con-tigo E pierde su cabdal,
        de aquesta rrayz mala nasçe todo el mal,
        es la mala cobdiçia pecado mortal.

229   lo mas e lo mejor, lo que es mas preçiado,
        desque lo tiene omne çiero E ya ganado,
        nunca deue dexarlo por vn vano coydado;
        quien dexa lo que tiene faze grand mal rrecabdo.

AQUI FABLA DEL PECADO DE LA SSOBERUIA

230   Soberuia mucha traes ha do miedo non as;
        piensas, pues non as miedo, tu de que pasaras,
        las joyas para tu Amiga de que las conplaras;
        por esto rrobas E furtas, por que tu penaras.

231   ffazes con tu soberuia acometer malas cosas,
        rrobar a camineros las joyas preçiosas,
        forçar muchas mugeres cassadas e esposas,
        virgenes E solteras, vyudas E rreligiosas.

232   Por tales malefiçios manda los la ley matar,
        mueren de malas muertes, non los puedes tu quitar,
        lyeua los el diablo por el tu grand abeytar,
        fuego jnfernal arde do vuias assentar.

233   Por tu mucha soberuia feziste muchos perder,
        primero muchos angeles, con ellos lucifer,
        que por su grand soberuia e su des-agradesçer
        de las sillas del cielo ovieron de caer.

THE FABLE OF THE MASTIFF WHO WAS CARRYING HIS PIECE OF MEAT IN HIS MOUTH

226   A hungry mastiff was walking beside a river,
carrying a hunk of meat in his mouth.
The water's reflection showed him a second piece of meat.
As he tried to seize it, he dropped the piece he had in the
river.

227   The deceptive reflection and his vain covetousness
made the mastiff lose the meat.
He did not get what he wanted, coveting was evil.
Thinking he would gain, he lost what he already had.

228   Every day these things happen to the covetous man;
he thinks he will gain from you, and loses his nest egg.
All evil grows from this rootstock,
covetousness is a mortal sin.

229   Once a man is sure he possesses
the highest and best, of greatest value,
it should never be exchanged for some vain longing.
If a man leaves what he has, he makes a poor profit.

THE SIN OF PRIDE

230   You have no fear, your pride is great.
Fearless, you consider which rules to break –
perhaps jewellery for your lady friend? But how to buy it?
So you rob and steal, but how you will suffer.

231   Evil deeds arise from the sin of pride,
like robbing travellers of their precious gems,
ravishing endless women, wives,
virgins and spinsters, widows and nuns.

232   The law decrees death to punish these evil deeds;
men die a dreadful death, from which you cannot free them.
The devil takes them because of your great deceit,
the fires of hell burn wherever you settle.

233   Many have been lost through your great pride,
first many angels, Lucifer among them,
who in pride and ingratitude
fell from their heavenly seats.

234 Maguer de su natura buenos fueron criados,
por la su grand soberuia fueron e son dañados;
quantos por la soberuia fueron e son dañados
non se podrian escreuir en mill priegos contados.

235 quantas fueron e son batallas e pelleas,
jnjurias e varajas e contiendas muy feas,
amor, por tu soberuia se fazen, bien lo creas,
toda maldat del mundo es do quier que tu seas.

236 El omne muy soberuio E muy denodado,
que non ha de dios miedo nin cata aguisado,
antre muere que otro mas fraco e mas lazrado,
contesçel commo al asno con el cavallo armado.

ENSSIENPLO DEL CAUALLO E DEL ASNO

237 Yva lydiar en canpo el cavallo faziente
por que forço la dueña el su señor valiente;
lorigas bien levadas, muy valiente se siente;
mucho delantel yva el asno mal doliente.

238 Con los pies e con las manos e con el noble freno,
el cavallo soberuio fazia tan grand sueno,
que a las otras bestias espanta como trueno:
el asno con el miedo quedo e nol fue bueno.

239 Estava rrefusando el asno con la grand carga,
andaua mal e poco, al cauallo enbargava.
derribole el cavallo en medio de la varga;
diz: "don villano nesçio, buscad carrera larga."

240 Dio salto en el canpo, ligero, aperçebido;
coydo ser vencedor E fynco el vencido;
en el cuerpo, muy fuere, de lança fue ferido,
las entrañas le salem, estaua muy perdido.

241 desque salyo del canpo, non valya vna çermeña;
a arar lo pusieron e a traer la leña,
a vezes a la noria, a vezes a la açenia;
escota el soberuio el amor de la dueña.

242 Tenia del grand yugo dessolladas las ceruiçes,
del jnogar a vezes fynchadas las narizes,

234   Although they were created good by nature,
        great pride condemned them, and still does.
        The number condemned through pride, still condemned,
        would fill more than a thousand complete pages.

235   How many battles and fights were there, are there still,
        insults and quarrels and ugly struggles.
        Love, these are caused by your pride, believe me,
        all the world's evil resides where you are.

236   The very proud and stubborn man,
        who does not fear God, nor acts with wisdom,
        shall die before the weak and wretched,
        as the story of the ass and the war-horse shows.

THE FABLE OF THE HORSE AND THE ASS

237   The war-horse was going to fight in the field,
        as his valiant lord had ravished a lady.
        The horse's armour fitted well, he felt bold and brave.
        Away ahead trudged the long-suffering ass.

238   With all four hooves and the finest bridle,
        the proud horse made such a racket
        that it scared the other beasts like thunder.
        The frightened ass stopped dead in its tracks.

239   The ass was sliding backwards with his heavy load,
        he was struggling painfully and blocked the horse's way.
        The horse knocked him aside in the middle of the slope.
        He said: "You stupid peasant, find a wider road."

240   He leapt lightly on to the battlefield, prepared for the fray;
        he thought he was the victor, but he ended up the
                                                    vanquished.
        Cruelly wounded by a lance,
        his guts poked out, he was all but lost.

241   When he left the battlefield he wasn't worth a sour pear.
        He was set to plough and carry wood,
        sometimes he worked the waterwheel, sometimes the mill.
        His pride paid the price for the love of the lady.

242   His neck was chafed raw by the heavy yoke,
        his nostrils flared wide with the effort of kneeling,

rrodillas desolladas, faziendo muchas prizes,
ojos fondos, bermejos, commo pies de perdizes.

243   los quadriles salidos, somidas las yjadas,
el espinazo agudo, las orejas colgadas;
vido lo el asno nesçio, Rixo bien tres vegadas.
diz: "conpañero soberuio ¿do son tus enpelladas?

244   ¿Do es tu noble freno e tu dorada silla?
¿Do es tu soberuia? ¿Do es la tu rrensilla?
sienpre byvras mesquino e con mucha mansilla,
vengue la tu soberuia tanta mala postilla."

245   Aqui tomen ensyenpro e lyçion de cada dia
los que son muy soberuios con su grand orgullya.
que fuerça e hedat e onrra, salud e valentia
non pueden durar syenpre, vanse con mançebia.

AQUI FABLA DEL PECADO DE LA AVARIZIA

246   Tu eres avarizia, eres escaso mucho;
al tomar te alegras, el dar non lo as ducho.
non te fartaria duero con el su agua ducho;
ssyenpre me ffallo mal, cada que te escucho.

247   Por la grand escaseza fue perdido el Rico
que al poble Sant lazaro non dio solo vn çatico;
non quieres ver nin amas poble grand nin chico,
nin de los tus thesoros non le quieres dar vn pico.

248   Maguer que te es mandado por santo mandamiento
que vistas al desnudo E fartes al fanbriento,
E des al poble posada; tanto eres avariento,
que nunca lo diste a vno, pidiendo telo çiento.

249   Mesquino, ¿tu que faras, el dia de la afruenta,
quando de tus averes E de tu mucha rrenta
te demandare dios de la despenssa cuenta?
non te valdran thesoros nin Reynos çinquaenta,

250   quando tu eras poble, que tenias grand dolençia,
estonçes sospirauas E fazias penitençia,
pidias a dios que te diesen Salud e mantenençia,
E que partirias con pobles e non farias fallencia.

his knees were rubbed raw by constant prayer,
his eyes were hollow and red, the colour of partridge feet.

243   His haunches stuck out, his flanks sank,
his spine showed through, his ears drooped down.
When the stupid ass saw him he laughed heartily,
and said: "Well, my proud companion, no pushing and
                                            shoving?

244   Where is your fine bridle and gilded saddle?
Where is your pride? Where is your fighting nature?
You shall always be a wretch and live in great mortification.
All those scabs will conquer your pride."

245   This story is a daily lesson and example
to those who are incurably proud.
Strength and time, honour, health and valour
do not last forever, they pass away with youth.

THE SIN OF AVARICE

246   You are Avarice itself, avaricious in abundance;
you love to take, but are not used to giving.
The full torrent of the River Duero is not enough for you,
I always have problems when I listen to you.

247   The rich man's great avarice damned him, for he gave not
even a small piece of bread to poor Saint Lazarus.
You have no interest in the poor or destitute,
nor would you give one penny of your treasure away.

248   Although the holy commandments order you
to clothe the naked and feed the hungry
and give shelter to the poor, you are so avaricious
that though a hundred ask, not even one receives.

249   Miser, what will you do on Judgement Day
when God asks for the account of how
you have spent your wealth and income?
Then not all the treasure or kingdoms in the world will help
                                                        you.

250   When you were poor, when you were suffering,
then you sighed and were repentant.
You asked God then for health and sustenance,
said you would share with the poor without fail.

251   oyo dios tus querellas E dio te buen consejo,
      Salud e grand rriqueza e thesoro sobejo;
      quando vees el poble, caesete el çejo,
      fazes commo el lobo dolyente en el vallejo.

ENXIENPLO DEL LOBO E DE LA CABRA E DE LA GRULLA

252   El lobo a la cabra comiala por merienda,
      atravesosele vn veso, estaua en contienda,
      afogar se queria, demandava corrienda,
      fisicos e maestros, que queria fazer emienda.

253   Prometio al que lo sacase thesoros e grand Riqueza.
      vino la grulla de somo del alteza,
      sacole con el pico el veso con ssotileza;
      el lobo finco sano, para comer sin pereza.

254   Dyxo la grulla al lobo quel quisiese pagar.
      el lobo dixo: "¡como! ¿yo non te pudiera tragar
      el cuello con mis dientes sy quisiera apertar?
      pues Sea te soldada, pues non te quise matar."

255   byen ansy tu lo fazes, agora que estas lleno
      de pan e de dineros que forçaste de lo ageno;
      non quieres dar al poble vn poco de çenteno,
      mas ansi te ssecaras como rroçio E feno.

256   En fazer bien al mal cosa nol aprouecha;
      omne desagradesçido bien fecho nunca pecha;
      el buen conosçemiento mal omne lo dessecha,
      el bien que omne le faze, diz que es por su derecha.

AQUI FABLA DEL PECADO DE LA LUXURIA

257   Syenpre esta loxuria a do-quier que tu estas,
      adulterio E forniçio toda via desseas,
      luego quieres pecar con qual quier que tu veas,
      por conplyr la loxuria enguinando las oteas.

258   ffeciste por loxuria al profeta dauid,
      que mato a urias, quando le mando en la lyd
      poner en los primeros, quando le dixo: "yd,
      leuad esta mi carta a jaab E venid."

259   Por amor de berssabe, la mujer de vrias,
      fue el Rey dauid omeçida e fizo a dios falliaz,

251   God heard your pleas and gave you good advice,
health and great wealth, abundant treasure.
But when you see the poor, you frown and look grave,
and act like the wolf in pain down in the dale.

THE FABLE OF THE WOLF, THE GOAT AND THE CRANE

252   The wolf ate up a goat for tea.
A bone got stuck, he struggled and fought.
About to choke to death, he frantically summoned
doctors and surgeons, vowing to make amends.

253   He promised treasure, riches to whoever removed the bone,
so the crane flew down from the heights
and cleverly picked out the bone with its bill.
The wolf was cured, he could eat with ease.

254   The crane asked the wolf for payment,
and the wolf replied: "What! I could have crushed
your neck with my teeth if I had clenched them.
Consider yourself paid, as I didn't kill you."

255   You do the same, now you are full
with bread and money, robbed by force.
You will not give the poor even a little rye,
and so you will dry up like dew and hay.

256   Doing good to the wicked is of no benefit;
an ungrateful person never repays a good deed.
A bad man will not acknowledge good conduct,
but says the good deed done is his right.

THE SIN OF LECHERY

257   Lechery follows close by, wherever you are.
You always long to commit adultery and fornication.
You want to sin at once, with anyone you see,
you wink at girls and leer with a view to lechery.

258   You made the Prophet David kill
Uriah for lust, ordering him to go first
in the ranks of battle, saying: "Go,
take my letter to Joab and come back."

259   For love of Bathsheba, Uriah's wife,
King David turned murderer, failed God,

por ende non fizo el tenpro en todos los sus dias,
fizo grand penitençia por las tus maestrias.

260 ffueron por la loxuria çinco nobles cibdades
quemadas e destruydas, las tres por sus maldades,
las dos non por su culpa mas por las veçindades:
por malas vezindades se pierden eredades.

261 Non te quiero por vesino nin me vengas tan presto.
al sabidor virgillio, commo dize en el testo,
engañolo la duena quando lo colgo en el cesto,
coydando que lo sobia a su torre por esto.

262 Por que le fizo desonrra E escarnio del rruego
el grand encantador fizole muy mal juego;
la lunbre de la candela encanto E el fuego,
que quanto era en rroma en punto morio luego.

263 Anssy que los rromanos, fasta la criatura,
non podien aver fuego, por su desaventura;
synon lo ençendian dentro en la natura
de la muger mesquina, otro non les atura.

264 Sy daua vno a otro fuego o la candela,
amatauase luego, e venien todos a ella;
ençendien ally todos commo en grand çentella:
ansy vengo virgillio su desonrra e querella.

265 despues desta desonrra E de tanta verguença,
por fazer su loxuria vergilio en la dueña,
descanto el fuego, que ardiesse en la leña,
fizo otra marauilla quel omne nunca ensueña.

266 Todo el suelo del Ryo de la çibdad de Roma,
tiberio, agua cabdal, que muchas aguas toma,
fizole suelo de cobre, Reluze mas que goma;
a dueñas tu loxuria desta guisa las doma.

267 desque peco con ella sentiose escarnida,
mando fazer escalera de torno, enxerida
de navajas agudas, por que a la sobida
que sobiese vergilio acabase su vida.

268 El ssopo que era fecho por su escantamente,
nunca mas fue a ella, nin la ovo talente:

and so the temple was never built in his lifetime.
He did great penance for your evil wiles.

260   Lust was the scourge of five noble cities,
burned and destroyed, three for their evil deeds
and two for the sins of their neighbours –
inheritances are lost through bad neighbours.

261   I do not want you as my neighbour, keep away.
As the books say, Virgil the sage was deceived by a woman,
when she dangled him in a basket, but not
to lift him to her tower and have her, as he thought.

262   She dishonoured him, mocked his pleas,
so the great magician played an evil trick.
He enchanted all candle flames and fires,
so all there were in Rome went out at once.

263   Neither Romans nor any living thing
had the gift of fire, to their misfortune,
unless it was kindled in the sex
of the wretched woman – no other endured.

264   If fire or candle was given, exchanged,
it went out at once, and they all went to her
to be lit by her flame in a great blaze.
So Virgil avenged his dishonour and complaint.

265   After such dishonour and shame,
to satisfy his lust for the woman,
Virgil lifted the spell from the fire that burnt in the wood
and performed a second miracle beyond man's dreams.

266   The whole bed of the river in the city of Rome,
the mighty Tiber, where many waters meet,
he turned to copper, which shone brighter than clear resin.
Your lust holds sway over women like this.

267   When he had sinned with her, she felt mortified.
She had a winding stairway built,
set with sharpest knives, to catch Virgil unawares
if he went upstairs and finish him off.

268   He found out what she had done through his magic;
he never went to her nor wanted her again.

ansy por la loxuria es verdadera mente
el mundo escarnido E muy triste la gente.

269 de muchos ha que matas non se vno que sanes;
quantos en tu loxuria son grandes varraganes,
matanse a sy mesmos, los locos alvardanes,
contesçeles commo al aguila con los nesçios truhanez.

ENSIENPLO DEL AGUILA E DEL CAÇADOR

270 El aguila cabdal canta sobre la faya,
todas las otras aves de ally las atalaya;
non ay pendola della que en tierra caya,
sy vallestero la falla preçiala mas que saya.

271 Saetas e quadrillos, que trae amolados,
con pendolas de aguila los ha enpendolados;
fue, commo avia vsado, a ferir los venados,
al aguila cabdal diole por los costados.

272 Cato contra sus pechos el aguila ferida,
e vido que sus pendolas la avian escarnida;
dixo contra si mesma vna Razon temida:
"de mi salyo quien me mato e me tiro la vida."

273 El loco, el mesquino, que su alma non cata,
vsando tu locura e tu mala barata,
destruye a su cuerpo e a su alma mata,
que de sy mesmo sale quien su vida desata.

274 omne, ave o bestia, a que ammor Retiente,
desque cunple luxuria luego se arrepiente,
entristeze en punto, luego flaquesa siente,
acortase la vida: quien lo dixo non miente.

275 ¡Quien podrie dezir quantos tu loxuria mata!
¡quien dirie tu forniçio e tu mala barata!
al que tu ençendimiento e tu locura cata,
el diablo lo lieua quando non se rrecabda.

AQUI FABLA DEL PECADO DE LA JNVIDIA

276 Eres pura enbidia, ¡en el mundo, non ha tanta!,
con grand çelo que tienes omne de ti se espanta;

This is how lust truly mocks
the world and saddens its people.

269   You kill many but I know no one who is cured.
Those who are proud and filled with your lust
kill themselves, the crazy fools.
The stupid buffoons are like the eagle in this story.

THE FABLE OF THE EAGLE AND THE HUNTER

270   The noble eagle screams from the rocky heights,
he watches over all the other birds from his vantage point.
If an eagle feather falls to earth and is found
by a crossbowman, he values it above his tunic.

271   The sharp tapered arrows and darts the hunter carried
were feathered with eagle's feathers.
He went out as usual to hunt some deer,
he hit the noble eagle in the side.

272   The wounded bird looked at its breast
and saw that its own feathers had mocked it.
It uttered a fearful thought to itself:
"Out of me came what killed me, what took my life."

273   The madman, the wretch who does not watch over his soul,
indulging in your madness and evil confusion,
destroys his body and kills his own soul.
He is the cause of his own downfall.

274   Man, bird or beast who is tempted by love
repents of lust afterwards,
grows sad, feels weak,
his life grows short – and that's the truth.

275   Who can say how many are killed by your lechery?
Who can recount your fornication and deceitful offers?
Whoever catches fire with your lust and falls into your
madness,
the devil takes him unawares.

THE SIN OF ENVY

276   You are pure envy, the world holds not as much;
your great jealousy is a source of fear to men.

sy el tu amigo te dize fabla ya, quanta
tristeza e sospecha tu coraçon quebranta.

277 El çelo syenpre nasçe de tu enbydia pura,
temiendo que a tu amiga otro le fabla en locura;
por esto eres çeloso e triste con rrencura,
ssyenpre coydas en çelos, de otro bien non as cura.

278 Desque uvia el çelo en ty arraygar,
ssospiros e corages quieren te afogar,
de ti mesmo nin de otro non te puedes pagar,
el coraçon te salta, nunca estas de vagar.

279 Con çelo e ssospecha a todos aborresçes,
leuantas les baraja, con çelo enfraquesçes,
buscas malas contiendas, fallas lo que meresçes,
contesçe te como acaesçe en la rred a los peçes.

280 Entras en la pelea, non puedes della salyr,
estas fraco e syn fuerça non te puedes Refertyr.
nin la puedes vençer nin puedes ende foyr,
estorua te tu pecado, façe te ally moryr.

281 Por la envidia cayn a su hermano abel
matolo, por que yase dentro en mongibel;
jacob a esau, por la enbidia del,
ffurtole la bendiçion, por que fue rrebtado del.

282 ffue por la enbydia mala traydo jhesu xpisto,
dios verdadero e omne, fijo de dios muy quisto,
por enbydia fue preso E muerto e con-quisto;
en ty non es vn byen nin fallado nin visto.

283 Cada dia los omes por cobdiçia porfian,
con envidia e çelo omnes e bestias lydian,
a do-quier que tu seas los çelos ally cryan,
la envydia los parte, envidiosos los crian.

284 Por que tiene tu vesino mas trigo que tu paja,
con tu mucha envidia leuantas le baraja;
anssy te acaesçe, por le leuar ventaja,
como con los paueznos contesçio a la graja.

If your friend brings you gossip about a woman,
sadness and suspicion break your heart.

277   Jealousy is ever born of your pure envy,
fearing another will talk of passion to your lady.
Then you are filled with jealousy, sadness, rancour,
jealousy and nothing else fills your mind.

278   Once jealousy takes root in you,
you suffocate with sighs and fits of rage,
ill-content with yourself and everyone else.
Your heart skips a beat, you are never at ease.

279   You hate everyone in your jealousy and suspicion,
you pick quarrels, lose weight,
go looking for trouble and find what you deserve,
just like fishes caught in a net.

280   You enter the fray, but you can't get out;
you are thin and weak, you cannot strike back.
You cannot win the fight, but neither can you flee;
sin thwarts you and leaves you to die.

281   Cain killed his brother Abel out of envy,
which is why he resides in Mount Etna's inferno.*
Through envy, Jacob stole Esau's birthright
because of the quarrel between them.

282   Jesus Christ was betrayed by evil envy,
the true God and man, beloved Son of God.
Through envy he was taken prisoner, killed and conquered.
There is no good to be found, nor seen in you.

283   Every day men persist in cupidity,
men and beasts fight in envy and jealousy.
Wherever you are, jealousy grows,
envy gives birth to it, the envious raises it.

284   If your neighbour has more corn than you have straw,
you pick a fight out of envy,
first to gain the advantage, as it happened
in the fable of the young peacocks and the crow.

ENXIENPLO DEL PAUON E DE LA CORNEJA

285   Al pauon la corneja vydol fazer la Rueda,
dixo con grand envidia: "yo fare quanto pueda
por ser atan fermosa"; esta locura coeda:
la negra por ser blanca contra sy se denueda.

286   Pelo todo su cuerpo, su cara E su çeja,
de pendolas de pauon vistio nueva pelleja,
fermosa, e non de suyo, fuese para la iglesia:
algunas ffazen esto, que fizo la corneja.

287   graja enpavonada, como pauon vestida,
vydo se byen pintada e fuese enloqueçida,
a mejores que non ella era desagradesçida.
con los pauesnos anda la tan desconosçida.

288   El pauon de tal fijo espantado se fizo,
vydo el mal engaño E el color apostizo,
pelole toda la pluma E echola en el carrizo:
mas negra paresçia la graja que el erizo.

289   Anssy con tu envidia ffazes a muchos sobrar,
piereden lo que ganaron por lo ageno coblar,
con la envidia quieren por los cuerpos quebrar,
non fallaran en ti synon todo mal obrar.

290   quien quiere lo que non es suyo E quiere otro paresçer,
con algo de lo ageno aora rresplandesçer,
lo suyo E lo ageno todo se va a perder;
quien se tiene por lo que non es loco es; va a perder.

AQUI FABLA DEL PECADO DE LA GULA

291   la golossyna traes, goloso, Laminero;
querries a quantas vees gostar las tu primero,
enfraquesçes, pecado, eres grand venternero,
por cobrar la tu fuerça eres lobo carniçero.

292   desque te conosçi nunca te vy ayunar,
almuerças de mañana, non pierdes la yantar;
syn mesura meriendas; mejor quieres çenar;
sy tienes que o puedes a la noche çahorar

293   Con la mucha vianda e vino creçe la frema,
duermes con tu amiga, afoga te postema,

THE FABLE OF THE PEACOCKS AND THE CROW

285   The crow saw the peacock spreading his tail
and said with great envy: "I will do my best
to be as beautiful as that," a crazy thought.
When black strives to be white, harm will be done.

286   She plucked her whole body, her head, her eyebrows,
and put on a new set of peacock feathers.
Beautiful, though not herself, she set off to church.
There are some women who do what the crow did.

287   The peacock crow, decked out like a peacock,
knew she was beautiful and was beside herself.
She was haughty to her betters and strutted,
unrecognized, among the young peacocks.

288   The peacock himself was horrified at such a peachick.
He saw the dirty trick and the false colouring,
he stripped her of her plumage and threw her in the reeds.
The crow seemed blacker than the darkest hedgehog.

289   In this way your envy is the downfall of so many.
They lose what they have gained to win what is others',
they are fit to burst with envy,
but all they will find in you is evil deeds.

290   If a man wants what is not his, or wants to change
his appearance and shine with something not his own,
he will lose what he has and what belongs to others.
It is a foolish thing to be what one is not – all will be lost.

THE SIN OF GLUTTONY

291   You bring tit-bits to eat, you greedy glutton,
but you are always first to try all you set eyes on.
You grow thin, you devil, you ravening beast,
to regain your strength you become a meat-eating wolf.

292   I've never seen you fast, as long as I've known you;
breakfast in the morning, lunch never missed out,
tea unrestrainedly taken, with an even bigger dinner,
and if there's enough food and room, you eat a late supper.

293   A lot of meat and wine increases phlegm,
you sleep with your lady, and choke with quinseys,

lyeua te el dyablo, en el jnfierno te quema;
tu dizes al garçon que coma byen e non tema.

294   Adan, el nuestro padre, por gula e tragonia,
       por que comio del fruto que comer non deuia,
       echole del parayso dios en aquesse dia;
       por ello en el jnfierno desque morio yazia.

295   mato la golosyna muchos en el desierto,
       de los mas mejores que y eran por çierto,
       el profeta lo dize que te rrefierto,
       por comer e tragar sienpre estas boca abierto.

296   ffeciste por la gula a lot, noble burges,
       beuer tanto que yugo con sus fijas, pues ves
       a fazer tu forniçio; Ca do mucho vino es,
       luego es la logxuria E todo mal despues.

297   Muerte muy Rebatada trae la golossyna
       al cuerpo muy goloso e al alma mesquina;
       desto ay muchas fablas e estoria paladina;
       desir telo he mas breue por te enbiar ayna.

ENSSIENPLO DEL LEON E DEL CAVALLO
298   Vn cavallo muy gordo pasçia en la defesa;
       venie el leon de caça, pero con el non pesa;
       el leon tan goloso al cavallo sopessa:
       "vassallo," dixo, "mio, la mano tu me besa."

299   al leon gargantero rrespondio el cavallo,
       dyz: "tu eres mi Señor e yo tu vasallo
       en te besar la mano yo en eso me fallo,
       mas yr a ty non puedo, que tengo vn grand contrallo.

300   ayer do me ferrava, vn ferrero mal-dito,
       echo me en este pie vn clauo tan fito,
       enclauo me; ¡ven, Señor, con tu diente bendito
       saca melo e faz de my como de tuyo quito!"

301   abaxose el leon por le dar algund confuerto,
       el cavallo ferrado contra sy fizo tuerto,
       las coçes el cavallo lançço fuerte en çierto,
       diole entre los ojos, echole frio muerto.

the devil takes you to burn in hell.
Yet you tell young men to eat well and fear nothing.

294   Adam our father, in greed and gluttony,
        ate the fruit forbidden to him,
        and God threw him out of paradise at once.
        When he died he went to Hell for it.

295   Gluttony killed many in the desert,*
        killed all the best there were, without doubt.
        The prophet spoke the words I'm telling you;
        your mouth is always wide open for food and drink.

296   Through gluttony you made Lot, that noble townsman,
        drink so much that he lay with his daughters
        and fornicated, for where a lot of wine is drunk,
        lust creeps in, and all other evils with it.

297   Gluttony brings very sudden death
        to the greedy body and wretched soul,
        as many fables and well-known tales tell.
        I will quickly tell you a short anecdote, so you don't tarry.

THE FABLE OF THE LION AND THE HORSE
298   A very fat horse was grazing in the pasture.
        A lion came hunting, but the horse took no notice.
        The greedy lion sized up the horse's weight:
        "Vassal," he said, "kiss my hand."

299   The horse answered the gluttonous lion,
        saying: "You are my lord and I am your vassal.
        I am certainly glad to kiss your hand
        but have great difficulty in coming over to you.

300   Yesterday, while I was being shoed, a cursed blacksmith
        forced a nail so deep into this hoof
        that he drove the nail too far in. Come, sir, take it out
        with your blessed teeth and do with me as you will."

301   The lion bent down to give the shod horse
        some relief, but the horse made a big mistake.
        He kicked out furiously at the lion,
        and got the lion between the eyes so he fell stone dead.

302   El cavallo, con nel miedo, fuyo aguas byuas;
      avia mucho comido de yeruas muy esquiuas,
      yua mucho cansado, tomaron lo adyuas:
      anssy mueren los locos golosos do tu y vaz.

303   El comer syn mesura E la grand venternia,
      otrossy mucho vino con mucha beuerria,
      mas mata que cuchillo, ypocras lo desia;
      tu dizes que quien byen come, byen faze garçonia.

AQUI FABLA DEL PECADO DE LA VANA GLORIA
304   Yra e vana gloria traes, en el mundo non ay tanta;
      mas orgullo e mas bryo tyenes que toda españa;
      sy non se faze lo tuyo tomas yra E saña;
      enojo E mal querençia anda en tu conpaña.

305   Por la grand vana gloria nabuco-donossor,
      donde era poderoso e de babylonia señor,
      poco a dios preçiaua nin avia del temor;
      tyro le dios su poderio e todo su honor.

306   El ffue muy vil tornado E de las bestias egual,
      comia yeruas montessas commo buey paja E al;
      de cabellos cobyerto como bestia atal,
      vñas crio mayores que aguila cabdal.

307   Rencor E homeçida criados de ti son:
      vos ved que yo soy fulano de los garçones garçon.
      dizes muchos baldones, asy que de rrondon,
      matanse los bauiecas desque tu estas follon.

308   Con la grand yra sansson, que la su fuerça perdio,
      quando su muger dalyda los cabellos le corto
      en que avia la fuerça, E desque la byen cobro,
      a sy mesmo con yra e a otros muchos mato.

309   Con grand yra e saña saul que fue Rey,
      el primero que los jodios ovieron en su ley,
      el mesmo se mato con su espada; pues vey
      sy devo fyar en ti; a la fe non ansy lo crey.

310   quien byen te conosçiere de ty non fyara,
      el que tus obras viere de ty se arredrara,
      quanto mas te vsare menos te preçiara,
      quanto mas te prouare menos te amara.

302   The frightened horse fled like a rushing torrent,
       but he had eaten too much harmful grass;
       he quickly tired, his throat grew inflamed,
       he died, like all foolish gluttons under your sway.

303   Eating with no restraint, excessive greed
       and too much wine, too much imbibing,
       kills more folk than the knife, so Hippocrates says,
       but you say a hearty eater performs better.

THE SIN OF VAINGLORY

304   You bring wrath and vainglory, more than the world's stock,
       more pride and vigour than the whole of Spain.
       If your will is not done, you are angry and enraged,
       ire and ill-will walk in your company.

305   Because of great vanity Nebuchadnezzar,
       all-powerful lord of Babylon,
       valued and feared God very little.
       Yet God took away his power and his honour.

306   He became vile and low, like a beast,
       he ate mountain grass and straw like an ox,
       all covered in hair like a wild animal,
       with nails longer than the noble eagle's talons.

307   Rancour and murder are your servants.
       "See, I am So-and-So, a lad among lads."
       You speak nothing but insults, then all of a sudden
       fools kill each other when you start to cause trouble.

308   Samson's great rage lost him his strength
       when his lover Delilah cut off his hair,
       the source of his power. Then when it grew back,
       he killed himself and many others in anger.

309   In mighty rage, great anger, Saul,
       first king of the Jews, according to their law,
       took his own life with his sword – so should I
       trust you? I think not, by all that's holy.

310   Anyone who knows you would never trust you;
       seeing your works, they would retreat.
       The better you are known the less you are valued;
       the more you are put to the test, the less you are loved.

ENSIENPLO DEL LEON QUE SE MATO CON YRA

311   Yra E vana gloria al leon orgulloso,
      que fue a todas bestias cruel e muy dañoso,
      mato a sy mesmo yrado et muy sañoso;
      dezir te he el enxienpro, sea te prouechoso.

312   El leon orgullo con yra e valentya,
      quando era mançebo todas las bestias corria;
      a las vnas matava e a las otras feria;
      vino le grand vejedat, flaqueza e peoria.

313   ffueron aquestas nuevas a las bestias cosseras,
      fueron muy alegres por que andauan solteras,
      contra el vynieron todas por vengar sus denteras,
      avn el asno nesçio venie en las delanteras.

314   Todos en el leon ferien E non poquyllo,
      el javalyn sañudo dauale del col-millo,
      ferianlo de los cuernos el toro y el novillo,
      el asno pereçoso en el ponie su syllo.

315   dyole grand par de coçes, en la fruente gelas pon;
      el leon con grand yra trauo de su coraçon,
      con sus vñas mesmas murio E con al non.
      yra e vana gloria dieronle mal gualardon.

316   El omne que tiene estado, onrra E grand poder,
      lo que para sy non quiere, non lo deue a otros fazer,
      que mucho ayna se puede todo su poder perder,
      E lo quel fizo a otros dellos tal puede aver.

AQUI DIZE DEL PECADO DE LA ACIDIA

317   De la açidia eres messonero E posada,
      nunca quieres que de bondat faga nada,
      desque lo vees baldio dasle vida penada,
      en pecado comiençan e en-tristesan acabada.

318   Nunca estas baldio; aquel que vna ves atas
      fazes le penssar engaños, muchas malas baratas,
      deleytase en pecados E en malas baratas;
      con tus malas maestrias almas e cuerpos matas.

319   Otrosy con açidia traes ypocresia,
      andas con grand synplesa penssando pletisia,

THE FABLE OF THE LION WHO KILLED HIMSELF WITH RAGE

311   Wrath and vanity were the downfall of the proud lion,
who was cruel and injurious to all the other beasts.
He killed himself in rage and anger –
I will tell you the story for your own benefit.

312   The proud lion, with wrath and vainglory
hunted all other beasts when he was young.
Some he killed and some he wounded;
old age overtook him, weakness and decline.

313   This news reached the swift-running beasts;
they were filled with joy at their new-found freedom.
They rose up against him to avenge their anger,
even the foolish ass came in the front line.

314   They all injured the lion, and not a little.
The enraged wild boar gored with his tusk,
bulls old and young wounded with their horns,
the lazy ass set his seal upon him.

315   He gave him gigantic kicks right between the eyes.
In his dire rage the lion seized his own heart
and died by his own claws, not any others:
wrath and vainglory gave him a dread reward.

316   A man who has status, honour, great power,
should not do to others what he would not wish for himself;
he may very quickly lose all his power,
and get his just deserts, as he dished out to others.

THE SIN OF SLOTH

317   You are both innkeeper and inn to sloth,
never wanting a man to act out of goodness.
As soon as you see him idle, you make his life a misery,
it starts in sin and ends in sadness.

318   You, though, are never idle. The person you ensnare
is led to think of deceit, evil deeds,
he delights in sin and disorderly conduct.
Your wiles and tricks kill body and soul.

319   Along with sloth you bring hypocrisy,
you proceed with great simplicity, thinking of love suits,

pensando estas triste, tu ojo non se ersia,
do vees la fermosa oteas con rraposya,

320 de quanto bien pedricas non fases dello cosa,
en-gañas todo el mundo con palabra fermosa,
quieres lo que el lobo quiere de la Rapossa;
abogado de fuero ¡oy fabla prouechossa!

AQUI FABLA DEL PLEITO QUEL LOBO E LA RRAPOSSA QUE OVIERON ANTE DON XIMIO ALCALDE DE BUGIA

321 Ffurtava la Raposa a su vezina el gallo,
veya lo el lobo, mandava le dexallo,
desia que non deuia lo ageno furtarllo,
el non veya la ora que estouiese en-tragallo.

322 lo que el mas fazia a otros lo acusava,
a otros rretraya lo quel en sy loaua,
lo que el mas amaua aquello denostaua,
desie que non feziesen lo quel mas vsaua.

323 Enplazola por fuero el lobo a la comadre,
fueron ver su juyzio ante vn sabydor grande:
don ximio avia por nonble, de buxia alcalde,
era sotil e sabio, nunca seya de valde.

324 ffizo el lobo demanda en muy buena manera,
acta e byen formada, clara e byen çertera,
tenie buen abogado, ligero e sotil era,
galgo que de la rrapossa es grand abarredera:

325 "Ante vos el mucho honrrado e de grand sabidoria,
don xymio, ordinario alcalde de bugia,
yo el lobo me querello de la comadre mia,
en juysio propongo contra su mal fetria.

326 E digo que agora en el mes que paso de feblero,
era de mill e tresientos en el ano primero,
rregnante nuestro Señor el leon masillero,
que vino a nuestra çibdat por nonble de monedero,

327 En cassa de don cabron, mi vassallo e mi quintero,
entro a ffurtar de noche por çima del fumero;

but thinking makes you sad, your eyes are downcast,
yet you see a beautiful girl and leer slyly like a fox.

320   You never do anything that you preach,
deceiving the whole world with honeyed words.
You want what the wolf wanted of the vixen –
advocate of common law, hear this salutary tale!

THE TALE OF THE LAWSUIT BETWEEN THE WOLF AND THE VIXEN HEARD BEFORE SIR MONKEY, JUDGE FROM BOUGIE IN ALGERIA

321   The vixen stole her neighbour the cockerel.
The wolf saw her and ordered her to stop.
He said she should not steal what was not hers,
and could not wait to gobble it up himself.

322   He accused others of what he did most,
and criticized in them what he praised in himself;
he insulted and reviled what he loved the most,
forbade the things he frequently allowed himself.

323   The wolf summoned the vixen to court
and the case was heard before a great sage –
Sir Monkey was his name, the judge of Bougie.
He was subtle and wise, never passed judgement in vain.

324   The wolf laid his charge in a most proper way,
legally formulated, clear and correct.
He had a good lawyer, quick and subtle,
a greyhound, great scourge of all foxes.

325   "Before you, most honoured fount of wisdom,
Sir Monkey, current judge of Bougie,
I, a wolf, lodge complaint against my neighbour,
and press my charges before the court against her wrongful
deeds.

326   And I state that in the month of February past,
in the year twelve hundred and sixty-three AD
in the reign of our Lord, the valiant lion,
who came to our city as royal minter,

327   she entered by night, at the top of the chimney, to steal from
the house of Mr Ram, my vassal and tenant farmer.

saco furtando el gallo, el nuestro pregonero,
leuolo E comiolo a mi pessar en tal ero.

328 de aquesto la acuso ante vos el buen varon,
pido que la condenedes por sentençia e por al non,
que sea enforcada e muerta como ladron,
esto me ofresco prouar so pena del talyon."

329 Seyendo la demanda en juyzio leyda,
ffue sabya la gulpeja e byen aperçebida:
"Señor," diz, "yo so syenpre do poco mal sabyda,
dat me vn abogado que fable por mi vida."

330 Respondio el alcalde: "yo vengo nueva mente
a esta vuestra çibdat, non conosco la gente;
pero yo te do de plazo que fasta dias veynte
ayas tu abogado, luego al plaso vente."

331 leuantosse el alcalde esa ora de judgar,
las partes cada vna pensaron de buscar
qual dineros, qual prendas para al abogado dar;
ya sabya la rraposa quien le avia de ayudar.

332 El dia era venido del plaso asignado,
vyno dona marfusa con vn grand abogado,
vn mastyn ovejero de carrancas çercado,
el lobo quando lo vyo fue luego espantado.

333 Este grand abogado propuso pa su parte:
"alcalde Señor don ximio, quanto el lobo departe,
quanto demanda E pide, todo lo faz con arte,
que el es fyno ladron e non falla quel farte.

334 E por ende yo propongo contra el esençion
legitima e buena, por que su petiçion
non deue ser oyda, nin tal acusaçion
el fazer non la puede, ca es fyno ladron.

335 A mi acaescio con el muchas noches e dias
que leuava furtadas de las ovejas mias,
vy que las dellogaua en aquellas erias,
ante que las comiese yo gelas tome frias.

336 muchas veses de furto es de jues condenado,
por sentençia E por derecho es mal enfamado;

Our defendant stole the cockerel, our town crier,
taking him, to my sorrow, and eating him in the ploughed
field.

328   She stands accused of this before you, good sir.
I request her condemnation, legally and uncompromisingly,
to be hung till she is dead, like a thief.
I claim proof of this, upon pain of my own conviction."

329   The charge was read out in court,
but the vixen was clever and well-advised.
"Sir," she said, "I am always a little slow on the uptake;
give me a lawyer to defend my life."

330   The judge replied: "I have come to your city
for the first time, and I know no one,
but I give you twenty days to find
your lawyer, after which you must return."

331   Then the judge arose from the court.
Each party thought to provide
either money or items of value to give their lawyer.
The vixen already knew who would help her.

332   The day of assignation came,
and cunning Mrs Fox arrived with a great lawyer.
He was a shepherd mastiff, with a spiked collar.
When the wolf saw him, he was terrified.

333   The great lawyer then spoke forth:
"Lord Judge, Sir Monkey, whatever the wolf may say,
whatever he wants or demands, it is all deceit.
He is a subtle thief, nothing will satisfy him.

334   Therefore I impose on him legal exception,*
fair and legitimately, against his petition,
which should not be heard, nor can he make
such an accusation, as he's a cunning thief himself.

335   Many days and nights the same thing happened
to me, as he carried off my very own sheep.
I saw him slit their throats in these very fields,
but I took them away cold before he could eat them.

336   He has often been convicted of theft,
and dishonoured by sentence and by law,

por ende non deue ser del ninguno acussado,
nin en vuestra abdiençia oydo nin escuchado.

337   otrosy le opongo que es descomulgado
      de mayor descomunion por costiçion de llegado,
      por que tiene barragana publica e es casado
      con su muger doña loba que mora en vil forado.

338   ssu mançeba es la mastina que guarda la ovejas,
      por ende los sus dichos non valen dos arvejas,
      nin le deuen dar rrespuesta a sus malas conssejas;
      asolued a mi comadre, vayase de las callejas."

339   El galgo e el lobo estauan encogidos,
      otorgaron lo todo con miedo e amidos;
      diz luego la marfusa: "Señor, sean tenidos
      en Reconvençion, pido que mueran e non sean oydos."

340   Enceraron Racones de toda su pofia,
      pidieron al alcalde que les asignse dia
      en que diese sentençia qual el por bien tenia,
      E asignoles plaze despues de la epifania.

341   don ximio fue a su cas, con el mucha conpaña,
      con nel fueron las pares, conçejo de cucaña,
      ay van los abogados de la mala picaña;
      por boluer al alcalde, ninguno non lo engaña.

342   las partes cada vna a su abogado escucha,
      presentan al alcalde qual salmon e qual trucha,
      qual copa, qual tasa en poridat aducha;
      arman se çancadilla en esta falsa lucha.

343   venido es el dia para dar la sentençia,
      ante el juez las partes estauan en presençia,
      dixo el buen alcalde: "aved buena abenençia,
      ante que yo pronuncie e vos de la sentençia."

344   Pugnan los avogados E fazen su poder
      por saber del alcalde lo que quierre fazer,
      que sentençia daria o qual podria ser;
      mas non podieron del cosa saber nin entender.

345   De lexos le fablauan por le fazer desir,
      algo de la sentençia, por su coraçon descobrir;

so he should accuse no one
nor be heard at this court in your presence.

337 Therefore I decree he should be excommunicated
by constitution issued by papal legate
because he keeps a mistress openly, yet he is
married to Mrs Wolf, who lives in Vilforado.*

338 His mistress is the mastiff that guards the sheep,
so you can see that what he says is not worth two tares.
His evil tales should get no response.
Absolve my friend, the vixen, let her go free."

339 The greyhound and the wolf both cringed at once;
all this they granted, amid fear and ill-will.
Then the sly vixen said: "Sir, they should be held
by counterclaim. I am filing for their death, without a
                                                    hearing."

340 Their claims ended amid great dispute,
they asked the judge to set a day
to pass sentence as he saw fit.
He set a day after Epiphany.

341 Sir Monkey went to his house with a great crowd
of followers. Both parties went with him, a council of rogues;
there go the lawyers, full of tricks and deceit,
but however hard they try, the judge is not fooled.

342 Each party listens to his lawyer,
presents the judge with salmon, with trout,
secretly bringing cups and goblets.
They trip each other up in this false fight.

343 The day came when sentence could be passed,
the parties stood before the judge.
The good judge said: "Before I make pronouncement,
I give you permission to come to agreement between you."

344 The lawyers struggled and did all in their power
to work out what the judge wanted to do,
what sentence he would give, or what would happen,
but they could not find out or understand a thing.

345 With great care he was pressed to reveal
the sentence, to show his hand.

el mostraua los dientes, mas non era rreyr,
coydauan que jugaua e todo era rrenir.

346 dixieron las partes a los sus abogados
que non podrian ser en vno acordados,
nin querian abenencia para ser despechados;
pyden que por sentençia fuesen de ally lybrados.

347 El alcalde letrado e de buena çiençia
vso bien de su ofiçio E guardo su conçiençia;
estando assentado assentado en la su abdiençia
Rezo el por sy mesmo escripta tal sentençia:

348 "En el nonble de dios," el judgador desia,
"yo, don ximio, ordinario alcalde de bugia,
vista la demanda que el lobo fasia,
en que a la marfusa furto le aponia,

349 E vistas las escusas e las defensiones
que puso la gulharra en sus exenpçiones,
e vista la rrespuesta e las rreplicaçiones
que propusso el lobo en todas sus rrasones,

350 E visto lo que pide en su rreconvençion
la comadre contra el lobo çerca la conclusion,
visto todo el proçeso E quantas rrasones en el son,
E las partes que pyden sentençia E al non,

351 Por mi examinado todo el processo fecho,
avydo mi conssejo, que me fizo prouecho,
con omnes sabydores en fuero e en derecho,
dyos Ante mis ojos, nin Ruego nin pecho,

352 fallo que la demanda del lobo es byen çierta,
bien acta e byen formada, bien clara e abyerta;
fallo que la Raposa es en parte byen çierta
en sus deffenssiones E escusa e rrefierta.

353 la exençion primera es en sy perentoria,
mas la descomunion es aqui dilatoria;
dire vn poco della que es grand estoria;
¡abogado de rromançe, esto ten en memoria!

354 la exepçion primera muy byen fue llegada
mas la descomunion fue vn poco errada,

He showed them his teeth, but he wasn't laughing:
they thought he was joking, but he was grinding his molars.

346 Both parties and their lawyers
     failed to be reconciled on anything,
     nor did they want an agreement, only to end up paying.
     They asked sentence to be passed to prevent this.

347 The learned judge, full of wisdom,
     performed his task well, kept his moral sense.
     While seated in the court, he read
     the sentence he had written out himself.

348 "In the name of God," the judge began,
     "I, Sir Monkey, current judge of Bougie,
     in view of the claim made by the wolf,
     in which he accuses the vixen of theft,

349 and in view of the excuses and defence
     given by the vixen by way of exception,
     and in view of the answer and replies
     given by the wolf on all matters,

350 and in view of what the vixen requests
     in her counterclaim against the wolf,
     and in view of the entire case, and all the arguments,
     and the request for a sentence by both parties and nothing
                                                              else,

351 I have examined the entire case,
     consulted wise men, to great advantage,
     learned in both traditional and canon law.
     God is before my eyes, not requests or payment.

352 I find that the wolf's case is correct,
     very fitting and well presented, very clear and open.
     I find the vixen is partly right
     in her defence, excuse and reply.

353 The first legal exception is in itself peremptory,
     but excommunication here is dilatory.
     I will say a few words on the subject, as it is a long story.
     Lawyers who read only vernacular, bear this in mind!

354 The first legal exception was very well stated,
     but excommunication was a little in error,

que la costituçion deuiera ser nonblada
E fasta nueve dias deuiera ser provada.

355 Por cartas o por testigos o por buen jnstrumente,
de publico notario, deuiera syn fallymiente
esta tal dilatoria prouar se clara mente;
sy pon perentoria esto otra mente.

356 Quando la descomunion por dilatoria se pone,
Nueve dias de plaso para el que se opone
por perentoria; esto guarda, non te encone,
que a muchos abogados se olvida e se pospone,

357 Es toda perentoria la escomunion atal
quando se pon contra testigos en pleito criminal,
contra juez publicado que su proçesso non val;
quien de otra guisa lo pone, yerralo e faze mal.

358 fallo mas, que la gulpeja pide mas que non deue pedir,
que de egual, en criminal, non puede Reconvenyr;
por exepçion non puedo yo condepnar nin punir,
nin deue el abogado tal petiçion comedyr.

359 Maguer contra la parte o contra el mal testigo
sea exepçion prouada, nol faran otro castigo;
desecharan su demanda, su dicho non val vn figo,
la pena ordinaria non avra, yo vos lo digo.

360 sy non fuere testigo falso o sy lo vieren variar;
Ca entonçe el alcalde puede le atormentar,
non por la exepçion mas por que lo puede far;
en los pleitos criminales su ofiçio ha grand lugar.

361 Por exepçion se puede la demanda desechar,
E pueden se los testigos tachar e Retachar;
por exeçion non puedo yo condepnar nin matar,
nin puede el alcalde mas que el derecho mandar.

362 Por quanto yo fallo por la su conffesion
del lobo ante mi dicha E por otra cosa non,
fallo que es prouado lo que la marfusa pon,
por ende pongo sylençio al lobo en esta saçon.

363 Pues por su confesion e su costunbre e vso
es magnifiesto e cierto lo que la marfusa puso,

as its constitutional origin should have been described
and proven within nine days.

355   By letter and witness or by the right instrument
       of the notary public, this dilatory excommunication
       should have been clearly and unfailingly proven.
       If it is peremptory, that is another matter.

356   When excommunication becomes dilatory,
       the defendant has nine days only;
       if peremptory, the time is longer, so take note
       and don't get angry, as many lawyers forget and overlook it.

357   Excommunication is always peremptory
       if put before witnesses in a criminal proceedings
       and before a public judge whose rulings are invalid.
       If it is stated otherwise, it is an error and wrong is done.

358   I find, moreover, that the vixen asks for more than she may,
       for she cannot make a criminal counterclaim against an
                                                          equal;
       by legal exception I cannot condemn or punish,
       nor should a lawyer even consider such a petition.

359   In spite of proven exception of the party
       or of false witness, there shall be no further punishment.
       The claim will be refused, it is not worth a fig.
       Ordinary punishment will not be meted, I say to you.

360   Unless a witness is false, or the testimony varies,
       in which case the judge may have torture applied.
       Not by exception, but because it is within his authority –
       his office has great power in criminal proceedings.

361   By exception the claim can be rejected,
       the witnesses can challenge and challenge again;
       by exception I cannot condemn or kill;
       a judge can only decree the law.

362   But by virtue of my findings in the wolf's confession
       made before me, for this reason and no other,
       I find the vixen's claim to be proven
       and therein silence the wolf this very moment.

363   Since by his confession, his habits and deeds,
       what the crafty vixen said is manifest and clear,

pronuncio que la demanda quel fizo e propuso
non le sea rresçebida Segund dicho he de suso.

364 Pues el lobo confiesa que fizo lo que acusa
E es magnifiesto e çierto que el por ello vsa,
non le deue rresponder en juysio la marfusa;
rresçibo sus defensiones e la buena escusa.

365 Non le preste lo que dixo, que con miedo e quexura
fizo la conffesion cogido en angostura,
Ca su miedo era vano e non dixo cordura,
que ado buen alcalde judga, toda cosa es segura.

366 do lyçençia a la Raposa, vayase a la saluagina,
pero que non la asueluo del furto tan ayna,
pero mando que non furte el gallo a su vesina."
Ella diz que non lo tenie, mas que le furtaria la gallyna.

367 Non apellaron las partes, del juysio son pagados,
por que non pagaron costas nin fueron condenados,
esto fue por que non fueron de las partes demandados,
nin fue el pleito constestado, por que fueron escusados.

368 ally los abogados dyxieron contra el jues
que avya mucho errado E perdido el su buen pres,
por lo que avia dicho E suplido esta ves;
non gelo preçio don ximio quanto vale vna nues.

369 dixo les que byen podia el en su pronunçiaçion
conplir lo que es derecho E de constituçion,
que el de fecho ageno non fazia mension,
tomaron los abogados del ximio buena liçion.

370 dixieron le otrosy vna derecha rracon:
que fecha la conclusyon en criminal acusaçion
non podia dar lyçençia para aver conpusiçion,
menester la sentençia çerca la conclusion.

371 a esto dixo el alcalde vna sola Responssion:
que el avie poder del Rey, en su comision,
espeçial para todo esto, E conplida jurysdiçion.
aprendieron los abogados en esta disputaçion.

I pronounce that the charge he levelled and preferred
shall not be accepted, as I have already said.

364 Since the wolf confesses to what he did accuse,
and as it is manifestly clear to me that this is true,
the vixen should not answer him in court.
I accept her defence and fair excuse.

365 I do not hold with what he said, that the confession
was made under physical and moral duress;
his fear was vain and he spoke nonsense,
but where a good judge presides, all things are safe.

366 I give permission to the vixen. She may hunt
wild game, but I do not absolve her of theft so quickly,
but order her not to steal her neighbour's cockerel."
She replied she no longer had it, but would steal his hen
instead.

367 The parties did not appeal, content with the judgement,
because they paid no costs and were not convicted.
This was because none was claimed by the parties,
nor was the trial contested, because they were pardoned.

368 Then the lawyers said that the judge
had made a big mistake and lost his good reputation
by virtue of his words and understanding.
Sir Monkey did not care two hoots what they said.

369 He told them that in his judicial statement
he had complied with law and constitution,
had added nothing foreign to the case.
The lawyers learnt a good lesson from the monkey.

370 They then spoke reasonably to him, saying
that once a criminal suit was concluded,
he could not give permission for any settlement.
A sentence was necessary when the conclusion was near.

371 The judge gave a single answer to all this:
that he had a king's power by special
commission on this case, total jurisdiction.
The lawyers learnt something from this dispute.

AQUI FFABLA DE LA PELEA QUEL ARÇIPRESTE OVO CON
DON AMOR

372   Tal eres como el lobo, rretraes lo que fazes,
estrañas lo que ves E non el lodo en que yazes,
eres mal enemigo a todos quantos plases,
fablas con grand synpleza por que muchos engañes.

373   a obla de piedad nunca paras mientes,
nin visitas los presos nin quieres ver dolientes,
synon solteros sanos, mancebos e valyentes;
ssy loçanas encuentras, fablas les entre los dientes.

374   Rezas muy byen las oras con garçones folgaynez,
"*cum his qui oderunt paçem*", fasta que el salterio afines,
diçes: "*ecce quan bonum*", con sonajas e baçinez,
"*Jn notibus estolite*", despues vas a matynes.

375   Do tu Amiga mora comienças a leuantar,
"*domine labia mea*", en alta boz a cantar,
"*primo dierum onium*", los estormentos tocar,
"*nostras preçes ut audiat*", E fazes los despertar.

376   desque sientes a ella, tu coraçon espaçias,
con la maytinada "*cantate*", en las friurias laçias,
"*laudes aurora lucis*", das les grandes graçias,
con "*miserere mey*" mucho te le engraçias.

377   El salyendo el sol, comienças luego prima,
"*deus jn nomine tuo*", Ruegas a tu saquima
que la lieue por agua e que de a toda çima;
va en achaque de agua a verte la mala esquima,

378   E sy es tal que non vsa andar por las callejas,
que la lyeue a las vertas por las rrosas bermejas;
ssy cree la bauieca sus dichos e conssejas,
"*Quod eva tristis*" trae de "*quicunque vult*" Redruejas.

THE ARCHPRIEST'S BATTLE WITH LOVE

372 You are like the wolf, reproving in others the things you do,
     you throw the mud where you lie in each other's faces,
     you are the evil enemy of all those you please,
     speaking with simplicity to catch them in your snares.

373 You never even think of pious works,
     nor visit prisoners, nor help the suffering,
     only single, healthy, lusty, valiant men.
     If you encounter beautiful women, you whisper to them.

374 You sing the hours with dubious louts, "*cum his qui oderunt
                paçem*" (with those who hated peace) till the end of the psalter.
     You say: "*ecce quan bonum*" (that was good) with timbrels
                                              and chamber pots.
     "*In notibus estolite*" (in the night lift up your hands), then
                                              you go to matins.*

375 Where your lady lives you start to raise a racket,
     singing loudly "*domine labia mea*" (Lord, my lips)
     "*primo dierum onium*" (at the earliest hour), you play your
                                              instruments,
     "*nostras preçes ud audiat*" (may our pleas be heard), and
                                              arouse them all.

376 When you see her your heart is joyful,
     "*cantate*" (you sing) Matins in the bitter cold,
     then "*laudes aurora lucis*" (Lauds, O light of dawn), giving
                                              her great thanks,
     with "*miserere mey*" (Have mercy on me), you gain her
                                              good will.

377 As the sun rises, you then begin Prime;
     "*deus jn nomine tuo*" (In the name of the Lord) you ask
                                              your go-between
     to take her to fetch water and come to the climax.
     The wicked whore shall see you on the pretext of fetching
                                              water.

378 And if she's unused to street-walking,
     take her to the gardens for scarlet roses.
     If she's gullible enough to believe the bawd's advice,
     "*Quod eva tristis*" (like sorrowful Eve), she will bear the fruit
                "*quicunque vult*" (of whomsoever hath desire).

379 E sy es dueña tu amiga que desto non se conpone,
tu catolica a ella cata manera que la trastorne,
"*os, lynga, mens*", la enuade, seso con ardor pospone;
va la dueña a terçia, caridat "*a longe pone*".

380 Tu vas luego a la iglesia por le dezir tu Razon,
mas que por oyr la missa nin ganar de dios perdon;
quieres la misa de los novios syn gloria e syn son;
coxqueas al dar ofrenda, byen trotas el comendon.

381 acabada ya la missa Rezas tan byen la sesta,
que la vieja que tiene a tu amiga presta.
comienças: "*jn verbum tuum*", e dizes tu de aquesta:
"*feo sant sant vter*", por la grand misa de fiesta.

382 dizes: "*quomodo dilexi*" nuestra fabla varona,
"*ssusçipe me secundum*", que ¡para la mi corona!
"*luçerna pedibus meys*" es la vuestra persona.
ella te dise: "*¡quam dulçia!*", que rrecubdas a la nona.

383 vas a Rezar la nona con la duena loçana:
"*mirabilia*", comienças, dizes de aquesta plana:
"*gressus meos dirige*" rresponde doña fulana:
"*justus est domine*"; tañe a nona la canpana.

384 Nunca vy sancristan que a visperas mejor tanga,
todos los jnstrumentos toca con la chica manga;
la que viene a tus visperas, por byen que se rremanga,
con "*virgam virtutis tue*" fazes que de ay Retangan.

385 "*Sede a destris meys*", dizes a la que viene;
cantas: "*letatus sum*", sy ally se detiene;
"*illyc enim asçenderunt*", a qualquier que ally se atiene;
la fiesta de seys capas contigo la pasqua tiene.

379 And if your lady friend will not agree to this,
your bawd will seek a way to change her mind.
"*os, lynga, mens*" (mouth, tongue, mind) overcome her,
         ardour sets reason aside.
She shall go to pray the third hour, "*a longe pone*" (set me a
         law) in love.

380 Then you go to church at once to say your piece,
rather than listen to Mass or ask God's pardon.
You want the lover's Mass, with no Gloria or music;
you drag yourself to the collection plate, but hurry at the
         commendation of souls.

381 When Mass is over, you sing the Sextus;
the old hag has your lady ready and waiting.
You begin "*jn verbum tuum*" (In your word I have trusted)
         and say to her:
"*[Factus sum sicut] uter*" (I am swollen like a wineskin) at
         this great festival Mass.*

382 You say "*quomodo dilexi*" (how greatly I esteem) your
         conversation, lady,
"*ssusçipe me secundum*" (Have me), then, by my tonsure,
your body is "*luçerna pedibus meys*" (a light unto my feet).
She replies: "*quam dulçia!*" (How good!), come back at Nones.

383 You go to pray Nones with the lovely lady.
"*mirabilia*" (Marvellous) you begin, clearly.
"*gressus meos dirige*" (Guide my steps) Miss So and So replies.
"*justus est domine*" (Lord, it is upright) – the Nones bell strikes.

384 I have never seen a sacristan play so well at Vespers.
You play on all instruments with the barest means.
The lady you invite to Vespers, however she resists,
with "*virgam virtutis tue*" (the rod of your virtue) you make
         her perform again.

385 "*Sede a destris meys*" (sit on my right hand) you say to any
         woman who comes,
and sing "*letatus sum*" (Happy am I) if she does not leave;
"*illyc enim asçenderunt*" (the path is ascended), if any
         woman lingers.
She'll have a real festival with you, Christmas and Easter all
         in one.

386   Nunca vy cura de almas que tan byen diga conpletas;
      vengan fermosas o feas, quier blancas quier prietas,
      digan te: "*conortamos*", de grado abres las puertas;
      despues: "*custodinos*", te rruegan las encubiertas.

387   ffasta el "*quod parasti*" non la quieres dexar:
      "*ante facien onium*", sabes las alexar;
      "*In gloria plebys tue*", fazes las aveytar;
      "*salue rregina*", dises, sy de ti se ha de quexar.

AQUI FABLA DE LA PELEA QUE OVO EL ARÇIPRESTE CON
DON AMOR

388   Con açidya traes estos males atantos,
      muchos otros pecados, antojos e espantos;
      non te pagas de omes castos nin dignos santos,
      a los tuyos das oblas de males e quebrantos.

389   El que tu obla trae es mitroso puro,
      por conplyr tus deseos fazes lo erege duro,
      mas cree tus lysonjas, el neçio fadeduro,
      que non la fe de dios, vete, yo te conjuro.

390   Non te quiero, amor, nin codbiçio tu fijo,
      fazes me andar de balde, dises me: "digo, digo";
      tanto mas me aquexas quanto yo mas aguijo;
      non me val tu vanagloria vn grano de mijo.

391   Non as miedo nin verguença de Rey nin Reyna,
      mudas te do te pagas cada dia Ayna,
      huesped eres de muchos, non duras so cortina;
      como el fuego andas de vesina en vesina.

392   Con tus muchas promesas a muchos envelyñas,
      en cabo son muy pocos a quien byen adelyñas,
      non te menguan lysonjas mas que fojas en vyñas,
      mas traes neçios locos que ay pyñones en piñas.

386   I never saw a priest of souls who said Compline better,
whether beautiful or ugly, dark or fair,
they all say: "*conortamos*" (convert us) and you gladly open
the door.
Then after, "*custodinos*" (protect us), the covered ones ask.

387   Until the "*quod parasti*" (that which you have prepared) is
over, you will not leave them,
"*ante facien onium*" (before the eyes of all people) you lead
them discreetly,
"*In gloria plebys tue*" (to the glory of thy people) you make
them kneel;
"*salue, rregina*" (All hail, Queen), you say, if they complain.

THE ARCHPRIEST'S BATTLE WITH LOVE CONTINUES

388   It is sloth that brings so many ills,
many other sins, caprices, and fears;
you have no time for chaste, worthy or holy men,
you give evil works and afflictions to your own kind.

389   Whoever does your work is a liar and perjurer,
to comply with your wishes you make him a hardened
heretic.
The foolish wretch rather believes your flattery
than the faithful word of God – get out, I beg you.

390   I do not care for you, Love, nor for Covetousness, your son.
You make me act in vain, saying: "I give the orders."
The faster I go, the more you harass me.
I don't value your vainglory one grain of millet.

391   You neither fear nor are ashamed before king or queen,
you go where you like each and every day.
The guest of many, though you never lie low,
you spread between women and their neighbours like fire.

392   All your promises drive many to madness,
very few are set on the right path.
You know more flattering words than there are leaves on a
vine,
you create more stupid fools than there are kernels in a pine
cone.

393   fazes como folguym en tu mesma manera,
        atalayas de lexos e caças la primera,
        al que quieres mata ssacas los de carrera,
        de logar encobyerto sacas çelada fiera.

394   Tyene omne su fija de coraçon amada,
        loçana e fermosa, de muchos deseada,
        ençerrada e guardada e con vycios criada;
        do coyda algo en ella tyene nada.

395   Coydan se la cassar como las otras gentes,
        por que se onrren della su padre e sus parientes;
        como mula camursia agusa rrostros e dientes,
        Remeçe la cabeça, a mal seso tiene mientes.

396   Tu le rruyes a la oreja E das le mal conssejo,
        que faga tu mandado E sigua tu trebejo;
        los cabellos en rrueda, el peyne E el espejo,
        que aquel mingo oveja non es della parejo.

397   El coraçon le tornas de mill guisas a la ora;
        ssy oy cassar la quieren cras de otro se enamora;
        a las vezes en saya, a las vezes en alcandora,
        rremira se la loca ado tu lo-cura mora.

398   El que mas a ty cree anda mas por mal cabo,
        a ellos e a ellas, a todos das mal rramo
        de pecado dañoso, de al non te alabo,
        tristeza e flaqueza al de ty non Recabdo.

399   das muerte perdurable a las almas que fieres,
        das muchos enemigos al cuerpo que rrequieres,
        fazer perder la fama al que mas amor dieres,
        a dios pierde e al mundo, amor, el que mas quieres.

400   Estruyes las personas, los averes estragas,
        almas, cuerpos e algos commo huerco las tragas,
        de todos tus vassallos fazes neçios fadragas;
        prometes grandes cosas, poco e tarde pagas.

401   Eres muy grand gigante al tienpo del mandar,
        eres enano chico quando lo as de dar,
        luego de grado mandas, bien te sabes mudar,
        tarde das e Amidos byen quieres demandar.

393   You act like a highwayman with your deceitful manner,
       you spy from a distance and hunt the first comer.
       You lead the one you will kill off the beaten track;
       she falls into the trap, like a wild beast in a hidden place.

394   A man has a daughter, deeply loved,
       lovely, so beautiful, desired by many,
       shut away and protected, brought up in luxury.
       He thinks he has something but he really has nothing.

395   They would like her married, like other folk,
       to do honour to her parents and relatives.
       Like an unruly mule she bares her teeth,
       tosses her head, her mind on foolish things.

396   You whisper in her ear and offer bad advice
       to follow your wishes and play your evil game.
       Hair spread like a peacock's tail, comb and mirror in hand,
       the daftest sheep is not her equal.

397   You turn her heart in a thousand different ways;
       if today they want her to marry, tomorrow she falls for
                                                         another.
       At times she wears a tunic, at times a white shirt,
       duped by your madness, she never stops admiring herself.

398   Anyone who believes you makes the worst errors.
       You bring bad luck to men and women.
       I can only praise you for harmful sin.
       You give nothing else but sadness and weakness.

399   The souls you wound die an eternal death,
       the body you visit and misuse has many enemies.
       Whoever you afflict with love loses their reputation;
       Love, whoever you love most loses God and the world.

400   You destroy people, you devour possessions,
       soul, body and property are all swallowed up into hell,
       you make foolish wretches of all your vassals,
       promising great things, but paying little and late.

401   You are a mighty giant when you make promises,
       but a tiny dwarf when it's your turn to give.
       You make willing promises, but you easily forget.
       You give late and unwillingly, but you know how to ask.

402   de la loçana fazes muy loca E muy bova,
       fazes con tu grand fuego commo faze la loba,
       el mas astroso lobo al enodio ajoba,
       aquel da de la mano e de aquel se encoba.

403   ansy muchas fermosas contigo se enartan,
       con quien se les antoja, con aquel se apartan;
       quier feo, quier natyo, aguisado non catam,
       quanto mas a ty creen, tanto peor baratan.

404   fazes por muger fea perder omne apuesto,
       pierde se por omne torpe duena de grand Respuesto,
       plase te con qual quier do el ojo as puesto,
       byen te pueden desir antojo por denuesto.

405   Natura as de diablo; ado quier que tu mores
       fazes tenblar los omnes, e mudar sus colores,
       perder seso e fabla, sentyr muchos dolores,
       traes los omnes çiegos que creen en tus loores.

406   a bletador semejas quando tañe su brete,
       que canta dulçe, con engaño, al ave pone abeyte,
       fasta que le echa el laço quando el pie dentro mete;
       assegurando matas; ¡quita te de mi, vete!

ENSSSIENPLO DEL MUR TOPO E DE LA RANA
407   Contesçe cada dia a tus amigos con-tigo,
       commo contesçio al topo que quiso ser amigo
       de la rrana pyntada, quando lo leuo con-sygo;
       entiende byen la fabla E por que te lo digo.

408   Tenia el mur topo cueva en la rribera;
       creçio tanto el rrio que maravilla era,
       çerco toda su cueva, que non salya de fuera;
       vyno a el cantando la rrana cantadera:

409   "Señor enamorado," dixo al mur la Rana,
       "quiero ser tu amiga, tu muger e tu çercana,
       yo te sacare a saluo agora por la mañana,
       poner te he en el otero, cosa para ti sana.

410   yo se nadar muy byen, ya lo ves por el ojo;
       ata tu pie al mio, sube en mi ynojo,

402   You turn a beautiful girl into a crazy fool.
       Your great consuming fire reminds me of the she-wolf:
       she always takes the lowest, most wretched mate,
       abandons the most handsome and hides herself from him.

403   Many lovely women are deceived by you like this,
       going off with whoever takes their fancy,
       some ugly, some wretched, they do not choose wisely.
       The more they believe you, the worse bargain they get.

404   The handsome man is lost to an ugly woman.
       A lady of great wealth is lost to a dull man.
       You take pleasure in whoever you chance to see –
       to call you capricious is an appropriate insult.

405   You have the devil's nature – wherever you reside
       men tremble and lose their colour,
       lose their reason and power of speech, suffer much pain.
       They believe in your praise and become blind.

406   You are like a fowler playing his pipe.
       He plays softly, deceptively, fooling the bird,
       whose foot touches the trap, then the noose ensnares it.
       In reassuring, you kill – leave me alone, get out!

THE FABLE OF THE MOLE AND THE FROG

407   Every day, the same happens to you and your friends
       as happened to the mole who wanted to befriend
       the beautiful but false frog when she took him with her.
       Try to understand this story correctly and my reason for
                                                        telling it.

408   The mole lived in a hole in the river-bank.
       The river swelled to a miraculous degree,
       surrounding his hole entirely, so he couldn't get out.
       The singing frog came dancing up to him.

409   "Mr Lover," said the frog to the mole,
       "I wish to be your friend, your wife, your relative,
       I will get you out safe and sound, now, this morning,
       I will put you on the hill, a good place for you.

410   You can see clearly how well I can swim.
       Tie your foot to mine and get up on my knee.

sacar te he bien a saluo, non te fare enojo;
poner te he en el otero o en aquel rrastrojo."

411   byen cantava la rrana con fermosa rraçon,
mas al tiene pensado en el su coraçon;
creo se lo el topo, en vno atados son;
atan los pies en vno, las voluntades non.

412   Non guardando la Rana la postura que puso,
dio salto en el agua, somiese fasia yuso;
el topo quanto podia tiraua fasia suso,
qual de yuso qual suso andauan a mal vso.

413   Andaua y vn milano volando desfranbrido
buscando que comiese; esta pelea vydo,
abatiose por ellos, subyo en apellydo,
al topo e a la rrana leuolos a su nido.

414   Comiolos a entranbos, non le quitaron la fanbre;
asy faze a los locos tu falsa vedegabre,
quantos tyenes atados con tu mala estanble,
todos por ti peresçem, por tu mala enxanbre.

415   a los neçios e neçias que vna vez enlaças,
en tal guisa les travas con tus fuertes mordaças,
que non han de dios miedo nin de sus amenasas,
el diablo los lyeva presos en tus tenasas.

416   Al vno e al otro eres destroydor,
tan byen al engañado como al enganador,
commo el topo e la rrana peresçen o peor;
eres mal enemigo, fazes te amador.

417   Toda maldad del mundo E toda pestilençia,
sobre la falsa lengua mitirosa aparesçençia,
dezir palablas dulses que traen abenençia,
E fazer malas oblas e tener mal querençia.

418   Del bien que omne dize sy a sabyendas mengua,
es el coraçon falso e mitirosa la lengua;
confonda dios al cuerpo do tal coraçon fuelga,
lengua tan enconada dios del mundo la tuelga.

419   Non es para buen omne creer de lygero
todo lo quel dixieren, piense lo bien primero;

I will get you out safely, without hurting you,
I'll put you on the hill, or in that stubble over there."

411   The frog croaked in a most persuasive way,
but she really had something else in mind.
The mole believed her – and they tied themselves together.
Yet though their feet were tied, their wills were not.

412   The frog did not keep her part of the agreement.
She leapt into the water, diving downwards –
the mole fought against her, pulling upwards,
downwards, upwards, then disaster struck.

413   A hungry kite was flying above them,
searching for food. Seeing their struggle,
he swooped down towards them with a war-cry.
He took the frog and the mole back to his nest.

414   He ate them both, but they didn't satisfy his hunger,
just like the poison you give to fools, Love.
All those you knit together with your evil yarn,
all perish amid your noxious swarm.

415   The foolish men and women, once entangled,
are seized between your powerful jaws,
and no longer fear God nor his warnings.
The devil takes them prisoner, out of your clutches.

416   You are the destroyer of everyone,
both deceiver and deceived.
They perish like the mole and the frog, or worse.
You are an evil enemy, in the guise of a lover.

417   All the evil in the world, all the pestilence,
lies and deceit come from your false tongue.
Speaking sweet words which bring accord,
you do evil deeds and harbour ill-will.

418   The good that men speak is knowingly a lie,
and comes from a false heart and deceitful tongue.
May God confound the body in which such a heart beats,
may God take away such a malevolent tongue.

419   A good man does not believe all he is told,
but first weighs up all that is said.

non le conviene al bueno que sea lyjongero,
en el buen desir sea omne firme e verdadero.

420   So la piel ovejuna traes dientes de lobo,
al que vna vez travas lievas telo en Robo,
matas al que mas quieres, del byen eres encobo,
echas en flacas cuestas grand peso e grand ajobo.

421   Plaze me byen, te digo, que algo non te devo,
eres de cada dia logrero E das a Renuevo,
tomas la grand vallena con el tu poco çeuo,
mucho mas te diria Saluo que non me atrevo.

422   Porque de muchas dueñas mal querido seria,
E mucho garçon loco de mi profaçaria;
por tanto non te digo el diezmo que podria,
pues calla te e callemos, amor vete tu vya.'

AQUI FABLA DE LA RESPUESTA QUE DON AMOR DIO AL
ARÇIPRESTE.

423   El amor con mesura dio me rrespuesta luego;
dyz: 'açipreste, Sañudo non seyas, yo te rruego,
non digas mal de amor en verdat nin en juego,
que a las vezes poca agua faze abaxar grand fuego.

424   Por poco mal desir se pierde grand amor,
de pequeña pellea nasçe muy grand rrencor,
por mala dicha pierde vassallo su Señor,
la buena fabla sienpre faz de bueno mejor.

425   Escucha la mesura, pues dixiste baldon,
non deue amenaçar el que atyende perdon,
do byen eres oydo escucha mi Razon,
ssy mis dichos fazes non te dira muger non.

426   ssi tu fasta agora cosa non rrecabdaste;
de dueñas e de otras que dizes que ameste,
torna te a tu culpa pues por ti lo erreste,
por que a mi non veniste nin viste nin prometiste.

427   quisyste ser maestro ante que discipulo ser,
e non sabes la manera commo es de aprender;
oy e leye mis castigos e sabe los byen fazer,
Recabdaras la dueña E sabras otras traer.

The good man should not use flattery,
but speak only good, with conviction and truth.

420   You hide wolf's teeth under sheep's clothing.
Once you seize someone, you take them as booty.
You kill the one you love the most, hiding what is good.
You place a great weight on weak shoulders.

421   I am glad to say I owe you nothing.
You are a usurer, charging more interest daily;
you reel in a great whale with your meagre bait.
I could say a great deal more, but do not dare,

422   because many women would dislike me for it,
and many crazy lads would denounce me.
So I will not say one tenth of what I might – say nothing
and we shall both be silent – Love, go on your way!'

HOW LOVE ANSWERED THE ARCHPRIEST
423   Then Love replied in measured tones:
'Archpriest, I beg you, don't be angry,
speak no ill of love, in truth or in jest,
as sometimes just a little water puts out a roaring fire.

424   Great love is lost by a few wrong words,
and great rancour stems from a trivial fight.
The vassal loses his lord through evil words.
Good speech always makes a fine thing even better.

425   Listen to moderation, since you have reproached me.
You should not threaten if you hope for pardon.
I have listened patiently, now you listen to me.
If you follow my advice, no woman will refuse you.

426   If you have had no success up to now
with ladies, or others, whom you say you loved,
the fault lies with you, so look where you went wrong,
as you did not come to me, nor put me to the test.

427   You wanted to be master before you were disciple,
and you do not know how to learn.
Hear and read my advice, and know how to use it.
You will win your lady and attract others to you.

428   Para todas mugeres tu amor non conviene,
        non quieras amar duenas que a ty non avyene;
        es vn amor baldio, de grand locura viene,
        syenpre sera mesquino quien Amor vano tyene.

429   sy leyeres ovydio, el que fue mi criado,
        en el fallaras fablas que le ove yo mostrado;
        muchas buenas maneras para enamorado,
        panfilo e nason yo los ove castigado.

430   sy quisyeres amar dueñas o otra qual quier muger,
        muchas cosas avras primero de aprender;
        para que ella te quiera en su amor querer,
        sabe primera mente la muger escoger.

431   Cata muger fermosa, donosa e loçana,
        que non sea mucho luenga otrosi nin enana;
        sy podieres non quieras amar muger villana,
        que de amor non sabe, es como bausana.

432   busca muger de talla, de cabeça pequeña,
        cabellos amarillos, non sean de alheña,
        las çejas apartadas, luengas, altas en peña,
        ancheta de caderas, esta es talla de dueña.

433   ojos grandes, fermosos, pyntados, Relusientes,
        E de luengas pestañas, byen claras e Reyentes,
        las orejas pequeñas, delgadas; paral mientes
        sy ha el cuello alto, atal quieren las gentes.

434   la naryz afylada, los dientes menudiellos,
        eguales e bien blancos, vn poco apartadillos,
        las ensivas bermejas, los dientes agudillos,
        los labros de la boca bermejos, angostillos.

435   la su boca pequena, asy de buena guisa,
        la su faz sea blanca, syn pelos, clara e lysa;
        puna de aver muger que la veas syn camisa,
        que la talla del cuerpo te dira esto a guisa.

436   A la muger que enbiares de ti sea parienta,
        que bien leal te sea, non sea su seruienta,
        Non lo sepa la dueña por que la otra non mienta,
        Non puede ser quien mal casa que non se arrepienta.

428   Your love is not for all women –
       don't bother with those who do not suit you.
       Your love will be in vain, it is a mistake,
       vain love will always make you wretched.

429   If you read the words of Ovid, who was my servant,
       there you will find the things I taught him,
       the correct behaviour for a lover.
       I have advised both Pamphilus and Ovid.

430   If you want to love a lady, or any other woman,
       you will have to learn a great deal first.
       If you want a woman to fall for you,
       first you must learn how to choose the right woman.

431   Look for a beautiful woman, gay and lively,
       neither too short nor too tall,
       and try not to fall in love with a peasant girl,
       who knows nothing of love, she's like a scarecrow.

432   Look for a woman with a good figure and a small head,
       blonde-haired, but not dyed with henna.
       Eyebrows well apart, long and arched;
       her hips should be nice and broad, as a lady should be.

433   Her eyes should be large, well-set, bright and shining,
       with beautiful, long, visible eyelashes.
       Her ears should be small, not thick. Notice if
       her neck is long, as this is how men like it.

434   Her nose should be slender, her teeth nice and small,
       even and white, slightly separated,
       with red gums and quite sharp teeth
       between her full, scarlet lips.

435   Her mouth should be small, as fashion dictates,
       her face should be pale, clear, smooth and hairless.
       Try to find a woman you can see without
       her shirt on, to tell if her figure suits you.

436   The woman who is your go-between should be related,
       she will be quite loyal to you; don't choose the lady's servant.
       Don't let the lady know this, as her servant will tell the truth.
       There is no bad match which is not repented. *

437 puña, en quanto puedas, que la tu mensajera
     sea bien rrasonada, sotil e costumera,
     sepa mentir fermoso e siga la carrera,
     ca mas fierbe la olla con la su cobertera.

438 si parienta non tienes atal, toma viejas,
     que andan las iglesias e saben las callejas,
     grandes cuentas al cuelo, saben muchas consejas,
     con lagrimas de moysen escantan las orejas.

439 son grandes maestras aquestas pauiotas,
     andan por todo el mundo, por plaças e cotas,
     a dios alçan las cuentas, querellando sus coytas,
     ¡ay! ¡quanto mal saben estas viejas arlotas!

440 toma de vnas viejas que se fasen erveras,
     andan de casa en casa e llaman se parteras;
     con poluos e afeytes, e con alcoholeras,
     echan la moça en ojo e çiegan bien de ueras.

441 E busca mensajera de vnas negras pecas,
     que vsan mucho frayres, monjas e beatas;
     son mucho andariegas e merescen las çapatas;
     estas trota conventos fasen muchas baratas.

442 do estas mugeres vsan mucho se alegran,
     pocas mugeres pueden dellas se despagar,
     por que a ty non mienta sabe las falagar,
     ca tal escanto vsan que saben bien çegar.

443 de aquestas viejas todas esta es la mejor;
     rruegal que te non mienta, muestral buen amor,
     que mucha mala bestia vende buen corredor,
     e mucha mala rropa cubre buen cobertor.

444 si dexiere que la dueña non tiene mienbros muy grandes,
     nin los braços delgados, tu luego lo demandes
     sy ha los pechos chycos; si dise "si" demandes
     contra la fegura toda, por que mas çierto andes.

445 si dis que los sobacos tiene vn poco mojados,
     e que ha chycas piernas e luengos los costados,
     ancheta de caderas, pies chicos, socavados,
     tal muger non la fallan en todos los mercados.

437   Strive as far as you can to find a messenger
       who is discreet, subtle and patient,
       knowing how to bend the truth and persevere to the end,
       because a pan with its lid on boils faster.

438   If you don't have such a relative, use one of those old women
       who frequent churches and know all the alleyways,
       who wear long rosaries round their necks. They are full
       of good advice, and weave a spell on ladies' ears with
                                                   Moses' tear beads.*

439   These old charlatans are past masters.
       They go all over the place, to the squares, up the hills,
       raising their beads up to God, lamenting their troubles.
       What a lot of bad things these old scoundrels know!

440   Choose an old woman who sells medicinal herbs.
       They go from house to house, claiming to be midwives,
       with powders, cosmetics, pots for eye make-up,
       to cast the evil eye and cause true blindness.

441   Look for a messenger with dark freckles,*
       the kind much used by friars, nuns and pious women.
       They cover a lot of miles, they earn their shoes,
       these convent-trotters do a lot of business.

442   Where these women practise there is great rejoicing;
       few women can free themselves from their clutches.
       You must learn to flatter them, so they don't lie to you;
       because they use such enchantment, they know how to blind.

443   Of all these old women, this kind is the best.
       Ask her to be truthful to you, show her the love of friendship,
       for many poor beasts are sold by a good broker,
       and a lot of tatty clothes hide a good go-between.

444   If she tells you the lady does not have long limbs,
       or slim arms, you must then ask her if
       the lady's breasts are small. If the reply is yes,
       ask about her whole figure, to give you a better idea.

445   If she says the lady's armpits are a little damp,
       that her legs are short and her body is long,
       with broadish hips, small, shapely feet,
       then you won't find a woman like that at every market.

446   en la cama muy loca, en casa muy cuerda,
     non oluides tal dueña mas della te enamora;
     esto que te castigo con ouidio concuerda,
     e para aquesta cata la fyna avancuerda.

447   tres cosas non te oso agora descobryr;
     son tachas encobiertas de mucho mal desir;
     Pocas son las mugeres que dellas pueden salyr;
     sy las yo dexiese començarien a rreyr.

448   guarte que non sea bellosa nin barbuda;
     ¡atal media pecada el huerco la saguda!
     sy ha la mano chyca, delgada, bos aguda,
     atal muger si puedes de buen seso la muda.

449   en fin de las rrasones fas le vna pregunta;
     si es muger alegre, de amor se rrepunta,
     si a sueras frias, ssy demanda quanto barrunta,
     al omne si drise "Si", a tal muger te ayunta.

450   atal es de seruir e atal es de amar,
     es muy mas plasentera que otras en doñear;
     si tal saber podieres e la quisieres cobrar,
     fas mucho por seruir la en desir e en obrar.

451   de tus joyas fermosas cada que dar podieres;
     quando dar non quisieres o quando non touieres,
     promete e manda mucho maguer non gelo dieres,
     luego estara afusiada, far[a] lo que quisieres.

452   syrue la, non te enojes, syruiendo el amor creçe.
     el seruiçio en el bueno nunca muere nin peresçe;
     sy se tarda, non se pierde, el amor nunca fallese,
     que el grand trabajo todas la cosas vençe.

453   gradesçe gelo mucho lo que por ti feziere,
     pongelo en mayor de quanto ello valyere,
     non le seas rrefertero en lo que te pediere,
     nin le seas porfioso contra lo que te dixiere.

454   Requiere a menudo a la que bien quisieres,
     non ayas miedo della quanto tienpo tovyeres,
     verguença non te enbargue quando con ella estodieres,
     peresoso non seas ado buena asina vyeres.

446   Passionate in bed, but prudent in household matters,
don't forget a lady like this, keep her in mind.
My advice matches Ovid's words,
so find the finest string in the bow to hunt for you.

447   There are three things I dare not reveal to you now,
hidden faults, and much maligned;
few women can escape from them.
If I say what they are, they would start to laugh.

448   Mind that she isn't hairy or bearded,
Hell would shake at such a she-devil!
If she has small, thin hands and a sharp voice,
be sensible, find another.

449   Last of all, ask her a question – does she have
a happy disposition? She will speak ill of love
if the saddle blanket she sits on is cold. If she wants
what she gets a sniff of, says "Yes" to a man, this is the
                                        woman to cleave to.

450   Serve and love a woman like this,
she will be far more pleasant to court than any other.
If you can get to know such a woman, then want
to conquer her, serve her in words and in actions.

451   Give her all the loveliest jewels you can,
and when you cannot or would not give,
promise her a great deal, without giving it.
Soon she will have confidence in you and do as you wish.

452   Serve her, don't be angry, love grows through service,
in the good man service never perishes, never dies;
love never fails, it is not lost, though may be slow in coming,
if love takes its time, hard work always conquers all things.

453   Be very grateful for what she does for you,
give it greater value than it really has.
Don't haggle over what she asks of you,
nor argue obstinately over what she says.

454   Woo the one you love, as often as you can,
don't be afraid of her when you find time to be with her,
don't be overcome with shyness when you are near her,
don't be lazy if an opportunity for love presents itself.

455   quando la muger vee al peresoso covardo
        dise luego entre sus dientes: "¡oyste, tomare mi dardo!"
        con muger non enpereçes, nin te enbueluas en tabardo,
        del vestido mas chico sea tu ardit alardo.

456   son en la grand peresa miedo E covardia,
        torpedat e vilesa, ssusiedat e astrossya;
        por la pereza pyerden muchos la mi conpania,
        por peresa se pierde muger de grand valya.

ENSSIENPLO DE LOS DOS PEREZOSOS QUE QUERIAN CASSAR CON VNA DUEÑA

457   Dezir te la ffasaña de los dos peresosos,
        que querian casamiento e andavan acusiossos,
        amos por vna dueña estaua codyçiossos,
        eran muy byen apuestos E veras quan fermosos:

458   El vno era tuerto del su ojo derecho,
        Ronco era el otro, de la pierna contrecho,
        el vno del otro avya muy grand despecho,
        coydando que tenian su cassamiento fecho.

459   dyxo les la dueña que ella queria casar
        con el mas peresosso, E aquel queria tomar;
        esto desie la dueña queriendo los abeytar.
        ffabro luego el coxo, coydo se adelantar:

460   Dyxo: "sseñora, oyd primero la mi Razon;
        yo soy mas peresosso que este mi conpanon.
        por peresa de tender el pie fasta el escalon
        cay del escalera, fynque con esta ligion.

461   Otrossy yo passava nadando por el Ryo,
        fasia la syesta grande, mayor que ome non vydo,
        perdia me de sed; tal peresa yo crio,
        que por non abrir la boca de sed perdy el fablar mio."

462   Desque callo el coxo, dixo el tuerto: "Señora,
        chica es la peresa que este dixo agora,
        desir vos he la mia, non vistes tal ningud ora,
        nin ver tal la puede omne que en dios adora.

463   yo era enamorado de vna duena en abryl;
        estando delante ella, sossegado e muy omyl,

455   When a woman sees a lazy coward,
she says to herself: "Gee up! my arrow is poised."
Don't be lazy with a woman, don't wear a heavy cloak,
dress in something lightweight to reveal your ardour.

456   Fear and cowardice lie in great laziness,
stupidity and meanness, filth and wretchedness.
Laziness lost many the pleasure of my company,
laziness loses a woman of great worth.

THE FABLE OF THE TWO LAZY MEN WHO WANTED TO MARRY THE SAME WOMAN

457   I must tell you the tale of the two lazy men
who wanted to marry, full of zeal.
They both desired the same woman,
they were very elegant and handsome, as you'll see.

458   One was boss-eyed in the right eye,
the other was quite hoarse, with a lame leg.
They scorned each other greatly,
each thinking his own marriage was a certainty.

459   The lady told them that she wished to marry
the lazier of the two and take him as her own,
but she said it thinking to deceive them.
The lame one spoke, trying to get in first,

460   saying: "Madam, hear what I have to say first.
I am far lazier than my companion here.
Too lazy to put my foot on the next step,
I fell down the stairs and ended up with this injury.

461   I was also swimming in the river
one hot afternoon, the hottest ever known.
I was dying of thirst, but I had become so lazy
that I lost my voice through not opening my mouth."

462   As soon as the lame man stopped talking, the boss-eyed
man spoke: "Madam, his laziness is nothing compared to
mine.
I shall tell you about it, I have never seen its like,
nor will a God-fearing man see greater laziness.

463   I was in love with a lady one April,
standing before her, calm and humble,

vyno me desçendimiento a las narizes muy vyl;
por peresa de alympiar me perdy la duena gentil.

464 Mas vos dire, Señora, vna noche yasia
en la cama despierto, e muy fuerte llouia,
daua me vna gotera del agua que fasia,
en el mi ojo muy Resia amenudo feria;

465 yo ove grand peresa de la cabeça Redrar,
la gotera que vos digo, con su mucho Rezio dar,
el ojo de que soy tuerto ovo melo de quebrar;
deuedes, por mas perèsa, duena, con-migo casar."

466 "Non se," dixo la duena, "destas peresas grandes
qual es la mayor dellas, anbos pares estades;
veo vos, torpe coxo, de qual pie coxeades,
veo, tuerto susio, que sienpre mal catades;

467 buscad con quien casedes, que la dueña non se paga
de peresoso torpe nin que vilesa faga."
por ende mi amigo, en tu coraçon non yaga
nin tacha nin vylesa de que dueña se despaga.

468 ffaz la vna vegada la verguença perder,
por aquesto faz mucho sy la podieres aver;
desque vna vez pierde verguenca la muger
mas diabluras faze de quantas omne quier.

469 Talente de mugeres quien le podria entender,
sus malas maestrias e su mucho mal saber,
quando son ençendidas E mal quieren fazer,
alma e cuerpo e fama todo lo dexan perder.

470 Desque la verguença pierde el tafur al tablero,
sy el pellote juga, jugara el braguero;
desque la cantader dize el cantar primero,
syenpre le bullen los pies e mal para el pandero.

471 Texedor E cantadera nunca tyenen los pies quedos,
en el telar e en la dança syenpre bullen los dedos;
la muger syn verguença, por darle diez toledos,
non dexaria de fazer sus antojos asedos.

when a foul discharge trickled down my nose.
Being too lazy to wipe it off, I lost the gentle lady.

464   I can tell you more Madam – one night I lay
awake in bed, and it was pouring with rain.
A series of drops from leaking rain water
kept hitting me in the eye, over and over.

465   I was too lazy to move my head,
and the leak fell so accurately and directly
that my eye, the bad one, was totally damaged.
So on account of my greater laziness, Madam, marry me."

466   "I can't decide," said the lady, "whose laziness is greater,
they seem to be quite equal to me.
I can see, you foolish cripple, which leg you limp on, and
I can see that your vision is very poor, you filthy, one-eyed
creature.

467   Look for someone else to marry, as no lady will tolerate
a stupid, lazy man who resorts to vile deeds."
So, my friend, let no stain, nor baseness
lie in your heart, to cause a lady displeasure.

468   Make her lose her shame just once,
strive for this, if you would have her.
Once a woman loses her shame, she will do
as many wild and foolish things as a man might want.

469   Who can understand the character of women?
Who knows their evil skills and wicked wisdom,
when they are aflame and seek to do evil,
soul, body and reputation, everything is lost.

470   As soon as the card cheat feels no shame at the gaming table,
if he bets his cloak, he will bet his underwear too.
As soon as the singer sings her first song,
her feet tap to the beat, her tambourine gets banged non-
stop!*

471   The weaver and singer never keep their feet still,
their toes always tap whether weaving or dancing.
The shameless woman will not leave off
her unfortunate whims, not for ten cities as fine as Toledo.

472 Non olvides la dueña, dicho te lo he de suso;
muger, molyno E huerta syenpre querie grand vso,
non se pagan de disanto en poridat nin a escuso,
nunca quiere olvido, provador lo conpusso.

473 çierta cossa es esta quel molyno andando gana,
huerta mejor labrada da la mejor mançana,
muger mucho seguida syenpre anda loçana;
do estas tres guardares non es tu obra vana.

ENXIENPLO DE LO QUE CONTEÇIO A DON PITAS PAYAS,
PYNTOR DE BRETAÑIA

474 Del que olvydo la muger te dire la fazaña,
sy vieres que es burla dyme otra tan mañana.
Era don pitas pajas vn pyntor de bretaña,
casose con muger moça, pagavase de conpaña;

475 Ante del mes conplido dixo el: "Nuestra dona,
yo volo yr a frandes, portare muyta dona."
Ella diz: "Mon señer, andat en ora bona,
non olvidedes vuestra casa nin la mi persona."

476 dyxo don pitas pajas: "dona de fermosura,
yo volo fazer en vos vna bona fygura,
por que seades guardada de toda altra locura."
Ella diz: "monssener, fazet vuestra mesura."

477 Pyntol so el onbligo vn pequeno cordero,
fuese don pytas pajas a ser novo mercadero;
tardo alla dos anos, mucho fue tardinero;
fasia sele a la dona vn mes año entero.

478 Commo era la moça nueva mente casada,
auie con su marido fecha poca morada,
tomo vn entendedor E poblo la posada,
desfizo se el cordero, que del non fynca nada.

479 quando ella oyo que venia el pyntor,
mucho de priessa enbio por el entendedor;
dixole que le pyntase commo podiesse mejor,
en aquel logar mesmo vn cordero menor.

472   But don't forget your lady, as I told you before;
       woman, mill and orchard always benefit from hard work.
       A woman is not content to stay in hiding on saint's days,
       she does not want to be forgotten, as the minstrel wrote in
                                                    his song.

473   One thing is certain – a working mill earns money,
       a well-tended orchard yields better apples,
       a woman much pursued always looks lovely.
       If you remember these three things, you will not strive in
                                                    vain.

THE TALE OF PITAS PAYAS, THE PAINTER FROM BRITTANY

474   I will tell you a story about a man who forgot a woman,
       if you see the joke, tell me a better one.
       Pitas Payas was a painter from Brittany,
       he married a young girl, as he liked to have company.

475   Before a month had passed, he said: "Milady,
       I have to go to Flanders, but I'll bring you lots of presents."
       She replied: "Good sir, go, and good luck,
       don't forget your house, nor me, your wife."

476   Pitas Payas said: "Beautiful lady,
       I am going to paint a picture on you,
       to keep you safe from all other folly."
       She replied: "Sir, do as you wish."

477   He painted a little lamb on her belly.
       So Pitas Payas left to learn his trade as merchant.
       He stayed away for two whole years, a great delay,
       one month seemed a whole year to the girl.

478   Since she was newly-wed,
       she had not lived with her husband long.
       She took a lover, who filled her husband's place,
       the lamb was rubbed off, so no trace remained.

479   When she heard news that the painter was returning,
       she quickly sent for her lover.
       She asked him to paint a little lamb
       as best he could, in the place where the other had been.

480   Pyntole con la grand priessa vn eguado carnero,
        conplido de cabeça, con todo su apero;
        luego en ese dia vino el menssajero,
        que ya don pytas pajas desta venia çertero.

481   quando fue el pyntor de frandes venido,
        ffue de la su muger con desden Resçebido;
        desque en el palaçio con ella estudo,
        la señal quel feziera non la echo en olvido.

482   dixo don pitas pajas: "madona sy vos plas,
        mostrat me la figura e ajan buen solas."
        diz la muger: "monseñer, vos mesmo la catat;
        fey y ardida mente todo lo que vollaz."

483   Cato don pitas pajas el sobredicho lugar,
        E vydo vn grand carnero con armas de prestar:
        "¿como es esto, madona, o como pode estar
        que yo pynte corder E trobo este manjar?"

484   Commo en este fecho es syenpre la muger
        sotil e mal sabyda, diz: "¿como, mon sseñer,
        en dos anos petid corder non se fazer carner?
        vos veniesedes tenplano E trobariades corder."

485   Por ende te castiga, non dexes lo que pides;
        non seas pitas pajas, para otro non errides;
        con dezires fermosos a la muger conbydes;
        desque telo prometa, guarda non lo olvidez.

486   Pedro leuanta la lyebre E la mueve del couil,
        non la sygue nin la toma, faze commo casador vyl;
        otro pedro que la sygue E la corre mas sotil,
        tomala: esto contesçe a caçadores mill.

487   dyz la muger entre dientes: "otro pedro es aqueste
        mas garçon e mas ardit quel primero que ameste;
        el primero apost deste non vale mas que vn feste,
        con aqueste e por este fare yo, sy dios me preste."

488   otrosi quando vyeres a quien vsa con ella,
        quier sea suyo o non, fablale por amor della;

480   In his great haste he painted an adult ram,
        endowed with a splendid head and pair of horns.
        That day a messenger came to say
        that Pitas Payas was nearly home.

481   When the painter had arrived from Flanders,
        his wife treated him with disdain.
        When they were together in their room,
        he remembered the sign he had painted on her.

482   Said Pitas Payas: "My lady, please
        show me the picture and let's have a good time."
        The woman replied: "Good sir, just look at it –
        do whatever you like down there."

483   Pitas Payas looked in the aforesaid place
        and saw a huge ram with excellent horns.
        "What is this, my lady, how can this be?
        I painted a lamb, and now I find this lump of meat?"

484   In these matters a woman is always cunning
        and subtle. She said: "Whatever do you mean, sir?
        Doesn't a little lamb grow into a ram in two years?
        If you had come back sooner, you would have found the
                                                        lamb."

485   So I advise you, don't leave what you desire,
        don't be like Pitas Payas, don't arouse her for another.
        Appeal to her with flattering words, as soon as
        she gives you her promise, take care not to forget her.

486   Tom, Dick or Harry flushes the hare, chases it from its form,
        but doesn't follow it or catch it; he acts like a poor hunter.
        Another Tom, Dick or Harry will follow it and rout it with
                                                        more subtlety,
        then catch it – this happens to hundreds of hunters.

487   The woman whispers: "This Dick is another kettle of fish,
        more manly and full of ardour than the other one I loved.
        After this one, the first isn't worth a fig,
        I'll stick with this one, with God's help."

488   Also, when you see whom she is familiar with,
        intimate or not, speak to him for love of her.

sy podieres dal ago non le ayas querella,
ca estas cosas pueden a la muger traella.

489   Por poquilla cosa del tu aver quel dyerez,
seruir te ha leal mente, fara lo que quisieres;
fara por los dineros todo quanto de pidieres,
que mucho o poco dal cada que podieres.

ENXIENPLO DE LA PROPIEDAT QUEL DINERO HA
490   Mucho faz el dinero, E mucho es de amar,
al torpe faze bueno E omne de prestar,
ffaze correr al coxo E al mudo fabrar,
El que non tiene manos dyneros quiere tomar.

491   ssea vn ome nesçio E rudo labrador,
los dyneros le fazen fidalgo e sabydor,
quanto mas algo tiene tanto es mas de valor,
el que non ha dineros non es de sy Señor.

492   sy tovyeres dyneros avras consolacion,
plazer e alegria, del papa Racion,
conpraras parayso, ganaras saluaçion;
do son muchos dineros esta mucha bendiçion.

493   yo vy en corte de Roma, do es la santidad,
que todos al dinero fazen grand homildat,
grand onrra le fazian con grand solepnidat,
todos a el se omillan commo a la magestat.

494   fazie muchos priores obispos E abbades,
arçobispos, doctores, patriarcas, potestades;
a muchos clerigos nesçios davales dinidades,
fazie de verdat mentiras e de mitiras verdades.

495   fazia muchos clerigos e muchos ordenados,
muchos monges e mongas, Religiosos sagrados,
el dinero los daua por byen examinados,
a los pobres desian que non eran letrados.

496   daua muchos juysios, mucha mala sentençia;
con muchos abogados era su manteneçia,
en tener pleitos malos E fazer abenençia,
en cabo por dineros avya penitençia.

If you can, give him something; don't pick a quarrel,
as these things can attract a woman.

489 Even if the gift you give him is small,
he will serve you loyally and do as you wish.
Try to give something, big or small, whenever you can;
he will do whatever you ask of him, for money.*

THE FABLE OF THE ATTRIBUTES OF MONEY

490 Money can do many things and is greatly loved.
It makes the dimwit good and worthy,
it makes the lame run and the dumb speak.
The man who has no hands longs to hold money.

491 A man may be a base and stupid labourer,
but money makes him noble and wise.
The more he has, the more he is of value;
a man without money is not master of himself.

492 If you have money, you will have consolation,
pleasure and happiness, a prebend from the Pope.
You will buy paradise, will earn salvation;
where there is a lot of money, there is also great blessing.

493 When I was at the court of Rome, where holiness resides,
I saw that everyone treated money with great reverence,
did it great honour amid great solemnity.
Everyone bowed down to it, as they do before the Virgin's
image.

494 It created many priors, bishops and abbots,
archbishops, doctors, patriarchs, potentates.
It gave dignity to many stupid clergymen,
it turned truth into lies, and lies into truth.

495 It created many clergymen and members of orders,
many monks and nuns, holy religious people,
money made them well-read,
and the poor were considered illiterate.

496 It passed many judgements, many dicey sentences,
it was the sustenance of many lawyers, through which
they brought unjust lawsuits, and made wrongful agreements.
In the end, absolution was given for money.

497 El dinero quebranta las cadenas dañosas,
tyra çepos e gruillos E cadenas peligrosas;
el que non tyene dineros echan le las posas;
por todo el mundo faze cosas maravillosas.

498 yo vy fer maravillas do el mucho vsaua,
muchos meresçian muerte que la vida les daua,
otros eran syn culpa E luego los matava,
muchas almas perdia E muchas salvaua.

499 fazer perder al pobre su case e su vyña,
sus muebles e Rayses todo lo des-alyña,
por todo el mundo anda su sarna e su tyña,
do el dinero juega ally el ojo guiña.

500 El faze caualleros de neçios aldeanos,
condes e Ricos omnes de algunos vyllanos;
con el dinero andan todos los omnes loçanos;
quantos son en el mundo le besan oy las manos.

501 vy tener al dinero las mejores moradas,
altas e muy costosas, fermosas e pyntadas,
castillos, heredades E villas entorreadas,
todas al dinero syruen E suyas son conpladas.

502 Comia muchos manjares de diuerssas naturas,
vistia los nobles paños, doradas vestiduras,
traya joyas preçiosas en vyçios E folguras,
guarnimientos estraños, nobles caualgaduras.

503 yo vy a muchos monges, en sus predycaciones,
denostar al dinero E a sus tenptaçiones,
en cabo por dynero otorgan los perdones,
asueluen el ayuno, ansy fazen oraçiones.

504 Pero que le denuestan los monges por las plaças,
guardando lo en covento en vasos e en taças,
con el dinero cunplen sus menguas e sus Raças;
mas condesyguos tyenen que tordos nin picaças.

505 Commo quier que los frayles E clerigos dyzen que aman a
                                                    dios seruir,
sy varruntan que el rrico esta ya para moryr,
quando oyen sus dineros que comiençan a Retenir,
qual dellos lo leuaran comyençan luego a Renir.

497   Money breaks harmful chains, it frees from the stocks,
      from ankle-irons, from perilous prisons.
      Men who have no money are handcuffed,
      all over the world it does wonderful things.

498   I saw many marvels where money was available,
      many deserved death, but it gave them life;
      others, though, were blameless, yet it killed them.
      It lost and saved many souls.

499   It makes the poor man lose his house and his vine,
      all his worldly goods are thrown into disorder.
      Its itching, its ringworm spreads throughout the world,
      where money plays, the eye winks.

500   It makes knights of foolish villagers,
      counts and wealthy men of some country folk.
      When men have money, they are self-assured,
      the whole world kisses its hand nowadays.

501   Money can buy the best dwelling places,
      tall and costly, beautifully decorated,
      castles and country estates, towns with towers;
      they all served the money they were bought with.

502   It bought many rare delicacies to eat,
      it provided fine clothing, gilded raiment,
      it brought precious jewels, with pleasure and luxury,
      strange trappings, noble mounts.

503   I saw many monks in their preaching
      denigrate money and its temptations,
      yet pardons are granted for money,
      fasting is absolved and prayers are spoken.

504   Although monks despise it in public,
      they horde it in glasses and cups in the monastery.
      Money heals all their misery,
      they have more hidey-holes than thrushes or magpies.

505   Wherever friars take no money,
      they give their accomplices a knowing wink.
      Their stewards take it quickly – but since
      they say they are poor, why do they need treasures?

506　Monges, frayles, clerigos, non toman los dineros,
　　　byen les dan de la çeja do son sus parçioneros,
　　　luego los toman prestos sus omes despenseros;
　　　pues que se dizen pobles, ¿que quieren thessoreroz?

507　Ally estan esperando qual avra mas Rico tuero,
　　　non es muerto, ya dizen "pater noster" a mal aguero,
　　　commo los cuervos al asno quando le desuellan el cuero:
　　　"cras, cras nos lo avremos, que nuestro es ya por fuero."

508　Toda muger del mundo E duena de altesa
　　　pagase del dinero E de mucha Riqueza;
　　　yo nunca vy fermo-sa que quisyese poblesa;
　　　do son muchos dineros y es mucha noblesa.

509　El dinero es alcalde E jues mucho loado,
　　　este es conssejero E sotil abogado,
　　　alguaçil E meryno, byen ardyt, es-forçado,
　　　de todos los ofiçios es muy apoderado.

510　En suma telo digo, tomalo tu mejor;
　　　el dinero del mundo es grand rreboluedor,
　　　señor faze del syeruo, de señor seruidor;
　　　toda cosa del sygro se faze por su amor.

511　Por dineros se muda el mundo e su manera;
　　　toda muger cobdyçiosa de algo es falaguera,
　　　por joyas E dineros Salyra de carrera.
　　　el dar quebranta peñas, fyende dura madera,

512　Derrueca fuerte muro E derriba grant torre,
　　　a coyta E a grand priessa el mucho dar acorre,
　　　non ha syeruo cabtivo que el dinero non le aforre,
　　　el que non tyene que dar su cavallo non corre.

513　las cosas que son graues fazelas de lygero,
　　　por ende a tu vieja se franco e llenero,
　　　que poco o que mucho non vaya syn logrero,
　　　non me pago de joguetes do non anda el dinero.

514　Sy algo non le dyeres, cosa mucha o poca,
　　　sey franco de palabla, non le digas Razon loca;
　　　quien non tiene miel en la orça tengala en la boca;
　　　mercador que esto faze byen vende e byen troca.

506   Monks, clergymen, friars, who wish to serve God,
if they sniff out a dying rich man,
when they hear his money start to tinkle,
they begin to argue over who shall have it.

507   There they are, waiting to see who will get the biggest share,
the man is not yet dead and they chant "Our Father", a bad
omen,
like the crows when they skin an ass,
"Tomorrow, tomorrow we'll have it, it's already ours by law."

508   All women of the world and high-born ladies
love money and great riches;
I never saw a beautiful woman who wanted to be poor;
where money is, there is great nobility.

509   Money is mayor, a praiseworthy judge,
it is counsellor and subtle lawyer,
beadle and king's judge, bold and energetic.
It wields the power in all offices.

510   To sum up, I say, understand this right:
money makes the world go round,
makes a lord out of a servant, and servant of a lord,
everything in the world is done for love of money.

511   For money the world and its ways waver,
all women who covet possessions use flattery,
woman changes her nature for jewels and money,
giving shatters crags, rends the hardest wood.

512   It demolishes the strongest walls and highest towers,
giving a lot lends succour to those in trouble.
There is no servant, no captive, that money does not free;
if a man has nothing to give, his horse won't run.

513   Money makes light of serious matters,
so be frank and generous with your old woman,
she will not do much, nor even little, without her pay.
I don't like love games which do not involve money.

514   If you don't give her anything, whether a little or a lot,
be generous in your speech and don't say foolish things.
If you have no honey in the jar, use honeyed words,
the merchant who learns this sells and trades well.

515   sy sabes estromentos byen tañer o tenplar,
        sy sabes o avienes en fermoso cantar,
        a las vegadas poco, en onesto lugar,
        do la muger te oya non dexes prouar.

516   Sy vna cosa sola a la muger non muda,
        muchas cosas juntadas facer te han ayuda;
        desoue lo oye la dueña mucho en ello coyda,
        non puede ser que a tienpo a byen non te rrecubda.

517   con vna flaca cuerda non alçaras grand trança,
        nin por van solo "farre" non anda bestia manca,
        a la peña pesada non la mueve vna palanca,
        con cuños E almadanas poco a poco se arranca.

518   Prueua fazer lygerezas e fazer valentya;
        quier lo vea o non, saber lo ha algud dia;
        non sera tan esquiua que non ayas mejoria;
        non cansses de seguir la, vençeras su porfia.

519   El que la mucho sygue, El que la mucho vsa,
        en el coraçon lo tyene, maguer se le escusa;
        pero que todo el mundo por esto le acusa,
        en este coyda syenpre, por este faz la musa.

520   quanto es mas sosañada, quanto es mas corrida,
        quanto por omne es magada e ferida,
        tanto mas por el anda loca, muerta E perdida;
        non coyda ver la ora que con el seya yda.

521   Coyda su madre cara que por la sosañar,
        por corrella e ferilla e por la denostar,
        que por ende sera casta e la fara estar:
        estos son aguijones que la fazen saltar.

522   deuia pensar su madre de quando era donsella,
        que su madre non quedaua de ferir la e corrella,
        que mas la ençendia, E pues devia por ella
        judgar todas las otras e a su fija bella.

523   Toda muger nasçida es fecha de tal massa,
        lo que mas le defienden aquello ante passa,

515   If you know how to tune and play instruments,
       if you can sing a beautiful song, sometimes
       in the proper place, where the lady can
       hear you, don't fail to try it out.

516   If one thing alone does not move a woman,
       several things together have a better effect.
       As soon as the lady hears it, she will think a lot about it,
       and it will turn out well for you in the end.

517   You will not raise a large beam with a thin rope,
       and a lame animal won't walk at just one "gee-up".
       A stick will not budge a heavy rock,
       it needs wedges and mallets to move it bit by bit.

518   Try to show your skills and daring.
       Whether she sees it or not, she'll find out about it one day.
       She won't be so aloof that you make no progress.
       Don't give up her pursuit and you will conquer her
                                                    stubbornness.

519   If you persist in following her, and make her familiar with
                                                                you,
       she will keep you in her heart, in spite of her denials.
       But everyone will reproach her for it,
       and it will prey on her mind and make her pensive.

520   The more she is taunted, the more ashamed she becomes,
       the more a man hurts her and beats her,
       the more crazy she becomes for him, lost, dying,
       she thinks there will never be a chance to go off with him.

521   Her mother puts on a scornful face,
       to nag her and taunt her and denounce her,
       to make her chaste and still,
       but these are the spurs which make her jump.

522   Her mother should remember when she was younger,
       how her mother in turn would chide and nag,
       only to arouse her, and she should judge other women
       and her own lovely daughter in this way.

523   Every woman born is made of the same stuff,
       what she most defends she'd as soon transgress,

aquello la ençiende E aquello la traspassa;
do non es tan seguida anda mas floxa, laxa.

524 A toda cosa brava grand vso la amansa:
la çierua montesyna mucho corrida canssa,
caçador que la sigue tomala quando descanssa,
la dueña mucho braua vsando se faz manssa.

525 Por vna vez al dia que omne gelo pida,
çient vegadas, de noche, de amor es rrequerida,
doña venus gelo pide por el toda su vyda,
en lo quel mucho piden anda muy ençendida.

526 Muy blanda es el agua, mas dando en piedra dura,
muchas vegadas dando, faze grand cavadura;
por grand vso el rrudo sabe grand letura,
muger mucho seguida olvida la cordura.

527 guarda te non te abuelvas a la casamentera;
donear non la quieras, ca es vna manera
por que te faria perder a la entendera,
ca vna congrueca de otra sienpre tyene dentera.

DE COMMO EL AMOR CASTIGA AL ARÇIPRESTE QUE AYA
EN SY BUENAS CONSTUNBRES, E SSOBR TODO QUE SE
GUARDE DE BEUER MUCHO VINO BLANCO E TYNTO

528 Buenas costunbres deues en ty syenpre aver,
guardate sobre todo mucho vino beuer,
que el vino fizo a loc con sus fijas boluer,
en verguença del mundo, en saña de dios caer.

529 fizo cuerpo E alma perder a vn hermitano
que nunca lo beuiera, prouolo por su daño,
rretentolo el diablo con su sotil engaño,
fizole beuer el vino; oye en-sienpro estraño:

530 Era vn hermitano, quarenta Años avya,
que en todas sus oblas en yermo a dios seruia;
en tienpo de su vyda nunca el vyna beuia,
en santidat e en ayuno e en oracion beuia.

531 Tomaua grand pesar el diablo con esto,
penso commo podiese partyrle de aquesto,

for it arouses and torments her.
When she is not pursued, she is weary and indolent.

524   Familiarity tames all wild things,
and much running tires the mountain hind,
the huntsman catches her when she is exhausted.
The unapproachable woman softens at the familiar.

525   If a man seeks her love once a day,
love seeks her a hundred times at night.
Venus begs for her all of her life,
the woman is kindled by repeated asking.

526   Water is very soft, but if it washes over
hard rocks many times, it wears a great hollow.
With constant practice, the ignorant man gains great
                                                     learning,
and a hotly pursued woman loses her good sense.

527   Take care not to get involved with a matchmaker,
do not court her, since that is one thing
which would make you lose your lover,
for a concubine is always jealous of others.

HOW LOVE ADVISES THE ARCHPRIEST TO BEHAVE RESPECTABLY AND ABOVE ALL NOT TO DRINK TOO MUCH RED AND WHITE WINE

528   You must always behave properly,
and above all avoid drinking too much wine.
Wine drove Lot to lie with his daughters, and brought
the shame of the world and the anger of God upon him.

529   A hermit lost body and soul through wine
who had never been accustomed to drink – he drank
at his peril. The devil tempted him with a cunning trick,
forcing him to drink wine – listen to this strange tale.

530   There was a hermit, who had served God
in all his deeds for forty years in a barren place.
He had never drunk wine in his life.
He lived in holiness and fasting, and in prayer.

531   The devil was very vexed to learn this,
and thought of how he could lure him away.

vyno a el vn dia con sotylesa presto:
"¡dyos te salue buen omne!" dixol con ssynple gesto.

532 Marauillose el monge, diz: "a dios me acomiendo;
dy me que cosa eres, que yo non te entyendo;
grand tienpo ha que esto aqui a dyos seruiendo,
nunca vy aqui omne, con la cruz me defyendo."

533 Non pudo el dyablo a su persona llegar,
seyendo arredrado començolo a Retentar,
diz: "aquel cuerpo de dios que tu deseas gustar,
yo te mostrare manera por que lo puedas tomar.

534 Non deves tener dubda que del vyna se faze
la sangre verdadera de dios, en ello yaze
sacramento muy sano, prueva si te plase."
el diablo al monge armado lo enlase.

535 dyxo el hermitano: "non se que es vyno."
rrespondio el diablo presto por lo que vino,
dyz: "aquellos taverneros que van por el camino
te daran asaz dello, ve por ello festino."

536 fizole yr por el vyno E desque fue venido
dixo: "saca dello e beue, pues lo as traydo,
prueva vn poco dello E, desque ayas beuido,
veras que mi conssejo te sera por byen avydo."

537 beuio el hermitano mucho vyno syn tyento;
commo era fuerte, puro, sacol de entendimiento,
desque vydo el dyablo que ya echaua çemiento,
armo sobrel su casa e su aparejamiento.

538 "Amigo," dyz, "non sabes de noche nin de dia
qual es la ora çierta, nin el mundo como se guia;
toma gallo que te muestre las oras cada dia,
con el alguna fenbra, que con ellas mejor cria."

539 Ceyo su mal conssejo, ya el vino vsaua;
el estando con vyno, vydo commo se juntaua
el gallo a las fenbras, con ellas se deleytaua;
cobdiçio fazer forniçio desque con vyno estaua.

So he went to him one day, with premeditated trickery:
"May the Lord preserve you, good man!" he said with a
kind expression.

532   The monk was astounded, and said: "I commend myself to
God.
Tell me what thing you are, as I do not understand you.
I have served God for a long time
and have never seen a man here – the cross is my defence."

533   The devil could not get at him,
and, withdrawing, began to tempt him again,
saying: "The body of God which you would like to enjoy,
I'll show you how you can taste it.

534   You should have no doubt that wine is
the true blood of God – it contains
a holy sacrament. Try it if you like."
The devil set up a snare to catch the hermit.

535   The hermit said: "I don't know what wine is."
The devil answered speedily, for this was his aim,
"The innkeepers along the road
will give you plenty – hurry and get some."

536   He made him go to get wine and when he returned,
the devil said: "Cross yourself and drink, since you
have brought it, try a little, and when you have drunk some,
you will see my advice was good."

537   The hermit drank a lot of wine without restraint.
It was strong and pure and took away his reason.
When the devil saw it was taking effect
he built his house on its foundations.

538   "My friend," he said, "you don't know what time it is,
night or day, nor how the world goes by.
Get a cockerel to tell the time for you each day
and a hen too, as they are easier to look after then."

539   He believed the evil advice – now he was used to wine.
In his cups, he saw how the cockerel mated
with the hen and took great delight in it.
Since he was drunk, the hermit longed to fornicate.

540 ffue con el la cobdyçia Rays de todos males,
loxuria e soberuia, tres pecados mortales;
luego el omeçida: estos pecados tales
trae el mucho vino a los decomunales.

541 desçendyo de la hermita, forço a vna muger,
ella dando muchas bozes non se pudo defender,
desque peco con ella temio mesturado ser,
matola el mesquino e ovo se de perder.

542 Commo dize el proverbyo, palabla es byen çierta,
que non ay encobyerta que a mal non rrevierta;
ffue la su mala obra en punto descobyerta,
esa ora fue el monge preso E en rrefierta.

543 descobrio con el vyno quanto mal avya fecho,
fue luego justiçiado commo era derecho,
perdio cuerpo e alma el cuytado mal trecho.
en el beuer demas yaz todo mal prouecho:

544 faze perder la vysta E acortar la vyda,
tyra la fuerça toda sys toma syn medida,
faze tenbrar los mienbros, todo seso olvida,
a do es el mucho vyno toda cosa es perdida.

545 ffaze oler el fuelgo, que es tacha muy mala,
vele muy mal la boca, non ay cosa quel vala,
que-ma las assaduras, el fygado tras-cala;
si amar quieres dueña del vyno byen te guarda.

546 los omnes enbriagos ayna envejeçen,
fazen muchas vylezas, todos los aborrescen,
en su color non andan, secanse e en-magresçen,
a dios lo yerran mucho, del mundo des-fallesçen.

547 Ado mas puja el vyno quel seso dos meajas,
fazen rroydo los beodos commo puercos e grajas,
por ende vyenen muertes, contyendas e barajas;
el mucho vyno es bueno en cubas e en tinajas.

548 Es el vino muy bueno en su mesma natura,
muchas bondades tiene sy se toma con mesura,
Al que demas lo beue sacalo de cordura,
toda maldat del mundo fase e toda locura.

540   Along with covetousness, the root of all evil,
went lust and pride, three mortal sins,
then murder followed. Such sins are
wrought by too much wine upon the intemperate.

541   He went down from the hermitage and took a woman by
force.
She cried out, but could not defend herself.
Once he had sinned with her, he feared accusation,
so the wretch killed her and was lost forever.

542   As the proverb says, and its words are true,
"There is nothing hidden which does not result in evil".
His dreadful deed was discovered straightaway
and the monk was imprisoned and put on trial.

543   He disclosed how much evil he had committed due to wine,
and was executed according to the law.
The unfortunate evildoer lost body and soul –
only disadvantage lies in too much drink.

544   A man loses his sight, his life is shortened,
all his strength is sapped if he drinks unrestrained,
his limbs start to shake, he loses his mind,
everything is lost where there is too much wine.

545   The breath smells foul, a serious fault,
the mouth has an evil odour which nothing can remove.
It burns the innards and attacks the liver.
If you want to love a lady, don't bother with wine.

546   Drunkards also age more quickly,
they lose their colour, shrivel and get thin,
they do all manner of mean things, everyone loathes them.
They stray far from God and from the world too.

547   When wine takes precedence over common sense,
drunken men make noises like pigs and rooks,
and it all ends in death, battles and quarrels.
A lot of wine is best in barrels and jars.

548   In itself wine is a good thing,
bringing many blessings if drunk in moderation,
but a man who drinks too much loses his good sense,
and brings about all the evil and madness in the world.*

549		por ende fuy del vino e fas buenos gestos;
		quando fablares con dueñas, dile doñeos apuestos,
		los fermosos rretraheres tien para desir aprestos,
		sospirando le fabla, ojos en ella puestos.

550		Non fables muy apriesa nin otrosi muy paso,
		Non seas rrebatado nin vagaroso, laso,
		de quanto que pudieres non le seas escaso,
		de lo que le prometieres non la trayas a traspaso.

551		quien muy ayna fabla ninguno non lo entiede,
		quien fabla muy paso enojase quien le atiende,
		El grant arrebatamiento con locura contiende,
		el mucho vagaroso de torpe non se defiende.

552		nunca omne escaso rrecabda de ligero,
		nin acaba quanto quiere si le veyen costumero;
		a quien de oy en cras fabla non dan por verdadero,
		al que manda e da luego a esto lo an primero.

553		En todos los tus fechos en fablar e en Al,
		escoge la mesura e lo que es cumunal;
		Cummo en todas cosas poner mesura val,
		asi syn la mesura todo paresçe mal.

554		Non quieras jugar dados nin seas tablajero,
		Ca es mala ganançia, peor que de logrero;
		El judio al año da tres por quatro, pero
		el tablax de vn dia dobla el su mal dinero.

555		des que los omnes estan en juegos ençendidos,
		des-pojan se por dados, los dineros perdidos;
		Al tablagero fincan dineros e vestidos,
		do non les come se rrascan los tahures amidos.

556		los malos de los dados dise lo maestre rroldan,
		todas sus maestrias e las tachas que an,
		mas alholis rrematan, pero non comen pan,
		que corderos la pascua nin ansarones san juan.

557		Non vses con vellacos ny seas peleador,
		Non quieras ser caçurro nin seas escarnidor,

549   So flee from wine and act calmly.
When you speak to a lady, praise her suitably,
have skilful refrains ready, the right words to say.
Speak with a sigh, and keep your eyes on her.

550   Don't speak too fast, nor too slow,
don't be impetuous, nor lazy nor listless,
don't be stingy in giving what you can,
don't delay what you promise her.

551   No one understands a person who speaks too fast,
and if you speak too slow, the listener gets impatient.
Reckless haste walks hand in hand with madness,
and slowness is equated with stupidity.

552   A stingy man never succeeds easily,
nor achieves his ends if seen to be lazy.
Putting off till tomorrow what can be done today suggests
insincerity;
the man who promises, then gives promptly, receives most
praise.

553   In all your actions, speech and so on,
be moderate and ordinary.
Moderation has value in all ways,
without it everything seems bad.

554   Don't play at dice or gamble,
for it is evil gain, worse than that of a usurer.
A Jew will lend at three for four a year,*
but a day's winnings doubles a gambler's bad money.

555   When men are excited by gambling
they strip themselves bare for dice and lost money.
Money and clothes are a gambler's life.
Card cheats scratch where they do not itch.

556   Master Roland speaks of the evils of dice,*
and all their tricks and faults.
They destroy more public granaries, though they eat no
bread,
than lambs at Easter or geese on Saint John's day.

557   Don't rub shoulders with louts, nor pick a fight,
don't be coarse or mocking,

nyn seas de ti mismo e de tus fechos loador,
Ca el que mucho se alaba de si mismo es denostador.

558 Non seas mal desiente nin seas enbidioso,
a la muger que es cuerda non le seas çeloso,
si algo nol prouares nol seas despechoso,
Non seas de su algo pedidor codiçioso.

559 ante ella non alabes otra de paresçer,
ca en punto la faras luego entristeçer,
cuydara que a la otra querrias anti vençer,
poder te ya tal achaque tu pleyto enpeesçer.

560 de otra muger non le digas, mas a ella alaba,
el trebejo dueña non lo quiere en otra aljaba,
rrason de fermosura en ella la alaba;
quien contra esto fase tarde o non rrecabda.

561 Non le seas mintroso, sey le muy verdadero,
quando juegas con ella non seas tu parlero,
do te fablare de amor sey tu plasentero,
ca el que calla e aprende este es mansellero.

562 ante otros de acerca tu muchos Non la cates,
Non le fagas senales, a ti mismo non mates,
Ca muchos lo entieden que lo prouaron antes;
de lexos algarea, quedo, non te arrebates.

563 sey commo la paloma, linpio e mesurado,
sey commo el pauon, loçano, sosegado,
sey cuerdo e non sanudo, nin triste nin yrado,
en esto se esmera el que es enamorado.

564 de vna cossa te guarda quando amares vna,
non te sepa que amas otra muger alguna,
sy non todo tu afan es sonbra de luna,
E es como quien siebra en rrio o en laguna.

565 Pyenssa consyntyra tu cavallo tal freno,
que tu entendera amase a frey moreno;
pues piensa por ty mesmo e cata byen tu seno,
E por tu coraçon judgaras el ajeno.

566 Sobre todas las cosas fabla de su bondat;
non te alabes della, que es grand torpedat;

nor boastful of yourself or your deeds,
for he who praises himself reviles himself.

558   Don't be slanderous or envious,
don't be jealous of a wise woman,
if you can't prove anything against her, don't be malicious,
don't be an envious petitioner of her wealth.

559   Don't praise another woman in her presence,
as you will immediately upset her.
She will think you want to win the other, not her,
and this accusation might hinder your case.

560   Don't speak of other women to her, just praise her,
she won't want her chess-piece in another bag.
Praise her for her beauty – for if you don't
you will succeed late or not at all.

561   Don't be deceitful, only honest;
when you are joking with her, don't talk too much.
When she speaks to you of love, show your pleasure.
A man who is quiet and listens is the victor.

562   Don't stand and gaze at her in the presence of others,
and don't make signs at her, don't harm your own position,
as many will understand who have tried it before.
Assail her calmly, from afar, don't pressure her close up.

563   Be like a dove, clean and temperate,
be like a peacock, proud and calm,
be wise, not irascible, nor sad or irate,
a man in love takes great care over this.

564   Be careful of one thing when you love someone –
don't let her know that you love any others,
or all your efforts are moonshadows,
and as if you sowed seed in the river or lake.

565   Think whether your horse would tolerate such a bit,
if your lover were involved with some Casanova,
then consider carefully and think how you'd feel,
and your heart will show you how to judge others.

566   More than anything speak of her goodness;
don't boast about her, which is very foolish.

muchos pierden la dueña por desir neçedat;
que quier que por ti faga ten lo en poridat.

567 ssy muchos le ençelares mucho fara por ty,
do falle poridat de grado departy,
de omne mesturero nunca me entremety,
a muchos de las dueñas por estos los party.

568 Como tyene tu estomago en sy mucha vyanda,
tenga la porydat que es mucho mas blanda;
caton, sabyo Romano, en su lybro lo manda,
diz que la buena poridat en buen amigo anda.

569 Tyrando con sus dientes descubre se la çarça,
echanla de la vyña, de la huerta e de la haça;
alçando el cuello suyo descobre se la garça,
buen callar çient sueldos val en toda plaça.

570 a muchos faze mal el omne mesturero,
a muchos des – ayuda e a sy primero,
rresçelan del las dueñas e dan le por fasañero:
por mala dicha de vno pyerde todo el tablero.

571 Por vn mur muy pequeno que poco queso priso,
diçen luego: "los mures han comido el queso."
sea el mal andante sea el mal apresso
quien a ssy E a otros muchos estorua con mal sesso.

572 de tres cossas que le pidas a la muger falaguera,
dar te ha la segunda sy le guardas la prymera,
sy las dos byen guardares tuya es la terçera;
non pierdas a la dueña por tu lengua parlera.

573 ssy tu guardar sopieres esto que te castigo,
cras te dara la puerta quien te oy çierra el postigo,
la que te oy te desama cras te querra Amigo;
faz conssejo de Amigo, fuye de loor de enemigo.

574 Mucho mas te diria sy podiese aqui estar,
mas tengo por el mundo otros muchos de pagar,
pesa les por mi tardança, a mi pessa del vagar,
Castiga te castigando E sabras a otros castigar.'

Many lose their lady through saying stupid things;
whatever she does for you, keep it a secret.

567 If you keep her secrets, she will do a lot for you,
where I found trust, I gladly spoke of it.
I never had any dealings with a gossiping man,
I have turned many women away from their men on this
score.

568 In the same way that your stomach holds a lot of meat,
fill it with secrets, which are easier to digest.
Cato, the wise Roman, decrees this in his book,
saying that keeping a secret is the sign of a good friend.

569 The briar shows itself by scratching with its thorns,
it is torn out of the vineyard, the orchard, the fields;
the heron shows itself by raising its long neck –
silence is golden in any place.

570 The gossiping man does harm to many,
he does not help them or himself;
women fear and distrust him and take him as an exaggerator.
The whole gaming table loses through one piece of bad luck.*

571 One tiny mouse eats a little piece of cheese,
and they say: "The mice have eaten the cheese."
Bad luck and misfortune to the man who
harms himself and others by lack of good sense.

572 If you ask an affectionate woman for three things,
she will give you the second if you can keep the first secret.
If you can keep them both secret, the third is yours.
Don't lose the lady through being too talkative.

573 If you can remember my advice, tomorrow the door
will be opened, though the secret entrance is shut today.
The lady who does not love you today will love you
tomorrow.
Follow a friend's advice and flee from an enemy's praise.

574 I could tell you a great deal more if I could stay,
but I have to see to many others throughout the world.
They are waiting impatiently, and it grieves me to linger.
Learn through your own mistakes and you will be able
to teach others.'

575   Yo, Johan Ruyz, el sobre dicho acipreste de hita,
       pero que mi coraçon de trobar non se quita,
       nunca falle tal dueña como a vos amor pynta,
       nin creo que la falle en toda esta cohyta.

DE COMO EL AMOR SE PARTIO DEL ARÇIPRESTE E DE
COMMO DOÑA VENUS LO CASTIGO

576   Partyose amor de mi E dexo me dormir,
       desque vyno al alua començe de comedyr
       en lo que me castigo; E, por verdat desir,
       falle que en sus castigos syenpre vse beuir.

577   Marauille me mucho desque en ello pensse,
       de commo en seruir dueñas todo tienpo non canse,
       mucho las guarde syenpre, nunca me alabe,
       ¿qual fue la Racon negra por que non Recabde?

578   Contra mi coraçon yo mesmo me torne,
       porfiando le dixe: 'agora yo te porne
       con dueña falaguera, e desta vez terne
       que sy byen non abengo, nunca mas aberne.'

579   My coraçon me dixo: 'faz lo e Recabdaras,
       sy oy non Recabdares torna y luego cras;
       lo que en muchos dias acabado non as,
       quando non coydares a otra ora lo avras.'

580   fasaña es vsada, prouerbio non mintroso:
       mas val rrato acuçioso que dia peresoso,
       parti me de tristesa, de cuydado dañoso,
       busque e falle dueña de qual so deseoso.

581   de talle muy apuesta, de gestos amorosa,
       doñegil, muy loçana, plasentera e fermosa,
       Cortes e mesurada, falagera, donosa,
       graçiosa e Risuena, amor de toda cosa.

582   la mas Noble figura de quantas yo auer pud,
       biuda, rrica es mucho, e moça de juuentud;
       E bien acostunbrada, es de calataut,
       de mi era vesina, mi muerte e mi salut.

583   fiia de algo en todo e de alto linaje,
       poco salie de casa segunt lo an de vsaje;

575   I, Juan Ruiz, aforesaid Archpriest of Hita,
whose heart never ceases to write poetry,
never found a lady like the one Love described,
nor am I likely to, in these surroundings.

HOW LOVE TOOK HIS LEAVE OF THE ARCHPRIEST, AND
THE ADVICE OF VENUS

576   Love finally left me and let me sleep.
When dawn came, I thought over
his advice and, to tell the truth,
I realized I often lived as he described.

577   I was amazed when I considered
how I never tired of serving women.
I always kept their secrets, never boasted,
so what was the cursed reason for my failure?

578   I turned to my own heart and said to it
obstinately: 'Now I will give you the company
of an affectionate woman, and this time I believe
that if I am not successful, I never shall be.'

579   My heart replied: 'Do it and you will succeed;
if not today, then try again tomorrow.
What you have not achieved for a long time
you shall have when you least expect it.'

580   There is a well-known saying, a truthful proverb:
'Brief pleasure is better than a day of sloth.'
I left sadness behind and harmful thoughts,
I searched, and found the kind of woman I desire.*

581   She had an elegant figure, loving gestures,
was feminine, sexy, attractive, beautiful,
courteous and thoughtful, obliging and pleasant,
witty and cheerful, love in every way.

582   The noblest character I could ever find,
a widow, very rich, yet young,
well mannered too; she was from Calatayud
and was my neighbour, my death and my health.

583   Noble in everything and of worthy lineage,
she rarely left the house, like most women in her position.

fuy m[e] a doña venus que le leuase mensaje,
Ca ella es comienço e fin deste viaje.

584   ella es nuestra vida e ella es nuestra muerte,
enflaqueçe e mata al rresio e al fuerte,
por todo el mundo tiene grant poder e suerte,
todo por su consejo se fara ado apuerte.

585   'Señora doña venus, muger de don amor,
Noble dueña, omillome yo vuestro seruidor,
de todas cosas sodes vos e el amor señor,
todos vos obedesçen commo a su fasedor.

586   Reys, duques e condes, e toda criatura
vos temen e vos seruen commo a vuestra fechura;
conplit los mis deseos e dat me dicha e ventura,
Non me seades escasa nin esquiua nin dura.

587   Non uos pidre grant cosa para vos me la dar,
Pero a mi cuytado es me graue de far,
sin vos yo non la puedo començar ni acabar;
yo sere bien andante por lo uos otorgar.

588   so ferido e llagado, de vn dardo so perdido,
en el coraçon lo trayo ençerrado e ascondido;
Non oso mostrar la laga, matar me a si la oluido,
e avn desir non oso el nonbre de quien me ferio.

589   la llaga non se me dexa a mi catar nin ver,
ende mayores peligros espera que an de seer,
Reçelo he que mayores dapnos me padran rrecreçer,
fisica nin melesina non me puede pro tener.

590   ¿qual carrera tomare que me non vaya matar?
¡Cuytado yo! ¿que fare, que non la puedo yo catar?
derecha es mi querella, rrason me fase cuytar,
pues que non fallo nin que me pueda prestar.

591   E por que muchas de cosas me enbargan e enpeçen,
he de buscar muchos cobros segunt que me pertenesçen;
las artes muchas vegadas ayudan, oras fallesçen,
por las artes biuen muchos, por las artes peresçen.

592   si se descubre mi llaga qual es, donde fue venir,
si digo quien me ferio, puedo tanto descobrir

I went to Venus and asked her to take a message,
as she is the beginning and end of this journey.

584 She is our life and death,
the robust and strong become thin and die,
throughout the world she has great power and honour,
with her advice everything can be attained.

585 'Madam, Venus, wife of Love,
noble lady, I, your servant, humble myself.
In all things you and Love rule.
All obey you as if you were their maker.

586 Kings, dukes, counts, all creatures
fear and serve you as your creations.
Fulfil my desires, bring me happiness and luck,
don't be mean, or hard and harmful.

587 I do not ask you to give me so much,
but in my distress it is important to do so,
I cannot start or finish without you,
but I will be so happy if you bestow it on me.

588 I am hurt, am wounded, lost because of an arrow,
it is locked up, hidden in my heart.
I dare not show the wound, but I shall die if I ignore it,
though I dare not speak the name of the one wounding me.

589 The wound cannot be seen or examined,
and I suspect great danger lies ahead.
I fear that greater harm shall befall me,
neither the art of medicine nor pills and potions can do any
good.

590 What path shall I take that will not slay me?
What torture! What can I do, as I cannot see her?
My complaint is just, I am right to suffer,
since I can find no good advice to help me.

591 Because so many things hinder and obstruct me,
I must find a remedy to help.
Often ingenuity can help, but sometimes not.
Many live by it, but many perish.

592 If my wound is revealed, its nature, whence it came,
if I say who has injured me, I may reveal so much

que perdere melesina so esperança de guarir;
la esperança con conorte sabes a las veses fallir.

593   E si encubre del todo su ferida e su dolor,
si ayuda non demanda por auer salut mijor,
por ventura me vernia otro peligro peor,
morria de todo en todo: nunca vy cuyta mayor.

594   mijor es mostrar el omne su dolençia e su quexura
Al monge e al buen amigo, quel daran por auentura
melesina e consejo por do pueda auer fulgura,
que non el morir syn dubda e beuir en grant Rencura.

595   El fuego mas fuerte quexa ascondido, encobierto,
que non quando se derrama, esparsido e descobierto,
Pues este es camino mas seguro e mas çierto,
en vuestras manos pongo el mi coraçon abierto.

596   Dona endryna, que mora aqui en mi vezindat,
de fermosura e donayre e de talla e de beldat,
sobra e vençe a todas quantas ha en la çibdat;
sy el amor non me engaña, yo vos digo la verdat.

597   esta dueña me ferio de saeta en-arbolada,
atrauiesa me el coraçon, en el la tengo fyncada;
toda mi fuerça pyerdo E del todo me es tirada,
la llaga va cresiendo, del dolor non mengua nada.

598   A persona deste mundo yo non la oso fablar,
por que es de grand lynaje E duena de grand solar,
es de mejores paryentes que yo e de mejor lugar,
en le dezir mi deseo non me oso aventurar.

599   Con arras e con dones rrueganle cassamientos,
menos los preçia todos que a dos viles sarmientos;
ado es el grand lynaje ay son los alçamientos,
ado es el mucho algo son los desdeñamientos.

600   Ryqua muger e fija de vn porquerizo vyl
escogera marido qual quisiere entre dos mill.
pues ansy aver non puedo a la duena gentil,
aver la he por trabajo E por arte sotil.

601   Todas aquestas noblesas me fasen querer,
por aquesto a ella non me oso atrever;

that I shall lose my cure in the hope of recovery;
hope and comfort, as you know, at times are lacking.

593 And if I conceal all of my wound and pain,
if I do not ask for help, for better health,
perhaps another greater danger will assail me.
I am dying little by little, I have never suffered so.

594 It is better for a man to speak of his pain and suffering
to the doctor and to a good friend, who will give him
medicine and advice on finding some relief,
or he will doubtless die or live in great rancour.

595 The brightest fire complains more when hidden, covered up,
than when it runs where it pleases in the open.
Since this is the surest, safest road,
I place my open heart in your hands.

596 Endrina,* who lives here in my neighbourhood,
exceeds, surpasses every woman in the city
in beauty and grace, in figure and beauty.
Unless love deceives me, I speak the truth.

597 This woman hit me with a poisoned dart,
which pierced my heart and there remains.
It cannot be removed, though I use all my strength,
the wound gets bigger, the pain does not cease.

598 I dare tell no one in the world,
since she is of high birth and noble lineage;
her family and home are far above me,
and so I dare not speak of my desire.

599 With money pledged, and gifts, men beg her hand,
but she values them less than the humble vineshoot;
the higher the lineage, the greater the arrogance,
but scorn is great when blood is blue.

600 Both a wealthy woman and a swineherd's daughter
will choose the husband they want from thousands.
I will not win her that way,
but only by hard work and subtle wit.

601 All these qualities increase my love for her,
I do not trust myself in her presence.

otro cobro non fallo que me pueda acorrer
sy non vos, doña venus, que lo podedes fazer.

602   atrevy me con locura E con amor afyncado,
muchas vezes gelo dixe que fynque mal denostado.
non preçia nada, muerto me trae coytado;
sy non fuese tan mi vesina non seria tan penado.

603   quanto mas esta omne al grand fuego llegado,
tanto muy mas se quema que quando esta alongado;
esto me trae muerto, perdido E penado;
¡asy señora doña venus ssea de vos ayudado!

604   ya ssabedess nuestros males E nuestras penas parejas;
sabedes nuestros pelygros, sabedes nuestras conssejas,
non me dades rrespuesta nin me oen vuestras orejas.
oyt me vos mansa mente las mis coytas sobejas.

605   ¿Non veen los vuestros ojos la mi triste catadura?
tyra de mi coraçon tal saeta e tal ardura,
conortad me esta llaga con juegos e folgura,
que non vayan syn conorte mi llaga e mi quexura.

606   ¿qual es la dueña tan braua E tan dura
que al su seruidor non le faga mesura?
afynco vos pidiendo con dolor e tristura,
el grand amor me faze perder salud e cura.

607   El color he ya perdido, mis sesos des-falleçen;
la fuerça non la tengo, mis ojos non paresçen;
sy vos non me valedes mi menbrios desfalleçen.'
Respondio doña venus: 'seruidores vençen;

608   ya fueste conssejado del amor mi marydo,
del en muchas maneras fuste aperçebydo,
por que le fuste sanudo contigo poco estudo,
de lo quel non te dixo de mi te sera rrepetido.

609   sy algo por ventura de mi te fuere mandado
de lo que mi marido te ovo conssejado.
Seras dello mas çierto, yras mas segurado:
mejor es el conssejo de muchos acordado.

610   Toda muger que mucho otea o es rrysueña,
dyl syn miedo tus deseos, non te enbargue verguueña,

I can find no other solace
than you, Venus, who alone can help me.

602   Deep-rooted love and its madness made me bold,
I spoke many times to her of love, but was reviled.
She cared nothing for me, I am dying of grief,
I would not feel so tormented, if she were not my neighbour.

603   If a man is close to a raging fire,
he is more likely to get burnt than at a distance.
I would not be suffering so if I were further away,
Oh, Venus, please help me!

604   You know our ills and greatest suffering,
you know when we are in danger, and all our fears,
won't you answer me, or even listen?
Please listen gently to my many cares.

605   Can't your eyes see my doleful appearance?
Pull out this arrow, this burning, from my heart,
comfort my wound with soothing ointment and pleasure,
do not leave my wound, or my complaints, uncomforted.

606   What lady, even the wildest and hardest in the world,
would not take pity on her servant?
I kneel before you in pain and sadness.
The strength of my love drains my health, my cure is lost.

607   I am pale and wan, my senses are failing,
I am weak, my eyes are sunken and hollow,
without your aid my limbs lack strength.'
Venus replied: 'Those who serve, conquer.

608   My husband, Love, just gave you advice,
and you were well-informed by him.
He stayed only a short time because of your anger,
and what he didn't say, I shall teach you.

609   If by chance I instruct you to do something
which my husband has already advised,
you will be more sure of it, will be more confident:
advice agreed by all is better.

610   If any woman looks round about her, smiles a lot,
tell her your wishes without fear, don't be embarrassed.

apenas de myll vna te lo niegue, mas desdeña;
amar te ha la dueña que en ello pienssa e sueña.

611 Syruela, non te enojes, siruiendo el amor creçe,
seruiçio en el bueno nunca muere nin pereçe,
si se tarda non se pierde, el amor non falleçe,
el grand trabajo todas las cosas vençe.

612 El amor leo a ovydyo en la escuela,
que non ha muger en el mundo, nin grande nin mocuela,
que trabajo e seruiçio non la traya al espuela;
que tarde o que ayna crey que de ty se duela.

613 Non te espantes della por su mala Respuesta,
con arte o con seruiçio ella la dara apuesta,
que syguiendo e seruiendo en este coydado es puesta;
El omne mucho cauando la grand peña acuesta.

614 si la primera onda del mar ayrada
espantase al marynero quando vyene torbada,
nunca en la mar entrarie con su nave ferrada;
non te espante la dueña la primera vegada.

615 jura muy muchas vezes el caro vendedor
que non dara la mercaduria sy non por grand valor;
afyncando lo mucho el artero conplador
lyeva la mercadorya por el buen corredor.

616 syrue la con arte E mucho te achaca,
el can que mucho lame sin dubda sangre saca;
maestria e arte de fuerte faze flaca,
el conejo por maña doñea a la vaca.

617 a la muela pesada de la peña mayor
maestria e arte la arrancan mejor,
anda por maestria lygera enderedor,
mover se ha la dueña por artero seruidor.

618 Con arte se quebrantan los coraçones duros,
tomanse las çibdades, derribanse los muros,
caen las torres altas, alçan pesos duros,
por arte juran muchos e por arte son perjuros.

619 Por arte los pescados se toman so las ondas,
E los pies enxutos corren por mares fondas,

Perhaps one in a thousand will deny you, take no notice,
if a lady thinks and dreams of love, then she will love you.

611   Serve her, don't grow tired, love grows with service,
which never perishes or dies in a good man.
All is not lost if progress is slow, love will not fail.
Hard work always conquers all things.

612   Love taught Ovid when he was at school.
There is no woman in the world, young or old,
who is not spurred on by work and service;
sooner or later, you can believe she will sympathize with you.

613   Don't be alarmed by her negative response,
she will soon give a better one if you use skill and service,
persevering and serving will change her thoughts,
a lot of shovelling demolishes the biggest mountain.

614   If the sailor were intimidated
by the first wave of an angry sea,
his iron-clad ship would never set out.
Don't let the woman intimidate you at first.

615   The high-priced salesman swears constantly
that he will sell his merchandise only at great cost,
but the skilful buyer should persevere,
and purchase the goods through a broker.

616   Serve her with great skill, and you will draw closer to her.
The dog who licks and licks will undoubtedly draw blood.
Skill and wiles make the strong woman weak.
The rabbit courts the cow with cunning.

617   The heaviest millstone can be pulled
up the steepest slope with skill and wiles.
It rolls freely with a bit of cleverness.
The lady cannot fail to be moved, if you serve her with skill.

618   The hardest hearts are softened by shrewdness,
cities are taken, walls demolished,
the highest towers fall, heavy loads are raised,
many swear by cunning, and many are perjured.

619   Using skill, fish are caught beneath the waves
and dry feet run over deepest seas.

con arte E con seruiçio muchas cosas abondas,
por arte non ha cosa a que tu non rrespondas.

620 ome poble, con arte, pasa con chico ofiçio,
E la arte al culpado salualo del malefiçio;
el que llorava poble, canta Ryco en vyçio,
faze andar de cauallo al peon el seruiçio.

621 los Señores yrados de manera estraña,
por el mucho seruiçio pierden la mucha saña;
con buen seruiçio vençen cavalleros de españa,
pues vençerse la dueña non es cosa tan maña.

622 Non pueden dar los parientes al pariente por herençia
el mester e el ofiçio, el arte e la sabiençia;
nin pueden dar a la dueña el amor la querençia
todo esto da el trabajo, el vso e la femençia.

623 Maguer te diga de non E avn que se ensañe,
non canses de seguir la, tu obra non se dañe.
fasiendo le seruiçio tu coraçon se bañe;
non puede ser que non se mueva canpana que se tañe.

624 con aquesto podras a tu amiga Sobrar,
la que te era enemiga mucho te querra amar,
los logares ado suele cada dia vsar,
aquellos deues tu mucho amenudo andar.

625 sy vieres que ay lugar, dile jugetes fermosos,
palabras afeytadas con gestos amorosos;
con palabras muy dulçes, con desires sabrosos,
creçem mucho amores e son desseosos.

626 quiere la mancebya mucho plaser con-sigo,
quiere la muger al ome alegre por Amigo,
al sañudo e al torpe non lo preçian vn figo,
tristesa e Rensilla paren mal enemigo.

627 El alegria al omne fazelo apuesto e fermoso,
mas sotil e mas ardit, mas franco e mas donoso;
non olvides los sospiros, en esto sey engañoso,
non seas mucho parlero, non te tenga por mintroso.

628 Por vna pequeña cosa pierde amor la muger,
E por pequeña tacha que en ty podria aver,

You shall have in abundance, using skill and good offices,
nothing is impossible for you, if you have skill.

620   A poor man, with skill, gets by in a humble profession,
skill saves the guilty from harm. The man who weeps
in poverty shall sing with riches and pleasure.
Through service, the foot-soldier rides on horseback.

621   Men who are sorely angered
lose their anger through constant service.
The knights of Spain conquer by good service –
so winning a lady is not such a great thing.

622   Relations cannot pass on occupation and office,
skill and knowledge, through inheritance,
nor can they give love and desire of woman.
This comes with work, familiarity and perseverance.

623   Even if she says "No", even if she is angry,
don't cease to serve her, your work will not come to nothing.
If you serve her, your heart will be bathed in delight –
a bell which rings cannot be still.

624   You can win over your lady friend like this.
Once your enemy, she will love you greatly.
You should often walk in places
which she visits each day.

625   If you have the opportunity, tell her a good story,
using words enhanced by loving gestures.
Gentle words and pleasant tales
will make love grow along with desire.

626   Young women long for pleasure,
women want a happy man as a friend,
they don't care two hoots for the dull or angry.
Sadness and quarrelling make for enemies.

627   Happiness makes a man elegant and handsome,
more subtle, more ardent, more generous and giving.
But don't forget to sigh, act out the part,
don't be too talkative, or be taken to be a liar.

628   A woman's love can be lost over a trifle,
some small fault you may have.

tomara tan grand enojo que te querra aborresçer;
a ty mesmo contesçio E a otros podra acaesçer.

629 Ado fablares con ella, sy vieres que ay lugar,
vn poquillo como a miedo non dexes de jugar;
muchas vezes cobdiçia lo que te va negar,
dar te ha lo que non coydas, sy non te das vagar.

630 Toda muger los ama, omnes aperçebydos,
mas desea tal omne que todos byenes conplidos;
han muy flacas las manos, los calcañares podridos,
lo poco e lo mucho façen lo como amidos.

631 Por mejor tyene la dueña de ser vn poco forçada
que desir: "faz tu talente", como desvergonçada;
con poquilla de fuerça fynca mal desculpada;
en todas las animalyas esta es cosa prouada.

632 Todas fenbras han en sy estas maneras:
al comienço del fecho syenpre son rreferteras,
muestran que tienen saña e son rregateras,
amenasan mas non fieren, en çelo son arteras.

633 Maguer que faze bramuras la duena que se doñea,
nunca el buen doñeador por esto enfaronea;
la muger byen sañuda e quel omne byen guerrea,
los doñeos la vençen por muy braua que sea.

634 El miedo e la verguença faze a las mugeres
non fazer lo que quieren byen como tu lo quieres.
non fynca por non querer, cada que podieres
toma de la dueña lo que della quisieres.

635 de tuyo o de ageno vele byen apostado,
guarda non lo entyenda que lo lyeuas prestado,
que non sabe tu vesino lo que tyenes condesado,
encubre tu poblesa con metyr colorado.

636 El pobre con buen seso E con cara pagada
encubre su pobreza e su vyda lazrada,
coge sus muchas lagrimas en su boca çerrada;
mas val que fazer se pobre a quien nol dara nada.

She may fly into a rage and loathe you,
it has already happened to you and may happen to others.

629 When you speak to her, if you see a chance,
keep up the game, little by little, with caution.
Often she desires what she denies you.
If you don't relax, she will give what you don't expect.

630 All women love men who are well-prepared,
and will desire this kind of man above all other good things.
Women's hands may be thin, their heels diseased,
they act with ill-will in things great and small.

631 A woman would rather have to be persuaded
a little than say "Do as you wish" like a shameless hussy.
With a little force, she feels more exonerated.
This is true of all the animal kingdom.

632 All females behave this way –
at the start they are reluctant,
they show they are wary, are angry,
they threaten without wounding, passion makes them
                                                    cunning.

633 Although the woman courted may make a fuss,
the good lover should never become lazy.
The outraged woman, hostile to her man,
will be conquered by attention, however untamed.

634 Fear and shame stop women
from doing what they want, or what you want,
but it is not through lack of wanting – whenever you can,
take what you desire from the woman.

635 When you see her, be elegant, well turned-out,
in your clothes or in others', but don't tell her if they are
                                                    borrowed.
Don't let your neighbours know what you have got hidden,
cover your poverty with a well-embroidered fib.

636 The poor man conceals his poverty and squalor
with good sense and a contented expression,
he catches his many tears in his closed mouth.
It is better than revealing his poverty to someone who will
                                                    give nothing.

637 las mentyras a las de veses a muchos aprouechan,
la verdat a las de vezes muchos en daño echa,
muchos caminos ataja desuiada estrecha,
ante salen a la peña que por carrera derecha.

638 quando vyeres algunos de los de su conpana,
faz les muchos plazeres fabla les bien con maña,
quando esto la duena su coraçon se baña;
Seruidor ligongero a su señor engaña.

639 ado son muchos tyzones e muchos tysonadores,
mayor sera el fuego e mayores los ardores;
ado muchos le dixieren tus bienes e tus loores,
mayor sera tu quexa E sus desseos mayores.

640 En quanto estan ellos de tus bienes fablando,
luego esta la dueña en su coraçon penssando,
sy lo fara o non, en esto esta dubdando;
desque vieres que dubda ve la tu afyncando.

641 ssy nol dan de las espuelas al cauallo faron,
nunca pierde faronia nin vale vn pepion;
asno coxo quando dubda, corre con el aguijon;
a muger que esta dubdando afynquela el varon.

642 Desque estan dubdando los omes que han de fazer,
poco trabajo puede sus coraçones vençer,
torre alta desque tyenbla non ay synon caer;
la muger que esta dubdando lygera es de aver.

643 ssy tyene madre vieja tu amiga de beldat,
non la consyntira fablar contigo en poridat;
es de la mançebya celosa la vejedat,
Sabe lo E entyendelo por la antiguedat.

644 mucho son mal sabydas estas viejas Risoñas,
mucho son de las moças guardaderas celosas,
sospechan E barruntan todas aquestas cosaz,
byen sabe las parانças quien paso por las losas.

645 Por ende busca vna buena medianera,
que sepa sabia mente andar esta carrera,

637   At times it is advantageous to lie,
      as the truth can cause great harm on occasions.
      A narrow byway shortens a long road,
      you reach the hilltop sooner than by going straight.

638   When you see some of those she knows,
      be pleasant to them, talk to them with sly intent.
      When the lady hears of it, she will be glad.
      A flattering servant deceives his master.

639   Where there are sparks and people to kindle,
      the greater the fire, the faster the burning.
      If many praise you and speak of your wealth,
      the stronger your pleas and her desire.

640   While others are speaking of your goodness,
      then the lady will be pondering in her heart
      whether to give in or not, she will be hesitating.
      When you see this, go ahead, urge her on.

641   If you don't spur on a lazy horse,
      it will never lose its vice or be worth a farthing.
      If an ass is lame when it hesitates, it will run when it feels
                                                      the spur;
      a man should give encouragement to a wavering woman.

642   When women vacillate, men have only
      a little work to do to win their hearts.
      Once a high tower starts to wobble, it has no choice but to
                                                      fall.
      It is easy to win the woman who hesitates.

643   If your lovely lady has an elderly mother,
      she will not allow her to speak with you in confidence.
      Age is jealous of youth,
      it knows and understands from its own experience.

644   These quarrelsome old women are pretty shrewd,
      and jealously guard young girls in their care.
      They suspect and sniff out all these sorts of things;
      if you have been caught in a trap, you know where the snares
                                                      lie.

645   So, find yourself a good go-between,
      who can walk this path wisely,

que entienda de vos anbos byen la vuestra manera,
qual don amor te dixo tal sea la trotera.

646   guardate non la tengas la primera vegada,
non acometas cosa por que fynque espantada,
syn su plaser non sea tanida nin trexnada,
vna ves echale çeuo que venga segurada.

647   asaz te he ya dicho non puedo mas aqui estar;
luego que tu la vieres comiençal de fablar,
mill tienpos e maneras podras despues fallar;
el tyenpo todas cosas trae a su lugar.

648   Amigo, en este fecho ¿que quieres mas que te diga?
sey sotil e acucioso e avras tu amiga.
non quiero aqui estar, quiero me yr mi vya.'
fuese doña venus, a mi dexo en fadigna.

649   ssy le conortan non lo sanan al doliente los joglares,
el dolor creçe E non mengua oyendo dulçes cantares,
consejo me dona venus mas non me tyro pesares,
ayuda otra non me queda synon lengua e parlares.

650   Amigos, vo a grand pena E so puesto en la fonda,
vo a fablar con la dueña, ¡quiera dios que bien me Responda!
puso me el marinero ayna en la mar fonda,
dexo me solo e señero, syn Remos, con la blaua onda.

651   Coytado sy escapare, grand miedo he de ser muerto;
oteo a todas partes e non puedo fallar puerto;
toda la mi esperança e todo el mi confuerto
esta en aquella sola que me trahe penado e muerto.

652   ya vo Rasonar con ella, quierol dezir mi quexura
por que por la mi fabla venga a fazer mesura;
desiendole de mis coytas entendera mi Rencura;
a vezes de chica fabla vinie mucha folgura.

who understands your ways well.
Find a messenger like Love described to you.

646   Be careful not to touch the lady on the first occasion,
don't do anything to frighten her off.
Don't touch or caress her unless it gives her pleasure.
Once the bait is cast, she will surely be caught.

647   I have told you enough and can stay here no longer.
As soon as you see her, start talking to her.
Afterwards you will find endless ways and means.
Time brings everything to its conclusion.

648   My friend, what else can I say on this subject?
Be subtle and diligent and you will have your sweetheart.
I cannot stay, I must be on my way.'
So Lady Venus departed, leaving me in low spirits.

649   Although they comfort him, the minstrels never cure the
                                  sufferer;
the pain grows, never lessens, on hearing sweet singing.
Venus advised me, but did not ease my troubles –
there is no other help left, except to talk.

650   My friends, I am anguished, I am in the ocean depths.
I shall go to speak to my lady, may it please God to let her
                                  respond!
The sailor left me straightaway in the ocean depths,
he left me alone and apart, without oars, amid the raging
                                  waves.

651   Poor unfortunate – will I escape? I have great fear of death,
I look all round but cannot see a port,
all my hopes and comfort lie
in her who is the cause of my moribund sorrow.

652   I shall go to talk to her, I want to tell her my pain,
and through my words she will take notice of me.
If I tell her my suffering, she will understand my bitterness;
at times great pleasure comes from few words.

AQUI DIZE DE COMO FUE FABLAR CON DONA ENDRINA
EL ARÇIPRESTE

653 ¡Ay dios E quam fermosa vyene doña endrina por la plaça!
¡que talle, que donayre, que alta cuello de garça!
¡que cabellos, que boquilla, que boquilla, que color, que
buen andança!
con saetas de amor fyere quando los sus ojos alça.

654 Pero tal lugar non era para fablar en amores;
a mi luego me venieron muchos miedos e tenblores;
los mis pies e las mis manos non eran de si senores,
perdi seso, perdi fuerça, mudaron se mis colores.

655 Vnas palabras tenia pensadas por de desir,
el miedo de las conpañas me facian al departir,
apenas me conosçia nin sabia por do yr,
con mi voluntat mis dichos non se podian seguir.

656 ffablar con muger en plaça es cosa muy descobierta;
a beses mal perro atado tras mala puerta abierta.
bueno es jugar fermoso, echar alguna cobierta,
ado es lugar seguro es bien fablar cosa çierta.

657 'Señora, la mi sobrina, que en toledo seya,
se vos encomienda mucho, mill saludes vos enbya;
sy ovies lugar e tienpo por quanto de vos oya,
desea vos mucho ver E conosçer vos querria.

658 querian alla mis parientes cassar me en esta Saçon,
con vna donçella muy rrica fija de don pepion;
a todos dy por rrespuesta que la non queria non,
de aquella seria mi cuerpo que tiene mi coraçon.'

659 abaxe mas la palabra, dixel que en juego fablaua,
por que toda aquella gente de la plaça nos miraua.
desque vy que eran ydos, que omne ay non fyncaua,
començel dezir mi quexura del amor que me afyncaua.

660 [Hay una laguna de dos líneas en todos los textos.]
otro non sepa la fabla, desto jura fagamos;
do se çelan los amigos son mas fieles entramos.

HOW THE ARCHPRIEST WENT TO TALK TO ENDRINA

653   Oh, Lord! How beautiful Endrina is walking across the
                              square!
    What a figure! What elegance, with her long, heron-like neck!
    What hair, what a lovely mouth, her complexion, the way
                          she walks!
    When she raises her eyes they fire wounding arrows of love.

654   But it was not the place to speak of love.
    I was filled with fear and trembling.
    My feet and hands seemed not to belong to me,
    I lost all reason, strength, lost all my colour.

655   I had thought of things I wanted to say,
    but fear of other people made me diverge,
    I scarcely knew myself nor where to go –
    my speech would not comply with my will.

656   Speaking to a woman in a square is very obvious,
    at times a bad dog is tied behind an open door . . .
    It is best to make pleasantries, put on a show,
    it is better to speak the truth in a safe place.

657   'Madam, my cousin who lives in Toledo
    asks to be remembered to you and sends best wishes.
    If you have the time and place, from what she has heard of
                          you,
    she would be glad to meet and get to know you.

658   My family there wanted to marry me
    to a wealthy lady, the daughter of Mr Farthing.
    I told them all that I certainly did not love her, no,
    that my body would belong to whoever had my heart.'

659   I lowered my voice, said I was speaking in jest
    because everyone in the square was watching.
    When I saw they had left, that no one remained,
    I began to speak to her of the love which tormented me.

660   [Lines 660a–b are missing in all manuscripts.]
    no one else should know of our conversation, let's swear an
                          oath,
    when friends keep things secret, the more faithful they are.

661 en el mundo non es cosa que yo ame a par de uos;
     tienpo es ya pasado de los años mas de dos
     que por vuestro amor me pena; amo vos mas que a dios.
     Non oso poner presona que lo fable entre nos.

662 Con la grant pena que paso vengo a uos desir mi quexa,
     vuestro amor he deseo que me afinca e me aquexa,
     Nos me tira, nos me parte, non me suelta, non me dexa,
     tanto me da la muerte quanto mas se me abaxa.

663 rreçelo he que non oydes esto que uos he fablado;
     fablar mucho con el sordo es mal seso e mal Recabdo;
     cret que uos amo tanto que non ey mayor cuydado;
     esto sobre todas cosas me traye mas afincado.

664 señora, yo non a me treuo d desir uos mas rrasones,
     fasta que me rrespondades a estos pocos sermones;
     desit me vuestro talante veremos los Coraçones.'
     ella dixo: 'vuestros dichos non los preçio dos piñones,

665 bien asi enganan muchos a otras muchas endrinas;
     el omne tan engañoso asi engaña a sus vesinas.
     non cuydedes que so loca por oyr vuestras parlillas;
     buscat a quien engañedes con vuestras falsas espinas.'

666 yo le dixe: 'ya, sañuda, anden fermosos trebejos;
     son los dedos en las manos pero non son todos parejos,
     todos los omnes non somos de vnos fechos nin cosejos,
     la peña tiene blanco e prieto pero todos son conejos.

667 a las vegadas lastan justos por pecadores,
     a muchos enpeesçen los ajenos errores,
     fas mal culpa de malo a buenos e a mejores;
     deuen tener la pena a los sus fasedores;

668 el yerro que otro fiso a mi non faga mal,
     Auet por bien que uos fable ally so aquel portal,
     Non uos vean aqui todos lo que andan por la calle;
     aqui vos fable vno ally vos fablare al.'

669 paso o paso don endrina so el portal es entrada,
     bien loçana e orgullosa, bien mansa e sosegada,

661   There is nothing in the world I love as much as you.
       It has been a long time now, two years past,
       that I have suffered with love – I love you more than God.
       I dare not have an intermediary to speak between us.

662   I am suffering so much that I must tell you my anguish.
       Love and desire for you, which torments and grieves me,
       it will not lessen, leave me, release me, nor depart.
       The more elusive it is, the nearer to death I lie.

663   I am afraid you are not listening to what I have to say.
       There is no sense or discretion in speaking to the deaf.
       Believe that my greatest care is my love for you,
       which torments me above all things.

664   Madam, I dare say no more
       until you respond to what I have told you.
       Tell me how you feel, let us reveal our hearts.'
       She replied: 'I don't give two hoots for your words.

665   Many other Endrinas have been deceived in this way.
       Deceitful man takes in his woman neighbours.
       Don't think I am silly enough to listen to your ditties,
       look for someone else to deceive with the false thorns of
                                                your words.'*

666   I said: 'Now, such anger, let us talk of happy things.
       There are five fingers on a hand, but they are not all the same.
       Not all men are made the same way or think the same
                                                thoughts.
       The fur in a coat may be black and white, but it is all made
                                                of rabbit.

667   Sometimes the righteous pay the price for the sinners,
       and others' mistakes hinder many.
       The good and the best get wrongly blamed,
       but the penalty should be for those who do wrong.

668   Another's error ought not to harm me.
       Let's stand over there in the porch so we can talk properly.
       We won't be seen by every passer-by,
       and I can say things there that I cannot standing here.'

669   Little by little Endrina moved into the porch,
       beautiful and proud, calm and relaxed.

los ojos baxo por tierra, en el poyo asentada;
yo torne en la mi fabla que tenia començada:

670   'escuche me, señora, la vuestra cortesia,
vn poquillo que uos diga la muerte mia;
Cuydades que vos fablo en engaño e en folia,
E non se que me faga contra vuestra porfia.

671   a dios juro, señora, para aquesta tierra,
que quanto vos he dicho de la verdat non yerra;
estades enfriada mas que la nief de la sierra,
e sodes atan moça que esto me atierra.

672   fablo en aventura con la vuestra moçedat,
cuydades que uos fablo lisonga e vanidat,
non me puedo entender en vuestra chica hedat;
querriedes jugar con la pella mas que estar en poridat.

673   pero sea mas noble para plasenteria,
E para estos juegos hedat e mançebia,
la vegedat en seso lieua la mejoria,
a entender las cosas el grand tienpo las guia.

674   a todas las cosas fase el grand vso entender,
el arte e el vso muestra todo el saber,
sin el vso e arte ya se va pereçer,
do se vsan los omnes pueden se conoçer.

675   yd e venit a la fabla otro dia, por mesura,
pues que oy non me creedes o non es mi ventura;
yt e venid a la fabla, esa creençia atan dura
vsando oyr mi pena entenderedes mi quexura.

676   otorgat me ya señora, aquesto de buena miente,
que venga es otro dia a la fabla sola miente,
yo pensare en la fabla e sabre vuestro talente;
al non oso demandar, vos venid segura miente.

677   por la fabla se conosçen los mas de los coraçones,
yo entendere de uos algo E oyredes los mis rrasones;
yt e venid a la fabla, que mugeres e varones
por las palabras se conosçen, e son amigos e conpañones.

She lowered her eyes and sat on the stone seat.
I began to finish what I had started saying earlier.

670   'Please have the goodness, madam, to listen to me,
while I tell you that I am dying.
You are worried that my words are deceit and foolishness,
and I don't know what I can do about your obstinacy.

671   I swear to God and by this land,
that everything I have told you is the truth.
You are colder than the mountain snow,
and you are so young that I am overcome.

672   I speak to your youthfulness in vain.
You think I speak to flatter and in vanity.
Your youth makes my words hard to understand –
you would rather be playing ball than talking of love.

673   Though youth is better for pleasure,
and for games like these,
age goes hand in hand with good sense,
time guides the understanding of these things.

674   Familiarity helps us understand all things,
ingenuity and practice lead to all knowledge.
Without these, a person would perish.
When people are on familiar terms, they can get to know
each other.

675   Go, then, and come back another day, out of politeness,
since you do not believe me today, or I am out of luck.
Go home and then come back to talk. When I tell you
again of my suffering, your rigid attitude will come to
understand my complaint.

676   Please grant me this gladly,
that you will come another day just to talk.
I will think about it, and would like to know your mind.
I ask no more, except that you definitely come.

677   Most hearts learn about each other through talking.
I will understand something of you and you shall hear what I
have to say.
Go now and come another day – men and women
know each other through words, as friends and companions.

678 pero que omne non coma nin comiença la mançana,
  es la color e la vista alegria palançiana;
  es la fabla e la vista de la dueña tan loçana
  al omne conorte grande e plasenteria bien sana.'

679 esto dixo doña endrina, esta dueña de prestar:
  'onrra es e non desonrra en cuerda miente fablar,
  las dueñas e mugeres deuen su rrepuesta dar
  a qual quier que las fablare o con ellas rrasonare.

680 quanto esto uos otorgo a uos o a otro qual quier,
  fablat uos, salua mi onrra, quanto fablar uos quigeredes;
  de palabras en juego direlas si las oyere,
  non uos consintre engaño cada que lo entendiere.

681 estar sola con uos solo, esto yo non lo faria,
  non deue la muger estar sola en tal conpañia;
  naçe dende mala fama, mi desonrra seria.
  ante testigos que nos veyan fablar uos he algund dia.'

682 'señora, por la mesura que agora prometedes,
  non se graçias que lo valan quantas uos mereçedes,
  a la merçed que agora de palabra me fasedes,
  egualar non se podrian ningunas otras merçedes.

683 pero fio de dios que a vn tienpo verna
  que qual es el buen amigo por las obras parescera;
  querria fablar, non oso, tengo que uos pesara.'
  ella dixo: 'pues desildo e vere que tal sera.'

684 'señora, que me prometades, de lo que de amor queremos,
  que sy ouiere lugar e tienpo, quando en vno estemos,
  segund que lo yo deseo vos e yo nos abraçemos;
  para uos non pido mucho ca con esto pasaremos.'

685 esto dixo doña endrina: 'es cosa muy prouada
  que por sus besos la dueña finca muy engañada,
  ençendemiento grande pone el abraçar al amada,
  toda muger es vençida des que esta Ioya es dada;

686 esto yo non uos otorgo saluo la fabla de mano;
  mi madre verna de misa, quiere me yr de aqui tenprano,
  non sospeche contra mi que ando con seso vano;
  tienpo verna que podremos fablar nos, uos e yo, este verano.'

678   Even if a man does not eat or start an apple,
its colour and shape give exquisite pleasure.
The words and sight of such a beautiful woman
are a great comfort and healthy pleasure to man.'

679   Endrina, so lovely in every way, replied:
'It is honourable, not dishonour, to speak wisely.
Women should give their answer to
anyone who speaks and debates with them.

680   I will grant you this, you or anyone,
by my honour, speak, as much as you wish.
If you play tricks on me, I shall do the same to you.
No deceit I am aware of will go unheeded.

681   I would not be alone with you,
for no woman should be alone in such company,
as a bad reputation will follow, and my dishonour.
I will speak to you one day, before witnesses.'

682   'Madam, for the favour you promise me,
I do not know how to thank you.
Truly, no other favour can equal
the words you have just promised me.

683   I trust in God that time will show
the good friend by his works.
I would like to speak – I dare not – I fear you will not like it.'
She said: 'Well, tell me, and I will see what I think.'

684   'Madam, promise me, because of love,
that if the time and place were right, and we together,
as I wish, that we might embrace each other.
I only ask this, which shall be enough.'

685   Endrina answered: 'It is a proven thing
that a woman suffers deception for her kisses.
To embrace the woman beloved arouses great passion,
and all women are conquered once this jewel is given.

686   I grant you no more than to talk, for now.
My mother will soon be back from Mass, I must go quickly.
She must not suspect that I am thinking foolish things –
there will be time for us to talk this spring.'

687 fuese mi señora de la fabla su via,
des que yo fue naçido nunca vy mejor dia,
solas tan plasentero e tan grande alegria,
quiso me dios bien giar e la ventura mia.

688 Cuydados muchos me quexan, a que non fallo cosejo;
si mucho vso la dueña con palabras de trebejo,
puede seer tanta la fama que saliria a conçejo,
asi perderia la dueña, que sera pesar sobejo.

689 si la non sigo, non vso, el amor se perdera;
sy veye que la oluido, ella otro amara.
El amor con vso creçe, desusando menguara,
do la muger oluidares ella te oluidara.

690 do añadieres la leña creçe syn dubda el fuego,
si la leña se tirare el fuego menguara luego;
el amor e la bien querençia creçe con vsar juego;
si la muger oluidares, poco preçiara tu Ruego.

691 cuydados tan departidos creçen me de cada parte,
con pensamientos contrarios el mi coraçon se parte.
E a la mi mucha cuyta non se consejo nin arte;
el amor do esta firme todos los miedos departe.

692 muchas vezes la ventura con ssu fuerça e poder
a muchos omnes non dexa su proposito fazer,
por esto anda el mundo en leuantar e en caer;
dios e el trabajo grande pueden los fados vençer.

693 ayuda la ventura al que bien quiere guiar,
E a muchos es contraria, puede los mal estoruar;
el trabajo e el fado suelen se aconpañar,
pero syn dios todo esto non puede aprouechar.

694 Pues que syn dios non puede prestar cosa que sea,
el guie la mi obra, el mi trabajo prouea.
por que el mi coraçon vea lo que dessea;
el que 'amen' dixiere lo que cobdiçia lo vea.

695 hermano nin Sobrino non quiero por ayuda,
quando aquel fuego vinie, todo coraçon muda;

687   My lady stopped talking and went on her way.
       It was the best day of my life, since I was born,
       such delightful solace and great joy.
       God guided me and my good fortune.

688   Many cares crowded in on me, for which I was given no
                                                         advice.
       If I saw her a lot and spoke playfully to her,
       it might become public knowledge
       and I would lose the lady, which would be the greatest
                                                         sorrow.

689   If I didn't follow her, spend time with her, I'd lose her.
       If she thought I had forgotten her, she would love another.
       Love grows with familiarity and wanes with neglect.
       If you forget a woman, she will forget you.

690   If you pile on wood, the fire will burn brighter,
       if you take the wood off, then the fire burns low.
       Love and affection increase with familiarity –
       if you forget a woman, your entreaties will be scorned.

691   All these cares assailed me from all sides,
       my heart was torn with conflicting thoughts,
       and I did not know how to ease my trouble with counsel or
                                                         cure.
       When love is strong, all fears are dispelled.

692   Often the power and strength of Fortune
       prevent men from doing as they wish.
       By this the world rises and falls,
       but God and hard work can conquer fate.

693   Fortune helps the man it wants to guide
       and hinders many that it works against.
       Hard work and chance usually go hand in hand,
       but there is no profit without God's help.

694   Since nothing avails without God,
       He guides my work and oversees it,
       and knows what my heart desires.
       He who says 'Amen' shall see what he covets.

695   I do not want the help of a brother or cousin,
       when the fire strikes, all hearts change.

vno a otro non guarda lealtad nin la cuda;
amigança, debdo e sangre la muger lo muda.

696 El cuerdo con buen seso pensar deue las cosas,
escoja las mejores E dexe las dañosas;
para mensajeria personas sospechosas
nunca son a los omnes buenas nin prouechosas.

697 busque trota conventos qual me mando el amor,
de todas las maestrias escogi la mejor,
dios e la mi ventura que me fue guiador;
açerte en la tyenda del sabio corredor.

698 falle vna vieja qual avia menester,
artera e maestra e de mucho saber;
doña venus por panfilo non pudo mas fazer,
de quanto fizo aquesta por me fazer plazer.

699 Era vieja buhona destas que venden joyas.
estas echan el laço, estas cavan las foyas,
non ay tales maestras commo estas viejas troyas.
estas dan la maçada; sy as orejas oyas.

700 Como lo han vso estas tales buhonas,
andan de casa en casa vendiendo muchas donas,
non se rreguardan dellas, estan con las personas,
ffazen con el mucho viento andar las athonas.

701 desque fuy en mi casa esta vieja sabida,
dixele: 'madre señora, tan bien seades venida,
en vuestras manos pongo mi salud e mi vida,
sy vos non me acorredes mi vida es perdida.

702 oy dezir sienpre de vos mucho bien e aguisado,
de quantos bienes fazedes al que a vos viene coytado;
como ha bien e ayuda quien de vos hes ayudado.
por la vuestra buena fama E por vos enbiado.

703 quiero fablar con-vusco bien en como penitençia,
toda cosa que vos diga, oydla en paçiençia;
sinon vos, otro non sepa mi quexa e mi dolençia.'
diz la vieja: 'pues desidlo e aved en mi creençia.

704 Comigo Segura mente vuestro coraçon fablat.
fare por vos quanto pueda, guardar he vos lealtal;

Loyalty and care go by the board,
friendship, kinship and blood ties, women alter it all.

696   The wise man should think things over,
choosing the best and avoiding the harmful.
Unreliable people are neither good
nor beneficial to men as messengers.

697   I searched for a go-between as Love instructed,
and of all the most skilled, I picked the best.
God and Fortune were my guides.
I struck good fortune at the clever broker's shop.

698   I found an old woman of the kind I needed,
cunning and skilful and very knowledgeable.
Venus could not have done more for Pamphilus
than she did to bring me pleasure.

699   She was an old pedlar who sold jewellery,
the kind who set the trap; they dig the ditches,
there are none better than these old bawds,
they do the damage – if you have ears, listen.

700   These hucksters habitually go
from house to house, selling numerous gifts.
No one suspects them, they mix with all social classes,
they make the mill work with the stir they create.

701   When this knowing old woman came to my house
I said: 'Mother, you are welcome.
My health and life are in your hands –
if you cannot help me, my life is lost.

702   I have always heard good about you and your wisdom,
of all the good you do to those who are in trouble,
how goodness and help is given to those you assist,
so I sent for you because of your good reputation.

703   I want to talk to you as if in penitence,
listen patiently to all I say.
Let no one other than you know my pain and suffering.'
The old woman said: 'Speak, then, and trust me.

704   You can surely speak your heart to me
and I will do all I can for you and stay loyal.

ofiçio de corredores es de mucha poridat,
mas encubiertas encobrimos que meson de vesindat.

705 Sy a quantas desta villa nos vendemos las alfajas
ssopiesen vnos de otros, muchas serian las barajas;
muchas bodas ayuntamos que viene arrepantajas,
muchos panderos vendemos que non suenan las sonajas.'

706 yo le dixe: 'amo vna dueña sobre quantas yo vy,
ella, si me non engaña, paresçe que ama a mi,
por escusar mill peligros fasta oy lo encubri,
toda cosa deste mundo temo mucho e temi.

707 De pequena cosa nasçe fama en la vesindat;
desque nasçe, tarde muere, maguer non sea verdat,
syenpre cada dia cresçe con enbia e falsedat;
poca cossa le enpeçe al mesquino en mesquindat.

708 aqui es bien mi vesina; Ruego vos que alla vayades,
E fablad entre nos anbos lo mejor que entendades,
encobrid todo aquesto lo mas mucho que podades,
açertad aqueste fecho pues que vierdes las voluntades.'

709 dixo: 'yo ire a su casa de esa vuestra vesina,
e le fare tal escanto e le dare tal atal-vina
por que esa vuestra llaga sane por mi melesina.
desid me quien es la dueña.' yo le dixe: 'doña endrina.'

710 'la çera que es mucho dura e mucho brozna e elada,
desque ya entre las manos vna ves esta masnada,
despues con el poco fuego çient vezes sera doblada;
doblar se ha toda dueña que sea bien escantada.'

711 Dixo me que esta dueña era byen su conosçienta.
yo le dixe: 'por dios, amiga, guardat vos de soberuienta.'
ella diz: 'pues fue casada creed que se non arrepienta,
que non ay mula de aluarda que la troxa non consienta.

712 Mienbre se vos, buen amigo, de lo que desir se suele:
que çiuera en molyno el que ante viene muele,
mensaje que mucho tarda a muchos omnes desmuele,
el omne aperçebido nunca tanto se duele.

The go-between must keep confidences.
We keep more secrets than the local inn.

705 If all those we sell jewellery to in this town
knew all about each other, what quarrels there would be.
We arrange a lot of matches, which end in repentance,
we sell a lot of tambourines, but their timbrels do not sound.'

706 I said: 'I love a woman like no other I have ever seen,
and if she doesn't deceive me, she loves me too.
To avoid no end of danger, I have kept silent till today.
I fear, have always feared, the things of this world.

707 Rumours start about the smallest neighbourhood thing,
and once they start, they take time to die down, true or not.
They tend to grow through envy and falsity.
It takes very little to make the unfortunate more wretched.

708 My neighbour lives over there – please go
and speak on my behalf as best you can.
Conceal my dealings as far as possible.
Since we are both willing, make sure you hit the mark.'

709 She replied: 'I will go to your neighbour's house
and cast such a spell and give her such a love potion
that your wound will be healed by my medicine.
Tell me who the lady is.' I said: 'Her name is Endrina.'

710 'Wax which is very hard, brittle and cold,
once softened and kneaded in the hands
will bend a hundredfold with slight heat,
and any well-enchanted woman will do so too.'

711 She told me that the lady was well-known to her,
so I warned: 'For heaven's sake, beware of giving a sudden
shock.'
She said: 'Well, she was married before, I assure you she
won't have regrets,
there is no pack mule who will not carry its load.

712 Remember, dear friend, the old saying
that the grain in the hopper is milled by the first comer,
a late message can dishearten many men.
The well-prepared man never suffers like that.

713   Amigo, non vos durmades, que la dueña que desides
      otro quiere casar con ella, pide lo que vos pedides;
      es omne de buen lynaje, viene donde vos venides;
      vayan ante vuestros rruegos que los ajenos conbites.

714   yo lo trayo estoruando por quanto non lo afynco,
      ca es omne muy escaso pero que es muy Rico;
      mando me por vestuario vna piel e vn pellico,
      dio melo tan bien parado que nin es grande nin chico.

715   El presente que se da luego, sy es grande de valor,
      queblanta leyes e fueros e es del derecho Señor;
      a muchos hes grand ayuda, a muchos estoruador;
      tienpo ay que aprouecha E tienpo ay que faz peor.

716   Esta dueña que desides, mucho es en mi poder;
      sy non por mi, non la puede omne del mundo aver;
      yo se toda su fasienda E quanto ha de fazer,
      por mi conssejo lo faze mas que non por su querer.

717   Non vos dire mas rrasones que asas vos he fablado;
      de aqueste ofiçio byuo non he de otro coydado,
      muchas veses he tristesa del laserio ya pasado,
      por que me non es agradesçido nin me es gualardonado.

718   ssy me dieredes ayuda de que passe algun poquillo,
      a esta dueña e a otras moçetas de cuello aluillo,
      yo fare con mi escanto que se vengan paso a pasillo,
      en aqueste mi farnero las traere al sarçillo.'

719   yo le dixe: 'madre señora, yo vos quiero byen pagar,
      el mi algo E mi casa a todo vuestro mandar;
      de mano tomad pellote e yd, nol dedes vagar,
      pero ante que vayades quiero vos yo castigar.

720   Todo el vuestro cuydado sea en aqueste fecho,
      trabajat en tal manera por que ayades prouecho,
      de todo vuestro trabajo avredes ayuda e pecho,
      pensat bien lo que fablaides con seso e con derecho.

721   Del comienço fasta el cabo pensat bien lo que digades,
      fablad tanto E tal cosa que non vos arepintades;
      en la fyn esta la onrra e la desonrra bien creades,
      do bien acaba la cosa ally son todas bondades.

713   My friend, don't fall asleep, for another wants to marry
        the lady you speak of – he asks for the same as you.
        He is a man of high birth, he comes from the same place too;
        let your demands come first, before other invitations.

714   I have got him on hold, will not advance his case,
        for he is a stingy man although he's very rich.
        He sent me a fur and a pelisse to wear,
        it fits me so well, it's neither too big nor too small.

715   The present given, if it is of great value,
        breaks rules and statutes and governs the law.
        It can help a great deal, or be a great hindrance.
        At times it is an advantage, at times it does harm.

716   The lady you talk of is very much in my power,
        no man in the world can have her without my help.
        I know all about her affairs and what she must do
        she does on my advice, rather than at her wishes.

717   I shall say no more, I've spoken enough,
        I live from this work, I care for nothing else.
        I am often sad at my past suffering
        for I am not thanked or recompensed.

718   If you could see your way to help me get by,
        both this lady and other girls with nice white necks,
        I will make them come little by little with my spell,
        will gather them into my basket with my weeding hook.'

719   I said to her: 'Mother, I want to pay you well,
        my property and my house is at your command.
        For the moment take this cloak and go, let's not waste time,
        but before you leave, here is some advice.

720   Put every effort into this affair,
        work so as to gain benefit from it,
        you shall have help and payment for all your work,
        think carefully of what you will say, rightly and wisely.

721   Think carefully of your words from start to finish,
        only say what you will not regret.
        Honour and dishonour lie at the end,
        when a thing ends well, therein lies all goodness.

722 Mejor cosa es al omne, al cuerdo e al entendido,
     callar do non le enpeçe E tyenen le por sesudo,
     que fablar lo que non le cunple por que sea arrepentido;
     o piensa bien lo que fablas o calla, faz te mudo.'

723 la buhona con farnero va taniendo cascaueles,
     meneando de sus joyas, sortijas E alfileres;
     desia por fasalejas: '¡conprad aquestos manteles!'
     vydola doña endrina, dixo: 'entrad, non Reçeledes.'

724 Entro la vieja en casa, dixole: 'Señora fija,
     para esa mano bendicha quered esta sortija;
     si vos non me descobrierdes desir vos he vna pastija
     que pensse aquesta noche.' Poco a poco la aguja.

725 'Ffija, sienpre estades en casa ençerrada,
     sola envejeçedes, quered alguna vegada
     Salyr, andar en la plaça con vuestra beldat loada;
     entre aquestas paredes non vos prestara nada.

726 En aquesta villa mora muy fermosa mançebia,
     mançebillos apostados e de mucha loçania,
     en todas buenas costunbres creçen de cada dia,
     nunca puede ome atan buena conpañia.

727 Muy byen me rresçiben todos con aquesta pobledat,
     El mejor e el mas noble de lynaje e de beldat
     es don melon de la verta, mançebillo de verdat,
     a todos los otros sobra en fermosura e bondat.

728 Todos quantos en su tyenpo en esta tierra nasçieron,
     en rriquesas e en costunbres tanto como el non crecieron;
     con los locos faze se loco, los cuerdos del byen dixieron;
     manso mas que vn cordero, nunca pelear lo vyeron.

729 El sabio vençer al loco con conssejo non es tan poco,
     con los cuerdos estar cuerdo, con los locos fazer se loco.
     el cuerdo non enloqueçe por fablar al Roça poco;
     yo lo piensso en mi pandero muchas veçes que lo toco.

730 Mançebillo en la villa atal non se fallara,
     non estraga lo que gana, antes lo guardara;

722   It is better if a man, wise or skilful,
      stays silent when he can and gives an impression of
                                  knowledge,
      than if he speaks and later regrets what he said.
      Think well of what you will say or be quiet, stay silent.'

723   The pedlar goes off with her basket, jingling her bells,
      dangling her jewellery, rings and pins,
      saying: 'Tablecloths for sale, swap them for towels.'
      Endrina saw her and said: 'Come in, don't be timid.'

724   The old woman went in and said to her: 'Young lady,
      have this ring for your blessed finger.
      If you don't give me away, I'll tell you a story
      I made up last night.' Little by little she spurs her on.

725   'My dear, you're always shut up at home,
      you will get old on your own. Why not go out
      once in a while and walk in the square?
      Your famous beauty will do nothing for you within these
                                  four walls.

726   There are some very handsome men in this town,
      elegant, lively young men,
      their good manners improve every day –
      you never saw such good company.

727   They all treat me very well in my poverty.
      The best and noblest in birth and looks
      is Lord Melon of the Kitchen Garden, a real fine lad,
      better than all others in goodness and good looks.

728   None of those born during his time in this area
      could exceed him in wealth and good manners.
      He acts mad with the mad, the prudent speak well of him.
      Never known to fight, he's more docile than a lamb.

729   It's no mean task for a wise man's brains to conquer a fool,
      showing wisdom with the wise and madness with the fool.
      The prudent man does not grow foolish by talking to
                               someone frivolous.
      I think of this a lot when I'm tapping my tambourine.

730   You won't find another young man like him in the town.
      He does not squander what he earns, but saves it.

creo byen que tal fijo al padre semejara,
en el beserillo vera omne el buey que fara.

731 El fijo muchas vezes commo el padre prueua,
en semejar fijo al padre non es cosa tan nueua;
el coraçon del ome por el coraçon se prueua,
grand amor e grand ssaña non puede sser que non se mueua.

732 ome es de buena vyda E es byen acostunbrado,
creo que casaria el con vusco de buen grado;
ssy vos lo bien sopiesedes qual es e quan preçiado
vos queriades aquesto que yo vos he fablado.

733 a veçes luenga fabla tiene chico prouecho,
quien mucho fabla yerra, diselo el derecho;
E de comienço chico viene granado fecho,
a veze cosa chica faze muy grand despecho.

734 E a vezes pequeña fabla bien dicha e chico Ruego
obra mucho en los fechos, a vezes rrecabda luego,
e de chica çentella nasçe grand llama de fuego,
e vienen grandes peleas a veses de chico juego.

735 syenpre fue mi costunbre e los mis pensamientos
leuantar yo de mio e mouer cassamientos,
fablar como en juego tales somouimientos,
fasta que yo entienda e vea los talentos.

736 agora señora fija desit me vuestro coraçon,
esto que vos he fablado sy vos plase o si non,
guardar vos he poridat, çelare vuestra rraçon;
syn miedo fablad con-migo quantas cosas son.'

737 Respondiole la dueña con mesura E byen:
'buena muger, dezid me qual es ese o quien,
que vos tanto loades e quantos bienes tyen;
yo penssare en ello, si para mi con-vyen.'

738 Dixo trota conventos: '¿quien, fija, es? fija Señora,
es aparado bueno que dios vos traxo agora,
mançebillo guisado, en vuestro barrio mora;
don melon de la verta. ¡quered lo en buen ora!

I think such a son takes after his father.
The yearling calf hints at the ox it will be become.

731 The son often turns out like the father.
There is nothing new in such a resemblance.
A man's heart is revealed in his deeds.
A heart cannot be unmoved by great love and great anger.

732 He leads a good life and has good habits,
I think he would willingly marry you.
If you knew what he was like, how well-esteemed,
you would love the man I am describing.

733 At times a lot of words have little benefit.
"To talk too much is to err," says the refrain.
Sometimes a little thing causes great displeasure
and great things have modest beginnings.

734 Sometimes a few well-chosen words and questions
have a great effect on things, at times they soon bring
                                    successful outcomes.
Huge flames, strong fire grows from a tiny spark,
and serious quarrels sometimes arise from harmless teasing.

735 It has always been my custom and my thought
to arrange marriages on my own initiative,
and make such suggestions as if in jest,
until I see and understand inclinations and desires.

736 So now, young lady, tell me what is in your heart,
and whether what I've said pleases you or not.
I will keep a secret, keep your confidence,
speak freely to me without fear.'

737 The lady answered with restraint and well-chosen words:
'My good woman, tell me who this person is
that you praise so much, in all his wealth.
I will think about it to see if it suits me.'

738 Trotaconventos* replied: 'Who is it, young lady?
It is a great gift given you by God,
an ideal young man, who lives in this very district,
Lord Melon of the Kitchen Garden. Love him now, at the
                                    right time.

739   creed me, fija señora, que quantos vos demandaron,
        a par deste maçebillo ningunos non llegaron;
        el dia que vos nasçites fadas aluas vos fadaron,
        que para esse buen donayre atal cosa vos guardaron.'

740   Dixo doña endrina: 'callad ese predicar,
        que ya esse parlero me coydo engañar,
        muchas otras vegadas me vyno a Retentar,
        mas de mi el nin vos non vos podredes alabar.

741   la muger que vos cree las mentiras parlando,
        E cree a los omnes con mentiras jurando,
        sus manos se contuerçe, del coraçon travando,
        que mal se laua la cara con lagrimas llorando.

742   Dexa me de tus Roydos, que yo tengo otros coydados,
        de muchos que me tyenen los mis algos forçados;
        non se viene en miente desos malos rrecabdos,
        nin te cunple agora desir me esos mandados.'

743   'A la fe,' dyxo la vieja, 'desque vos veen bilda,
        sola, syn conpañero, non sodes tan temida,
        es la vyda sola mas que vaca corrida;
        por ende aquel buen omne vos ternia defendida.

744   Este vos tiraria de todos esos pelmasos,
        de pleitos e de afruentas, de verguenças e de plasos;
        muchos disen que coydan parar vos tales lasos,
        fasta que non vos dexen en las puertas llumasos.

745   guardat vos mucho desto, Señora doña endrina,
        sy non contesçer vos puede a vos mucho ayna
        commo la abutarda, quando la golondryna
        le daua buen conssejo, commo buena madrina.

ENXIENPLO DE LA ABUTARDA E DE LA GOLONDRINA

746   Era se vn caçador muy sotil paxarero,
        ffue senbrar cañamones en vn viçioso ero,
        para fazer sus cuerdas E sus lazos el rredero;
        andaua el abutarda çerca en el sendero.

747   Dixo la golondrina a tortolas e a pardales
        e mas al abutarda estas palabras tales:

739 Believe me, my lady, whoever has asked for your hand
is not a patch on this young man.
Good fairies blessed you on the day you were born,
and have preserved him for you by their good grace.'

740 Endrina answered: 'Stop all this talking,
since he has already tried to deceive me with his words.
He has tempted me many other times,
but neither of you can boast of getting me.

741 The woman who believes such lying words
and believes men who swear their love
will wring her hands and clutch her heart,
and wash her face with the tears she cries.

742 Stop such chatter, as I have got other worries
about my own property, which is being taken by force.
Don't remind me of foolish involvements,
or tell me these messages now.'

743 'Well, really,' said the old woman, 'since you have been a
widow,
alone, with no companion, you have been less esteemed.
A widow is more alone than a cow run through the streets.
A good man would defend and protect you.

744 He would set you free from all those annoyances
about lawsuits and offences, embarrassments and terms.
Many say they are casting such snares,
and will even take the hinges off the doors.

745 Beware of this, Endrina, madam,
and mind that the same thing does not happen to you
that happened to the bustard when the swallow
gave him sound advice, like a good god-mother.

THE FABLE OF THE BUSTARD AND THE SWALLOW

746 Once there was a hunter, a clever bird-catcher,
who went to sow hemp seed in a fertile field
in order to make his hunting ropes and snares.
The bustard was walking nearby on the path.

747 The swallow warned the turtle-doves and linnets
and also spoke to the bustard:

"comed aquesta semiente de aquestos eriales,
que es aqui senbrado por nuestros males grandes."

748 fezieron grande escarnio de lo que les fablaua,
dixieron que se fuese, que locura chirlaua.
la semiente nasçida, vyeron como rregaua
el caçador el canamo e non las espantaua.

749 Torno la golondrina e dixo al abutarda
que arrancase la yerua que era ya pujada;
que quien tanto la rriega e tanto la escarda,
por su mal lo fasia, maguera que se tarda.

750 dixo el abutarda: "loca, sandia, vana,
syenpre estas chirlando locura de mañana;
non quiero tu conssejo, vete para villana,
dexa me esta vegada tan fermosa e tan llana."

751 fuese la golondrina a casa del caçador,
fizo ally su nido quanto pudo mejor;
commo era grytadera E mucho gorjeador,
plogo al paxarero que era madrugador.

752 Cogido ya el cañamo E fecha la parança
fuese el paxarero, commo solia, a caça;
prendio al abutarda, leuola a la plaça.
dixo la golondrina: "ya sodes en pelaça."

753 Juego los ballesteros pelaron le las alas,
non le dexaron dellas sinon chicas e rralas;
non quiso buen conssejo, cayo en fuertes palas.
guardat vos, doña endrina, destas paraças malas.

754 que muchos se ayuntan e son de vn conssejo
por astragar lo vuestro e fazer vos mal trebejo;
juran que cada dia vos leuaran a conçejo,
commo al abutarda vos pelaran el pellejo.

755 Mas este vos defendera de toda esta contienda,
ssabe de muchos pleitos e sabe de leyenda,
ayuda e deffiende a quien sele encomienda;
si el non vos defiende non se quien vos defienda.'

"Eat up the seed in those fields,
as it is sown here to catch us."

748   They made a great mockery of what she said,
and told her to go away as she was chirping nonsense.
When the seed sprouted, they saw how the hunter
watered the hemp and they were not afraid.

749   The swallow came back and told the bustard
to pull out the grass that had grown up,
because the hunter watered and weeded it so much
to do the bustard harm, though the effect was not
                                    immediate.

750   The bustard said: "Mad, crazy, empty-headed,
you're always chirping some nonsense in the morning.
I don't need your advice, off you go, you peasant.
Leave me in this beautiful, flat, fertile field."

751   The swallow went to the hunter's house
and built her nest there as best she could.
She sang a lot, a burbling song
which pleased the hunter, because he rose at dawn.

752   When the hemp was gathered and the snare was made,
the bird-catcher went to hunt as usual.
He caught the bustard and took it to market.
The swallow said: "Now you're in mortal danger."

753   Then the archers took his long wing feathers
and only left the small sparse ones.
He would not listen to good advice and fell into dire straits.
Beware, Endrina, of traps like these.

754   Many men are united in the aim
of devouring what is yours and playing you a dirty trick.
They swear daily they will take you before the town council,
they would strip you of your feathers like a bustard.

755   But this man will defend you against all these difficulties,
he knows about lawsuits and about the law,
he helps and defends anyone who will commend themselves
                                       to him;
if he doesn't defend you, then I don't know who will.'

756 començo su escanto la vieja coytral;
     'quando el que buen siglo aya seya en este portal,
     daua sonbra a las casas e rrelusie la cal;
     mas do non mora omne la casa poco val.

757 asi estades, fiia, biuda e mançebilla,
     sola e sin conpanero commo la tortolilla;
     deso creo que estades amariella e magrilla,
     que do son tadas mugeres nunca mengua rrensilla.

758 dios bendixo la casa do el buen omne cria,
     sienpre an gasajado plaser e alegria;
     por ende tal mançebillo para uos lo querria,
     ante de muchos dias veriedes la mejoria.'

759 Renpondiole la dueña, diz: 'non me estaria bien
     casar ante del año, que a bivda non conuien,
     fasta que pase el año de los lutus que tien,
     casarse; ca el luto con esta carga vien.

760 sy yo ante casase seria enfamada,
     perderia la manda que a mi es mandada,
     del segundo marido non seria tan onrrada,
     ternie que non podria sofrir grand tenporada.'

761 'Fiia,' dixo la vieja, 'el año ya es pasado,
     tomad aqueste marido por omne e por velado;
     andemos lo, fablemos lo, teng[a]mos lo çelado;
     hado bueno que uos tienen vuestras fadas fadado.

762 ¿que prouecho uos tien vestir ese negro paño,
     andar en-vergonçada e con mucho sosaño?
     señora, dexar duelo e faset el cabo de año;
     nunca la golondrina mejor consejo ogaño.

763 xergas por mal señor, burel por mal marido
     a caualleros e a dueñas es prouecho vestido,
     mas deuen lo traer poco e faser chico rroydo:
     grand plaser e chico duelo es de todo omne querido.'

764 Respondio doña endrina: 'dexat, non osaria
     faser lo que me dezides nin lo que el querria,

756   The decrepit old crone began to weave her magic.
       'When he who now rests in paradise stood in this doorway,
       he shaded the houses, and the whitewash was bright.
       But where there is no man, the house is worth little.*

757   So, daughter, you are young and widowed,
       alone without a companion like the little turtle-dove.
       I think you have grown thin and yellow because of it.
       Where there are only women together, there is always strife.

758   God blessed the house where the good man lived.
       There was always hospitality, pleasure and happiness.
       This is why I'd like this young man for you.
       You would see an improvement in just a short time.'

759   The lady replied: 'It would not be seemly
       to marry before a year has passed, it's not appropriate
       for a widow to marry till the year of mourning is over,
       this is the usual obligation.

760   If I married before then I would be shamed,
       and would lose the inheritance owing to me.
       My second husband would not respect me so much,
       he would think I could not wait such a long time.'

761   'My dear,' said the old woman, 'the year's already past.
       Take this man as your husband.
       Let's go to him, talk to him, keep it all secret.
       Fate has dealt you some good fortune.

762   What is the advantage of dressing in black,
       and going about in shame and ridicule?
       Leave your mourning clothes behind, put an end to the year
                                                   with Mass.
       The swallow never gave better advice this year.

763   Frieze* to mourn a bad man, sackcloth for a bad husband,
       seemly clothes for gentlemen and ladies,
       yet they should wear them briefly and curtail their weeping.
       Lengthy pleasure and short mourning are what everyone
                                                        wants.'

764   Endrina answered: 'Stop, I wouldn't dare
       do what you suggest nor what he would like.

non me digas agora mas desa ledania,
non me afinques tanto luego el primero dia.

765   yo non quise fasta agora mucho buen casamiento,
de quantos me Rogaron sabes tu mas de çiento,
sy agora tu me sacas de buen entendemiento,

[Aqui faltan seis cuartetas en todos los textos.]

766   assentose el lobo, estudo atendiendo,
los carneros valyentes vinieron bien corriendo,
cogieron le al lobo en medio en el feriendo;
el cayo quebrantado, ellos fueron fuyendo.

767   a cabo de grand pieça leuantose estordido,
dixo: 'diome el diablo el ageno Roydo,
yo ove buen aguero, dios avia melo conplido,
non quise comer tosino agora soy escarnido.'

768   ssalio de aquel plado, corrio lo mas que pudo,
vyo en vnos fornachos rretoçar amenudo
cabritos con las cabras, mucho cabron cornudo.
'a la fe,' diz, 'agora se cunple el estornudo.'

769   quando vyeron al lobo fueron mal espandados,
Salieron a rresçebir le los mas adelantados.
'¡ay, Señor guardiano!' dixieron los barbados.
'byen venido seades a los vuestros criados,

770   quatro de nos queriamos yr vos a conbydar,
que nuestra santa fiesta veniesedes a onrrar,
desir nos buena missa e tomar buena yantar;
pues que dios vos aduxo, quered la oy cantar.

771   ffiestas de seys capas E de grandes clamores
fazemos byen grande, syn perros e syn pastores;
vos cantad en boz alta, rresponderan los cantores,
ofreçeremos cabritos, los mas e los mejores.'

772   Creo se los el neçio, començo de Avllar,
los cabrones e las cabras en alta boz balar;
oyeron lo los pastores aquel grand apellidar,
con palos e con mastines vinieron los a buscar.

Don't recite any more of this litany to me,
don't pressure me so much on the very first day.

765 I've not been interested in marriage up to now,
though you know hundreds have asked for my hand.
If you now start turning my head,

[There are six stanzas missing from all manuscripts at this
point.]*

766 The wolf sat down waiting.
The valiant rams came running along
and hit him in the middle, wounding him.
He fell down, injured, and they fled.

767 After a long while he got to his feet, bewildered,
and said: 'The devil made me mistake the sound,
I had a good omen, God has fulfilled it.
I didn't want to eat bacon, now I am mocked.'

768 He went from the meadow, ran as far as he could,
and saw kids frisking about in the caves
with the nanny-goats and a number of horned billy-goats:
'Truly,' he said, 'the omen of the sneeze is now fulfilled.'

769 When they saw the wolf, they were terrified,
the leaders came forward to meet him:
'Ah, Mr Guardian!' said the bearded ones,
'welcome to your humble servants.

770 Four of us want to invite you
to honour our holy feast-day,
say a good Mass for us and have a good meal.
Since God has brought you, please sing it today.

771 We are celebrating a festival of great solemnity
and make a great deal of noise, without dogs or goatherds.
You sing in a loud voice and the singers will respond.
We will offer up kids, the best we can find.'

772 The idiot believed them and started to howl,
while the billy- and nanny-goats bleated loudly.
The goatherds heard the tremendous uproar
and came to the rescue with their sticks and their mastiffs.

773   salyo mas que de passo, fizo ende rretorno,
       pastores e mastines troxieron lo en torno,
       de palos e de pedradas ouo vn mal sojorno,
       dixo: 'diome el diabro cantar missa en forno.'

774   fuese mas adelante, çerca de vn molino
       fallo vna puerca con mucho buen cochino:
       '¡ea!' diz, 'ya desta tan buen dia me vino,
       que agora se cunple el mi buen adeuino.'

775   dyxo luego el lobo a la puerca byen ansi:
       'dios vos de paz, comadre, que por vos vine yo aqui;
       vos e vuestros fijuelos ¿que fazedes por ay?
       mandad vos E fare yo, despues governad a mi.'

776   la puerca, que se estaua so los sauses loçanos,
       fablo contra el lobo, dixo dechos non vanos.
       diz: 'señor abbad conpadre, con esas santas manos
       bautisat a mis fijuelos, por que mueran xristianos.

777   despues que vos ayas fecho este sacrifiçio,
       ofreçer vos los he yo en graçias e en seruiçio,
       E vos faredes por ellos vn salto syn bolliçio,
       conbredes e folgaredes a la sonbra, al vyçio.'

778   abaxose el lobo ally so aquel sabse
       por tomar el cochino que so la puerca yaze;
       diole la puerca del rrosto, echole en el cabçe;
       en la canal del molino entro, que mal le plaçe.

779   Toxo lo enderedor a mal andar el rrodesno,
       salyo mal quebrantado, paresçia pecadesno;
       bueno le fuera al lobo pagarse con torresno,
       non oviera tantos males nin perdiera su presno.

780   Omne cuerdo non quiera el ofiçio danoso;
       non deseche la cosa de que esta deseoso;
       de lo quel pertenesçe non sea des-deñoso;
       con lo quel dios diere paselo bien fermoso.

781   algunos en sus cassas passan con dos sardinas,
       en agenas posadas demandan gollorias,

773   The wolf ran off as fast as he could, but he came back,
       as the goatherds and mastiffs had him surrounded.
       He had a terrible time with their sticks and stones
       and cried: 'The devil is making me sing this Mass in Hell.'

774   He went on further and came near a mill,
       where he found a sow with lots of piglets.
       'Ha!' he said, 'now things are improving,
       and my good augury is coming true.'

775   Then the wolf spoke to the sow, saying:
       'May God give you peace, old lady, as I have come here for
                                                           you.
       You and your children, what are you doing here?
       Give me my orders and I will obey, then later you can feed
                                                           me.'

776   The sow, who was under the leafy willows,
       spoke out to the wolf in no mean terms:
       'Mr Abbot, my friend, with these holy hands
       baptize my sons, so that they might die as Christians.

777   When you have made this baptismal sacrifice,
       I must offer them to you in thanks and service,
       and you shall take them as your prey without a fight,
       eat and enjoy them in the shade, at your ease.'

778   The wolf went down beneath the willows
       to take the piglet lying under the sow.
       The sow thrust at him with her snout and threw him in the
                                                           stream,
       and he went into the mill-race, much to his displeasure.

779   The whirling water turned him round and round
       and he came out badly battered, he looked like a devil;
       the wolf would have done better to make do with bacon,
       he would not have suffered such ills nor lost his honour.

780   A wise man does not want a harmful job,
       he does not cast aside the thing he desires,
       nor disdain what belongs to him.
       He should be happy with what God gives him.

781   Some make do with a couple of sardines at home,
       and in other houses demand delicacies to eat;

des-echan el carnero, piden las adefinas,
desian que non conbrian tozino sin gallynas.

[Entre las cuartetas 781 y 782 faltan dos folios en S,
equivalentes a treinta y dos cuartetas. Ninguno de los
manuscritos conserva este texto.]

782   fijo el mejor cobro de quantos vos avedes,
      es oluidar la cosa que aver non podedes;
      lo que non puede ser nunca lo porfiedes,
      lo que fazer se puede por ello trabajedes.'

783   '¡ay de mi! ¡con que cobro tan malo me venistes!
      ¡que nuevas atan malas, tan tristes me troxistes!
      ¡ay vieja mata amigos, para que melo dixistes!
      tanto byen non me faredes quanto mal me fesistes.

784   ¡ay, viejas pytofleras, mal apresas seades!
      el mundo rrevoluiendo a todos engañades
      mityendo aponiendo, desiendo vanidades,
      a los nesçios fazedes las mentyras verdades.

785   ¡ay! que todos mis mienbros comiençan a tremer,
      mi fuerça e mi seso e todo mi saber,
      mi salud e mi vyda e todo mi entender,
      por esperança vana todo se va a perder.

786   ¡ay! coraçon quexoso, cosa des aguisada,
      ¿por que matas el cuerpo do tyenes tu morada?
      ¿por que amas la dueña que non te preçia nada?
      coraçon, por tu culpa, byviras culpa penada.

787   Coraçon que quisiste Ser preso E tomado
      de dueña que te tyene por de mas oluidado,
      posiste te en presion e sospiros e cuydado,
      penaras ¡ay! coraçon tan oluidado, penado.

788   ¡ay, ojos, los mis ojos! ¿por que vos fustes poner
      en dueña que non vos quire nin catar, nin ver?
      ojos, por vuestra vista vos quesistes perder,
      penaredes, mis ojos, penar e amortesçer.

789   ¡Ay, lengua syn ventura! ¿por que queredes desir?
      ¿por que quieres fablar? ¿por que quieres departyr

they refuse mutton and ask for rich stew,
they say they will not eat bacon without chicken.

[There are thirty-two stanzas missing from all manuscripts
at this point.]

782   My son, the best remedy you can take
is to forget the thing you cannot have.
Do not persist in seeking what cannot be –
work for what can be achieved.'

783   'Ah, no! What an awful remedy you bring!
What bad news, what sad tidings you bear!
You old killer of friends, why did you tell me!
You cannot do the same amount of good as the harm you
                                        have done.

784   Bad luck curse you, you old good-for-nothing!
With the world in disarray, you trick everyone,
lying, accusing, speaking vain things,
making lies appear like truths to fools.

785   Oh! all my limbs begin to tremble,
my strength and my reason, all my knowledge,
my health and my life and all my understanding,
everything is lost in the vainest of hopes.

786   Oh! my troubled heart, senseless thing,
why kill the body in which you reside?
Why love a lady who does not care two pins for you?
My heart, your life of pain is all your fault.

787   My heart who longed to be the prisoner, taken by
a lady who at most has forsaken you,
you are now in prison, sighing and careworn,
and you will sorrow, oh, forgotten, anguished heart.

788   Oh eyes, my eyes! Why did you look
at a woman who does not wish to see you?
Eyes, you are lost because of what you saw,
sorrow, eyes of mine, sorrow, and grow dim.

789   Oh luckless tongue! Why did you speak,
why talk, why long for conversation

con dueña que te non quiere nin escuchar nin oyr?
¡ay, cuerpo tan penado, commo te vas a moryr!

790 Mugeres aleuosas, de coraçon traydor,
que non avedes miedo, mesura nin pauor,
de mudar do queredes el vuestro falso amor,
¡ay! muertas vos veades de tal Rauia e dolor.

791 Pues que la mi Señora con otro fuer casada,
la vida deste mundo yo non la preçio nada,
mi vida e mi muerte, esta es señalada;
pues que aver non la puedo mi muerte es llegada.'

792 Diz: 'loco, ¿que avedes que tanto vos quexades?
por ese quexo vano nada non ganades,
tenprad con el buen seso el pesar que aydes,
alynpiat vuestras lagrimas, pensad que fagades.

793 grandes artes de muestra el mucho menester,
pensado los peligros podedes estorçer,
quiça el grand trabajo puede vos acorrer,
dios e el vso grande fazen los fados boluer.'

794 yo le dixe: '¿qual arte, qual trabajo, qual sentido
Sanara golpe tan grand, de tal dolor venido?
pues a la mi señora cras le dan marido,
toda la mi esperanca pereçe e yo so perdido.

795 ffasta que su marido pueble el çementerio,
non casaria con-migo, ca seria adulterio;
en nada es tornado todo el mi laçerio,
veo el daño grande E de mas el haçerio.'

796 dixo la buena vieja: 'en ora muy chiquilla
sana dolor muy grand e sale grand postilla,
despues de las muchas luuias viene buen orilla,
en pos de los grandes nublos grand sol e sonbrilla.

797 vyene salud e vyda despues de grand dolençia,
vienen muchos plaseres despues de la tristençia.
conortad vos, amigo, e tened buena creençia,
cerca son vuestros gozos de la vuestra querençia.

798 Doña endrina es vuestra e fara mi mandado,
non quiere ella casar se con otro ome nado,

with a woman who does not wish to listen, not hear?
Oh! anguished body, what a death you'll have!

790   Treacherous women, with betraying hearts,
you have no fear, or moderation, no horror,
of exchanging your false love as you wish –
Oh, die, then, of rage and pain!

791   Once my lady is married to another,
I shall not value the life of this world,
my life and death is mapped out,
and since I cannot have her, death has come.'

792   She said: 'Fool, what are you making such a fuss for?
Nothing will be gained by this vain complaint.
Temper your sorrow with good sense,
dry your tears, think what you are going to do.

793   Great need teaches great cunning.
If you think, you can avoid the dangers.
Perhaps hard work will help you;
God and great persistence can change the course of fate.'

794   I said to her: 'What skill, what work, what sense
can cure so great a blow, such pain?
If my lady is to be given tomorrow in marriage,
all my hope has perished and I am lost.

795   Until her husband lies in the cemetery,
she cannot join with me, it would be adultery.
All my torment is turned to nothing.
I see the great harm and the shame to follow.'

796   The good old woman replied: 'In a short time
great pain is healed and a scab is formed.
Good weather follows heavy rain,
hot sun and deep shade come after the largest clouds.

797   Life and health come after great suffering,
and many pleasures follow great sadness.
Be comforted, my friend, have good faith,
great joy in your love lies close by.

798   Endrina is yours and will do as I say,
she doesn't want to marry another living man,

todo el su desseo en vos esta fyrmado,
sy mucho la amades mas vos tyene amado.'

799   'Señora madre vieja, ¿que me desides agora?
fasedes commo madre quando el moçuelo llora,
que le dise falagos por que calle esa ora,
por eso me desides que es mia mi señora.

800   ansy fazedes, madre, vos a mi por ventura,
por que pierda tristesa, dolor e amargura,
por que tome conorte e por que aya folgura;
¿desides me joguetes o fablades me en cordura?'

801   Estonçe dixo la vieja: 'ansy al amador
commo al aue que sale de manos del astor:
en todo logar tyene que esta el caçador
que la quiere leuar; syenpre tyene temor.

802   Creed que verdat digo, e ansy lo fallaredes;
sy verdat le dixistes e amor le avedes,
ella verdat me dixo, quiere lo que vos queredes;
perdet esa tristesa, que vos lo prouaredes.

803   la fyn muchas de vezes non puede rrecudyr
con el comienco suyo nin se puede seguir.
el curso de los fados non puede omne desir,
solo dios e non otro sabe que es por venir.

804   Estorua grandes fechos pequeña ocasyon,
desperar el omne es perder coraçon,
el grand trabajo cunple quantos deseos son,
muchas veses allega rriquesas a monton.

805   Todo nuestro trabajo E nuestra esperança
esta en aventura, esta en la balança,
por buen comienço espera omne la buena andança;
a veses viene la cosa pero faga tardança.'

806   'Madre, ¿vos non podedes conosçer o asmar
sy me ama la dueña o sy me querra amar?
que quien amores tyene non los puede çelar,
en gestos o en sospiros o en color o en fablar.'

807   'Amigo,' diz la vieja, 'en dueña lo veo
que vos quiere e vos ama e tyene de vos desseo;

all her longing lies in you.
If you love her a lot, she loves you more.'

799   'My dear old lady, what are you saying now?
You are playing the mother when her baby cries,
telling him sweet things to quieten him down,
that's why you say my lady belongs to me.

800   Are you perhaps doing the same to me
so that I am not sad, sorrowing and bitter,
to give me comfort and pleasure?
Are you telling me fibs or speaking in earnest?'

801   'The same thing happens to a lover,' she said,
'as happens to the bird who flies from the claws of a
goshawk – it thinks the hunter is everywhere,
always about to seize it, and it is always afraid.

802   Believe what I say, and you will see it is so.
If you are telling the truth and really love her,
she told me the truth too, and really wants the same as you.
Stop feeling sad, as you will find out the truth for yourself.

803   Often the end does not correspond
with its beginnings, nor can it be guessed.
Man does not know the course of fate.
Only God and none other knows what is to come.

804   A small accident can get in the way of great things,
but a man loses his heart if he despairs.
Hard work fulfils all desires
and often wealth piles up in heaps.

805   All our work and our hope
is at risk and in the balance.
A man hopes for good progress from a good start,
and sometimes the end is achieved, though late.'

806   'Mother, can you know or guess
whether the lady loves, or wants to love me?
If someone is in love, they cannot hide it,
in gestures and sighs, their colour, what they say.'

807   'My friend,' said the old crone, 'I see that
the lady loves you and desires you.

quando de vos le fablo e a ella oteo,
todo se le demuda el color e el desseo.

808   yo a las de vegadas mucho canssada callo,
ella me diz que fable e non quiera dexallo,
fago que me non acuerdo, ella va começallo,
oye me dulçe mente, muchas señales fallo.

809   En-el mi cuello echa los sus blaços entranbos,
ansy vna grand pieça en vno nos estamos,
sienpre de vos desimos, en al nunca fablamos,
quando alguno vyene otra rrazon mudamos.

810   los labrios de la boca tyenbranle vn poquillo,
el color se le muda bermejo e amarillo,
el coraçon le salta ansy amenudillo,
aprieta me mis dedos en sus manos quedillo.

811   Cada que vuestro nonbre yo le esto desiendo
oteame e sospira e esta comediendo,
avyua mas el ojo e esta toda bulliendo;
paresçe que con-vusco non se estaria dormiendo.

812   En otras cosas muchas entyendo esta trama,
ella non me lo niega, ante diz que vos ama;
sy por vos non menguare abaxar se ha la rrama,
E verna doña endrina sy la vieja la llama.'

813   'Señora madre vieja, la mi plasenteria,
por vos mi esperança syente ya mejoria,
por la vuestra ayuda creçe mi alegria,
non canssedes vos madre, seguilda cada dia.

814   tyra muchos prouechos a vezes la pereza,
a muchos aprouecha vn ardit sotilesa;
conplid vuestro trabajo e acabad la noblesa,
perder la por tardanca seria grand avolesa.'

815   'Amigo, Segund creo, por mi avredes conorte,
por mi verna la dueña andar al estricote,
mas yo de vos non tengo synon este pellote;
sy buen manjar queredes pagad bien el escote.

816   a veses non façemos todo lo que desimos,
E quanto prometemos, quisa, non lo conplimos,

When I talk of you and look at her,
her colour and general attitude changes.

808 Sometimes I get tired and stop talking
and she asks me to carry on and not to stop.
I pretend I can't really remember what I said, but she starts
it off again. She listens lovingly. There are other signs too.

809 She puts both arms around my neck
and we may stay like that for a while,
talking constantly of you, never anything else.
If someone comes, then we change the subject.

810 Her lips tremble slightly,
her colour goes from red to pale,
her heart beats fast, it leaps,
she squeezes my fingers with her hands, very gently.

811 Each time I say your name
she looks at me and sighs and considers,
her eyes sparkle and she gets restless.
I don't think she would spend much time asleep with you.

812 I understand what's happening in other ways too.
She makes no denials, but rather says she loves you.
If you don't falter, the branch will bend,*
and Endrina will come, if the old lady calls her.'

813 'Dear old mother, my great pleasure,
because of you there is an element of hope,
my happiness grows through your help.
Don't tire, old lady, pursue her daily.

814 Sometimes great profit is lost through laziness,
daring subtlety benefits many.
Finish your work, end your task,
to lose her through delay would be a great calamity.'

815 'My friend, I believe I will bring you comfort,
the lady will let herself be led by me.
But so far I've only had this cloak from you.
If you want a good meal, you must pay the bill.

816 At times we don't do all we say we will,
and what we promise, perhaps we don't fulfil.

al mandar somos largos E al dar escasos primos;
por vanas promisiones trabajamos e seruimos.'

817   'Madre, vos non temades que en mentyra vos ande,
ca engañar al poble es pecado muy grande,
yo non vos engañaria, nin dios nunca lo mande;
sy vos yo engañare, el a mi lo demande.

818   En lo que nos fablamos fyusa deuer avemos,
en la firme palabla es la fe que tenemos;
sy en algo menguamos do lo que prometemos,
es verguença e mengua, sy conplyr lo podemos.'

819   'Eso,' dixo la vieja, 'byen se dize fermoso;
mas el poble coytado syenpre esta temeroso
que sera soberuiado del Rico poderoso;
por chica rrason pierde el poble e el coytoso.

820   El derecho del poble pierde se muy ayna;
al poble e al menguado e a la poble mesquina
el rrico los quebranta, su soberuia los enclina,
non son mas preçiados que la seca sardina.

821   En toda parte anda poca fe e grand fallya
en-cubre se en cabo con mucha arteria,
non ha el aventura contra el fado valya,
a las vezes espanta la mar e faze buen orilla.

822   lo que me prometistes pongo lo en aventura,
lo que yo vos promety, tomad E aved folgura.
quiero me yr a la dueña, rrogar le he por mesura
que venga a mi posada a vos fablar segura.

823   sy por aventura yo solos vos podies juntar
Ruego vos que seades omne do fuer lugar;
el su coraçon della non sabe al amar
dar vos ha en chica ora lo que quereder far.'

824   fuese a casa de la dueña, dixo: '¿quien mora aqui?'
Respondiole la madre: '¿quien es que llama y?'
'Señora doña Rama, yo que por mi mal vos vy,
que las mis fadas negras non se parten de mi.'

825   dixo le doña Rama: '¿como venides, amiga?'
'¿commo vengo, señora? non se como melo diga,

We are good at making promises and bad at giving.
We old women work and serve for vain promises.'

817   'Mother, do not fear that I am lying to you,
for deceiving the poor is a great sin.
I would never deceive you, nor would God will it;
if I did, he would bring a suit against me.

818   We must have confidence in the things we say,
in the steadfast word lies the faith we hold.
If we fall short of something we promise,
it is a disgrace and short-coming, if we are able to fulfil it.'

819   'That,' said the old lady, 'sounds very pretty,
but the common people always fear
that they will be crushed by the rich and powerful.
The poor and unfortunate lose for no reason at all.

820   The poor person's rights are easily lost.
The rich man crushes the poor and unfortunate,
and the wretched pauper woman, they bow down at his
pride,
they are no more respected than a dried sardine.

821   Lack of faith and falsity stalk everywhere,
it ultimately conceals itself with great cunning.
Hazard cannot compete with Fate.
At times the sea threatens when the weather is good.

822   What you promised me, I am taking a risk with,
what I promised you, take and enjoy.
I must go to the lady and ask her as a favour
if she will come to my house to talk to you in safety.

823   If by chance I can bring you together alone,
I beg you to be a man when the opportunity presents itself.
Her heart does not know how to love incompletely,
soon you will have what you desire.'

824   She went to the lady's house and said: 'Who lives here?'
The mother replied: 'Who is calling?'
'It's me, Mrs Branch' (what a nuisance you're there,
bad luck still pursues me).

825   Mrs Branch said: 'How are you, my dear?'
'How am I? I don't know what to say –

corrida e amarga, que me diz toda enemiga
vno non se quien es, mayor que aquella vyga.

826 Anda me todo el dia como a çierua corriendo,
commo el diablo al Rico omne ansy me anda seguiendo,
quel lyeue la sortija que traya vendiendo.
esta lleno de doblas, fascas que non lo entyendo.'

827 Desque oyo esto la Rysona vieja
dexola con la fija e fuese a la calleja.
començo la buhona a desir otra consseja,
a la rraçon primera tornole la pelleja.

828 Diz: 'ya leuase el verco a la vieja Risona,
que por ella con-vusco fablar omne non osa;
pues ¿que?, fija Señora, ¿como esta nuestra cosa?
veo vos byen loçana, byen gordilla e fermosa.'

829 Preguntol la dueña: 'pues ¿que nuevas de aquel?'
diz la vieja: '¿que nueuas? ¿que se yo que es del?
mesquino e magrillo, non ay mas carne en el
que en pollo enverniso despues de sant migel.

830 El grand fuego non puede cobrir la su llama,
nin el grande amor non puede encobrir lo que ama.
ya la vuestra manera entyende la ya mi alma,
mi coraçon con dolor sus lagrimas derrama,

831 Por que veo e conosco en vos cada vegada
que sodes de aquel omne loçana mente amada.
su color amarillo, la su faz mudada,
en todos los sus fechos vos trahe antojada.

832 E vos del non avedes nin coyta nin enbargo,
desides me non, maguer que sienpre vos encargo
con tantas de mesuras de aquel omne tan largo;
que lo traedes muerto, perdido e penado.

833 sy anda o sy queda en vos esta pensando;
los ojos façia tierra, non queda sospirando,
apretando sus manos, en su cabo fablando,
¡Raviosa vos veades! ¿doled vos fasta quando?

I am bitter and persecuted by an enemy,
a man, I don't know who he is, bigger than that beam.

826   He's after me all day, as if he's running after a hind,
he pursues me like the devil after a rich man,
he wants a ring I was selling.
He's stinking rich, so I don't understand it.'

827   When the gossiping old woman heard this,
she left Trotaconventos with her daughter and went out
                                    into the street.
Then the pedlar began to speak of other things.
She changed tack completely with her first words.

828   She said: 'To Hell with the confounded old woman,
no man dares to talk to you because of her.
Well, then, my dear, how is our matter going?
You look lovely, beautiful and plump.'

829   The lady asked: 'Well, what news of him?'
The old woman replied: 'What news? How should I know
                              what's the matter with him?
He's thin and wretched, there's less flesh on him
than a winter chicken after the feast of St Michael.

830   The strongest fire cannot hide its flame,
nor can great passion conceal its object.
My soul understands the way you are acting,
my heart weeps tears of pain,

831   because I realize each time I see you
how madly in love with you he is.
His pale complexion, his changed face,
you are before his eyes in everything he does.

832   And you neither care nor sorrow for him,
always saying "No", although I insist,
with a generous show of courtesy on his part,
that he is dying, lost and bitter over you.

833   Whether he goes or stays, he is thinking of you,
he looks at the ground and never stops sighing,
clasping his hands, talking to himself.
I hope you go crazy! Suffer then! For how long . . .?

834 El mesquino sienpre anda con aquesta tristesa,
¡par-dios! ¡mal dia el vydo la vuestra grand duresa!
de noche e de dia trabaja syn peresa,
mas non le aprouecha arte nin sotilesa.

835 de tierra mucho dura fruta non sale buena,
¿quien, sy non el mesquino, sienbra en el arena?
saca gualardon poco grand trabajo e grand pena,
anda devaneando el pez con la ballena.

836 Primero por la talla el fue de vos pagado,
despues con vuestra fabla fue mucho enamorado,
por aquestas dos cosas fue mucho engañado,
de lo que le prometistes non es cosa guardado.

837 desque con el fablastes, mas muerto lo trahedes,
pero que avn vos callades, tan bien commo el ardedes
descobrid vuestra llaga, sy non ansy morredes;
el fuego encobyerto vos mata E penaredes.

838 dezid me de todo en todo bien vuestra voluntad,
¿qual es vuestro talente? desid me la verdat;
o byen lo fagamos o byen lo dexat,
que venir aca cada dia non seria poridat.'

839 'El grand amor me mata, el su fuego parejo,
pero quanto me fuerça apremia me sobejo;
el miedo E la verguença defienden me al trebejo;
a la mi quexa grande non le fallo conssejo.'

840 'fija, perdet el miedo que se toma syn Rason;
en casar vos en vno aqui non ay trayçion;
este es su deseo, tal es su coraçon,
de cassar se con-vusco a ley e a bendiçion.

841 Entyendo su grand coyta en mas de mill maneras,
dize a mi llorando palablas muy manselleras:
"doña endrina me mata e non sus conpañeras,
ella sanar me puede e non las cantaderas."

842 Desque veo sus lagrimas e quan byen lo de-parte,
con piedat e coyta yo lloro por quel farte,
pero en mi talante alegro me en parte,
por que veo que vos ama e vos quiere syn arte.

834 The poor soul is always full of sadness,
by heaven! it was an evil day when he saw how hard you
are!
He works relentlessly night and day
but no art or subtlety can help him.

835 Fruit does not grow well in hard ground.
Who, if not the wretched, sows in the sand?
He gets little reward and a great deal of work and sorrow.
The fish goes courting with the whale.

836 First he delighted in your good figure,
and then he fell in love with the way you talk.
But he was greatly deceived by these things,
you have not kept to what you promised him.

837 As soon as you spoke to him, the nearer to death he came.
But even though you are silent, you are burning up too.
Reveal your hidden wound, or else you too will die.
Hidden fire torments and takes your life.

838 Tell me exactly what you want, tell all,
what is your wish? Tell me the truth,
either we go ahead or leave it completely,
as my daily visits will no longer be discreet.'

839 'The depth of my love is killing me, with its intense flame,
how it urges me, pursues me.
Fear and shame prohibit the game,
I can find no good advice to ease my complaint.'

840 'My dear, have no fear, which is groundless.
There is no betrayal in being united.
This is his desire, the hope of his heart,
to marry you with legal and Church blessing.

841 I understand his great anguish in many ways.
He speaks pitiable words as he cries:
"Endrina is killing me, not her companions,
she alone can cure me, not any girls who sing."

842 When I see his tears, and how well he speaks,
I cry out of loyalty and anguish to give him satisfaction.
But inside part of me is glad,
because I see that he loves you guilelessly.

843   En todo paro mientes mas de quanto coydades,
       E veo que entre amos por egual vos amades,
       con el ençendymiento morides E penades;
       pues el amor lo quiere ¿por que non vos juntades?'

844   'lo que tu me demandas yo eso cobdicio,
       sy mi madre quiese otorgar el ofiçio;
       mas que nos al queramos por vos fazer seruicio,
       tal lugar non avremos para piazer E vyçio.

845   que yo mucho faria por mi amor de fyta,
       mas guarda me mi madre, de mi nunca se quita.'
       dixo trota conventos: '¡a la vyeja pepita,
       ya la cruz la leuase conl agua bendita!

846   El amor cobdiçioso quiebla caustras E puertas,
       vençe a todas guardas e tyene las por mueras
       dexa el miedo vano e sospechas non çiertas,
       las fuertes çerraduras le paresçen abyertas.'

847   dixo doña endrina a la mi vieja paga:
       'mi coraçon te he dicho, mi desseo e mi llaga,
       pues mi voluntad vees conseja me que faga;
       por me dar tu conssejo verguença en ty non aya.'

848   'Es maldat E falsia las mugeres engañar,
       grand pecado e desonrra en las ansy dañar,
       verguença que fagades yo he de çelar,
       mis fechos e la fama esto me faz dubdar.

849   Mas el que contra mi por acusar me venga,
       tome me por palabla, a la peor se tenga,
       faga quanto podiere, en ello se atenga;
       o callara vençido o vaya se por menga.

850   venga qual se quier comigo a departir,
       todo lo peor diga que podiere desir,
       que aquel buen mançebo, dulçe amor e syn fallyr,
       El sera en nuestra ayuda que lo fara desdesir.

851   la fama non sonara que yo la guardare byen,
       el mormullo e el Roydo que lo digan non ay quien,
       syn verguença es el fecho pues tantas carreras tyen,
       marauillo me, Señora, esto por que se detyen.'

843   I think about things and notice more than you imagine,
and I see that you both love each other equally.
You are both dying of passion and sorrow.
Since love desires it, why not be united?'

844   'What you ask of me is what I desire,
if my mother will give her consent.
If we wished for anything else, to please you,
we have no place for pleasure and enjoyment.

845   I would do a lot for my love from Hita,
but my mother watches over me and never leaves me.'
Trotaconventos said: 'I hope the old girl gets the pip,
may the cross take her, along with the holy water!

846   Greedy love breaks down doors and cloisters,
it overcomes all guards and leaves them for dead,
it leaves vain fear behind, and groundless suspicions,
the strongest locks seem to be open.'

847   Endrina answered the contented old crone:
'I have spoken my heart, my desire and pain.
Since you know my wishes, tell me what I should do,
there is no shame for you in giving me your advice.'

848   'It is evil and false to deceive women,
and a great sin and dishonour to harm them so.
I must hide any shame on your part,
but my actions and reputation make me undecided.

849   Yet if anyone accuses me, let him trap me with words,
may he reproach the worst thing I have said.
He can do as he wishes, I have nothing to fear,
he must be silent or go to the devil.

850   Let anyone come to argue with me,
let him say the worst things he can think of,
since that good young man, sweet, unfailing love,
he will help us and make him retract his words.

851   There will be no rumours, I'll take care of that,
no one will murmur, there will be no gossip.
The act has no shame, as there are many ways out.
I'm amazed, my dear, at why you hold back.'

852 'ïay dios!' dixo la dueña, 'el coraçon del amador
     ïen quantas guysas se buelue con miedo e con temor!
     aca e alla lo trexna el su quexoso amor,
     E de los muchos peligros non sabe qual es el peor.

853 dos penas desacordadas canssam me noche e dia.
     lo que el amor desea, mi coraçon lo querria;
     grand temor gelo defiende que mesturada seria.
     ïqual coraçon tan seguido de tanto non cansaria!

854 Non sabe que se faga, sienpre anda descaminado.
     Ruega e rrogando creçe la llaga del enamorado;
     con el mi amor quexoso fasta aqui he porfiado;
     mi porfya el la vençe, es mas fuerte apoderado.

855 Con aquestos pesares trae me muy quebrantada,
     su porfia e su grand quexa ya me trahe cansada,
     alegro me con mi tristesa, lasa, mas enamorada;
     mas quiero moryr su muerte que beuir penada.'

856 quanto mas malas palabras omne dise e las entyende,
     tanto mas en la pelea se abyua e se ençiende;
     quantas mas dulçes palablas la dueña de amor atyende,
     atanto mas doña venus la fla e la ençiende.

857 'E pues que vos non pododes amatar la vuestra llama,
     façed byen su mandado del amor que vos ama;
     fija, la vuestra porfia a vos mata e derrama,
     los plaseres de la vyda perdedes si non se amata.

858 vos de noche e de dia lo vedes, byen vos digo,
     en el vuestro coraçon al omne vuestro amigo.
     el a vos ansy vos trahe en su coraçon con-sygo,
     acabad vuestros desseos, matad vos con enemigo.

859 Tan byen a vos commo a el este coydado vos atierra,
     vuestras fazes E vuestros ojos andan en color de tierra,
     dar vos ha muerte a entranbos la tardança e la desira,
     quien non cree los mis dichos mas lo falle e mas lo yerra.

860 Mas çierto, fija Señora, yo creo que vos cuydades,
     oluidar o escusar aquello que mas amades;
     esto vos non lo penssedes nin coydedes nin creades
     que si non la muerte sola non parte las voluntades.

852   'Oh lord!' said the lady, 'the lover's heart,
how many problems it has, caused by fear and trembling!
Sorrowing love pulls it this way and that
and it does not know which danger is the greatest.

853   Two conflicting troubles wear me down night and day.
What love wants, my heart wants too.
Great fear prohibits it, for it will be discovered.
What heart so afflicted would not grow tired?

854   It no longer knows what it's doing, it is disorientated;
it prays, yet praying worsens the wound of love.
I have been stubborn till now with my troubled love,
he will conquer my obstinacy, for he is stronger and more
                                        powerful.

855   These thoughts have really torn me apart.
Stubbornness and great sorrow have exhausted me.
I am happy in my sadness, tired, but in love.
I would rather die its death than live a life of anguish.'

856   The more evil words a man says and understands,
the more he strives and contests the fight.
The more sweet words a lady expects from love,
the more Venus inflames and arouses her.

857   'And since neither of you can put out the flames that burn,
follow the commands of Love, who cares for you.
My dear, your stubbornness destroys, it kills you.
You will lose life's pleasures, if you don't stop it.

858   Night and day, I tell you, you see
him, your friend, in your heart;
he also keeps you in his heart; put an end to your desire,
which is killing you both like an enemy.

859   These thoughts frighten him as well as you.
Both your faces, your eyes, are the colour of earth.
The delay, the uncertainty, will be the end of you both.
If you don't believe me, the deeper you'll err.

860   My dear, I think you are trying
to forget or avoid what you love the most.
Don't think of this, nor meditate on it, nor believe it,
for only death can separate two joined wills.

861   verdat es que los plaseres conortan a las de veses,
        por ende, fija Señora, yd a mi casa a veses,
        jugaremos a la pella e a otros juegos Raeses,
        jugaredes e folgaredes e dar vos he ay ¡que nueses!

862   Nunca esta mi tyenda syn fruta a las loçanas,
        muchas peras e durasnos, ¡que çidras e que mancanas!
        ¡que castanas, que piñones e que muchas avellanas!
        las que vos queredes mucho estas vos seran mas sanas.

863   desde aqui a la mi tienda non ay synon vna pasada,
        en pellote vos yredes commo por vuestra morada,
        todo es aqui vn barrio e vesindat poblada,
        poco a poco nos yremos jugando syn rreguarda.

864   yd vos tan segura mente con-migo a la mi tyenda,
        commo a vuestra casa, a tomar buena meryenda;
        nunca dios lo quiera fija que de ally nasca contyenda,
        yremos calla callando que otre non nos lo entyenda.'

865   los omnes muchas vegadas, con el grand afyncamiento,
        otorgan lo que non deuen, mudan su entendimiento,
        quando es fecho el daño viene el arrepentymiento;
        çiega es la muger seguida, non tyene seso nin tyento.

866   Muger, liebre Seguida, mucho corrida, conquista,
        pierde el entendimiento, çiega e pierde la vista;
        non vee rredes nin lasos, en los ojos tyene arista;
        andan por escarneçerla, coyda que es amada e quista.

867   otorgole doña endrina de yr con ella fablar,
        a tomar de la su fruta e a la pella jugar.
        'Señora,' dixo la vieja, 'cras avremos buen vagar,
        yo me verne para vos quando vyere que ay logar.'

868   vyno me trota conventos, alegre con el mandado.
        'amigo,' diz, '¿como estades? yd perdiendo coydado;
        el encantador malo saca la culebra del forado,
        cras verna fablar con-vusco, yo lo dexo Recabdado.

861   The truth is that pleasure comforts at times,
so, young lady, come to my house sometimes.
We will play ball and other silly games,
you can play and have fun, what nuts I can give you!

862   My shop always has plenty of fruit for beautiful girls,
lots of pears and peaches, such citrons and apples!
Wonderful chestnuts, pine kernels, no end of hazelnuts!
The ones you like the best will do you most good.

863   It's only a little way to my shop,
come dressed as you are, as if you were at home.
This is all the same district, one neighbourhood,
we will play as we go, without fear.

864   Come safely with me to my shop,
enjoy a good tea, as if you were at home.
God in heaven knows, my dear, we want no quarrels there,
we will go nice and quietly, no one will cotton on.'

865   Often, when people are in a tight spot,
they allow things they should not, their understanding
                                changes.
When the damage is done, then they repent.
The woman pursued is blind, she has no sense or restraint.

866   Women, like hares pursued, are chased and conquered.
Understanding is lost, and so is sight,
she does not see snares and nets, she has chaff in her eyes.
Men are out to mock her, while she thinks she is loved and
                                desired.

867   Endrina agreed to go and chat with her,
to try her fruit and play ball games.
'Tomorrow,' said the old woman, 'we will have an
                                opportunity;
I will come for you, when I can pick the right moment.'

868   Trotaconventos returned happily with the news.
'My friend,' she said, 'how are you? Stop your suffering.
The evil enchanter brings the snake out of its hole.
Tomorrow she will come and talk to you, I've got it all
                                arranged.

869   byen se que diz verdat vuestro prouerbyo chico,
       que el rromero fyto que sienpre saca çatico;
       Sed cras omne, non vos tengan por tenico;
       fablad, mas Recabdat quando y yo no fynco.

870   Catad non enperesedes, acordad vos de la fablilla:
       quando te dan la cablilla acorre con la soguilla.
       rrecabdat lo que queredes, non vos tenga por çestilla,
       que mas val verguença en faz que en coraçon mansilla.'

DE COMMO DOÑA ENDRINA FUE A CASA DE LA VIEJA E
EL ARÇIPRESTE ACABO LO QUE QUISO

871   Despues fue de santiago otro dia seguiente,
       a ora de medio dia, quando yanta la gente,
       vyno doña endrina con la mi vieja sabiente,
       entro con ella en su tyenda byen sosegada mente.

872   Commo la mi vejesuela me avya aperçebydo,
       non me detoue mucho, para alla fuy luego ydo,
       falle la puerta çerrada mas la vieja byen me vydo:
       '¡yuy!' diz, '¿que es aquello que faz aquel rroydo?

873   ¿Es omne o es viento? creo que es omne, non miento;
       ¡vedes, vedes como otea el pecado carboniento!
       ¿es aquel? ¿non es aquel? el me semeja, yo lo siento.
       ¡a la fe!, aquel es don melon, yo lo conosco, yo lo viento.

874   aquella es la su cara e su ojo de beserro;
       ¡catat, catat commo assecha! ¡barrunta nos commo perro!
       ally rraviaria agora que non puede tirar el fierro.
       mas quebrantaria las puertas, meneala commo çencerro.

875   Cyerto aqui quiere entrar; mas ¿por que yo non le fablo?
       don melon, ¡tyrad vos dende! ¿troxo vos y el diablo?
       ¡non queblantedes mis pueras, que del abbad de sant paulo
       las ove ganado! ¿non posistes ay vn clauo?

876   ¡yo vos abrire la puerta! ¡esperat, non la quebredes,
       E con byen e con sosiego desid si algo queredes!
       ¡luego vos yd de mi puerta, non nos alhaonedes!
       entrad mucho en buen ora, yo vere lo que faredes.'

869   I know your little proverb is true,
that the persistent pilgrim always wins his bread.
But tomorrow, be a man in all things, don't be a wimp.*
Talk, but achieve your aims when I am not there.

870   Don't grow lazy, remember the saying,
"When you see the goat, get the rope ready."
Achieve your desires, don't be a fool,
better shame on your face than a blemish in your heart.'

HOW ENDRINA WENT TO THE OLD WOMAN'S HOUSE AND THE ARCHPRIEST ACHIEVED HIS DESIRES

871   It was the day after the feast of Saint James.
At midday, when people were having lunch,
Endrina went with my astute old lady
and entered her house quite quietly.

872   As my dear old lady had forewarned me,
I didn't take my time, but went there at once.
I found the door was shut, but the old woman saw me;
'Hey!' she cried, 'what is it, making all that noise?

873   Is someone there or is it the wind? I think someone really is
there; look, look, see how the devil stares!
Is it him? Or isn't it? It looks like him, I can feel it.
Heavens! It's Lord Melon, I know him, I can sniff him out.

874   That's his face and those are his calf's eyes.
Look, see how he is watching! He senses we're here, like a
                                             dog.
He must be in a rage, since he can't draw the bolt,
but he'll break down the door, he's shaking it like a cow-bell.

875   He certainly wants to get in – why don't I speak to him?
Lord Melon, get away from there! Has the devil brought
                                             you?
Don't break down my doors! I got them from the abbot
of Saint Paul's. You didn't put as much as a nail in them!

876   I'll open the door to you, wait! don't break it!
Tell me calmly and quietly what you want.
Then go away from my door, don't bother us.
Come in and welcome – I'll see what you get up to.'

877 '¡Señora doña endrina! ¡vos la mi enamorada!
vieja, ¿por esto teniades a mi la puerta çerrada?
¡tan buen dia es oy este que falle atal çellada!
dios E mi buena ventura mela touieron guardada.'

[Falta texto, treinta y dos estrofas aproximadamente, en los
codices.]

878 'quando yo saly de casa, pues que veyades las rredes,
¿por que fyncauades con el sola, entre estas paredes?
a mi non Retebdes, fija, que vos lo meresçedes;
El mejor cobro que tenedes, vuestro mal que lo calledes.

879 menos de mal sera que esto poco çeledes,
que non que vos descobrades E ansy vos pregonedes,
casamiento que vos venga, por esto non lo perderedes;
mejor me paresçe esto que non que vos enfamedes.

880 E pues que vos desides que es el daño fecho,
defyenda vos E ayude vos a tuerto e a derecho;
fija, a daño fecho aved rruego E pecho,
¡callad! ¡guardat la fama non salga de sotecho!

881 Sy non parlase la pycaça mas que la codorniz,
non la colgarian en la plaça, nin Reyrian de lo que dis;
castigad vos, amiga, de otra tal contra ys,
que todos los omnes fazen commo don melon ortiz.'

882 doña endrina le dixo: '¡ay, viejas tan perdidas!
a las mugeres trahedes engañadas, vendidas.
ayer mill cobros me dauas, mill artes, mill saldas;
oy que so escarnida, todas me son fallydas.

883 Sy las aves lo podiesen byen saber E entender
quantos laços les paran, non las podrian prender;
quando el laso veen ya las lyeuan a vender,
mueren por el poco çeuo, non se pueden defender.

884 ssy los peçes de las aguas, quando veen al ansuelo,
ya el pescador los tiene E los trahe por el suelo;
la muger vee su daño quando ya fynca con duelo,
non la quieren los parientes, padre, madre nin avuelo.

877   'Madam, Endrina! It's you, my love!
       Old woman! Was this why you kept the door shut?
       What a lucky day, that I should find this hiding-place!
       God and good fortune have kept her for me.

       [There are about thirty-two stanzas missing from all
       manuscripts at this point, relating to Endrina's seduction.]*

878   'When I went out, since you knew the traps,
       why did you stay inside alone with him?
       Don't blame me, young lady, you deserved it.
       The best thing you can do is keep quiet about your problem.

879   It's all to the good if you conceal it.
       Don't reveal yourself and make your dishonour public.
       That way you won't lose out on any marriage to come.
       This strikes me as better than shaming yourself.

880   And since you say that the harm is done,
       let him defend you and help you, right or wrong.
       My girl, if a wrong's been done, pray and be stout-hearted,
       be silent! Keep quiet, don't let it be public knowledge.

881   If the magpie talked as little as the quail,
       he wouldn't be hung in the square as a laughing stock.
       Prepare yourself for another similar situation,
       as all men behave like Lord Melon Ortiz.'

882   Endrina said: 'Oh! such a damnable old crone!
       You deceive and sell women –
       yesterday you told me a thousand solutions, wiles, ways out,
       today, now I'm a mockery, they have all failed me.

883   If the birds knew and could understand
       how many traps lie in wait, they wouldn't fall for them.
       When they see the snare, they are already about to be sold.
       They die with just a little bait, they cannot defend
                                                     themselves.

884   Yes, when all the fish see the hook,
       the fisherman has already got them and dragged them on to
                                                              land.
       A woman sees the harm when she is left with her sorrow.
       Her family do not want her, father, mother nor grandfather.

885 El que la ha desonrrada dexala, non la mantyene,
vase perder por el mundo, pues otro cobro non tyene.
pyerde el cuerpo e el alma, a muchos esto aviene;
pues otro cobro yo non he, asy fazer me convyene.'

886 Esta en los antiguos seso e sabyençia,
es en el mucho tienpo el saber e la çiençia.
la mi vieja maestra ovo ya conçiençia
E dio en este pleito vna buena sentençia:

887 'El cuerdo graue mente non se deue quexar,
quando el quexamiento non le puede pro tornar;
lo que nunca se puede Reparar nin emendar,
deuelo cuerda mente sofrir E endurar.

888 a las grandes dolençias, a las desaventuras,
a los acaesçimientos, a los yerros de locuras,
deue buscar conssejo, melesinas e curas;
el sabydor se prueua en coytas e en presuras.

889 la yra, la discordia a los amigos mal faz,
pone sospechas malas en cuerpo do yaz;
aved entre vos anbos corcordia e paz,
el pesar E la saña tornad lo en buen solaz.

890 Pues que por mi desides que el daño venido,
por mi quiero que sea el vuestro byen avydo:
vos sed muger suya e el vuestro marido;
todo vuestro deseo es byen por mi conplido.'

891 doña endrina e don melon en vno casados son,
alegran se las conpañas en las bodas con rrazon.
Sy vyllania he dicho aya de vos perdon,
que lo felo de estoria diz panfilo e nason.

DEL CASTIGO QUEL ARÇIPRESTE DA A LAS DUEÑAS E DE
LOS NONBLES DEL ALCAYUETA

892 Dueñas aved orejas, oyd buena liçion,
entendet bien las fablas, guardat vos del varon,
guardat vos non vos contesca commo con el leon
al asno syn orejas e syn su coraçon.

893 El leon fue doliente, doliale tiesta,
quando fue Sano della, que la traya enfiesta,

885   The one who dishonours her leaves her without support;
       she is lost, out in the world, there is no other way out.
       She loses body and soul – it happens to so many.
       As I have no other help, I shall have to do this.'

886   The ancients show great knowledge and wisdom.
       Both of these lie in age itself.
       My old woman knew this
       and judged the case fairly.

887   'The wise man should not complain seriously,
       when the complaint can do him no good.
       What cannot be repaired or put right
       must be wisely suffered and endured.

888   Advice, medicine, cures should be sought
       for great pain, misfortune,
       bad experiences and foolish errors.
       The wise man proves himself in sorrow and affliction.

889   Anger and discord is not good between the people who
       harbour them, they lead to evil suspicion.
       Let there be peace and harmony between you,
       then turn trouble and rage into pleasure.

890   Since you say the harm done was my fault,
       then I shall try to put it right.
       Be his wife and he shall be your husband.
       All your wishes shall be fulfilled through me.'

891   Endrina and Lord Melon were married,
       and the wedding guests were happy.
       If I have said anything vulgar, forgive me,
       for it was taken from Ovid's story of Pamphilus.

THE ARCHPRIEST GIVES SOME ADVICE TO WOMEN AND
DESCRIBES THE DIFFERENT NAMES GIVEN TO GO-
BETWEENS

892   Ladies, listen carefully and hear some good advice,
       understand the old proverbs, beware of men.
       Be careful you are not caught by the lion
       like the ass, who lost his ears and also his heart.

893   The lion was in pain, he had a terrible headache.
       When it was better he held his head up high

todas las animalias, yn domingo, en la syesta,
vynieron antel todos a fazer buena fyesta.

894   Estaua y el burro, fesieron del joglar,
commo estaua byen gordo començo a Retoçar;
su atanbor taniendo, bien alto a Rebusnar,
al leon e a los otros querialos atronar.

895   con las sus caçurias el leon fue sanudo,
quiso abrillo todo, alcançar non lo pudo,
su atanbor taniendo fuese, mas y non estudo;
Sentiose por escarnido el leon del orejudo.

896   El leon dixo luego que merçed le faria,
mando que lo llamasen que la fiesta onrraria;
quanto el demandase tanto le otorgaria.
la gulhara juglara dixo quel llamaria.

897   ffuese la Raposilla donde el asno andava
paçiendo en vn prado, tan byen lo saludaua:
'Señor,' dixo, 'confrade, vuestro solas onrra
a todos e agora non vale vna faua.

898   Mas valya vuestra abbuelbola e vuestro buen solas,
vuestro atanbor sonante, los sonetes que fas,
que toda nuestra fiesta; al leon mucho plas
que tornedes al juego en saluo e en pas.'

899   Creo falsos falagos, el escapo peor,
tornose a la fiesta baylando el cantador.
non sabya la manera el burro de Señor,
escota juglar neçio el son del atanbor;

900   Commo el leon tenia sus monteros armados
prendieron a don burro, como eran castigados.
al leon lo troxieron, abriol por los costados,
de la su segurança son todos espantados.

901   Mando el leon al lobo con sus vñas parejas
que lo guardase todo mejor que las ovejas.
quanto el leon traspuso vna o dos callejas,
el coraçon el lobo comio e las orejas.

and the animals all came before him
one Sunday, not long after lunch, to celebrate.

894 The donkey came too, and they made him the minstrel.
He was quite plump and began to frisk about,
banging his drum and braying loudly.
He nearly deafened the lion and all the other animals.

895 The lion grew angry with this mockery of a minstrel
and wanted to tear him open, but he couldn't reach him.
He had gone, still banging his drum.
The lion felt the long-eared donkey had made a fool of him.

896 He said he would like to reward the ass,
and asked him to be called to honour the celebration.
The lion promised to grant him anything he wished,
and the minstrel vixen said she would call him.

897 Off went the little fox to where the ass was standing,
grazing in a meadow. She greeted him warmly:
'Sir,' she said, 'my friend, you honoured us all with
entertainment, and now you're gone, nothing is worth a
bean.

898 Your joyful cries and good entertainment,
your resounding drum, the sounds it makes
were worth more than the whole festival – it would greatly
please
the lion if you would come back safely and peaceably.'

899 He believed the false flattery and came off worse.
The singer went back to the festival dancing,
not knowing the ways of his lord, the lion.
The foolish minstrel paid for the sound of his drum.

900 The lion had his mounted guards at the ready
who seized Mr Donkey as they had been instructed.
They brought him to the lion, who tore open his flanks.
They were all horrified at the lion's resolve.

901 The lion ordered the wolf, with his fearsome claws
to keep watch over the ass, better than he did over sheep.
When the lion had gone a couple of streets away
the wolf ate the ass's heart and its ears.

902   quando el leon vyno por comer saborado,
        pidio al lobo el asno que le avya encomendado;
        syn coraçon E syn orejas troxolo des-figurado;
        el leon contra el lobo fue sañudo e yrado.

903   dixo al leon el lobo quel asno tal nasçiera,
        que sy el coracon E orejas touiera,
        entendiera sus mañas e sus nuevas oyera,
        mas que lo non tenia e por end veniera.

904   assy, Señoras dueñas, entended el rromançe,
        guardat vos de amor loco, non vos prenda nin alcançe,
        abrid vuestras orejas, vuestro coraçon se lançe
        en amor de dios lynpio, vuestro loco nol trançe.

905   la que por des-aventura es o fue engañada,
        guarde se que non torne al mal otra vegada,
        de coraçon E de orejas non quiera ser menguada,
        en ajena cabeça sea byen castigada.

906   En muchas engañadas castigo e seso tome,
        non quieran amor falso, loco rriso non asome;
        ya oystes que asno de muchos lobos lo comen;
        non me maldigan algunos que por esto se encone.

907   de fabla chica, dañosa, guardese muger falagoera,
        que de vn grano de agraz se faze mucha dentera,
        de vna nues chica nasçe grand arbor de grand noguera,
        e muchas espigas nasçen de vn grano de çiuera.

908   Andan por todo el pueblo della muchos desires,
        muchos despues la enfaman con escarnios E rreyres;
        dueña, por te desir esto, non te asanes nin te ayres,
        mis fablas e mis fasañas Ruego te que byen las mires.

909   Entyende byen mi estoria de la fija del endrino;
        dixela por te dar ensienpro, non por que a mi vino.
        guardate de falsa vieja, de rriso de mal vesino,
        sola con ome non te fyes, nin te llegues al espino.

902 The lion returned for a tasty feast
     and asked the wolf for the ass left in his charge.
     He brought him back disfigured, without his ears and heart,
     and the lion was filled with rage at the wolf.

903 The wolf told the lion that the donkey had been born that
                                                         way,
     and that if he had had a heart and ears
     he would have understood the lion's tricks, heard the
                                                     rumours
     about him, but he didn't, and this is why he came back.

904 So, dear ladies, try to understand the tale,
     beware of foolish love, don't be caught, be touched by it.
     You have ears to hear – our hearts are elevated
     in the pure love of God. Worldly love shall not destroy them.

905 If a woman has been or is being deceived,
     take care not to make the same mistake twice.
     Don't lose your ears and heart,
     learn through someone else's head.

906 Use the example and wisdom of many deceived ladies.
     They do not want false love nor inane laughter.
     You have already heard how the ass with many masters is
                                            eaten by wolves.
     Those annoyed by this should not malign me.

907 A loving woman should shun harmful small-talk,
     one unripe grape can set your teeth on edge.
     A huge walnut tree grows from a little nut,
     and one grain of corn produces many ears.

908 Soon rumours fly all round the town about her,
     and she is defamed by many with mockery and laughter.
     Madam, don't be angry when I say this to you,
     I beg you to listen carefully to my words and stories.

909 Try to understand fully the story of Endrina, daughter of
                                                    the sloe;
     I told it to you as an example, not because it happened to me.
     Beware of false old women, of a bad neighbour's laughter.
     Don't trust a man to be alone with you, nor get too close to
                                                     the thorn.

910 Seyenedo yo despues desto syn amor e con coydado,
vy vna apuesta dueña ser en su estrado,
mi coraçon en punto leuo me lo forçado;
de dueña que yo vyese nunca ffuy tan pagado.

911 de talla la mejor de quantas yo ver pud,
niña de pocos dias, Ryca E de virtud,
fermosa, fijadalgo e de mucha joventud,
nunca vy tal commo esta, ¡sy dios me de salud!

912 apuesta E loçana e duena de lynaje,
poco salya de casa, era como saluase;
busque trota conventos que siguiese este viaje,
que estass son comienço para el santo pasaje.

913 Sabed que non busque otro ferrand garçia,
nin lo coydo buscar para mensajeria.
nunca se omne byen falla de mala conpania;
de mensajero malo ¡guarde me santa maria!

914 aquesta mensajera fue vieja byen leal;
Cada dia llegaua, la fabla, mas non al.
en esta pleytesia puso femençia tal
que çerca de la villa puso el arraval.

915 luego en el comienço fiz aquestos cantares,
leuogelos la vieja con otros adamares:
'Señora,' diz, 'conprad me aquestos almajares.'
la dueña dixo: 'plaz me desque melos mostrares.'

916 Començo a encantalla, dixole: 'Señora fija,
catad aqui que vos trayo esta preçiosa sortija.
dam vos esta [. . .],' poco a poco la aguija.
'Sy me non mesturardes, dire vos vna pastija.'

917 diz: 'yo se quien vos querria mas cada dia ver,
que quien le diese esta villa con todo su aver.
Señora, non querades tan horaña ser,
quered salyr al mundo a que vos dios fizo nasçer.'

918 encantola de guisa que la enveleño,
diole aquestas cantigas, la çinta le çynio,

910   After this I was without love but full of sorrow.
        I saw an elegant lady sitting in her parlour.
        My heart was immediately taken by storm,
        I had never seen such a lovely woman before.

911   She had the best figure I had ever seen,
        just a girl, but wealthy and virtuous.
        Beauty, nobility and youth she was,
        may God give me good health, I'd never seen her like!

912   As she was elegant, beautiful and of noble birth,
        she hardly ever left the house, she was inaccessible.
        I looked for a go-between to take me on this journey,
        for this is how the holy voyage begins.

913   You can imagine I didn't look for someone like Ferrand
                                                    García,
        nor searched for a similar messenger.
        Bad company is not good for a man,
        may the Holy Virgin keep me from bad messengers!

914   That old woman go-between was very loyal,
        every day she got the lady to come and talk, but no more.
        She put such a lot of effort into my suit
        that it seemed as if the outskirts of the town were in the
                                                            centre.

915   At the beginning I wrote these songs,
        and the old woman took them along with other lover's gifts.
        'My lady,' she said, 'buy this fine cloth from me,'
        and she replied: 'I'd be glad to, if you show me it.'

916   She began to bewitch the girl, saying: 'My dear,
        look at this beautiful ring I have brought you.
        Give me your [hand].' Little by little she urged her,
        'If you don't spill the beans, I'll tell you a story.

917   I know who would like to see you every day,
        more than all this town and its possessions.
        Please don't be so shy,
        come out into the world you were born into, by God's grace.'

918   She bewitched her, gave her love's poison,
        she gave her those songs, put a girdle round her waist

en dando le la sortyja del ojo le guiño,
somouiola ya quanto e byen lo adeliño.

919 Commo dise la fabla que del sabyo se saca,
que çedaçuelo nueuo tres dias en astaca,
dixo me esta vyeja, por nonbre ha vrraca,
que non querria ser mas Rapaça nin vellaca.

920 yo le dixe commo en juego: 'picaça parladera,
non tomes el sendero e dexes la carrera;
syrue do avras pro, pues sabes la manera;
que non mengua cabestro a quien tyene çiuera.'

921 Non me acorde estonçe desta chica parlylla,
que juga jugando dize el omne grand mansilla.
fue sañuda la vieja tanto que a marauilla,
toda la poridat fue luego descobrilla.

922 ffue la dueña guardada quanto su madre pudo,
non la podia aver ansi tan amenudo.
ayna yerra omne que non es aperçebydo;
o piensa byen que fables, o calla, faz te mudo.

923 prouelo en vrraca, do te lo por conssejo,
que nunca mal rretrayas a furto nin en conçejo
desque tu poridat yase en tu pellejo;
que commo el verdadero non ay tan mal trebejo.

924 a la tal mensajera nunca le digas maça;
byen o mal commo gorgee, nunca le digas pycaça,
señuelo, cobertera, al-madana, coraça,
altaba, traynel, cabestro nin almohaça.

925 garavato nin tya, cordel nin cobertor,
esco-fyna, avancuerda, nin Rascador,
pala, agusadera, freno, nin corredor,
nin badil, nin tenasas, nil ansuelo pescador.

926 Canpana, tarauilla, alcahueta nin porra,
xaquima, adalid, nin guya, nin handora.
nunca le digas trotera, avn que por ti corra;
creo que si esto guardares que la vieja te acorra.

927 Aguijon, escalera, nin abejon nin losa,
traylla, nin trechon, nin rregistro, nin glosa.

and winked as she gave her the ring.
She tempted her a little, guided her thoughts.

919   As the wise man's story tells us,
the new sieve must hang on the peg for three days.
The old woman, whose name was Urraca,* said
she no longer wanted to be predatory or wicked.

920   I said as if in jest: 'Chattering magpie,
don't leave the main road for the narrow path,
work where you are needed, since you know how;
if you have grain to feed an ox, then you'll have its halter.'

921   I attached no importance to this brief conversation,
it's easy to say hurtful things when you are joking.
The old woman was incredibly annoyed,
and immediately went and revealed the secret.

922   The lady was guarded by her mother as much as possible,
and I couldn't manage to have such frequent dealings with
                                                          her.
A man who is not shrewd soon makes mistakes.
Either think before you speak or stay silent.

923   I found this out with Urraca and give you this advice,
never speak ill either in secret or in public,
keep your secrets under your own skin,
there is no worse trick than a truthful one.

924   Of all names don't call her a mace,
and never a magpie, however she warbles on,
nor bait, lid, sledgehammer, cuirass,
doorknocker, shoelace, halter, nor currycomb.

925   Nor meathook, pillowcase, rope or cover,
rasp, bowstring, [. . .] nor scratcher,
spade, whetstone bridle nor broker,
nor fire shovel, nor tongs, nor fish hook.

926   Neither bell, millclapper, bawd nor club,
leading rope, leader, guide nor street-walker,
never call her convent-trotter, although she trots for you.
I believe that if you stick to this, the old bawd will help you.

927   Spur, staircase, nor bee nor flagstone,
neither leash, nor cudgel, notebook nor gloss.

desir todos sus nonbles es a mi fuerte cosa,
nonbles e maestrias mas tyenen que Raposa.

928   Commo dise vn derecho, que coyta non ay ley,
coytando me amor mi señor E mi Rey,
dolyendo me de la dueña, mucho esto me crey;
que estaua coytada commo oveja syn grey.

929   ove con la grand coyta Rogar a la mi vieja
que quisiese perder saña de la mala consseja;
la liebre del couil sacala la comadreja,
de prieto fasen blanco boluiendole la pelleja.

930   'a la he,' diz, 'açipreste, vieja con coyta trota,
E tal fasedes vos por que non tenedes otra;
tal vieja para vos, guardadla que conorta,
que mano besa ome que la querria ver corta.

931   Nunca jamas vos contesca e lo que dixe apodo,
yo lo desdire muy byen e lo des-fare del todo,
asy como se desfase entre los pies el lodo;
yo dare a todo çima e lo trahere a rrodo.

932   Nunca digas nonbre malo nin de fealdat,
llamat me buen amor e fare yo lealtat,
Ca de buena palabra paga se la vesindat,
el buen desir non cuesta mas que la nesçedat.'

933   Por amor de la vieja e por desir Rason,
buen amor dixe al libro e a ella todo saçon;
desque bien la guarde ella me dio mucho don;
non ay pecado syn pena, nin bien syn gualardon.

934   ffizo grand maestria E sotil trauesura,
fizo se loca publica andando syn vestidura.
dixo luego la gente: 'de dios mala ventura
ha vieja de mal seso que fase tal locura.'

935   dizen por cada canton: '¡que sea mal apreso
quien nunca vieja loca creyese tal mal seso!'
de lo que ante creyan fue cada vno rrepiso;
dixe yo: 'en mano de vieja nunca dy mejor beso.'

It's hard work for me to list all her names,
she has more names and tricks than a vixen.

928   As a saying goes: 'Suffering has no rules.'
With my lord and king, Love, tormenting me,
I suffered so much because of the lady, and that's the truth,
and she was melancholy too, like a sheep without its flock.

929   I was in such great anguish that I asked my old woman
if she would cease to be angry over my unfortunate remarks.
The weasel flushes the hare out from its hiding place,
black turns to white by reversing the pelt.

930   'It's true, archpriest,' she said, 'an old woman runs for
                                financial gain,
and you're saying that because you have no other.
Keep an old woman like me, she gives comfort,
you'd kiss the hand you would cut off.

931   Don't let it happen again – all my words make good sense,
I will go back on my word and cancel everything,
as mud is crushed under our feet.
I will bring things to a conclusion and set everything in
                                  motion.

932   Never call me ugly, cruel names,
call me "good love" and I will be loyal,
for the neighbourhood values a good word,
speaking well costs no more than foolishness.'

933   Out of love for the old woman and to speak wisely,
I called both her and the book 'good love' for all time.
When I looked after her well, she gave me a great deal;
there is no sin without sorrow, no good without its reward.

934   She showed great skill and subtle mischief,
she caused a public scandal walking about naked.
The people said: 'Evil fortune strike a crazy old woman
who does such mad things.'

935   People at every corner said: 'How luckless is the person
who believes such a foolish old woman!'
But what they all thought they repented of.
I said: 'Never a better-placed kiss than on that old woman's
                                  hand.'

936   ffue a pocos de dias amatada la fama,
       a la dueña non la guardan su madre nin su ama,
       torme me a mi vieja commo a buena Rama,
       quien tal vieja touiere, guardela commo al alma.

937   ffizose corredera, de las que benden joyas,
       ya vos dixe que estas paran cauas e foyas,
       non ay tales maestras commo estas vieja troyas;
       estas dan la maçada, si as orejas oyas.

938   otrosi vos dixe que estas tales buhonas
       andan de casa en casa vendiendo muchas donas,
       non se guarda dellas, estan con las personas,
       fazen con el su vyento andar las atahonas.

939   la mi leal vrraca, ¡que dios mela mantenga!
       tovo en lo que puso, non lo fas toda menga;
       diz: 'quiero me aventurar a que quier que me venga
       E fazer que la pella en Rodar non se tenga.

940   Agora es el tyenpo, pues que ya non la guardan,
       con mi buhonera de mi non se guardam,
       quanto de vos dixieron, yo fare que lo padan,
       Ca do viejos non lydian los cuervos non gradan.'

941   ssy la ensychiso o sy le dyo atyncar,
       o sy le dyo Raynela o sy le dyo mohalinar,
       o sy le dio ponçoña o algud adamar,
       mucho ayna la sopo de su seso sacar.

942   Commo faze venir el senuelo al falcon
       asy fizo venir vrraca la dueña al Ryncon;
       ca diz vos, amigo, que las fablas verdat son,
       se que el perro viejo non ladra a tocon.

943   Commo es natural cosa el nasçer e el moryr,
       ouo por mal pecado la dueña a ffallyr,
       murio a pocos dias, non lo puedo desir;
       ¡dios perdone su alma e quiera la rresçebyr!

944   Con el triste quebranto E con el grand pesar
       yo cay en la cama e coyde peligrar;
       pasaron byen dos dias que me non pud leuantar.
       dixe yo: '¡que buen manjar, sy non por el escotar!'

936   In a few days the gossip had died down.
       The lady was no longer watched by her mother or governess.
       I turned to the old woman as to a life-saving branch.
       If you have such an old woman yourself, protect her like
                                                    your soul.

937   She passed herself off as a jewellery seller,
       I've already told you how they dig the most difficult holes.
       It's hard to find an equal for these old bawds,
       they strike a telling blow! If you have ears, listen.

938   I also told you that these old girls
       go from house to house selling gifts freely;
       no one suspects them, they mingle with people,
       and their wind blows the mill-sails round.

939   My loyal Urraca, God protect the old magpie!,
       kept to her word, which is not true of everyone.
       She said: 'I'll take on whatever comes,
       I'll keep the ball rolling.

940   Now is the time, as she's not under lock and key,
       and they pay no attention to me peddling my wares.
       I'll make them suffer for what they said about you,
       if old women don't fight, the crows aren't happy.'

941   Perhaps she bewitched her or gave her an aphrodisiac,
       or some other love potions and filters,
       or perhaps poison, maybe a love token,
       she knew how to alter her state of mind.

942   As the falcon comes to the lure,
       so the old lady gave her the bait.
       The old sayings are true, my friend,
       I know an old dog doesn't bark for nothing.

943   But it is the law of nature to be born and to die,
       and – what sadness! – the lady passed away.
       She died in just a few days – I can hardly speak!
       May God forgive her soul and take her to Him!

944   I fell into bed and pined away
       with the sad shock and great anguish.
       I couldn't get up for at least two days.
       I thought: 'What a tasty piece, if not for the cost!'

DE LA VIEJA QUE VINO A VER AL ARÇIPRESTE E DE LO
QUE LE CONTESÇIO CON ELLA

945   El mes era de março, salido el verano,
        vino me ver vna vieja, dixo me luego de mano:
        'moço malo, moço malo, mas val enfermo que sano.'
        yo traue luego della, e fablele en seso vano.

946   Con su pesar la vieja dixo me muchas veses:
        'açipreste, mas es el rroydo que las nueses.'
        dixel yo: '¡diome el diablo estas vieja Raheses!
        desque han beuido el vino, disen mal de las feses.'

947   de toda laseria E de todo este coxixo
        fiz cantares caçurros de quanto mal me dixo;
        non fuyan dello las dueñas, nin los tengo por lixo,
        Ca nunca los oyo dueña que dellos mucho non rrixo.

948   a vos dueñas Señoras por vuestra cortesia,
        de-mando vos perdon, que sabed que non querria
        aver saña de vos, Ca de pesar morria;
        conssentyd entre los ssesos vna tal bauoquia.

949   Por melo otorgar, Señoras, escreuir vos he grand saçon
        de dicho E de fecho e de todo coraçon;
        non puede ser que non yerre omne en grand Raçon,
        el oydor cortes tenga presto El perdon.

DE COMO EL ARÇIPRESTE FUE A PROUAR LA SIERRA E DE
LO QUE LE CONTESCIO CON LA SSERRANA

950   prouar todas las cosas el apostol lo manda:
        fuy a prouar la syerra e fiz loca demanda,
        luego perdi la mula, non fallaua vyanda,
        quien mas de pan de trigo busca syn de seso anda.

951   El mes era de março, dia de sant meder,
        pasado el puerto de lacayo fuy camino prender,
        de nieue e de graniso non ove do me asconder;
        quien busco lo que non pierde, lo que tiene deue perder.

952   En çima deste puerto vyme en Rebata,
        falle vna vaquerisa çerca de vna mata,

AN OLD WOMAN VISITS THE ARCHPRIEST

945   It was the month of March, and spring was coming.
An old woman came to see me and spoke straightaway:
'Bad lad, bad lad, better ill than well.'
I grabbed hold of her and spoke lightheartedly.

946   She reproached me by repeating:
'Archpriest, there's much ado about nothing.'
I replied: 'The devil gives me these despicable old women
like you. When they've finished the wine, they criticize the
                                 dregs.'

947   I wrote some rough verses about how accursed I was,
and about all this worry and sorrow.
Don't despise them or throw them away as rubbish,
for no lady ever heard them without laughing a lot.

948   Dear ladies, I asked you out of courtesy
to pardon me, and know that I did not mean
to make you angry, or I would die of grief.
Permit me this one foolish act amid more sensible things.

949   As you have granted, ladies, I will write at length
about what people say and do, with all my heart.
Sometimes men make errors in a long text,
may the polite listener forgive them freely.

HOW THE ARCHPRIEST WENT TO EXPERIENCE THE MOUNTAINS AND WHAT HAPPENED WITH THE MOUNTAIN WOMEN

950   The Apostle decrees that we should try all things.
I went to experience the mountains, which was a foolish
                                undertaking.
I lost my mule on the way and could find no food.
If you search for more than daily bread, you have no sense.

951   It was March, Saint Emeterius's Day.*
I took the road to the Locoya Pass.
I had nowhere to hide from the hail and snow;
if you seek what you haven't lost, you'll lose what you have.

952   I was in a difficult situation when I came above this mountain
pass and found a cowgirl near some bushes.

preguntele quien era, Respondiome: 'la chata,
yo so la chata Resia que a los omnes ata.

953   yo guardo el portadgo E el peaje cogo,
el que de grado me paga, non le fago enojo;
el que non quiere pagar, priado lo despojo.
pagame, synon veras commo trillan Rastrojo.'

954   Detouo me el camino commo era estrecho,
vna vereda estrecha, vaqueros la avian fecho;
desque me vy en coyta, aResido, mal trecho,
'amiga,' dixel, 'amidos faze el can baruecho.

955   dexa me passar, amiga, dar te he joyas de sierra.
sy quieres, dime quales vsan en esta tierra.
Ca segund es la fabla: quien pregunta non yerra.
E por dios da me possada, que el frio me atierra.'

956   Respondiome la chata: 'quien pide non escoge,
prometeme que quiera antes que me enoje.
non temas syn das algo que la nieue mucho moje;
conssejate que te abengas antes que te despoje.'

957   Commo dize la vieja quando beue ssu madexa:
'comadre, quien mas non puede amidos moryr se dexa',
yo, desque me vy con miedo, con frio e con quexa,
mandele pacha con broncha e con çorron de coneja.

958   Echome a su pescueço por las buenas rrespuestas,
E a mi non me peso por que me lleuo acuestas,
escuso me de passar los arroyos E las cuestas;
fyz de lo que y passo las copras de yuso puestas.

CANTICA DE SSERRANA
959   Passando vna mañana por el puerto de mal angosto
salteome vna serrana a la asomada del rrostro.
'fade maja,' dix, '¿donde andas, que buscas o que demandas,
por aqueste puerto angosto?'

I asked her who she was and she replied: 'The Mountain Girl!
I am the sturdy shepherd girl who ties men up.

953   I keep the toll and collect the money.
If you pay gladly, I will do you no harm,
but if you don't, I will strip you instantly.
Pay me, or you will see how stubble is threshed.'

954   She blocked the path, which was narrow,
a mere trail made by muleteers.
When I realized my plight, frozen to the bone and hapless,
I said: 'My friend, the dog unwillingly walks through fallow
                         fields.

955   Let me pass, dear, I will give you some fashionable jewellery.
Tell me, if you like, what people wear in these parts.
As the saying goes, "If you ask first, there are no mistakes,"
and for the Lord's sake, give me shelter, for the cold is
                         getting the better of me.'

956   The mountain girl replied: 'Beggars can't be choosers,
promise me something and stop me from getting annoyed.
If you give me something, you'll have no fear of the snow.
I advise you to agree before I strip you.'

957   As the old woman says as she moistens her needle with spittle,
'My friend, when you're quite exhausted, you can do nothing
                         but die unwillingly.'
I was so cold, frightened and worried that I promised her
a pendant and a brooch, and a rabbit-skin bag.

958   She was so pleased she threw me round her neck.
I didn't mind that she carried me on her back;
she saved me from crossing streams and hillocks.
I wrote some verses to describe what happened.

SONG ABOUT THE MOUNTAIN GIRL

959   One morning as I walked
through the Malangosto Pass,
a mountain girl assailed me
as I showed my face over the rise.
'You son of a fairy,' she said, 'Where are you going?
What are you looking for? What do you want
in this narrow pass?'

960   Dixele yo a la pregunta: 'vome fasia sotos aluos.'
        diz: 'el pecado barruntas en fablar verbos tan blauos,
        que por esta encontrada que yo tengo guardada
        non pasan los omnes sanos.'

961   Parose me en el sendero la gaha rroyn, heda.
        'a la he,' diz, 'escudero, aqui estare yo queda,
        fasta que algo me prometas; por mucho que te arremetas,
        non pasaras la vereda.'

962   Dixele yo: 'por dios vaquera non me estorues mi jornada,
        tirate de la carrera que non trax para ty nada.'
        ella diz: 'dende te torna, por somo sierra trastorna,
        que non avras aqui passada.'

963   la chata endiablada, ¡que santillan la confonda!
        arrojome la cayada e Rodeome la fonda,
        en-avento me el dardo, diz: 'para el padre verdadero
        tu me pagaras oy la rroda.'

964   ffasia nieue e gransaua. diome la chata luego,
        fascas que me amenasaua: 'pagan sinon veras juego.'
        dixel yo: 'par dios, fermosa, desir vos he vna cosa:
        mas querria estar al fuego.'

965   Dyz: 'yo leuare a cassa e mostrar te he el camino,
        fazer te he fuego e blasa, darte he del pan e del vino.

960   I answered her question:
'I am going to Sotosalvos.'
She said: 'The devil will sniff you out
for saying such bold words,
for I am the one who guards
this wild region,
and no man passes in safety.'

961   The ugly, vile, deformed creature
barred my way:
'By faith, squire,' she said,
'I will not budge an inch
until you promise me something.
You will not pass along this path
however hard you try.'

962   I replied: 'For heaven's sake, cowgirl,
don't hinder my journey.
Get out of the road and let me past,
I haven't got anything for you.'
She replied: 'Then turn back,
go back through Somosierra,
for you won't get through here.'

963   That mountain girl had the devil in her,
may Saint Julian take her!
She threw her crook at me,
twirled around her sling
and fired a stone at me:
'By the name of our Father,
you're going to pay the toll today.'

964   It was hailing and snowing at the same time,
so after a moment the mountain girl said
in a menacing voice:
'Pay up or see what I'll do to you.'
I said to her: 'Heavens above, my lovely,
let me tell you something –
I'd rather be beside a nice warm fire.'

965   She said: 'I'll take you to my house,
let me show you the way,
I'll make you a fire and hot coals,

¡alae! promed algo e tener te he por fydalgo.
¡buena mañana te vino!'

966   yo con miedo E aresido, prometil vna garnacha
E mandel para el vestido vna bronca E vn pancha.
ella diz: 'dam mas amigo, anda aca, trete con-migo,
non ayas miedo al escacha.'

967   Tomome Resio por la mano, en su pescueço puso
commo a çuron lyuiano e leuon la cuesta ayusso:
'hadre duro, non te espantes, que byen te dare que yantes,
commo es de la sierra vso.'

968   Pusso me mucho ayna en vna venta con su enhoto,
dio me foguera de ensina, mucho gaçapo de ssoto,
buenas perdises asadas, fogaças mal amassadas
de buena carne de choto.

969   de buen vino vn quartero, manteca de vacas mucha,
mucho queso assadero, leche, natas e vna trucha.
dise luego: 'hade duro, comamos deste pan duro,
despues faremos la lucha.'

970   desque fuy vn poco estando, fuyme desatyrisiendo;
commo me yua calentando, ansy me yua sonrriendo.

I'll give you bread and wine.
By thunder! promise me a present
and I'll believe you're a gentleman.
It's a lucky morning for you!'

966   I was so frightened and cold
       I promised her a robe
       and a brooch and pendant
       to go on her dress.
       She said: Of course, my friend,
       pass, please do, come along with me,
       don't be afraid of the frost.'

967   She grabbed me quickly by the hand,
       flung me round her neck
       as if I were a little shepherd's pouch
       and carried me down the hill on her shoulders.
       'Don't be alarmed, you wally,
       I'll satisfy your appetite,
       as we do up in the mountains.'

968   We quickly came
       to her comfortable hut.
       She made up a blaze of holm-oak logs,
       gave me plenty of tender young rabbit,
       good roast partridges,
       large rough loaves of bread
       and some tasty kid;

969   a pint of good wine,
       masses of cow's-milk butter,
       cheese to eat hot,
       milk, cream and even a trout.
       Then she said: 'Well, old man,
       let's eat this hard bread,
       then we'll have some rumpy-pumpy.'

970   After I'd been there a while
       I began to thaw out a bit.
       As I grew warmer
       I began to relax and smile.
       The cowgirl saw me

oteo me la pastora, diz: 'ya conpañon, agora.
creo que vo entendiendo.'

971   la vaquera trauiessa diz: 'luchemos vn Rato,
lyeua te dende apriesa, desbuelue te de aques hato.'
por la muñeca me priso, oue de faser quanto quiso;
creo que ffiz buen barato.

DE LO QUE CONTESÇIO AL ARÇIPRESTE CON LA SSERRANA

972   despues desta ventura fuy me para ssegouia,
non a conprar las joyas para la chata novia;
fuy ver vna costilla de la serpiente groya
que mato al viejo rrando, segund dise en moya.

973   estude en esa çibdat e espendi mi cabdal.
non falle polco dulce nin fuente perhenal.
desque vy que la mi bolsa que se paraua mal,
dixe: 'mi casilla e mi fogar çient sueldos val.'

974   Torne para mi casa luego al terçer dya,
mas non vine por locoya, que joyas non traya;
coyde tomar el puerto que es de la fuent fria,
erre todo el camino commo quien lo non sabia.

975   Por el pynar ayuso falle vna vaquera,
que guardaua sus vacas en aquesa rribera.
'omillome,' dixe yo, 'sserana fallaguera,
o morar me he con-vusco o mostrad me la carrera.'

976   'Ssemejas me,' diz, 'sandio, que ansy te conbidas.
non te lleges a mi, ante telo comidas,
sy non yo te fare que mi cayada midas.
sy en lleno te cojo, byen tarde la oluidas.'

977   Commo dise la fabla, del que de mal nos quita:
escarua la gallyna E falla su pepita,
proue me de llegar a la chata maldita.
diome con la cayada en la oreja fyera.

978   Deribo me la cuesta ayuso E cay estordido;
ally proue que era mal golpe el del oydo.

and said: 'Aha, my friend, now
I think I understand you.'

971   The mischievous mountain girl
said: 'How about a bit of wrestling?
Get up this minute
and get your clothes off.'
She seized me by the wrist –
I had to do as she said.
I think she got a good deal.

WHAT HAPPENED TO THE ARCHPRIEST AND THE MOUNTAIN GIRL

972   After this little adventure I went to Segovia,
but not to buy jewellery for the lewd shepherdess.
I wanted to see the rib-bone of the great red serpent
which killed old Rando, as the story goes in Moya.*

973   I arrived at that city and spent all my money.
I did not find a sweet well nor an eternal fountain.
When I realized my money was running out,
I thought: 'House and home are worth a hundred stipends.'

974   After three days I returned home,
but I didn't go through Locoya, as I had no jewellery.
I decided to take the Fuentfría Pass,
but I lost my way like a complete stranger.

975   I found a cowgirl in the lower pine slopes,
she was guarding her cows by the riverside.
'Greetings, lovely mountain lass.
You must show me my way, else I must stay with you.'

976   'You sound daft, inviting yourself like that.
Don't come too close, just think first,
or else you'll feel the measure of my crook.
If I give you a good thwack, you won't forget it for a while.'

977   Like the fable of the man who won't turn his back on danger,
'the hen rakes around and ends up with the pip'.
I tried to approach the cursed misshapen creature,
and she dealt me an almighty blow on the ear with her crook.

978   She knocked me down the slope and I fell stunned.
A blow on the ear is not much fun.

'¡confonda dios,' dixe yo, 'çigueña en el exido
que de tal guisa coje çigoñinos en nido!'

979   desque ovo en mi puesto las sus manos yradas,
        dixo la descomulgada: 'non pises las aradas,
        non te ensañes del juego, que esto a las vegadas
        cohieren se en vno las buenas dineradas.'

980   Dyz: 'entremos a la cabaña, fferruzo non lo entienda,
        meter te he por camino e avras buena merienda;
        lieua te dende, cornejo, non busques mas contyenda.'
        desque la vy pagada leuante me corrienda.

981   Tomo me por la mano e fuemos nos en vno.
        era nona passada e so estaua ayuno;
        desque en la chosa fuymos non fallamos niguno.
        dixo me que jugasemos el juego por mal de vno.

982   'Pardios,' dixe yo, 'amiga, mas querria almosar,
        que ayuno E arreçido non ome podria solasar;
        sy ante non comiese non podria byen luchar.'
        non se pago del dicho e quiso me amenasar.

983   Pensso de mi e della. dixe yo: 'agora se prueua
        que pan E vino juega, que non camisa nueua.'
        escote la meryenda e party me dalgueua.
        dixe le que me mostrase la ssenda que es nueua.

984   Rogome que fyncase con ella esa tarde,
        ca mala es de amatar el estopa de que arde.
        dixe le yo: 'esto de priessa, ¡sy dios de mal me guarde!'
        assañose contra mi, resçele e fuy couarde.

985   ssacome de la choça E llegome a dos senderos,
        anbos son byen vsados e anbos son camineros;
        ande lo mas que pud ayna los oteros,
        llegue con sol tenplano al aldea de ferreros.

986   desta burla passada ffiz vn cantar atal,
        non es mucho fermoso creo que nin comunal.
        fasta que el libro entyendas del byen non digas nin mal,
        Ca tu entenderas vno e el libro dise al.

'God confound a female stork in the fields,' I said,
'if she kicks out her nestlings like that!'

979   Once she'd got her angry hands on me,
the bumpkin said: 'Don't trample over the newly ploughed
                                     land
and don't be angry at my trick. Sometimes
it can lead to great gains.

980   Let's go to the hut, Ferruzo* won't realize.
I'll set you on the right path and give you a tasty meal.
Get up now, my old cuckoo, don't pick another fight.'
As soon as I saw she was pleased, I got up in a hurry.

981   She took my hand and we were as one.
It was past Nones, later than three, and I was hungry.
Once we were inside the hut, we found no one there.
She wanted to play the game where only one loses out.

982   'Heavens above, my dear,' I said, 'I'd rather have lunch,
I'm so frozen and hungry I couldn't relax.
I can't make love on an empty stomach.'
She didn't like what I said and looked threatening.

983   She brought out enough food for two, so I said: 'Now I'll
                                     show
you how bread and wine pay better than a new shirt.'
I paid for my meal and left her side.
I asked her to show me the route I should follow.

984   She begged me to stay with her that afternoon,
it's hard to put out hemp once it's caught fire.
I told her: 'I'm in a hurry, may God keep me from harm!'
She became enraged, I took fright and took the coward's
                                     way out.

985   She brought me out of the hut and led me towards two paths.
Both were well used and easy to walk.
I walked as fast as I could over low hills
and reached the village of Ferreros in early-morning sun.

986   I wrote a song about my escapade,
not very lavish, but I think out of the ordinary.
Don't judge it until you understand the book,
for you will think one thing and the book will say
                                     something else.

987 ssyenpre se me verna miente
     desta sserrana valyente,
     gadea de rrio frio.'

988 a la fuera desta aldea, la que aqui he nonblado,
     encontrome con gadea, vacas guarda en el prado.
     yol dixe: '¡en buena ora sea de vos cuerpo tan guisado!'
     ella me rrespuso: 'ca la carrera as errado
     E andas commo Radio.'

989 'Radio ando, sseñora, en esta grand espessura.
     a las vezes omne gana o pierde por aventura;
     mas quanto esta mañana del camino non he cura,
     pues vos yo tengo, hermana, aqui en esta verdura,
     rribera de aqueste rrio.'

990 Ryome commo rrespuso la serrana tan sañuda.
     desçendio la cuesta ayuso, commo era atrevuda,
     dixo: 'non sabes el vso comos doma la rres muda,
     quiça el pecado puso esa lengua tan aguda,
     ¡si la cayada te enbyo!'

991 Enbiome la cayada aqui tras el pastorejo,
     fixo me yr la cuesta-lada, derribome en el vallejo.
     dixo la endiablada: 'asy apilan el conejo.

MOUNTAIN-GIRL SONG

987   I shall always remember
        that lusty mountain girl,
        Gadea of Riofrío.

988   Just outside the village,
        the one I have just named,
        I came across Gadea,
        guarding cows in the meadow.
        I said to her: 'Good to meet you,
        beautiful girl!'
        She retorted: 'Hey!
        you've come the wrong way
        and you are quite lost.'

989   'I am quite lost, mountain girl,
        amid this great mass of thickets.
        Sometimes a man gains
        and loses by chance.
        But, as for this morning,
        I'm not too worried about the road,
        as I have you, Miss,
        here in this field
        beside the river.'

990   I laugh at how
        the angry girl replied.
        She came down the slope,
        for she was bold
        and said: 'Don't you know
        how a dumb beast is tamed?
        Perhaps the devil gave you
        such a sharp tongue,
        watch if I don't give you a taste of my crook!'

991   She threw the crook at me
        here, behind my ear,
        and I fell sideways down the slope
        and into the ditch.
        The devilish girl said:
        'That's how you nab a rabbit;
        I'll wallop your saddle,' she said,

sobarte,' diz, 'el aluarda sy non partes del trebejo.
¡lyeuate, vete sandio!'

992   hospedome E diome vyanda, mas escotar mela fizo.
    por que non fiz quando manda, diz: '¡rroyn, gaho, enverniso!
    ¡commo fiz loca demanda en dexar por ty el vaqueriso!
    yot mostrare, sinon ablandas, commo se pella el eriso,
    syn agua E syn rroçio.'

DE LO QUE CONTESÇIO AL ARCIPRESTE CON LA SSERRANA

993   lunes antes del alua Commençe mi camino,
    falle çerca el cornejo do tajaua vn pyno,
    vna sserrana lerda, dire vos que me avino;
    coydos cassar con-migo commo con su vesino.

994   Preguntome muchas cosas, coydos que era pastor;
    por oyr de mal rrecabdo, dexos de su lavor.
    coydos que me traya rrodando en derredor,
    oluidose la fabla del buen conssejador,

995   que dize a su amigo, queriendol conssejar:
    'non dexes lo ganado por lo que as de ganar;
    sy dexas lo que tyenes por mintroso coydar,
    non avras lo que quieres, podor te has engañar.'

996   de quanto que paso fize vn cantar serrano,
    este de yuso escripto que tyenes sala mano.
    façia tyenpo muy fuerte pero era verano,
    pase por la mañana el puerto por sosegar tenplano.

CANTICA DE SERRANA

997   do la casa del cornejo, priner dia de selmana,
    encomedio de vallejo encontre vna serrana,

'if you don't stop this game.
Get up and go away, idiot!'

992 She invited me in and gave me meat,
but I had to pay for it.
Because I wouldn't do all she asked
she said: 'Pathetic, fool, simpleton!
What a daft thing
to leave the cowherd for you!
If you don't obey me, I'll show you
how a hedgehog rolls into a ball
without water or dew.'

WHAT HAPPENED TO THE ARCHPRIEST WITH THE
MOUNTAIN GIRL

993 Before dawn on Monday I went on my way,
and near the Dogwood Inn, cutting down a pine,
I found an ignorant mountain girl – let me tell you the tale.
She wanted to marry me, as she might a local.

994 She asked me a lot of questions, she thought I was a
                                                    shepherd.
She stopped work to hear deceitful words,
she thought I was madly in love with her,
and forgot the words of the wise counsellor

995 who gave some advice to his friend:
'Don't leave what you have got for what you have yet to get.
If you leave what you have for a vain whim,
you won't get what you want and may be deceived.'

996 I wrote a romantic song about what happened;
it comes next, you have it to hand.
It was a cold day, though it was spring;
I crossed the pass in the early morning so I could rest early.

SONG OF THE MOUNTAIN GIRL

997 In the middle of the valley,
on the first day of the week,
at the place they call Dogwood Inn,
I met a mountain girl
dressed in vivid vermilion,

vestida de buen bermejo, buena çinta de lana.
dixele yo ansy: '¡dios te ssalue hermana!'

998 diz: '¿que buscas por esta tierra? ¿commo andas
descaminado?'
dixe: 'ando por esta sierra do quirria cassar de grado.'
ella dixo: 'non lo yerra el que aqui es cassado,
busca e fallaras de grado.

999 Mas, pariente, tu te cata sy sabes de sierra algo.'
yol dixe: 'bien se guardar vacas, yegua en cerro caualgo.
se el lobo commo se mata; quando yo en pos el salgo,
antes lo alcanço quel galgo.

1000 sse muy bien tornear vacas E domar brauo nouillo.
Se maçar e faser natas E faser el odresillo;
bien se guytar las abarcas e taner el caramillo,
E caualgar blauo potrillo.

1001 sse faser el altybaxo E sotar a qual quier muedo,
non fallo alto nin baxo que me vença Segund cuedo;
quando a la lucha me abaxo, al que vna vez trauar puedo,
derribol si me denuedo.'

1002 Diz: 'aqui avras casamiento qual tu demandudieres.
Casar me he de buen talento contigo si algo dieres,
faras buen entendimiento.' dixel yo: 'pide lo que quisieres,
E dar te he lo que pidieres.'

1003 diz: 'dame vn prendero que sea de bermejo pano,
e dame vn bel pandero E seys anillos de estaño,

wearing a stout wool belt.
I greeted her: 'May the Lord save you, love.'

998 'What are you seeking in these parts?
How come you've lost your way?'
I said: 'I'm walking through the mountains,
and would gladly marry here.'
She replied: 'No one takes the wrong path
if he marries here.
Search and you will find what you want.

999 But, lad, think carefully
if you know anything at all about the mountains.'
I said to her: 'I'm a good cowherd,
and can ride a mare bareback.
I know how to kill a wolf.
When I go out hunting
I get to him faster than a greyhound.

1000 I'm an expert at driving cows
and can tame a fierce young bull.
I know how to churn milk and make cream,
and how to make a goatskin churning bag.
I can make a pair of twine sandals,
play the shepherd's pipes,
and ride a lively colt.

1001 I can do the "up and down" dance
or dance to any tune;
no man, tall or short, defeats me.
When I prepare to fight,
if I get him in a good hold
I can knock him over when I'm riled.'

1002 She spoke: 'You could marry anyone
you wished in these parts.
I will gladly marry you.
If you will give me some gifts,
you'd get a good deal.'
I replied: 'Ask for anything you like,
and I shall give it to you.'

1003 So she replied: 'Give me a hair clasp
of vermilion ribbon,

vn çamaron disantero e garnacho para entre el año,
E non fables en engaño.

1004　Dan çarçillos de heuilla de laton byen Relusiente,
E da me toca amarilla byen listada en la fruente,
çapatas fasta rrodilla e dira toda la gente:
bien caso menga lloriente.'

1005　yol dixe: 'dar te he esas cosas e avn mas si mas comides,
byen loçanas E fermosas; a tus parientes conbydes,
luego fagamos las bodas e esto non lo oluides,
que ya vo por lo que pides.'

DE LO QUE CONTESÇIO AL ARÇIPRESTE CON LA
SSERRANA E DE LAS FIGURAS DELLA
1006　Syenpre ha la mala manera la sierra E la altura;
sy nieua o si yela, nunca da calentura.
byen ençima del puerto fasia orrilla dura,
viento con grand elada, Rosio con grand friura.

1007　Commo omne non siente tanto frio si corre,
corri la cuesta ayuso, ca dis: 'quien da a la torre
antes dize la piedra que sale el al-horre.'
yo dixe: 'so perdido, sy dios non me acorre.'

1008　Nunca desque nasçi pase tan grand peligro
de frio; al pie del puerto falle me con vestiglo,
la mas grande fantasma que vy en este siglo.
yeguarisa, trifuda, talla de mal çeñiglo.

1009　Con la coyta del frio e de aquella grand elada,
rroguel que me quisiese ese dia dar posada.
dixo me quel plasia sil fuese bien pagada.
touelo a dios en merçed e leuome a la tablada.

and give me a fine tambourine,
six rings of tin,
a sheepskin jacket for best,
and a dress for every day.
And don't you dare deceive me.

1004   Give me earrings and a brass clasp
that gleams and shines,
and a yellow bonnet
with stripes at the front,
and some knee-high boots.
Then people will say:
"Menga Lloriente has married well!" '

1005   I told her: 'I will give you all of these
and more besides, if you can think of more
beautiful, fine things.
Invite your relatives,
let's have a wedding right away.
Don't forget anything,
as I'm going to get what you asked.'

WHAT HAPPENED WHEN THE ARCHPRIEST MET THE
MOUNTAIN GIRL AND WHAT SHE LOOKED LIKE

1006   The sierra and mountain heights have an evil climate,
it either snows or freezes and is never warm.
Above the pass the weather was foul,
high winds and ice, frost and severe cold.

1007   You feel much warmer if you run,
so I ran down the hill, remembering: 'A stone thrown
at a tower lands before the falcon flees.'
I thought: 'I'm lost, if God doesn't come to my aid.'

1008   I have never been so terrified of the cold
since the day I was born. Then at the foot of the pass
I met a monster, the worst apparition I'd ever seen,
the most muscular great mare, filthy and scruffy to look at.

1009   But I was so cold and the frost so intense
that I asked her if she could give me shelter.
She said she would gladly if I paid her well.
I thanked God for this and she took me to the Tablada Pass.

1010 ssus mienbros e su talla non son para callar,
ca byen creed que era vna grand yegua cavallar;
quien con ella luchase non se podria bien fallar;
sy ella non quisiese, non la podria aballar.

1011 Enl apocalipsi Sant Johan evangelista
no vido tal figura nin de tan mala vista.
a grand hato daria lucha e grand con-quista;
non se de qual diablo es tal fantasma quista.

1012 Avia la cabeça mucho grand syn guisa,
cabellos muy negros, mas que corneja lysa,
ojos fondos, bermejos, poco e mal deuisa.
mayor es que de yegua la patada do pisa.

1013 las orejas mayores que de añal burrico,
el su pescueço negro, ancho, velloso, chico,
las narizes muy gordas, luengas, de çarapico,
beueria en pocos dias cavdal de buhon Rico.

1014 Su boca de alana E los rrostros muy gordos,
dyentes anchos E luengos, asnudos e moxmordos,
las sobreçejas anchas e mas negras que tordos;
los que quieren casar se, aqui non sean sordos.

1015 Mayores que las mias tyene sus prietas baruas.
yo non vy en ella al, mas sy tu en ella escaruas,
creo que fallaras de las chufetas daruas;
valdria se te mas trillar en las tus paruas.

1016 Mas, en verdat, sy byen vy fasta la rrodilla,
los huesos mucho grandes, la çanca non chiquilla,
de las cabras de fuego vna grand manadilla,
sus touillos mayores que de vna añal novilla.

1017 mas ancha que mi mano tyene la su muñeca,
vellosa, pelos grandes, pero non mucho seca,
boz gorda e gangosa, a todo omne enteca,
tardia como Ronca, desdonada e hueca.

1018 El su dedo chiquillo major es que mi pulgar,
pienssa de los mayores si te podrias pagar.
sy ella algund dia te quisiese espulgar,
byen sentiria tu cabeça que son viga de lagar.

1010   Her limbs and figure were not to be ignored,
you must believe she was built like a cart-horse.
Love-making with her would be no fun;
if she didn't want to, you couldn't hold her down.

1011   In all of the Apocalypse of St John the Evangelist
there was never such a dreadful ugly creature.
She could fight and tumble a whole flock –
heaven knows if any devil could love such a sight.

1012   She had a huge head all out of proportion,
and short hair, smooth and black as a crane's,
deep-set, bright red eyes, very short-sighted,
and her footprints were bigger than a mare's.

1013   Her ears were bigger than a yearling donkey's,
her neck was broad, black, short and hairy,
her nose long and wide, like a curlew's beak.
She'd drink a whole lake full of water in just a few days.

1014   Her mouth was like a mastiff's, with a large, wide snout,
long, broad teeth, like a horse's, all higgledy-piggledy,
great, thick eyebrows, blacker than a blackbird.
Take great heed, if you are thinking of marriage.

1015   Her dark beard was thicker than mine.
This was all I could see, but if you delved deeper,
I think you would find more reason for laughter.
You'd do better tilling your own piece of ground!

1016   But if truth be told, I did see as far as her knee,
great bony frame, huge shanks,
a large crop of heat blisters on her legs,
and her ankles bigger than a two-year-old heifer's.

1017   Her wrists were broader than my hand,
with long, harsh hairs upon them, not dry,
a loud, nasal voice, unpleasant to hear,
hoarse and drawling, unrefined, hollow.

1018   Her little finger was bigger than my thumb;
imagine, if you'd like, her biggest ones –
if she ever decided to pick out your lice,
your head would feel her fingers like a wine press.

1019 Por el su garnacho tenia tetas colgadas,
      dauan le a la çinta pues que estauan dobladas,
      ca estando sensillas dar-l yen so las yjadas;
      a todo son de çitola andarian syn ser mostradas.

1020 Costillas mucho grandes en su negro costado,
      vnas tres veses contelas estando arredrado;
      digo te que non vy mas nin te sera mas contado,
      ca moço mesturero non es bueno para mandado.

1021 de quanto que me dixo, E de su mala talla,
      fize bien tres cantigas, mas non pud bien pyntalla.
      las dos son chançonetas, la otra de trotalla;
      de la que te non pagares, veyla e Rye e calla.

CANTICA DE SSERRANA
1022 Cerca la tablada,
      la sierra passada,
      falle me con aldara,
      a la madrugada.

1023 En çima del puerto
      coyde ser muerto,
      de nieue e de frio,
      e dese rroçio
      e de grand elada.

1024 a la deçida
      dy una corrida,
      falle vna sserrana
      fermosa, loçana,
      e byen colorada.

1025 dixe yo a ella:
      'omillome bella.'
      diz: 'tu que bien corres,
      aqui non te engorres,
      anda tu jornada.'

1026 yol dixe: 'frio tengo,
      e por eso vengo
      a vos, fermosura;
      quered por mesura
      oy darme posada.'

1019   Her tits hung down over her dress
       and reached to her waist, being enormously thick.
       If they'd been thinner, they'd have touched her flanks.
       They would swing to any beat without any help.

1020   Huge ribs poked out of her swarthy sides,
       I counted them at least three times – from a distance.
       I saw no more nor shall tell you more,
       a gossip does not make a good messenger.

1021   I wrote three songs about how she spoke
       and looked, but still couldn't portray her exactly.
       Two are light tunes to sing, the other a song for travellers.
       If you don't like one, listen, smile and be silent.

MOUNTAIN-GIRL SONG

1022   Near the Tablada Pass
       beyond the mountain range,
       I came across Alda
       in the early morning.

1023   Up above the pass,
       I feared that I should die
       of cold, from the snow,
       frost
       and bitter icy blast.

1024   As I dashed down
       a mountain slope
       I met a lovely
       mountain girl, lively
       and rosy-cheeked.

1025   I spoke to her, saying:
       'Greetings, my beauty.'
       She replied: 'You run very well,
       but don't hang around here,
       get on with your journey.'

1026   I answered: 'I am so cold,
       so I have come
       to you, pretty one.
       Please, out of courtesy,
       give me shelter today.'

1027 dixo me la moça:
'pariente, mi choça,
el que en ela posa
conmigo desposa,
e dan grand soldada.'

1028 yol dixe: 'de grado,
mas soy cassado
aqui en ferreros.
mas de mis dineros
darvos he, amada.'

1029 diz: 'trota conmigo.'
leuo me consigo
e dion buena lunbre,
commo es de constunbre
de sierra nevada.

1030 diome pan de çenteno,
tyznado, moreno,
e dyon vino malo,
agrillo e Ralo,
e carne salada.

1031 Dion queso de cabras:
'fidalgo,' diz, 'abras
ese blaço E toma
vn canto de soma,
que tengo guardada.'

1032 diz: 'huesped, almuerça.
e beue e esfuerça,
calyenta te e paga,
de mal nos te faga
fasta la tornada.

1033 quien dones me diere
quales yo pediere
avra bien de çena,
E lechiga buena
que nol, coste nada.'

1034 'vos que eso desides
¿por que non pedides
la cosa çertera?'

1027   The girl said to me:
       'Friend, anyone who stays
       in my hut with me
       marries me
       and pays me well.'

1028   I replied: 'Willingly,
       though I already have a wife,
       here in Ferreros.
       But I will give you money,
       sweetheart.'

1029   And then: 'Quick, come with me.'
       She took me with her
       and made a good fire
       as is the custom
       in the snowy mountains.

1030   She gave me rye bread,
       dark and blackened,
       gave me bad wine,
       bitter and thin,
       and salt meat.

1031   Then she gave me goat's cheese.
       'Sir,' she said, 'hold out your hand
       and take a piece of good bread
       I've kept aside.

1032   Eat, guest, eat,
       and drink, and take strength.
       Warm yourself, then pay me.
       No harm will come to you
       until you go back.

1033   Whoever gives me gifts,
       the ones I ask for,
       will have a good dinner
       and comfortable bed
       which will cost nothing.'

1034   'When you say this,
       why don't you ask me
       for something particular?'

Ella diz: '¡maguera!
¿e syn sera dada?

1035 pues dan vna çinta,
bermeja, byen tynta,
E buena camisa
fecha a mi guisa
con su collarada.

1036 E dan buenas sartas
de estaño e fartas,
E dame halia
de buena valya,
pelleja delgada.

1037 E dan buena toca
lystada de cota.
E dame çapatas
de cuello byen altas,
de pieça labrada.

1038 Con aquestas joyas,
quiero que lo oyas,
seras byen venido.
seras mi marido,
e yo tu velada.'

1039 'Serrana Señora,
talto algo agora
non trax por ventura,
mas fare fiadura
para la tornada.'

1040 dixo me la heda:
'do non ay moneda
non ay merchandia.
nin ay tan buen dia
nin cara pagada.

1041 Non ay mercadero
bueno sin dinero
e yo non me pago
del que non da algo,
nin le do la posada.

She replied: 'If only!
Will I get it then?

1035　Well, give me a bright
red girdle, well-dyed,
a good shirt
made the way I like,
with a yoke.

1036　And I'd like a good string
of tin beads, a lot of them,
and a good quality
jewel,
and a fine fur.

1037　Also a good bonnet
with nice stripes,
and boots, knee-high,
made all in one piece.

1038　Now understand this,
with these presents,
you will be welcome.
You will be my husband
and I your wife.'

1039　'Mistress mountain girl,
I did not bring
such wealth with me,
but I will promise
to bring these things when I return.'

1040　The ugly creature replied:
'There is no merchandise
where there is no money,
nor fine days
and happy faces.

1041　There is no good merchant
without money,
and I don't like
a man who gives me nothing,
nor do I give him shelter.

1042 Nunca de omenaje
pagan ostalaje;
por dineros faze
omne quanto plase,
cosa es prouada.'

DEL DITADO QUEL ARÇIPRESTE OFFRECIO A SANTA
MARIA DEL VADO

1043 Santiago apostol diz de todo bien conplido
e todo don muy bueno de dos bien escogido.
E yo, desque saly de todo aqueste Roydo,
torne Rogar a dios que non diese a oluido.

1044 Cerca de aquesta ssierra ay vn logar onrrado,
muy santo E muy deuoto, santa maria del vado.
fuy tener y vigilia, commo es acostunblado,
a onrra de la virgen ofreçile este ditado.

1045 ¡ay! noble Señora, madre de piedat,
luz lusiente al mundo, del çielo claridat,
mi alma E mi cuerpo ante tu magestat
ofresco con cantigas e con grand omildat.

1046 omillome Reyna, madre del Saluador,
virgen Santa e dina, oye a mi pecador.

1047 My alma E mi coyta e en tu alabança,
de ty non se muda la mi esperança;
virgen tu me ayuda e sy detardanca
rruega por mi a dios tu fijo mi Señor.

1048 Por que en grand gloria estas e con plaser,
yo en tu memoria algo quiero fazer:
la triste estoria que a jhesu yaser
fiso en presiones, en penas e en dolor.

1042 Promises do not
pay for hospitality.
A man does what he likes
when he has money.
It's a known fact.'

VERSES OFFERED BY THE ARCHPRIEST TO THE VIRGIN OF
THE FORD

1043 St James the Apostle says that perfect goodness
and all good gifts come from God our Father.
As soon as I had put such a muddle behind me
I turned to God and begged him not to forget me.

1044 Near to the mountain lies a devout, holy
and reverend place, the shrine of the Virgin of the Ford.
I went there to keep a vigil, as is the custom,
and wrote these verses in honour of the Virgin.

1045 To you, noble lady, Mother of mercy,
shining Light of the world and Light of Heaven,
I offer my body and soul before your majesty,
with these songs and great humility.

1046 I bow down before you, Queen,
Mother of the Saviour,
Virgin Holy and upright,
listen to this sinner.

1047 My soul ponders upon you,
and praises you,
my hope and trust in you
never changes.
Virgin, help me,
without delay,
pray for me to your Son, my Lord.

1048 Because you are great
in glory and joy,
I would create
something in your memory,
the sad story
in which Jesus lies
imprisoned, in anguish and suffering.

DE LA PASION DE NUESTRO SENOR JHESU XPISTO

1049 Myercoles a terçia el cuerpo de xpisto
     judea lo apreçia; esa ora fue visto
     quan poco la preçia al tu fijo quisto
     judas el quel vendio, su disçipulo traydor.

1050 Por treynta dineros fue el vendimiento
     quel Caen Señores del noble vngento,
     fueron plasenteros del pleyteamiento;
     dieron le algo al falso vendedor.

1051 a ora de maytines, dandole judas pas,
     los traydores gallynes, commo si fuese rrapas,
     aquestos mastines asy ante su fas
     trauaron del luego todos enderedor.

1052 Tu con el estando, a ora de prima,
     viste lo leuando feriendo que lastima.
     pilatos judgando escupenle en çima
     de su fas tam clara, del çielo rresplandor.

1053 a la terçera ora xpistus fue judgado,
     judgolo el atora, pueblo porfiado,
     por aquesto morra en cabtiuo dado,
     del qual nunca saldra nin avra librador.

1054 Disyendo le vaya, lieua lo a muerte,
     ssobre la su saya echaron le suerte,

THE PASSION OF OUR LORD JESUS CHRIST

1049   On Wednesday at nine in the morning,
        Christ's body
        was given a price by the Jews.
        At once it was clear
        how little valued
        was your beloved Son
        in the eyes of Judas, his traitorous disciple, who sold him.

1050   He sold him
        for thirty coins,
        owing to Judas
        for the precious unguent.
        They were well pleased
        with the transaction
        and gave the money to the deceitful vendor.

1051   At the hour of Matins
        as Judas gave him the kiss of peace,
        the villainous Jews,
        as if he were a robber,
        gathered round like mastiffs
        in His presence,
        and blocked His way all round.

1052   At the hour of Prime,
        you were with Him,
        you saw them take Him away,
        you pitied His wounds.
        Pilate was in judgement,
        as they spat in His face so bright, the radiance of Heaven.

1053   At the third hour
        Christ was judged
        by the Sanhedrin,
        obstinate people
        who remain
        in captivity because of this
        and will never be set free or liberated.

1054   They urged Him: 'Get on,'
        and took Him to His death.
        They cast lots

qual dellos la aya ¡pesar atan fuerte!
quien lo dirie dueña, qual fue destos mayor.

1055   a ora de sesta, fue puesto en la crus;
        grand coyta fue aquesta por el tu fijo dus,
        mas al mundo presta, que dende vino lus,
        claridat del çielo, por syenpre durador.

1056   a ora de nona morio, e constesçio
        que por su persona el sol escuresçio;
        dandol del escona la tierra estremeçio,
        ssangre E agua salio, del mundo fue dulçor.

1057   a la vesperada de crus fue desçendido,
        cupleta llegada, de vnguente vngido,
        de piedra tajada en sepulcro metydo,
        çenturio fue dado luego por guardador.

1058   Por aquestas llagas desta santa pasion,
        a mis coytas fagas aver consolaçion.
        tu que a dios pagas, da me tu bendiçion,
        que Sea yo tuyo por sienpre Seruidor.

over His robe
and who should have it,
such great sorrow!
Who can say, Lady,
which was worst?

1055   At the sixth hour
they nailed Him to the cross.
Such great suffering
for your gentle Son,
but He was given to the world
that light might come,
Heaven's radiance, everlasting.

1056   At the ninth hour
He died and it was told
that for Him
the sun grew dark.
When the spear pierced Him
the earth shook,
blood and water issued
from Him – the sweetness of the world.

1057   By the hour of Vespers
they took Him down from the cross.
When Compline came
He was embalmed with unguent
and laid in the sepulchre
hewn out of stone.
A centurion was given the task
of guarding Him.

1058   Through these wounds
of the Holy Passion,
bring consolation
for my suffering.
You who please God,
give me your blessing,
for I am yours,
your servant always.

DE LA PASION DE NUESTRO SEÑOR IHESU XPISTO

1059 Los que la ley de xpistus avemos de guardar
de su muerte deuemos doler nos e acordar.

1060 Cuentan los profetas lo que sse ouo a conplir;
primero jeremias como ovo de venir,
diz luego ysayas que lo avya de parir
la virgen que sabemos ssanta maria estar.

1061 Dize otra proffeçia de aquella vieja ley
que el cordero vernia e saluaria la ley;
daniel lo desia por xpistos nuestro Rey,
en dauit lo leemos, segud el mi coydar.

1062 Commo profetas disen, esto ya se conplio:
vino en santa virgen E de virgen nasçio,
al que todos bendiçen por nos todos morio,
dios e omne que veemos en el santo altar.

1063 Por saluar fue venido el lynaje vmanal,
ffue de judas vendido por mi poco cabdal,
fue preso e ferido de los jodios mal,
este dios en que creemos fueron açotar.

THE PASSION OF OUR LORD JESUS CHRIST

1059   We who must keep
the Law of Christ
must remember
and mourn His death.

1060   The prophecies recount
what was to happen.
First Jeremiah
told of His coming,
then Isaiah
foretold that a Virgin
would bear Him,
whom we know to be the Virgin Mary.

1061   Another prophecy
of the ancient Law
tells that the Lamb
would come to save His flock.
Daniel foretold it,
through Christ our King,
and we read it in David's book,
if I remember right.

1062   What the prophecies foretold
is now fulfilled.
He came to a Holy Virgin
and was born of her,
He we all bless,
who died for us,
both God and man whom we see
at the Holy Altar.

1063   He came to save
mankind
and was sold by Judas
for a trifle.
He was imprisoned and wounded
greatly by the Jews.
The God in whom we believe
was scourged by them.

1064   En su faz escopieron del çielo claridat,
       espinas le pusieron de mucha crueldat,
       en la crus lo sobieron syn toda piedat,
       destas llagas tenemos dolor e grand pessar.

1065   Con clauos enclauaron las manos e pies del,
       la su set abebraron con vinagre E fiel,
       las llagas quel llagaron son mas dulçes que miel
       a los que en el avemos esperança syn par.

1066   En cruz fue puesto por nos, muerto, ferido e llagado,
       despues fue abierto de ascona su costado,
       por estas llagas çierto es el mundo saluado,
       a los que creemos el nos quiera ssaluar.

DE LA PELEA QUE OUO DON CARNAL CON LA QUARESMA

1067   acercando sse viene vn tienpo de dios ssanto,
       ffuy me para mi tierra por folgar algund quanto,
       dende a siete dias era quaresma tanto,
       puso por todo el mundo miedo e grand espanto.

1068   Estando a la mesa con do jueues lardero,
       truxo A mi dos cartas vn lygero trotero;
       desir vos he las notas, ser vos tardinero,
       ca las cartas leydas dy las al menssajero.

1069   'De mi, santa quaresma, syerua del ssaluador,
       enbiada de dios a todo pecador,
       a todos los açiprestes E clerigos con amor,
       salud en jhesu xpisto fasta la pasqua mayor.

1070   ssabed que me dixieron que ha çerca de vn año
       que anda don carnal sañudo, muy estraño,

1064 They spat in His face,
      the Light of Heaven,
      and cruelly
      pierced Him with thorns,
      then put Him on the cross
      without mercy.
      And we suffer and ache
      for these wounds.

1065 They nailed Him
      by the hands and feet,
      also quenched His thirst
      with vinegar and gall.
      The wounds they gave Him
      are sweeter than honey
      and give us boundless hope
      in the Lord.

1066 He died on the cross for us,
      wounded and injured,
      His side opened
      with a spear.
      By these wounds the world was saved
      and those of us who believe in Him
      may He wish to save.

THE BATTLE BETWEEN CARNAL AND LENT

1067 One of God's holy times approached,
      and I returned home to rest awhile.
      There were only seven days till Lent
      and everyone was fearful and worried.

1068 I was at the dining table with Mr Thursday before Lent
      when a nimble messenger brought me two letters.
      I'll tell you what they said – it could take a while.
      I gave the letters back to the messengers when I'd read them.

1069 'From Holy Lent, servant of our Saviour,
      sent by God to all sinners,
      to all archpriests and clergy who are without love,
      with greetings in Jesus Christ until Easter Day.

1070 I must tell you that for about a year now
      Carnal has stalked through my lands,

astragando mi tierra, fasiendo mucho dapño,
vertyendo mucha ssangre, de lo que mas me asaño.

1071   E por aquesta Rason, en vertud obediençia,
vos mando firme mente, so pena de setençia
que por mi e por mi ayuno e por mi penitençia
que lo des-afiedes luego con mi carta de creençia.

1072   desid le de todo en todo que, de oy siete dias,
la mi persona mesma e las con-pañas mias
yremos pelear con el e con todas sus porfias;
creo que se me non detenga en las carneçerias.

1073   Dad la al menssajero esta carta leyda,
lyeuela por la tierra, non la traya escondida,
que non diga su gente que non fue aperçebida.
dada en castro de ordiales, en burgos Resçebida.'

1074   otra carta traya abyerta e ssellada,
vna concha muy grande de la carta colgada;
aquel era el sello de la duena nonbrada.
la nota es aquesta, a carnal fue dada:

1075   'De mi doña quaresma, justiçia de la mar,
alguaçil de las almas que se han de saluar,
a ty, carnal goloso, que te non coydas fartar,
enbyo te el ayuno por mi des-afiar.

1076   Desde oy en syete dias tu e tu almohalla
que seades con migo en el canpo alla batalla,
fasta el sabado santo dar vos he lyd syn falla;
de muerto o de preso non podras escapalla.'

1077   ley amas las cartas, entendy el ditado,
vy que venia a mi vn fuerte mandado,
ca non tenia amor nin era enamorado,
a mi e a mi huesped puso nos en coydado.

1078   do tenia a don jueues por huesped a la messa,
leuantose byen alegre de lo que non me pesa,
dixo: 'yo so el alfres contra esta mala presa,
yo justare con ella que cada año me sopesa.'

1079   Dio me muy muchas graçias por el buen conbyd,
fuese e yo fiz mis cartas, dixele al viernes: 'yd

angry and extravagant, wreaking great havoc
and even spilling blood, which has incensed me.

1071 For this reason, in the name of obedience
I order you firmly upon pain of legal sentence,
for me and on behalf of Fasting and Penitence,
to challenge him now with my letter of credence.

1072 Tell him earnestly that seven days from now,
I myself and my own companies
shall fight him and his renegades –
they will not hold out against us – not even the butchers.

1073 Once read, give this letter back to the messenger,
to promulgate throughout the land, not to hide away,
so his rabble cannot say they were not warned.
Written in Castro Urdiales* and formalized in Burgos.'

1074 He bore another letter, already opened,
sealed by a large shell which hung on the outside.
This was the seal of the aforementioned lady,
and it was addressed to Carnal as follows:

1075 'From Lent, Justice of the Sea,
bailiff of souls which must be saved,
to you, greedy Carnal, never sated with eating,
I send Mr Fasting to challenge you.

1076 Seven days from now, you and your army
shall join battle with me in the field.
I shall fight with you till Easter Saturday.
You shall not escape injury and death.'

1077 I read both the letters, gleaned their intent,
and saw I had been given the sternest of mandates,
for I was neither loved nor in love.
My dinner guest and I began to worry.

1078 As Mr Thursday before Lent was also at table,
he stood up gladly, for which I wasn't sorry.
He said: 'I will be the standard-bearer against this
unfortunate.
I will joust with her, for each year Lent pesters me.'

1079 He thanked me profusely for my invitation.
He left me to write my letters. I said to Mr Friday:

a don carnal mañana e todo esto le desit,
que venga apercebido el martes a la lyd.'

1080 las cartas Resçebidas, don carnal argulloso,
mostro en sy esfuerço, pero estaua medroso;
non quise dar Respuesta, vino a mi acuçioso,
truxo muy grand mesnada, commo era poderosso.

1081 desque vino el dia del plaso señalado,
vino don carnal que ante estaua esforçado,
de gentes muy guarnidas, muy byen aconpañado;
serie don alexandre de tal rreal pagado.

1082 Pusso en la delanteras muchos buenos peones,
gallynas e perdises, conejos e capones,
anades e lauancos, e gordos anssarones;
fasian su alarde çerca de los tysones.

1083 Estos trayan lanças de peon delantero,
espetos muy conplidos de fierro e de madero.
escudauan se todos con el grand tajadero;
en la buena yantar estos venian primero.

1084 En pos los escudados estan lo ballesteros,
las anssares, çeçinas, costados de carneros,
piernas de puerco fresco, los jamones enteros;
luego en pos de aquestos estan los caualleros.

1085 las puestas de la vaca, lechones E cabritos
ally andan santando e dando grandes gritos;
luego los escuderos, muchos quesuelos friscos,
que dan de las espuelas a los vinos byen tyntos.

1086 Traya buena mesnada Rica de jnfançones,
muchos buenos faysanes, los locanos pauones;
venian muy byen guarnidos, enfiestos los pendones,
trayan armas estrañas a fuertes guarniçiones.

1087 Eran muy byen labladas, tenpladas e byen fynas,
ollas de puro cobre trayan por capellynas,
por adaragas calderas, sartenes e cosinas;
Real de tan grand preçio non tenian las sardinas.

1088 vinieron muchos gamos e el fuerte jauali:
'Señor,' diz, 'non me escusedes de aquesta lyd a mi,

'Go to Carnal tomorrow and tell him all this,
and that he must come prepared for battle this Tuesday.'

1080 When he received the letters, proud Carnal
gave a show of strength, but inside he was fearful.
He would not reply, but came eagerly
bringing a great company with him to show his power.

1081 When the day of battle arrived
Carnal came early. He looked strong
and well-protected and was accompanied by his troops.
Such an army camp would have pleased Alexander the
Great.

1082 Many foot soldiers filled the front rank,
hens and partridge, rabbits and capons,
ducks both domestic and wild, fat geese too.
All formed their battle ranks near the burning embers.

1083 They carried foot soldiers' lances before them,
fine spits of iron and wood.
They shielded themselves with the large trencher –
these always come first at any good feast.

1084 Behind the shield-bearers came the archers,
dried, smoked goose, sides of mutton,
fresh legs of pork, whole hams.
Then after these came the knights:

1085 beefsteaks and chops of sucking pig and kid
all jostling and jumping, creating a fuss.
Then came the squires, the fresh black puddings,*
spurring on the good red wines.

1086 A splendid group of noblemen came after,
fine pheasants, lusty peacocks;
they were well-protected with their tail feathers spread,
and carried lofty weapons and strong armour.

1087 This was well-made, tempered and fine.
They wore pots of pure copper for helmets,
and for shields, kettles, frying pans and saucepans.
The sardines' camp was not nearly so good.

1088 There were many buck deer and wild boars:
'Sir, pray do not leave me out of the battle,

que ya muchas vegadas lydie con don aly,
vsado so de lyd, syenpre por ende valy.'

1089   Non avia acabado desir byen su verbo,
ahe vos ado viene muy lygero el çieruo:
'omillo me,' diz, 'señor, yo el tu leal syeruo,
por te faser seruiçio ¿non fuy por ende syeruo?'

1090   vino presta e lygera al alarde la lyebre:
'Señor,' diz, 'alla dueña yo le metre la fiebre,
dalle he la sarna e diuiesos que de lydiar nol mienbre;
mas querria mi pelleja quando alguno le quiebre.'

1091   vino el cabron montes con corços e torcasas,
desiendo sus bramuras e muchas amenasas:
'Señor,' dis, 'a la duena, sy con-migo la enlasas,
non te podra enpesçer con todas sus espinaças.'

1092   vino su paso a paso el buey viejo lyndero:
'Señor,' diz, 'a herren me echa oy el llugero,
non so para afrae en carrera nin ero,
mas fago te seruiçio con la carne e cuero.'

1093   Estaua don toçino con mucha otra çeçina,
çidierbedas e lomos, fynchida la cosina,
todos aperçebidos para la lyd malyna;
la dueña fue maestra, non vino tan ayna.

1094   Commo es don carnal muy grand enperador,
E tiene por todo el mundo poder commo señor,
aves E animalias por el su grand amor
vinieron muy omildes, pero con grand temor.

1095   Estaua don carnal Rica mente assentado,
a messa mucho farta en vn Rico estrado,
delante sus juglares, commo omne onrrado;
desas muchas vyandas era byen abastado.

1096   Estaua delante del su alferes homil,
el ynojo fyncado, en la mano el barril,
tañia amenudo con el el añafyl;
parlaua mucho el vino, de todos alguaçil.

for I have fought many times with Mr Moor,
I am used to battle and have fought well in the past.'

1089   He had hardly finished speaking
when the deer came up nimbly:
'I pay homage, Sir,' he said, 'I am your loyal servant.
It is my purpose to do you service.'

1090   The hare came fast and fleet to muster:
'Sir,' she said, 'I'll give the old lady a fever,
I'll give her mange and boils, she'll forget the fight,
she'll want to be in my skin when she is wounded.'

1091   The mountain goat came with the fallow deer and ring-
doves,
roaring and snorting menacingly:
'Sir,' he said, 'if we both engage the old coot
she won't reel you in with all her fish spines and spinach.'

1092   Slowly the fine old ox arrived:
'Sir,' he said, 'either send me to pasture or give me to the
ploughman,
I cannot fight on the road or in the pastures,
I'd serve you better as meat and leather.'

1093   Mr Bacon was there with many other smoked meats,
pork chops and loin; the cooking pot was full,
all in readiness for the battle against the Marines.
The lady was skilful – she came later.

1094   Carnal is a wealthy emperor
and has power in the world as lord.
Fowls and animals came in humility
and trembling, in their awe of him.

1095   Carnal was luxuriously seated.
His table was abundant, in an elegant room.
He had a good supply of all these meats
while minstrels played before him as before an honoured
man.

1096   His humble adjutant was before him,
on his knees, his hand ready by the wine barrel.
The goblet sounded often on the wood of the barrel,
the wine spoke at length, as it was everyone's beadle.

1097 Desque vino la noche mucho despues de çena,
que tenia cada vno ya la talega llena,
para entrar en la fasienda con la dueña serena
adormieron se todos, despues de la ora buena.

1098 Essa noche los gallos con grand miedo estouieron,
velaron con espanto nin punto non dormieron;
non avia marauilla que sus mugeres perdieron,
por ende se alboroçaron del Roydo que oyeron.

1099 fasa la media noche, en medio de las salas,
vino doña quaresma: '¡dios Señor, tu me valas!'
dieron bozes los gallos, batieron de las alas,
llegaron a don carnal aquestas nueuas malas.

1100 Commo avia el buen omne Sobra mucho comido,
con la mucha vianda mucho vino ha beuido,
estaua apesgado e estaua adormido,
por todo el su Real entro el apellido.

1101 Todos amodoridos fueron a la pelea,
pusieron las sus fases, ninguno non pletea;
la conpaña del mar las sus armas menea,
vinieron se a fferyr desiendo todos '¡ea!'

1102 El primero de todos que ferio a don carnal
fue el puerro cuelle aluo e ferio lo muy mal
fizole escopir flema, esta fue grand Señal.
touo doña quaresma que era suyo el Real.

1103 vino luego en ayuda la salada sardina,
firio muy Resia mente a la gruesa gallyna,
atrauesosele en el pyco, afogala ayna,
despues a don carnal falsol la capellyna.

1104 vinien las grandes mielgas en esta delantera,
los verdeles e xibias guardan la costanera,
buelta es la pelea de muy mala manera,
caya de cada cabo mucha buena mollera.

1105 De parte de valençia venien las anguillas,
salpresas e trechadas, a grandes manadillas,
dauan a don carnal por medio de las costillas;
las truchas de aluerche dauanle en las mexillas.

1097   When night fell, long after dinner,
       and everyone had too full a belly
       to enter battle with the serene lady,
       they all fell asleep, wishing each other goodnight.

1098   During the night the cockerels were filled with terror –
       they kept awake in fear and did not sleep a wink.
       It was not surprising, since they'd lost their wives!
       In the end they caused a riot due to the noise they heard.

1099   It was midnight when Lent came
       right through the halls and said: 'Lord God, protect me!'
       The cockerels crowed and flapped their wings.
       The bad news reached Carnal.

1100   Since the good man had eaten too much,
       and drunk a lot of wine with all the meat,
       he felt very heavy and sleepy
       as the war cry rang throughout his camp.

1101   Everyone drowsily went to battle,
       the troops lined up, no one argued,
       the marine troops wielded their arms,
       shouting 'Aargh!' as they entered the fray.

1102   The very first to wound Carnal
       was the white-necked leek; he dealt a nasty blow
       and made Carnal spit phlegm – it was a significant sign,
       for Lent believed the camp was hers.

1103   Then the salted sardine came up to help,
       seriously wounding the fat hen.
       It lodged in her beak and immediately choked her.
       Then the sardine pierced Carnal's helmet.

1104   Next, all the great dogfish lined up front,
       green fish and cuttlefish guarded the flanks,
       and the battle took a nasty turn.
       Many good heads rolled on both sides.

1105   The eels came from Valencia,
       salted, split and pickled, in great shoals.
       They attacked Carnal in the ribs,
       while trout from the Alberche went for his cheeks.

1106   Ay andaua el atun commo vn brauo leon,
       fallose con don tosino, dixole mucho baldon.
       synon por doña çeçina quel desuio el pendon
       dierale a don ladron por medio del coraçon.

1107   de parte bayona venien muchos caçones,
       mataron las perdizes, Castraron los capones.
       del Rio de henares venian los camarones,
       fasta en guadal-qui-vyl ponian su tendejones.

1108   Alli con los lauancos lydian baruos E peçes.
       diz la pixota al puerco: '¿do estas que non paresçes?
       sy ante mi te paras, dar te he lo que meresçes;
       ençierra te en la mesquita, non vayas a las preses.'

1109   ally vino la lyxa en aquel desbarato,
       traya muy duro Cuero con mucho garauato,
       E a costados e a piernas dauales negro Rato,
       ansi traua dellos Como si fuese gato.

1110   Recudieron del mar de pielagos E charcos
       conpañas mucho estranas e de diuersos marcos,
       trayan armas muy fuertes e ballestas e arcos,
       mas negra fue aquesta que non la de larcos.

1111   De sant ander vinieron las bermejas langostas,
       trayan muchas saetas en sus aljauas postas,
       ffasian a don carnal pagar todas las costas,
       las plasas que eran anchas fasian se le angostas.

1112   ffecho era el pregon del año jubileo,
       para saluar sus almas avian todos desseo,
       quantos son en la mar vinieron al torneo,
       arenques E vesugos vinieron de bermeo.

1113   Andava y la vtra con muchos conbatyentes
       feriendo e matando de las carnosas gentes;
       a las torcasas matan las sabogas valyentes,
       el dolfyn al buey viejo derribole los dientes.

1114   ssavalos E albures E la noble lanplea
       de Seuilla E de alcantara venian a leuar prea;
       sus armas cada vno en don carnal enprea,
       non le valia nada deçenir la correa.

1106   The tuna went about like a ferocious lion,
        encountered Mr Bacon and gave him the same abuse.
        If not for the cured meat, who deflected his banner,
        he'd have got Mr Lardy straight through the heart.

1107   Many small sharks came from Bayona,
        killing the partridges, castrating the capons.
        Little shrimps came from the River Henares
        and set up their tents as far as the Guadalquivir.

1108   Barbels and other fish fought the wild ducks.
        The hake asked the pig: 'Where are you? Come out!
        If I see you, I'll give you what you deserve,
        keep yourself shut up in the mosque, don't go to prayer.'

1109   The dogfish joined in the rout.
        He had a very hard hide covered with barbs,
        which tore at legs and sides,
        seizing hold of them like the claws of a cat.

1110   Out of the seas, from abysses and pools,
        came strange and varied companies.
        They carried heavy arms, crossbows and longbows.
        It was more terrible than the Battle of Alarcos.

1111   Vermilion lobsters came from Santander,
        carrying arrows in their quivers.
        They made Carnal pay dearly,
        the widest places seemed narrow to him.

1112   The proclamation of the jubilee year was made,
        and all men longed to save their souls.
        All the sea creatures came to the battle,
        herring and sea bream came from Bermeo.

1113   The great porgy fought with other troops,
        wounding and killing the fleshly ranks,
        the valiant shad slayed the ring-doves,
        and the dolphin smashed the old ox's teeth.

1114   More shad, with dace and the noble lamprey
        came from Seville and Alcántara to carry off their prey,
        each wielding their arms against Carnal.
        It did him no good to undo his belt.

1115   brauo andaua el tollo, vn duro vyllanchon,
tenia en la su mano grand maça de vn trechon,
dio en medio de la fruente al puerco e al lechon,
mando que los echasen en sal de vyllenchon.

1116   el pulpo a los pauones non les daua vagar,
nin a los faysanes non dexaua bolar,
a cabritos E a gamos queria los afogar,
como tiene muchas manos, con muchos puede lydiar.

1117   ally lidian las ostyas con todos los conejos,
con la liebre justauan los asperos cangrejos,
della e de la parte dan se golpes sobejos,
de escamas E de sangre van llenos los vallejos.

1118   ally lydia el conde de laredo muy fuerte,
congrio çeçial e fresco mando mala suerte,
a don carnal Seguiendo, llegandol a la muerte,
esta mucho triste, non falla quel confuerte.

1119   Tomo ya quanto esfuerço e tendio su pendon,
ardiz E denodado fuese contra don salmon,
de castro de vrdiales llegaua esa saçon,
atendiole el fidalgo, non le dixo de non.

1120   Porfiaron grand pieça e pasaron grand pena,
si a carnal dexaran dierale mal estrena,
mas vino contra el la gigante ballena,
abraçose con el, echolo en la arena.

1121   las mas de Sus conpñas eran le ya fallesçidas,
muchas dellas murieron E muchas eran foydas,
pero ansi apeado fasia grandes acometidas,
deffendiose quanto pudo con manos enfraqueçidas.

1122   Commo estaua ya con muy pocas conpañas,
el jaualyn E el çieruo fuyeron a las montanas,
todas las otras rreses fueron le muy estrañas,
los que con el fyncaron non valyan dos castañas.

1123   Synon fuese la çeçina con el grueso toçino
que estaua amarillo de dias mortesino,
que non podia de gordo lydiar syn el buen vino,
estaua muy señero, çecado e mesquino.

1115   The spotted dogfish, a great tough villain, walked boldly,
a huge mallet for pounding meat in his hand.
He got the hog and the sucking pig right between the eyes,
and ordered them to be salted in Velinchón salt.*

1116   The octopus gave the peacocks no rest,
nor even let the pheasants take flight.
It wanted to strangle the kids and the buck deer,
for it can take on all comers with its many arms.

1117   The oysters fought with the rabbits,
the hard-shelled crabs jousted with the hare.
Great blows were dealt on all sides,
and the valleys were filled with fish scales and blood.

1118   The count of Laredo* joined boldly in the fray,
both salted and fresh conger eel – he brought bad luck
to Carnal, pursuing him to the death.
There was no one to comfort him in his sorrows.

1119   Carnal took heart a little and raised his banner.
Bold and daring, he went for the salmon,
newly arrived from Castro de Urdiales.
The knight was waiting and did not say no.

1120   They fought for some time and suffered a lot.
If they abandoned Carnal, misfortune would strike,
then the giant whale came upon him,
threw itself at him and cast him in the sand.

1121   Most of his company were already dead.
Many had been killed and many had fled,
but on foot as he was, he put up a great fight,
defending himself with weakened hands.

1122   He had very little of his company left –
the wild boar and the deer had fled to the mountains.
All the other beasts were cruel and disloyal to him,
and those who remained were not worth a farthing.

1123   There was only the cured meat and fatty bacon,
old and deathly yellow in colour,
so fat it could not fight without wine.
Carnal was alone, surrounded and wretched.

1124   la mesnada del mar fiso se vn tropel,
       fyncaron las espuelas, dieron todos en el,
       non lo quisieron matar, ovieron duelo del,
       a el e a los suyos metieron en vn cordel.

1125   Troxieron los atados por que non escapasen,
       dieron los a la dueña ante que se aforrasen;
       mando luego la dueña que a carnal guardasen
       E a doña çeçina con el toçino colgasen.

1126   mandolos colgar altos, byen como atalaya,
       E que a descolgallos ninguno y non vaya;
       luego los enforcaron de vna viga de faya;
       el sayon yua desiendo: 'quien tal fizo tal aya.'

1127   Mando a don carnal que guardase el ayuno
       E que lo touiesen ençerrado ado non lo vea ninguno,
       si non fuese doliente o confesor alguno,
       E quel dyesen a comer al dia majar vno.

DE LA PENITENCIA QUEL FLAYRE DIO A DON CARNAL E DE COMMO EL PECADOR SE DEUE CONFESSAR E QUIEN HA PODER DO LO ABSOLUER

1128   vino luego vn frayle para lo convertyr,
       començole a predicar, de dios a departyr,
       ouose don carnal luego mucho a sentyr,
       demando penitençia con grand arrepentyr.

1129   En carta por escripto le daua sus pecados,
       con sello de poridat çerrados E sellados;
       rrespondiole el flayre quel non serian perdonados,
       çerca desto le dixo muchos buenos ditados.

1130   Non se fase penitencia por carta nin por escripto,
       sinon por la boca misma del pecador contrito;
       non puede por escripto ser asuelto nin quito,
       menester es la palabla del conffesor bendito.

1131   Pues que de penitençia vos fago mençion,
       rrepetir vos querria vna buena lyçion:
       deuedes creer firme mente, con pura deuoçion,
       que por la penitençia avredes saluaçion.

1124   The marine troops formed into a squad,
       spurred on their mounts and went straight for him.
       They had no wish to kill him, they took pity on him,
       and tied him and his troops up with rope.

1125   They brought the prisoners bound, so they couldn't escape,
       and gave them to Lent before they could get free.
       She ordered Carnal to be held,
       while cured meat was to be hung with Mr Bacon.

1126   She ordered them to be hung high up, like a look-out,
       and that no one should take them down.
       They were then strung up on a beam of beech.
       The executioner repeated: 'As you did, so shall be done to
                                                                you.'

1127   She ordered Carnal to fast for a while
       and be imprisoned without any visitors,
       unless he was ill or needed confession,
       and then he was to be served only one meal a day.

THE PENANCE GIVEN BY THE FRIAR TO CARNAL, HOW
THE SINNER SHOULD CONFESS AND WHO SHOULD
ABSOLVE HIM

1128   Then a friar came to convert him,
       he started to preach to him and talk of God.
       Carnal had much to regret,
       he begged the friar for penance amid a show of repentance.

1129   He listed his sins in a written letter
       closed and sealed with a secret seal.
       The friar told him they would not be pardoned,
       and related much of what was said on the subject.

1130   'You cannot do penance by letter or in writing,
       but only from the mouth of the contrite sinner.
       You cannot be absolved or exonerated in writing,
       you need the spoken word of the holy confessor.'

1131   Since I am talking to you about penance,*
       I'd like to give you a good lesson on the subject.
       You must truly believe, with great devotion,
       that you will win salvation through penance.

1132 Por que la penitençia es cosa preçiada
      non deuedes, amigos, dexar la oluidada;
      fablar en ella mucho es cosa muy loada;
      quanto mas la seguieremos, mayor es la soldada.

1133 Es me cosa muy graue en tan grand fecho fablar,
      es pielago muy fondo, mas que todo el mar;
      so rrudo E syn çiençia non me oso aventurar,
      saluo vn poquillo que oy disputar.

1134 E por aquesto que tengo en coraçon de escreuir,
      tengo del miedo tanto quanto non puedo desir:
      con la çiençia poca he grand miedo de fallyr;
      Senores, vuestro saber quiera mi mengua conplir.

1135 Escolar so mucho rrudo, nin maestro nin doctor,
      aprendi e se poco para ser demostrador,
      aquesto que yo dixiere entendet lo vos mejor,
      so la vuestra emienda pongo el mi error.

1136 En el santo decreto ay grand disputaçion
      si se fase penitençia por la sola contriçion,
      determina al cabo qual es la confesion,
      menester de todo en todo con la satysfaçion.

1137 verdat es todo aquesto do puede omne fablar,
      do ha tienpo E vida para lo emendar:
      do aquesto fallesçe, bien se puede saluar
      por la contriçion sola, pues al non puede far.

1138 quito quanto a dios que es sabidor conplido,
      mas quanto a la iglesia que non judga de ascondido,
      es menester que faga por gestos e gemido
      Sinos de penitençia que es arrepentido:

1139 En sus pechos feriendo, a dios manos alçando,
      sospiros dolorosos muy triste sospirando,
      sygnos de penitençia de los ojos llorando,
      do mas fazer non puede la cabeça enclinando.

1140 Por aquesto es quito del jnfierno mal lugar,
      pero que a purgatorio lo va todo a purgar;
      ally faz la emienda purgando el su errar
      con la misericordia de dios que lo quiere saluar.

1132   Because penance is a thing of great value,
       it should not be forgotten, my friends.
       To keep it ever present is very praiseworthy;
       the more closely we follow it, the greater our gain.

1133   It is a momentous thing for me to speak of such a topic,
       it is a deep, deep abyss, deeper than the sea.
       I am uncouth, unlearned, I only dare speak
       of the little I have heard in disputation.

1134   What I have in my heart to write down
       I fear more than I can say.
       My lack of knowledge makes me fear my mistakes.
       Good sirs, your learning will compensate for my short-
                                                     coming.

1135   I am a simple scholar, neither master nor doctor,
       I learnt and know little to be a teacher.
       You may understand what I have to say better than I do –
       so I offer my errors for your correction.

1136   In the holy Decretal there is great dispute
       over whether penance is done by contrition alone.
       In the end it states that confession
       is necessary, together with satisfaction.

1137   This is all true where man can speak
       and where he has time and life to put things right.
       But when he is moribund, then he can be saved
       by contrition alone, for he can do nothing else.

1138   Absolved in God's eyes, who sees and knows all,
       in terms of the Church, which does not judge things hidden,
       it is necessary for him to make signs of penance
       and repentance by gestures and a show of suffering.

1139   Beating one's chest, hands raised to God,
       sighing sadly and with great sorrow,
       signs of penance through eyes that weep,
       and if nothing else, bowed head.

1140   Through this, man is free from Hell, fearsome place,
       but he will pay for everything in Purgatory.
       There he will make amends and purge his errors
       through the mercy of God, who longs to save him.

1141   Que tal contriçion ssea penitençia byen llena,
        ay en la santa iglesia mucha prueua e buena;
        por contriçion e lagrimas la santa madalena,
        fue quita E absuelta de culpa e de pena.

1142   Nuestro Señor sant pedro, tan santa criatura,
        nego a jhesu xpisto con miedo E quexura;
        se yo que lloro lagrimas triste con amargura,
        de sastifaçion otra non fallo escriptura.

1143   El rrey don esechias de muerte condenado,
        lloro mucho contrito, a la pared tornado;
        de dios tan piadoso luego fue perdonado,
        quinçe años de vida anadio al culpado.

1144   Muchos clerigos synples que non son tan letrados
        oyen de penitençia a todos los errados,
        quier a sus parrochianos, quier a otros culpados,
        a todos los absueluen de todos sus pecados.

1145   En esto yerran mucho, que lo non pueden faser;
        de lo que faser non pueden, non se deuen entremeter;
        si el çiego al çiego adiestra o lo quier traer,
        en la foya dan entranbos e dentro van caer.

1146   ¿que poder ha en Roma el jues de cartajena,
        o que jusgara en françia el alcalde de rrequena?
        non deue poner omne su foz en miese ajena,
        fase injuria e dapno e meresçe grand pena.

1147   Todos los casos grandes, fuertes, agrauiados,
        a arçobispos e abispos e a mayores perlados,
        Segud comun derecho le son encomendados,
        saluo los que del papa son en si rreseruados.

1148   los que son rreseruados del papa espirituales,
        son muchos en derecho; desir quantos e quales
        serie mayor el rromançe, mas que dos manuales;
        quien saber los quisiere, oya las decretales.

1149   Pues que el arçobispo, bendicho e conssagrado,
        de palio e de blago e de mitra onrrado
        con pontifical, non es destos apoderado,
        ¿pot que el sinple clerigo es desto tan osado?

1141 There is much good evidence in the Holy Church
that such contrition is a full penance.
By contrition and tears the holy Mary Magdalene
was freed and absolved from blame and sorrow.

1142 Our master St Peter, that holy being,
denied Jesus Christ in fear and anguish.
I know he cried sad and bitter tears,
I find no other written word of satisfaction.

1143 King Hezekiah, condemned to death,*
cried in great contrition, turned to the wall.
He was then pardoned by ever-merciful God
who added fifteen more years to the accused king's life.

1144 Many simple clergy, who are not so learned,
hear the confession of all kinds of sinners,
whether their parishioners, or others condemned.
They absolve them all from all their sins.

1145 Here they err greatly, for they ought not do it.
What cannot be done should be left well alone.
If the blind lead the blind,
we shall all fall into the pit.

1146 What power does the judge of Cartagena have in Rome?
What will the mayor of Requena* judge in France?
A man should not use his scythe in others' cornfields,
it causes harm and injury and merits great punishment.

1147 All serious, important and grave cases
are commended to bishops and archbishops
and higher prelates, according to standard law,
save those which are reserved for the Pope alone.

1148 Those special cases reserved for the Pope
are many under law – to describe which and how many
would make a long diatribe, more than two theology
                                                     manuals.
Listen to the Decretals if you would like to know about them.

1149 Since the archbishop, blessed and consecrated,
and honoured with pallium, crozier and mitre,
with pontifical dress, has no power over these,
how can a simple clergyman be so bold?

1150   otrosi del obispo E de los sus mayores,
        son otros casos muchos de que son oydores,
        pueden bien asoluer los e ser dispenssadores,
        son mucho defendidos a clerigos menores.

1151   Muchos son los primeros e muchos son aquestos;
        quien quisier saber los, estudie do son puestos,
        trastorne byen los libros, las glosas e los testos;
        el estudio a los Rudos fase sabios maestros.

1152   lea en el especulo o en el rreportorio
        los libros de ostiense, que son grand parlatorio,
        el jnocençio quarto, vn sotil consistorio,
        el rrosario de guido, nouela e diratorio.

1153   Decretales mas de çiento, en libros E en questiones,
        con fueres argumentos E con sotiles Rasones,
        tyenen sobre estos casos diuersas opiniones;
        Pues, por non desir tanto, non me rebtedes, varones.

1154   vos, don clerigo synpre, guardat vos de eror,
        de mi parrochiano non seades confesor,
        de poder que non avedos non seades judgador,
        non querades vos penar por ajeno pecador.

1155   Syn poder del perlado o syn aver liçençia
        del su clerigo cura, non le dedes penitençia;
        guardat non lo absoluades, nin de des la sentençia
        de los casos que non son en vuestra pertenençia.

1156   Segund comun derecho aquesta es la verdat;
        mas en ora de muerte o de grand necesidat,
        do el pecador non puede aver de otro sanidat,
        a vuestros E ajenos oyd, absolued E quitad.

1157   En tienpo de peligro, do la muerte arapa,
        vos sodes para todo arçobispo E papa;
        todo el su poder esta so vuestra capa,
        la grand neçesidat todos los casos atapa.

1158   Pero que aquestos tales deuedes les mandar,
        que Si antes que muera si podieren fallar
        E puedan aver su cura para se confesar,
        que lo fagan e cunplan para mejor estar.

1150 Also, the bishop and high-ranking clergy
hear many cases themselves,
and may give absolution and dispensations.
These offices are quite forbidden to minor clergy.

1151 There are many of the first kind, many more of the latter.
If you wish to study them, read all about them,
turn books inside out, both gloss and text.
Study turns the unpolished man into a wise master.

1152 Read the Speculum and the Repertorium,
the Cardinal of Ostia's books, which form a large collection,
and Innocent IV's subtle compendium,
Guido's Rosary, the Law Supplement and Decretorium.*

1153 More than a hundred doctors, in books and in discussion,
with powerful arguments and subtle reasoning
hold various opinions on these cases,
but do not berate me for not saying more, sirs.

1154 You, Mr Ordinary Priest, guard against error,
don't be the confessor of my parishioner,
do not be judge where you have no authority,
do not pay the penalty for another's sins.

1155 Without a prelate's power and without permission
from his priest, do not give him penance.
Take care not to absolve him or pass sentence
in cases which are not in your jurisdiction.

1156 This is the truth in standard law,
but at the hour of death or in great need,
where no other solution can be found,
hear, absolve and pardon both your own and others.

1157 In times of danger, where death snatches man away,
you are archbishop and Pope to all.
All their power lies beneath your cape,
great need encompasses all cases.

1158 But still you must command such men
that if they speak before they die,
they should have their own priest for confession,
who should fulfil this duty for the sake of good.

1159 E otrosi mandatle a este tal dolyente,
que si dende non muere, quando fuere valiente,
que de los casos grandes, que vos distes vngente,
vaya a lauarse al Rio o a la fuente.

1160 Es el papa syn dubda la fuente perenal,
ca es de todo el mundo vicario general,
los Rios son los otros que han pontifical,
arçobispos e obispos, patriarca, cardenal.

1161 El frayle sobre dicho que ya vos he nonbrado
era del papa e del mucho priuado;
en la grand nesçesidat al cardenal aprisionado
absoluiole de todo quanto estaua ligado.

1162 Desque del santo flayre ovo carnal cofesado,
diole esta penitençia: que por tanto pecado
comiese cada dia vn manjar señalado
E non comiese mas e seria perdonado:

1163 'El dia del domingo por tu cobdiçia mortal
conbras garuanços cochos con aseyte e non al,
yras a la iglesia E non estaras en la cal,
que non veas el mundo nin cobdicies el mal.

1164 En el dia del lunes por la tu soberuia mucha,
conbras de las arvejas mas non salmon nin trucha,
yras oyr las oras, non prouaras la lucha,
nin bolueras pelea Segund que la as ducha.

1165 Por tu grand avariçia te que el martes
que comas los formigos e mucho non te fares,
el terçio de tu pan comeras o las dos partes,
para por dios lo otro todo te mando que apartes.

1166 Espinacas conbras el miercoles non espesas,
por la tu grand loxuria comeras muy pocas desas;
non guardaste casadas nin mongas profesas,
por conplir adulterio fasias grandes promesas.

1167 El jueues çenaras, por la tu mortal yra,
E por que te perjuraste desiendo la mentira,
lentejas con la sal; en Resar te rremira,
quando mejor te sepan, por dios de ti las tira.

1159   And also order this suffering wretch
that if he should not die, when he is well again,
he should go and wash in the river or fountain,
to wash away the serious cases over which you gave unction.

1160   There is no doubt that the Pope is the perennial fountain,
for he is the supreme vicar of the world;
the rivers are the others of pontifical rank,
archbishops and bishops, patriarch, cardinal.

1161   The friar I mentioned to you before
was the pope of the stomach and a great favourite.
In his great need he absolved the imprisoned Carnal
of everything which he had pending.

1162   When the holy friar had confessed Carnal
he gave him this penance – that for such great sin
he should eat a particular dish each day
and nothing more, then he would be pardoned.

1163   'For your mortal covetousness, on Sunday
you shall eat chick-peas cooked in oil, and no more.
You shall go to church and not linger in the street,
so as to see no one and not long to do evil.

1164   For your great pride, on Monday you shall eat
greens, but not salmon or trout.
You shall hear the Hours and not indulge in sex,
nor start up a fight, as you usually do.

1165   For your great avarice, on Tuesday I order you
to eat wheat siftings, but not to excess.
You may eat half a loaf of bread, or two thirds,
and give the last third to God's needy.

1166   On Wednesday you may eat a little spinach,
not too much, for your sin of rampant lechery.
You did not spare married women or professed nuns,
making extravagant promises to achieve your ends.

1167   For your mortal anger and your lying perjury,
on Thursday you shall dine on
salted lentils. Take care to pray, and
if you start to enjoy them, stop eating, in God's name.

1168 Por la tu mucha gula E tu grand golosina
      el viernes pan E agua comeras E non cosina,
      fostigaras tus carnes con santa disçiplina,
      aver te ha dios merçed e saldras de aqui ayna.

1169 Come el dya del sabado las fabas E non mas.
      por tu envidia mucha, pescado non comeras;
      commo quier que algund poco en esto lasraras,
      tu alma pecador ansi la saluaras.

1170 anda en este tienpo por cada çiminteryo,
      visita las iglesias, Resando el salterio,
      esta y muy deuoto al santo misterio,
      ayudar te ha dios e avras pro del laserio.'

1171 Dada la penitençia, fiso la confesion;
      estaua don carnal con muy grand deuoçion,
      desiendo: 'mia culpa', diole la absoluçion;
      partiose del el frayel dada la bendiçion.

1172 ffynco ally ençerrado don carnal el coytoso,
      estaua de la lid muy fraco E lloroso,
      doliente E mal ferido, costribado e dolioso,
      non lo vee ninguno xristiano rreligioso.

DE LO QUE SE FAZE MIERCOLES CORUILLO E EN LA QUARESMA

1173 Desque ovo la dueña vençido la fasienda,
      mouio todo el Real, mando coger su tyenda;
      andando por el mundo, mando faser emienda,
      los vnos a los otros, non se paga de contyenda.

1174 Luego el primero dia, el miercoles coruillo,
      en las casas do anda, cesta nin canistillo,
      non dexa, tajador, bacin nin cantarillo,
      que todo non lo muda sobre linpio librillo.

1175 Escudillas, sartenes, tinajas e calderas,
      cañadas e uarriles, todas cosas casseras,
      todo lo fyzo lauar a las sus lauanderas,
      espetos e griales, ollas e coberteras.

1176 Repara las moradas, las paredes Repega,
      dellas faze de nueuo e dellas enxaluega;

1168   Because of your greed and great gluttony,
       you shall eat bread and water on Friday, nothing cooked,
       and shall whip yourself with holy discipline.
       Then God shall have mercy and you will soon be free.

1169   On Saturday you shall eat beans and nothing else;
       because of your great envy, you shall not eat fish.
       However much you suffer in doing this,
       you will save your sinful soul.

1170   During this time, visit the graveyard,
       enter the churches praying from the Psalter,
       and be devout at Holy Mass.
       Then God will help you and your suffering will bear fruit.'

1171   When the penance was given, he made confession.
       Carnal repeated '*mea culpa*' with great
       devoutness and was given absolution.
       The friar blessed him and departed.

1172   Carnal lay wretched in his prison,
       weak and tearful from the battle,
       in pain and wounded, afflicted and suffering.
       No conscientious Christian would see him.

WHAT HAPPENED ON ASH WEDNESDAY AND IN THE
SEASON OF LENT

1173   When Lent had won the battle,
       she set the army marching, ordering her tents to be
                                                  dismantled.
       As she went through the land, she ordered everyone
       to make amends – she did not enjoy fighting.

1174   On the first day, which was Ash Wednesday,
       in every house she entered; no baskets big or small,
       no chopper, serving dish or pitcher escaped –
       everything was cleaned in an earthenware tub.

1175   Bowls, frying pans, jars and kettles,
       spits and platters, pots and lids,
       wine measures and barrels, all household utensils,
       she made her washerwomen wash everything.

1176   Dwellings were repaired, walls were patched,
       some were newly built, others whitewashed.

ado ella ver lo puede suzedat non se llega;
saluo a don carnal non se a quien non plega.

1177 Bien commo en este dia para el cuerpo Repara,
asi en este dia por el alma se para;
a todos los xristianos llama con buena cara
que vayan a la iglesia con conçiençia clara.

1178 A los que alla van con el su buen talente,
con çeniza los cruzan de Ramos en la fruente,
dizenles que se conoscan E les venga miente
que son çeniza e tal tornaran çierta mente.

1179 Al xristiano catholico dale el santo signo
por que an la cuaresma biua linpio e digno,
de mansa penitençia el pecador jndigno,
ablanda Robre duro con el su blando lino.

1180 En quanto ella anda estas oblas faziendo,
don carnal el doliente yua salud aviendo,
yua se poco a poco de la cama yrguiendo;
penso como fesiese, commo fuese rreyendo.

1181 Dixo a don ayuno el domingo de Ramos:
'vayamos oyr misa, señor, vos e yo anbos;
vos oyredes misa, yo rresare mis salmos;
oyremos pasion, pues que baldios estamos.'

1182 Resspondiole don ayuno que desto le plasia.
rresio es don carnal, mas flaco se fasia.
fueron a la iglesia, non a lo quel desia;
de lo que dixo en casa, ally se desdesia.

1183 fuyo de la iglesia, fuese a la joderia,
rresçebieron lo muy bien en su carneçeria,
pascua de pan çenseño estos les venia,
plogo a ellos con el e el vido buen dia.

1184 luego lunes de mañana, don rraby açelyn,
por le poner saluo, enprestole su Rosin;
pusose muy priuado en estremo de medellyn;
dixieron los corderos: 'vedes aqui la fyn.'

1185 Cabrones e cabritos, carneros e ovejas
dauan grandes balidos, desien estas conssejas:

She would have nothing to do with dirt.
She pleased everyone, except Carnal.

1177 In the same way that material things were repaired,
the soul was also prepared on that day.
She called all Christians, with her smiling face,
to go to church with a clear conscience.

1178 Those who go willingly and readily
have their foreheads crossed with the ash from holy wood.
She tells them to know themselves and remember
that they are ash and will certainly return to it once more.

1179 She gives the sign of the cross to the Catholic Christian,
that he might live purely and worthily during Lent.
She gives gentle penance to the unworthy sinner,
and softens hard oak with the sweet wood of the cross.

1180 While she was engaged on these good works,
the languishing Carnal was regaining his health,
and little by little sitting up in bed,
wondering how he could bring a smile to his face again.

1181 On Palm Sunday he said to Mr Fast:
'Let's go to Mass, Sir, you and I together;
you can hear Mass and I will pray my psalms.
We will hear the passiontide service, since we have nothing
          else to do.'

1182 Mr Fast replied that he would be glad to.
Carnal was robust, but made out he was weak.
They went to the church, but not for what he'd said.
What was said in the house was unsaid there.

1183 He escaped from the church and went to the Jewry.
He was very well received at their butcher's shop.
It was almost the Jewish Easter-tide.
They liked being with him and he had a good time.

1184 Then on Monday morning, Rabbi Acebin
lent Carnal his nag to help him to safety.
He rode like a flash to the depths of Medellín.*
All the lambs bleated: 'Baa! This is the end of me!'

1185 Billy-goats and kids, rams and ewes
all bleated loudly and spoke as follows:

'sy nos lyeuas de aqui, Carnal, por las callejas,
a muchos de nos otros tirara las pellejas.'

1186 Plados de medellyn, de caçres, de troxillo,
la bera de plasençia fasta valdemorillo,
E toda la serena El presto mançebillo
alboroço ayna, fizo muy grand portillo.

1187 El canpo de alcudia e toda la calatraua,
el canpo de fazaluaro, en vasayn entrava,
en tres dia lo andudo, semeja que bolaua,
el rroçin del rrabi con miedo byen andaua.

1188 Desquel vieron los toros yrisaron los çerros.
los bueys E vacas Repican los çençerros,
dan grandes apellidos terneras E beçerros:
'¡aba, aba, pastores, acorred nos con los perros!'

1189 Enbio las cartas, andar non pudo,
el por esas montañas en la sierra estudo,
e contra la quaresma estaua muy sañudo,
pero de venir solo non era atre-vudo.

1190 Estas fueron las cartas, el testo e la glosa:
'de nos don carnal, fuerte madador de toda cosa,
a ty quaresma fraca, magra E muy sarnosa,
non salud, mas sangria commo a mala flemosa.

1191 byen sabes commo somos tu mortal enemigo;
enbyamos nos a ty al armuerzo nuestro amigo,
que por nos te lo diga, commo seremos contigo
de oy en quatro dias que sera el domingo.

1192 Commo ladron veniste, de noche, a lo escuro,
estando nos dormiendo, yasiendo nos sseguro;
non te nos defenderas en castillo nin en muro,
que de ty non ayamos el cuero maduro.'

1193 la nota de la carta venia a todos nos:
'don carnal poderoso, por la graçia de dios,
a todos los xristianos e moros e jodios,
salud con muchas carnes, sienpre de nos a vos.

1194 Byen ssabedes, amigos, en commo ¡mal pecado!
oy ha siete selmanas que fuemos desafiado

'If Carnal takes us from here through the streets,
many of us will lose our skins.'

1186 Through the meadows of Medellín, Cáceres and Trujillo,
Vera in Plasencia, as far as Valdemorillo,
and all through the Serena region, that agile young man
made a great disturbance, opened a great breach.

1187 He passed through the fields of Alcudia and all Calatrava,
Hazálvaro too, until he came to Valsaín.*
All this took just three days – he seemed to be flying.
The rabbi's nag travelled fast in its fear.

1188 When the bulls saw him, their hackles rose.
Both bulls and cows rang their cow-bells,
calves and yearlings made a great din:
'Oh, oh, shepherds! come to help us with your dogs!'

1189 He sent his letters where he could not walk,
and roamed the mountain ranges
full of ire against Lent –
but he was not bold enough to go alone.

1190 This is the text and gloss of the letters:
'From Us, Carnal, powerful slayer of all things,
to you, Lent, thin, skinny, vile and mangy, we wish you
not health, but a blood-letting suitable for a sick phlegmy
woman.

1191 You know I am your mortal enemy.
I am sending my friend Mr Breakfast to you,
so that he can tell you how we are prepared for battle
four days from now, which will be Sunday.

1192 You came like a thief in the night, in darkness,
while we slept, thinking we were safe.
You cannot defend yourself behind castle walls,
for we will have your leathery hide.'

1193 The content of this letter was for everyone to read:
'I, Carnal, all powerful, by the grace of God,
greet all Christians, Moors and Jews
and wish you abundant meat, from us to you.

1194 You well know, my friends, how – cursed day! –
we were challenged seven weeks ago

de la falsa quaresma e de mar ayrado;
estando nos seguro fuemos della arrancado.

1195   Por ende vos mandamos, vista la nuestra carta,
que la des-afiedes antes que dende parta;
guardat la que non fuya, que todo el mundo en-arta;
enbiat gelo desir con dona merienda farta.

1196   E vaya el almueso que es mas aperçebido,
digale que el domingo antes del sol salido
yremos lydiar con ella fasiendo grand Roydo;
sy muy sorda non fuere, oyra nuestro apellido.

1197   nuestra carta leyda, tomad della traslado,
dalda a don almuerso, que vaya con el mandado,
non se detenga y, vaya luego priuado:
dada en torna vacas, nuestro lugar amado.'

1198   Escriptas son las cartas todas con sangre biua,
todos con el plaser cada vno do yua
desian a la quaresma: '¿donde te asconderas, catyua?'
ella esta Rason aviala por esquiva.

1199   Pero que ella non avia las cartas rrescebidas,
mas desque gelas dieron E le fueron leydas,
rrespondio mucho flaca, las mexillas caydas,
dixo: '¡dios me guarde destas nuevas oydas!'

1200   Por ende cada vno esta fabla decuere:
quien a su enemigo popa a las sus manos muere;
el que a su enemigo non mata, si podiere,
su enemigo matara a el, si cuerdo fuere.

1201   Disen los naturales que non son solas las vacas,
mas que todas las fenbras son de coraçon fracas,
para lydiar non firmes quanto en afrecho estacas,
saluo si son vellosas, ca estas son barracas.

1202   Por ende doña quaresma de flaca conplision
rresçelo de la lyd muerte o grand presion,
de yr a jerusalen avia fecho promisiom,
para pasar la mar puso muy grand mision.

1203   la dueña en Su Rybto puso dia ssabido
fasta quando lydiasen, byen lo avedes oydo;

by false Lent and the angry sea.
When we thought we were safe, she conquered us.

1195 So we order you, when you have read our letter,
to challenge her before she leaves these parts.
Stop her from fleeing, for she deceives everyone.
Send a message to be taken by Mrs High Tea, full to bursting.

1196 And let Mr Breakfast go, he's very shrewd.
Tell her that before sunrise on Sunday
we shall engage in battle against her with warlike din,
and if she's not deaf, she'll hear our call to fight.

1197 Once the letter is read, take a copy of it
and give it to Mr Breakfast, so he can take the order.
Don't hang about there, go quickly.
Written in Tornavacas, our beloved place.'

1198 All the letters were written in fresh blood.
Everyone went in great pleasure
and said aloud: 'Lent, where are you hiding, wretch?'
She thought the question most impertinent,

1199 since she had not yet received the letters.
But as soon as they arrived and were read,
she responded weakly, with sunken cheeks,
saying: 'May God spare me from this news!'

1200 So everyone should learn this proverb by heart:
'He who saves an enemy's life shall die at his hands.'
If a person does not kill an enemy while they can,
that enemy shall kill them, if he has any sense.

1201 Naturalists say that not only cows
but all females are weak-hearted,
not firm in battle, like a stick plunged into bran,
unless they are hairy and like female wild boars.

1202 So Lent, of weak disposition,
feared the battle, death or life in prison.
She vowed to go to Jerusalem,
and made great efforts to cross the sea.

1203 In her challenge the lady fixed a day
for the fighting to end, as you have heard.

por ende non avia por que lidiar con su vençido,
syn verguença, se pudo yr el plaso ya venido.

1204   lo al, es ya verano e non venian del mar
los pescados a ella para la ayudar,
otrosi dueña flaca non es para lydiar;
por todas estas Rasones non quiso esperar.

1205   El viernes de jndulgençias vistio nueva esclamina,
grande sonblero Redondo con mucha concha maryna,
bordon lleno de ymagenes, en el la palma fyna,
esportilla e cuentas para Resar ayna.

1206   los çapatos rredondos e bien sobre solados,
echo vn grand doblel entre los sus costados,
gallofas e bodigos lyeua y condesados;
destas cosas Romeras andan aparejados.

1207   De yuso del sobaco va la mejor alfaja,
calabaça bermeja mas que pyco de graja,
bien cabe su asunbre e mas vna meaja;
non andan los rromeros syn aquesta sofraja.

1208   Estaua demudada desta guisa que vedes,
el sabado por noche salto por las paredes,
diz: 'vos que me guardades creo que me non tomedes,
que a todo pardal viejo nol toman en todas Redes.'

1209   Ssalyo mucho ayna de todas aquestas calles,
diz: 'tu, carnal soberuio, meto que non me falles.'
luego aquesta noche llego a rronças valles.
¡vaya, e dios la guie por montes e por valles!

DE COMO DON AMOR E DON CARNAL VENIERON E LOS
SALIERON A RRESÇEBIR

1210   vigilia era de pascua, abril çerca pasado,
el sol era salido por el mundo Rayado,
fue por toda la tierra grand Roydo sonado,
de dos enperadores que al mundo han llegado.

1211   Estos dos enperadores amor E carnal eran,
a rresçebyr los Salen quantos que los esperan,
las aves e los arbores nobre tyenpo averan,
los que amor atyenden sobre todos se esmeran.

So she had no reason to fight the one she had conquered.
She could go without shame when the time expired.

1204   What's more, it was already spring and fish
would no longer leave the sea to help her,
and a weak female is no good in battle.
For all these reasons, she didn't want to wait.

1205   On Good Friday she dressed in a pilgrim's cloak,
and a large round hat covered with sea-shells,
and a pilgrim's staff with carved images, such as a fine palm,*
plus a basket and prayer beads too.

1206   She wore rounded, thick-soled sandals,
threw a great knapsack over her shoulder
and carried rolls and bread hidden.
Pilgrims usually carry these provisions.

1207   Under her arm she carried her most valued adornment,
a gourd as vermilion as a jackdaw's beak,
which easily held half a gallon, plus a smidgin more.
No pilgrim travels without this support!

1208   She was well disguised, as you can imagine,
and on Easter Saturday night she jumped over the wall,
saying: 'You can guard me, but I don't think you'll catch me;
an old sparrow can't be caught in any net.'

1209   She passed quickly through the streets,
saying: 'You, boastful Carnal, I bet you won't find me!'
Go, and may God guide you through mountains and valleys!
That night, she reached Roncesvaux.*

HOW PEOPLE WENT OUT TO GREET LOVE AND CARNAL AS THEY ARRIVED

1210   It was Easter Eve and, April nearly over,
the sun shone brightly over the world.
Throughout the land was heard great rumour
of two emperors who had just arrived.

1211   These emperors were Love and Carnal.
All those waiting went out to greet them,
as the trees and birds announced fine weather.
Those awaiting Love made a special effort.

1212   a don carnal rresçiben todos los carniçeros,
        E todos los rrabys con todos sus aperos,
        a el salen triperas taniendo sus panderos,
        de muchos que corren monte llenos van los oteros.

1213   El pastor lo atyende fuera de la carrera,
        taniendo su çapoña E los albogues espera,
        su moço el caramillo fecho de caña vera,
        taniendo el Rabadan la çitola trotera.

1214   Por el puerto asoma vna seña bermeja;
        en medio vna fygura, cordero me semeja.
        vienen derredor della, balando, mucha oveja,
        carneros E cabritos con su chica pelleja.

1215   los cabrones valyentes, muchas vacas E toros,
        mas vienen çerca della que en granada ay moros,
        muchos bueys castaños, otros hoscos e loros;
        non lo conplaria dario con todos sus thesoros.

1216   Venia don carnal en carro muy preciado,
        cobierto de pellejos e de cueros çercado,
        el buen enperador esta arremangado,
        en saya, faldas en çinta, e sobra byen armado.

1217   Traya en la su mano vn assegur muy fuerte,
        a toda quatro-pea con ella da la muerte,
        cuchillo muy agudo a las rreses acomete,
        con aquel las deguella e a desollar se mete.

1218   Enderedor traya, çeñida de la su çynta,
        vna blanca rrodilla, esta de sangre tynta;
        al cablon que esta gordo el muy gelo pynta,
        fase fase: ¡ve! valando en bos E doble quinta.

1219   Tenia coffya en la cabeça, quel cabello nol ssalga,
        queça tenie vestida blanca e Raby galga,
        en el su carro otro a par del non caualga,
        a la llybre que sale luego le echa la galga.

1220   Enderredor de ssy trahe muchos alanes,
        vaqueros e de monte e otros muchos canes,
        ssabuesos e podencos quel comen muchos panes,
        e muchos nocherniegos que saltan mata canes.

1212 All the butchers and rabbis greeted
Carnal, armed with their implements.
Tripe-sellers welcomed him sounding their tambourines,
the hills were covered with people out hunting.

1213 The shepherd awaited him away from the road,
he waited and played his pipes and his flute.
His boy played a reed pipe made from canes
and the head shepherd played the dance zither.

1214 A bright red banner rose up above the pass,
with a figure painted in the middle – a lamb, I think it was.
Behind it came many sheep, all bleating,
rams and little kids with their short coats.

1215 Then valiant billy-goats, cows and bulls;
more came to the banner than there are Moors in Granada.
A lot of chestnut oxen, some dark brown, some greyish
brown;
not even Darius with all his treasure could buy them.

1216 Carnal travelled in a priceless chariot,
covered in skins and lapped in leather.
The good emperor had rolled up his sleeves.
He wore a tunic and belt, and carried powerful weapons.

1217 He bore a strong axe in his hand
to kill any four-footed creature,
plus a razor-sharp knife, to cut the throat
of any beast he attacked and then skin it.

1218 Girdled round his waist he wore
a white cloth stained with blood,
bringing fearful forebodings to the plumpest goat,
who bleats and baas in melody and counterpoint.

1219 He had a butcher's hat on his head to keep his hair in,
and wore a white cloak, long as a greyhound's tail.
No equal rode with him in his chariot.
He set his greyhound at once on any hares that emerged.

1220 He gathered many mastiffs round about him:
sheepdogs and mountain dogs, and many other kinds,
bloodhounds and other hounds – they take a lot of feeding –
tracker dogs that can catch hares by night,

1221   ssogas para las vacas, muchos pessos e pessas,
       tajones e garavatos, grandes tablas e mesas,
       para las triperas gamellas e artesas,
       las alanas paridas en las cadenas presas.

1222   Rehalas de castilla con pastores de ssoria
       rreciben lo en sus pueblos, disen del grand estoria,
       taniendo las canpanas en disiendo la gloria;
       de tales alegrias non ha en el mundo memoria.

1223   Pesso el enperante en sus carneçerias,
       venian a obedeçerle villas E alcarias,
       dixo con grand orgullo muchas blauas grandias,
       començo el fidalgo a faser cauallerias.

1224   Matando e degollando E dessollando rresses,
       dando a quantos veniam castellanos E jngleses,
       todos le dan dineros e dellos le dan torneses,
       cobra quanto ha perdido en los pasados meses.

DE COMO CLERIGOS E LEGOS E FLAYRES E MONJAS E DUEÑAS E JOGLARES SALIERON A RECEBIR A DON AMOR

1225   Dia era muy ssanto de la pascua mayor,
       el sol era salydo muy claro E de noble color,
       los omnes e las aves e toda noble flor,
       todos van rresçebir cantando al amor.

1226   Resçiben lo las aves, gayos E Ruy Señores,
       calandrias, papagayos, mayores e menores,
       dan cantos plasenteros e dulçes ssabores,
       mas alegria fasen los que son mas mejores.

1227   rresçiben lo los arbores con rramos E con flores,
       de diuerssas maneras, de diuerssas collores,
       rresçiben lo omnes E dueñas con amores,
       con muchos jnstrumentos salen los atanbores.

1228   ally sale gritando la guitara morisca,
       de las boses aguda e de los puntos arisca,
       el corpudo laud que tyene punto a la trisca,
       la guitarra latyna con esos se aprisca.

1229   El rrabe gritador, con la su alta nota,
       cabel El orabyn taniendo la su rrota,

1221   ropes for the cows, many weights and scales,
chopping knives and meat-hooks, great butchering tables,
trenchers and troughs for his tripe-sellers,
bitches with new-born puppies, imprisoned in chains.

1222   Flocks from Castile with shepherds from Soria
welcomed him to their towns, where his fame had spread,
amid bells ringing and singing the Easter 'Gloria'.
The world could not recall such happiness.

1223   The emperor lodged at their butchers',
and towns and farms were subservient to him.
In his great pride he made many boastful speeches.
The knight began to show his valour,

1224   killing beasts, slitting their throats and skinning them,
and giving some to all comers, Castilian and English.
Everyone gave him some money, Spanish and French coins,
and he regained all he had lost in recent months.

HOW PRIESTS AND LAY BROTHERS, FRIARS AND NUNS, LADIES AND MINSTRELS CAME OUT TO GREET LOVE

1225   It was the holy day of Easter,
the sun was shining bright gold.
All men, birds and lovely flowers
went singing to greet Love.

1226   The birds greeted him, rooks and nightingales,
larks and parrots, large and small,
they sang beautiful songs of sweet delight.
The best singers created the greatest joy.

1227   The trees greeted him with branches and flowers
of different kinds and varied colours.
Men and women in love greeted him
and minstrels brought out many instruments.

1228   The Moorish guitar sang its lament,
high and harsh in tone.
The portly lute accompanies a rustic dance,
and the Western guitar joins with them.

1229   The crying rebec with its high notes,
and the rote playing the Arab 'alborayn' song.*

el salterio con ellos mas alto que la mota,
la vyuela de pendola con aquestos y ssota.

1230   Medio caño E harpa con el rrabe morisco,
entrellos alegrança el galipe françisco,
la flauta diz con ellos, mas alta que vn Risco,
con ella el tanborete, syn el non vale vn prisco.

1231   la viuela de arco ffas dulçes de vayladas,
adormiendo a vezes, muy alto a las vegadas,
boses dulses, saborosas, claras e bien pyntadas,
a las gentes alegra, todas las tyene pagadas.

1232   Dulçe caño entero sal con el panderete,
con sonajas de asofar fasen dulce sonete,
los organos y disen chançones e motete,
la hadedura aluardana entre ellos se entremete.

1233   Dulçema e axabeba, el fynchado albogon,
çinfonia e baldosa en esta fiesta sson,
el ffrançes odreçillo con estos se conpon,
la neçiacha manduria ally fase su son.

1234   Tronpas e añafiles ssalen con atanbales;
non fueron tyenpo ha plasenterias tales,
tan grandes alegrias nin atan comunales,
de juglares van llenas cuestas e eriales.

1235   las carreras van llenas de grandes proçesiones,
muchos omnes ordenados que otorgan perdones,
los legos segrales con muchos clerisones;
en la proçesion yua el abad de borbones.

1236   ordenes de çisten Con las de sant benito,
la orden de cruz niego con su abat bendito,
quantas ordenes son non las puse en escripto:
'¡venite, exultemus!' cantan en alto grito.

1237   orden de santiago con la del ospital,
calatraua e alcantara con la de buena val,
abbades beneditos en esta fiesta tal:
'¡te amore laudemus!' le cantan E al.

The psaltery also with them, higher than La Mota castle.*
The quill plectrum guitar dances in time.

1230   The Moorish psaltery and the harp with the Moorish rebec,
the French gavotte swings lively with them.
The flute speaks too, higher than a cliff,
along with the side drum, it's not worth a fig without it.

1231   The viol played with a bow moves sweetly down the scale;
at times it lulls, at times it is piercing,
sweet, notes that are tuneful, clear, well-played,
bringing people joy, pleasing everyone.

1232   The sweet zither plays with the tambourine,
and with brass timbrels, it makes a lovely sound.
Portable organs play songs and motet,
and the unversed strummer intrudes between them.

1233   Shawm and transverse flute, the large recorder,
the hurdy-gurdy and zither you play with a plectrum are at
                                                            the
celebration. The French bagpipe is played in harmony,
the foolish mandola adds its tune.

1234   Horns and Moorish trumpets come out with the kettledrums.
It's a long time since there was such rejoicing,
such great happiness is very rarely shared by all.
The hills and farmland were filled with minstrels.

1235   The streets are crowded with great processions,
many of the ordained are granting pardons,
secular priests with many acolytes,
the Abbot of the Borbones walks in the procession.*

1236   Cistercian orders alongside the Benedictines,
the Cluniac order with their blessed abbot;
there were so many I could not write them all down.
'venite, exultemus!' (Come, rejoice) they sing, in full voice.

1237   The Order of Saint James beside the Hospitallers' Order,
Calatrava and Alcántara with the order of Bonaval,
blessed abbots joined in the festival, singing:
'te amore, laudemus!' (Love, we praise thee) and nothing
                                                            else.

1238   ally van de ssant paulo los sus predicadores;
        non va y sant françisco, mas van flayres menores.
        ally van agostynes e disen sus cantores:
        '*¡exultemus E letemur!*' ministros E priores.

1239   los de la trinidat con los frayles del carmen,
        e los de santa eulalya, por que non se ensanen,
        todos manda que digam que canten e que llamen:
        '*¡benedictus qui venit!*' Responden todos: '*amen.*'

1240   ffrayles de sant anton van en esta quadrilla,
        muchos buenos cauallos e mucha malasilla.
        yuan los escuderos en la saya cortilla,
        cantando: 'andeluya!' anda toda la villa.

1241   Todas dueñas de orden, las blancas e las prietas,
        de çistel predicaderas e muchas menoretas,
        todas salen cantando, disiendo chansonetas:
        '*magne nobiscum domine*', que tañe a conpletas.

1242   De la parte del sol, vy venir vna seña,
        blanca, rresplandeçiente, mas alta que la peña,
        en medio figurada vna ymagen de dueña,
        labrada es de oro, non viste estameña.

1243   Traya en su cabeça vna noble corona,
        de piedras de grand preçio con amor se adona,
        llenas trahe las manos de mucha noble dona;
        non conplara la seña paris nin barçilona.

1244   a cabo de grand pieça vy al que la traye,
        estar rresplandeçiente, a todo el mundo rriye.
        non conpraria françia los paños que viste,
        el cauallo de españa muy grand preçio valie.

1245   Muchas vienen con el grand enperante,
        açiprestes E dueñas, estos vienen delante,
        luego el mundo todo e quanto vos dixe ante,
        de los grandes rroydos es todo el val sonante.

1246   Desque fue y llegado don amor el loçano,
        todos finojos fyncados besaron le la mano;

1238   The Dominicans, preachers of St Paul, were also there,
not the Franciscans, but minor friars.
The Augustinians were there, singing:
'*exultemus E letemur!*' (Let us rejoice and be filled with joy)
ministers and priors.

1239   The Trinitarians with the Carmelite friars,
and those of St Eulalia, to avoid indifference,
they all called for these words to be spoken, sung or shouted:
'*Benedictus qui venit!*' (Blessed is he who comes), and all
answer: 'Amen.'*

1240   The Friars of St Anthony were in this crowd,
a lot of good horses with a lot of bad saddles;
the squires in their short tunics joined in,
the whole town was there singing: 'Aleluya!'

1241   All ordained nuns, dressed in dark and light habits,
Cistercians, Dominicans and the Order of St Clare,
they were all chanting, singing songs without refrains:
'*magne nobiscum domine*' (Abide with us, Lord), the bells
are ringing for Compline.

1242   From where the sun rose in the East I saw a standard,
white, shining, high above the slopes.
In the centre was the picture of a woman,
worked in pure gold. She was not dressed in woollen clothes.

1243   She wore a noble crown on her head,
lovingly adorned with stones of great value.
In her hands were many rich gifts.
Neither Paris nor Barcelona could have paid for that banner.

1244   After a long while, I saw who carried it.
It was a resplendent sight, for he smiled at everyone.
All the money in France would not buy the clothes he wore,
his Spanish horse was worth a fortune.

1245   The great emperor brought many companies of people:
archpriests and ladies – these were in front –
then, it seemed, the whole world, all those I've mentioned
before, and the valley rang out to the great din.

1246   When lusty Love arrived at that place,
everyone kneeled to kiss his hand.

al que gela non besa, tenian lo por villano.
acaesçio grand contyenda luego en ese llano.

1247 Con quales possarie ovieron grand porfia,
querria leuar tal huesped luego la clerisia,
fueron le muy contrarios quantos tyenen fleylya,
tan bien ellas commo ellos querrian la mejoria.

1248 Dixieron ally luego todos los rreligiosos e ordenados:
'Señor, nos te daremos monesterios honrrados,
rrefitorios muy grandes e manteles parados,
los grandes dormitorios de lechos byen poblados.

1249 Non quieras a los clerigos por vesped de aquesta,
ca non tyenen moradas do touiesedes la fiesta,
Señor, chica morada a grand Señor non presta,
de grado toma el clerigo e amidos enpresta.

1250 Esquilman quanto puedem a quien seles allega,
non han de que te fagan seruiçios que te plegan,
a grand Señor conviene grand palaçio e grand vega,
para grand Señor non es posar en la bodega.'

1251 'Señor,' disen los clerigos, 'non quieras vestir lana,
estragarie vn frayle quanto el convento gana,
la su possaderia non es para ty sana,
tyenen muy grand galleta e chica la canpana.

1252 Non te faran Seruiçio en lo que dicho han,
mandan lechos syn rropa e manteles syn pan,
tyenen cosinas grandes, mas poca carne dam,
coloran su mucha agua con poco açafran.'

1253 'Señor, sey nuestro huesped,' disien los caualleros;
'non lo fagas, Señor,' disen los escuderos;
'dar te han dados plomados, perderas tus dineros,
al tomar vienen prestos, a la lid tardineros.

1254 Tyenden grandes alfamares, ponen luego tableros
pyntados de jaldetas, commo los tablajeros,
al contar las soldadas ellos vienen primeros,
para yr en frontera muchos ay costumeros.

Those who did not were thought mere country louts.
Next, a great argument arose on the plain.

1247   There was a tremendous dispute over his lodgings.
The secular clergy wanted to carry off such a prime guest,
but the monks and nuns quite opposed them;
both wanted the best for themselves.

1248   So all the ordained spoke to him as follows:
'Sir, we will give you our honoured monasteries,
large refectories and laden tablecloths,
great dormitories full of beds.

1249   You would not favour the clergy as hosts above us,
they do not have anywhere to hold your celebrations.
Their tiny dwellings are not fit for great lords;
the clergy take willingly but lend reluctantly.

1250   They fleece what they can from those who raise funds,
but they don't have the wherewithal to serve you and please
                                                        you.
A great lord needs a large palace and grounds,
he doesn't lodge in the wine cellar.'

1251   'Sir,' said the clergy, 'don't dress in wool,*
a friar would devour as much as the monastery earns.
Their lodgings could not possibly be healthy for you,
they have large wineskins and small prayer bells.

1252   They cannot give service as they said.
They promise beds with no bedclothes, tablecloths with no
                                                        bread.
Their saucepans are large, but they serve little meat;
they colour their watery soup with a touch of saffron.

1253   'Sir, be our guest,' say the knights;
'Don't do it, sir,' say the squires,
'they'll give you loaded dice, you'll lose your money.
They are ready to take, but tardy to fight.

1254   They spread out large rugs and set out the gaming tables
painted in yellow squares, just as if they were gamblers.
They come first to collect their pay,
but they are very slow to go to the frontier.

1255   Dexa todos aquestos, toma de nos Seruiçio.'
       las monjas le dixieron: 'Señor, non avrias viçio,
       son pobres bahareros de mucho mal bollyçio,
       Señor, vete con nusco, prueua nuestro çeliçio.'

1256   ally Responden todos que non gelo conssejauan,
       que amauan falsa mente a quantos las amauan,
       son parientas del cueruo, de cras en cras andauan,
       tarde cunplen o nunca lo que afiusiauan.

1257   Todo su mayor fecho es dar muchos sometes,
       palabrillas pyntadas, fermosillos afeytes,
       con gestos amorosos e engañosos jugetes,
       trahen a muchos locos con sus falsos rrisetes.

1258   Myo señor don amor, si el a mi creyera,
       el conbid de las monjas, aqueste rresçibiera;
       todo viçio del mundo E todo plaser oviera,
       sy en dormitorio entrara, nunca se arrepentiera.

1259   Mas commo el grand Señor non deue ser vandero,
       non quiso rresçebir el conbid rrefertero,
       dioles muchas graçias, estaua plasentero,
       a todos prometio merçed E a mi primero.

1260   Desque vy a mi señor que non tenia posada,
       E vy que la contyenda era y sosegada,
       fynque los mis ynojos antel e su mesnada,
       demandele merçed aquesta señalada:

1261   'Señor, tu me oviste de pequeno criado,
       el byen, si algo se, de ti me fue mostrado,
       de ti fuy aperçebido e de ti fuy castigado,
       en esta santa fiesta sey de mi ospedado.'

1262   Su mesura fue tanta que oyo mi petiçion,
       fue a la mi posada con esta procesion,
       todos le aconpañan con grand conssolaçion,
       tyenpo ha que non andude tan buena estaçion.

1263   ffueron se a sus posadas las mas de aquestas gentes,
       pero que en mi casa fyncaron los jnstrumentes.
       mi Señor don amor en todo paro mientes,
       Ca vido pequeñas cassas para tantos seruientes.

1255 Leave them all alone, be our guest instead.'
The nuns said: 'Sir, you will have no fun,
they are poor wretches only good for picking fights –
come with us, sir, try our hair-shirts.'

1256 The others all responded that they didn't advise it,
for nuns make bad lovers.
They are relatives of the raven, always crowing about
tomorrow,
but doing what they promise late or never.

1257 The best they can do is of little substance.
With pretty words, charming cosmetics,
they take in many fools with their false giggles,
tender gestures and deceitful trifles.

1258 Had my lord, Love, believed me,
he should have accepted the nuns' invitation.
He would have had all the delight and pleasure in the world,
he would never regret going into that dormitory.

1259 But since a great man should be impartial,
he would not accept any invitation causing strife.
He was very pleasant, thanking them kindly;
he promised a favour to everyone, and to me, first of all.

1260 When I realized my lord had no lodging
and saw that the argument had now abated,
I knelt before him and his company
and asked him the following favour:

1261 'Sir, you have raised me from a child,
and you showed me goodness, that I do know.
I was instructed by you, advised by you,
be my guest for this holy celebration.'

1262 He courteously listened to my request.
He went to my lodging with this procession.
Everyone accompanied him.
It was a long time since I'd walked so gladly.

1263 The rest of these people went to their lodgings,
but the instruments remained at my house.
My lord, Love, took everything in –
he thought the space too small for so many servants.

1264   Dyz: 'mando que mi tyenda fynque en aquel plado,
        ssy me viniere a ver algud enamorado
        de noche e de dia ally sea el estrado.'
        Ca todo tyenpo quiere a todos ser pagado.

1265   Desque ovo yantado fue la tyenda armada,
        nunca pudo ver omne cossa tan acabada,
        byen creo que de angeles fue tal cosa obrada,
        que omne terrenal desto non faria nada.

1266   la obra de la tyenda vos querria contar,
        aver se vos ha vn poco atardar la yantar,
        es vna grand estoria pero non es de dexar,
        muchos dexan la çena por fermoso cantar.

1267   El mastel en que se arma es blanco de color,
        vn marfyl ochauado, nuncal vistes mejor,
        de piedras muy preciosas çercado en derredor,
        alunbrase la tyenda de su grand rresplandor.

1268   en la çima del mastel vna piedra estaua;
        creo que era rroby, al fuego ssemejaua,
        non avia menester sol, tanto de sy alunbraua.
        de sseda son las cuerdas con que ella se tyraua.

1269   En suma vos lo cuento por non vos detener,
        do todo se escriue en toledo non ay papel.
        en la obra de dentro ay tanto de faser,
        que, si lo desir puedo, meresçia el beuer.

1270   luego a la entrada, a la mano derecha,
        estaua vna messa muy noble e muy fecha,
        delante ella grand fuego de si grand calor echa,
        tres comen a ella, vno a otro assecha.

1271   Tres caualleros comian todos a vn tablero,
        asentados al fuego, cada vno Señero;
        non se alcançarien con vn luengo madero,
        e non cabrie entrellos vn canto de dinero.

1272   El primero comia las primeras chereuias,
        comiença a dar çanahoria a bestias de estabrias;

1264 He said: 'I order my tent to be pitched in that meadow.
If some young man in love comes to visit,
my reception room shall be there night and day.
I want to please anyone at any time.'

1265 When he had dined, the tent was set up.
Such a perfect thing had never been seen before.
I think it was the work of angels,
no earthly man could do as much.

1266 I shall tell you what the tent was like,
so you must wait a bit longer for your lunch.
It's a long story, but not to be missed;
many people leave their dinner for a beautiful song.

1267 The tent pole was pure white in colour,
a shaft of octagonal ivory, you never saw better,
encrusted all round with very precious stones,
which lit up the tent in their splendour.

1268 At the top of the pole there was a precious stone,
a ruby I think it was, like fire,
no need for the sun, it lit everything around.
The tent ropes were made of silk.

1269 I'll be brief so as not to keep you;
if I wrote everything down, there'd be no paper left in
Toledo.
There is so much to say of the work of art within,
if I can tell it all, I'll earn a good drink.

1270 At the entrance, on the right,
stood a fine, well-made table.
Behind it a large fire gave out great heat.
Three people were seated round it eating, watching each
other.

1271 Three knights ate there, all at the same table,
seated at the fireside, each one quite alone.
One could not touch the other, even with the longest stick,
yet there was not the width of a coin's edge between them.

1272 The first was eating early parsnips,
and had just started feeding carrots to the stable animals,

da primero faryna a bueys de eryas,
ffase dias pequenos e mañanas frias.

1273 Comia Nueses primeras e asaua las castañas,
mandaua ssenbrar trigo e cortar las montañas,
matar los gordos puercos e desfaser las cabañas,
las viejas tras el ffuego ya disen las pastrañas.

1274 El Segundo comia carne salpresa,
estaua enturbiada con la niebra su mesa,
fase nueuo aseyte, con la blasa nol pesa,
con el frio a las de veses en las sus vnas besa.

1275 Comie el cavallero el toçino con verças,
enclaresçe los vinos con anbas sus almuesas,
anbos visten çamarras, querrien calientes quesas;
en pos deste estaua vno con dos cabeças,

1276 a dos partes otea aqueste cabeçudo,
gallynas con capirotada comia amenudo,
fasia çerrar sus cubas, fenchir las con enbudo,
echar de yuso yelos que guardan vino agudo.

1277 ffase a sus collaços faser los valladares,
rrefaser los pesebres, lynpiar los aluañares,
çerrar los silos del pan e seguir los pajares,
mas querrien estonçe peña que non loriga nin yjares.

1278 Estauan tres fijos dalgo a otra noble tabla,
mucho estauan llegados, vno a otro non fabla;
non se podrian alcançar con las vigas de gaola,
non cabria entre vno e otro vn cabello de paula.

1279 El primero de aquestos era chico enano,
oras triste, Sanudo, oras seye loçano;
tenia las yeruas nueuas en el plado ançiano,
partese del jnvierno e con el viene el verano.

1280 lo mas que este andaua era viñas podar,
E enxerir de escoplo e gauillas amondar;
mandaua poner viñas para buen vino dar,
con la chica alhiara nol pueden abondar.

and meal to the oxen in the ploughed fields.
He makes the days short and the early mornings chill.

1273 He was eating early nuts and roasting chestnuts,
ordering corn to be sown and wood to be cut on the
mountain,
fat pigs to be killed and herds to be split up for slaughter,
while old women spin their tales by the fire.

1274 The second was eating salted meat,
and his part of the table was thick with mist.
He was making new oil, sitting comfy by the fire,
while he blew on his fingers to warm them against the cold.

1275 This knight was eating stew with cabbage,
and clarifying wine with handfuls of chalk.
They were both wearing sheepskin jackets, they liked warm
clothing.
Beside the knight was a man with two heads;

1276 he looked in two directions at once,
and often ate chicken with a sauce of cheese, eggs and herbs.
He sealed his wine-casks and placed a funnel in them,
adding danewort to keep the wine in perfect condition.

1277 He ordered his servants to put up fences,
repair the mangers and clean out the drains,
close the grain silos and fill the straw lofts.
He preferred a warm pelt around his chest, instead of
armour.

1278 Three noblemen were seated round another fine table;
they were very close together but shared not a word.
They could not reach each other with a long pole or beam,
yet one of Paula's hairs would not have gone between.*

1279 The first one was a diminutive dwarf,
now sad and angry, now gay and laughing.
New grass is growing in the old meadow,
winter is taking its leave and spring is coming.

1280 He was about his business of pruning vines,
grafting with a chisel and thinning out shoots.
He ordered vines to be planted to produce good wine;
a small bottle is certainly not enough.

1281 El Segundo enbya a viñas cauadores,
echan muchos mugrones los amugronadores,
vid blanca fasen prieta los buenos enxeridores,
a omes, aves e bestias mete los en amores.

1282 Este tyene tres diablos presos en su cadena,
el vno enbiaua a las dueñas dar pena,
pesal en el lugar do la muger es buena,
desde entonçe comiença a pujar el avena.

1283 El Segundo diablo entra en los abades,
açiprestes e dueñas fablan sus poridades,
con este conpañero que les dan lybertades,
que pierden las obladas e fablen vanidades.

1284 antes viene cueruo blanco que pierdan asneria,
todos e ellas andan en modorria,
los diablos do se fallan llegan se a conpania,
fasen sus diabluras e su trauesura.

1285 Enbia otro diablo en los asnos entrar,
en las cabeças entra, non en otro lugar,
fasta que pasa agosto non dexan de rrebusnar,
desde ally pierden seso, esto puedes prouar.

1286 El terçero fidalgo esta de flores lleno,
con los vientos que fase grana trigo E çeteno.
fase poner estacas que dan aseyte bueno,
a los moços medrosos ya los espanta el trueno.

1287 Andan tres Ricos onbres ally en vna danca,
entre vno e otro non cabe punta de lança,
del primero al segundo ay vna grand labrança,
el segundo al terçero con cosa non le alcança.

1288 El primero los panes e las frutas grana,
figados de cabrones con rruy baruo armoçaua,
fuyan del los gallos, a todos los mataua,
los baruos e las truchas amenudo çenaua.

1289 buscaua cassa fria, fuya de la siesta,
la calor del estio doler fase la tyesta,
anda muy mas loçano que pauon en floresta,
busca yeruas e ayres en la sierra enfiesta.

1281 The second was sending men to dig the vineyards,
while others layered a lot of shoots.
A skilled grafter can grow a black grape from a white vine.
He made men, fowl and beast grow amorous.

1282 He had three devils imprisoned in chains.
He sent one to cause women trouble
and come to bear where a woman is best.
Now the oats are growing abundantly.*

1283 The second devil shakes up the abbots.
Archpriests and ladies tell each other secrets,
because of this companion who gives them freedom,
so they lose their offerings and say vain things.

1284 Crows will turn white before they stop playing the fool.
All of them, male and female, are in a dream.
The devils find them wherever they are and draw near;
they exploit their wickedness and rascally tricks.

1285 The other devil was sent to enter the asses.
He entered their heads – nowhere else –
they won't stop braying until after August.
They lose their sense, you can see it.

1286 The third nobleman is covered in flowers.
In the winds that blow the corn and rye grow.
He plants cuttings of olive branches to give good oil.
Now nervous children are frightened by thunder.

1287 Next three noblemen take part in a dance.
Between the first and the second lies a lot of farmland,
from the second to the third nothing can reach,
yet the point of a lance would not fit between them.

1288 The first ripened corn and fruit,
and lunched on goat's liver and rhubarb.
Chickens fled from him since he would eat them all.
He often dined on barbels and trout.

1289 He sought a cool house out of the midday heat.
The summer warmth made his head ache.
He searched for herbs and cool breezes in the high
                                                    mountains,
and was more mettlesome than a peacock in the woods.

1290   El Segundo tenia an su mano la foz,
        segando las çeuadas de todo el alfoz,
        comie las bebras nueuas e cogia el arroz,
        agraz, nueuo comiendo enbargole la boz.

1291   Enxeria los arbores con ajena cortesa,
        comia nueuos palales, sudaua syn peresa,
        boluia las aguas frias de su naturalesa,
        traya las manos tyntas de la mucha çeresa.

1292   El terçero andaua los çetenos trayendo,
        trigos e todas mieses en las eras tendiendo,
        estauan de los arbores las frutas sacodiendo,
        el tauano al asno ya le yua mordiendo.

1293   Comiença a comer las chiquitas perdices,
        sacan varriles frios de los pozos helyses,
        la mosca mordedor fas traher las narises,
        a las bestias por tierra e abaxar las çeruiçes.

1294   tres labradores vinien todos vna carrera,
        al Segundo atiende el que va en delantera,
        el terçero al Segundo atiendel en frontera,
        el que viene non alcança al otro quel espera.

1295   El primero comia vuas ya maduras,
        comia maduros figos de las fygueras duras,
        trillando e ablentando aparta pajas puras,
        con el viene otoño con dolençias e curas.

1296   El Segundo adoba e rrepara carrales,
        estercuela baruechos e sacude nogales,
        comiença a bendimiar vuas de los parrales,
        esconbra los Rastrojos e çerca los corrales.

1297   Pissa los buenos vinos el labrador terçero,
        fynche todas sus cubas commo buen bodeguero,
        enbya derramar la sienpre al ero,
        açerca se el jnvierno bien commo de primero.

1298   Yo fuy maruillado desque vy tal vision,
        coyde que soñaua pero que verdat son,
        rrogue a mi Señor que me diese rraçon,
        por do yo entendiese que era o que non.

1290 The second carried a sickle in his hand,
and reaped fodder throughout the district.
He ate the early figs and gathered rice.
He lost his voice because the grapes were not ripe.

1291 He grafted the trees with new bark,
ate new honeycomb, sweated freely.
He drank the cold water of fountains and springs.
His hands were stained red with cherry juice.

1292 The third went harvesting the rye,
spreading wheat and other corn over the threshing floors.
He shook the fruit down from the trees
while the horsefly bit the ass mercilessly.

1293 He begins to eat the youngest partridge,
and draw cold wine jugs from the wells of melted snow.
The horsefly irritates the noses of the animals,
making them kneel to rub them on the ground.

1294 Three farmworkers all came along the same road;
the one in front awaits the second,
while the second awaits the third, at the border,
but the one behind never reaches the one in front.

1295 The first was already eating ripe grapes
and ripe figs from the hardy fig trees;
threshing and winnowing, he separates the good, clean
straw,
bringing with him the autumn with its aches and pains.

1296 The second prepares and repairs wine-barrels,
manuring fallow land and shaking down walnuts.
He starts to harvest the grapes from the vines,
clears the stubble and fences in animal enclosures.

1297 The third worker treads the good wine,
filling all his barrels like a good cellarer.
He sends seed to be sown in the fields,
for winter approaches, as it did at the start.

1298 I marvelled when I saw this vision
and thought I was dreaming, though I was not.
I asked my lord to explain it to me,
and help me understand what it meant.

1299   el mi Señor don amor Commo omne letrado,
        en sola vna palabra puso todo el tratado,
        por do el que lo oyere sera çertificado;
        esta fue rrespuesta, Su dicho ableuiado:

1300   'El tablero, la tabla, la dança, la carrera,
        son quatro tenporades del año del espera,
        los omes son los meses, cosa es verdadera,
        andan e non se alcançan, atiendense en Ribera.'

1301   otras cossas estrañas, muy graues de creer,
        vy muchas en la tienda; mas por non vos detener,
        e por que enojo soso non vos querria ser,
        non quiero de la tienda mas prologo faser.

1302   Myo señor, desque fue su tyenda aparejada,
        vino dormir a ella, fue poca su estada;
        desque se leuanto non vino su mesnada,
        los mas con don carnal fasian su morada.

1303   Desque lo vy de espaçio, commo era su criado,
        atreui me e preguntel que el tyenpo pasado,
        ¿commo nunca me viera, o do avia morado?
        rrespondio me con sospiro e commo con coydado.

1304   Dyxo: 'en la jnvernada visite a sseuilla,
        toda el andalusia, que non fynco y villa,
        ally toda persona de grado se me omilla,
        andando mucho viçioso, quanto fue marauilla.

1305   Entrada la quaresma vine me para toledo,
        coyde estar viçioso, plasentero e ledo,
        falle grand santidat, fiso me estar quedo,
        pocos me rresçebieron nin me fesieron del dedo.

1306   Estaua en vn palaçio pyntado de almagra,
        vino a mi mucha duena, de mucho ayuno magra,
        con muchos pater nostres e con mucha oraçion agra,
        echaron me de la çibdat por la puerta de visagra.

1307   Avn quise porfiar, fuy me para vn monasterio;
        falle por la caustra e por el çiminterio
        muchas religiosas rresando el salterio;
        vy que non podia sofrir aquel laserio.

1299   My lord, Love, a man of letters,
       explained it all in a single verse,
       making it clear to anyone who listened.
       This was his answer, his brief summing-up:

1300   'The two dining tables, the dance, the road,
       are the four seasons of the solar year,
       the men are the months, and this is fact.
       They move but never touch, they wait for each other at
                                                   their limits.'

1301   In that tent I saw many other strange things,
       hard to believe, but so as not to delay
       and annoy you in any way,
       I will not say much more about it.

1302   When my lord saw his tent was ready,
       he came to sleep in it – but his stay was short.
       When he got up, he could not see his company;
       most of them were staying with Carnal.

1303   When I saw he was having a few quiet moments,
       I plucked up courage and asked him
       why he had not seen me recently, where he had been.
       He answered with a sigh, as if he had a lot of cares.

1304   He said: 'In the winter I visited Seville,
       all Andalusia, I didn't leave a city out.
       There, everyone gladly bowed before me.
       I had a very good time, which surprised me.

1305   At the beginning of Lent, I came to Toledo,
       thinking I would be content and happy.
       I found great holiness, which cooled me down.
       Very few welcomed me or beckoned to me.

1306   I was in a palace painted with red ochre.
       Many women came to me, thin with fasting,
       with a lot of "Our Fathers" and insistent prayer.
       They threw me out of the city at the Bisagra gate.

1307   But I was stubborn and went to a monastery,
       where I found many nuns praying the psalter
       in the cloisters and in the cemetery,
       and realized I couldn't bear such suffering.

1308 Coyde en otra orden fallar cobro alguno
   do perdiese laserio; non pud fallar ninguno.
   con oraçion e lymosna e con mucho ayuno
   rredrauan me de sy commo si fuese lobuno.

1309 En caridat fablauan, mas non mela fasien,
   yo veya las caras, mas non lo que desien;
   mercado falla omne en que gana sy se detyen,
   rrefez es de coger se el omne do se falla bien.

1310 Andando por la çibdat, rradio E perdido,
   dueñas e otras fenbras fallaua amenudo,
   con sus aue marias fasian me estar mudo;
   desque vy que me mal yua, fuy me dende sañudo.

1311 Saly desta laseria de coyta e de lastro,
   fuy tener la quaresma a la villa de castro,
   rresçebieron me muy byen a mi e a mi rrastro,
   pocos ally falle que me non llamasen padrasto.

1312 Pues carnal es venido quiero perder laseria,
   la quaresma catolica do aquesta quiteria,
   quiero yr ver alcala, morare ay la feria,
   dende andare la tyerra, dando a muchos materia.'

1313 Otro dia mañana antes que fues de dia,
   mouio con su mesnada amor e fue su via,
   dexome con cuydado, pero con allegria,
   este mi Señor sienpre tal constubre avia.

1314 Syenpre, do quier que sea, pone mucho coydado
   con el muy grand plaser al su enamorado;
   syenpre quiere alegria, plaser e ser pagado,
   de triste e de sanudo no quiere ser ospedado.

DE COMO EL ARÇIPRESTE LLAMO A SU VIEJA QUE LE
CATASE ALGUD COBRO

1315 Dia de quasy-modo, iglesias E altares
   vy llenos de alegrias de bodas e cantares;
   todos avien grand fiesta, fasien grandes yantares,
   andan de boda en boda clerigos e juglares.

1316 los que ante son solos, desque eran casados,
   veya los de dueñas estar aconpañados;

1308   I thought I would find solace in another order
        and cease to suffer. I could find none.
        With prayer and alms and great fasting,
        they kept their distance as if I were a wolf.

1309   They spoke of charity, but showed me none.
        I saw their faces, but not what they were saying.
        Men find a market and gain if they stay.
        It is foolish to leave a place where you are at ease.

1310   I wandered through the city, lost and alone,
        and often came across fine ladies and other women.
        Their "Ave Marias" kept me silent.
        When I realized things were going badly, I left angrily.

1311   I was freed from this suffering and sorrow,
        as I went to the town of Castro for Lent,
        and my followers and I were very well received.
        Very few folk there called me stepfather.

1312   Now Carnal has come, I don't want to feel sad any more,
        I give Catholic Lent to St Quitit.*
        I want to see Alcalá and stay for the fair,
        from there cover the area and give people something to talk
                                                                about.'

1313   The next morning, before daybreak,
        Love moved on with his company,
        and left me in a state of both sorrow and joy,
        as it was his custom to do.

1314   Wherever he goes he causes great pain,
        and great pleasure to the lover.
        He always seeks happiness, pleasure and contentment,
        and will not be hosted by the sad and angry man.

HOW THE ARCHPRIEST ASKED HIS OLD GO-BETWEEN TO
FIND SOLACE FOR HIM

1315   On the Sunday after Easter I saw churches
        and altars overflowing with joy, weddings and song.
        Everyone was having a party, with lavish feasts.
        Clergy and minstrels went from one wedding to another.

1316   Those who were single before, once married
        were in the company of ladies.

pense commo oviese de tales gasajados,
ca omne que es solo sienpre pienso cuydados.

1317 ffyz llamar trota conventos, la mi vieja sabida;
presta e plasentera de grado fue venida.
rroguel que me catase alguna tal garrida,
Ca solo syn conpaña era penada vida.

1318 Dixo me que conosçia vna byuda loçana,
muy rrica e byen moça e con mucha vfana.
diz: 'açipreste, amad esta; yo ire alla mañana
E si esta rrecabdamos nuestra obra non es vana.'

1319 con la mi vejesuela enbiele ya que
con ellas estas cantigas que vos aqui Robre.
ella non la erro e yo non le peque;
si poco ende trabaje, muy poco ende saque.

1320 assaz fizo mi vieja quanto ella faser pudo,
mas non pudo trabar, atar, nin dar nudo;
torno a mi muy triste e con coraçon agudo.
diz: 'do non te quieren mucho, non vayas amenudo.'

DE COMO EL ARÇIPRESTE FUE ENAMORADO DE VNA
DUEÑA QUE VIDO ESTAR FAZIENDO ORAÇION

1321 Dia era de sant marcos, ffue fiesta señalada,
toda la santa iglesia fas proçesion onrrada,
de las mayores del año, de xristianos loada;
acaeçiome vna ventura, la fiesta non pasada.

1322 vy estar vna dueña fermosa de veltad,
rrogando muy deuota ante la majestad;
rrogue a la mi vieja que me oviese piadat,
E que andudiese por mi passos de caridat.

1323 Ella fiso mi rruego, pero con antipara.
dixo: 'non querria esta que me costase cara
commo la marroquia que me corrio la vara;
mas el leal amigo al byen e al mal se para.'

1324 ffue con la pleytesia, tomo por mi afan,
fisose que vendie joyas, Ca de vso lo han;
entro en la posada, rrespuesta non le dan,
non vido a la mi vieja ome, gato nin can.

I wondered how I could enjoy such pleasure,
for a man who is alone is always sad and pensive.

1317 I summoned Trotaconventos, my clever old lady,
and she came gladly, ready and willing.
I asked her to find me a lovely woman like those,
for it was a sad life alone with no company.

1318 She told me she knew a lively widow,
rich and young and full of vigour.
'Archpriest, have her – I will go over there tomorrow,
and if we succeed, our work is not in vain.'

1319 I sent a little something with my old dear,
and also the songs I have written down for you here.
She did not lead her astray and I did not sin –
I didn't put much into it and got very little out too.

1320 The old woman did the best she could,
but she grasped nothing, no knot was tied.
She came back to me very sad and downhearted,
saying: 'Don't keep going where you are not wanted.'

HOW THE ARCHPRIEST FELL IN LOVE WITH A WOMAN HE SAW PRAYING

1321 It was St Mark's day, a religious festival,
all the holy church was in honourable procession,
praised by the Christians as a high point of the year.
I had an adventure, before the festival was over.

1322 I saw a lovely woman, a beauty,
praying devoutly before Christ's majesty,
so I asked my old woman to take pity on me
and walk in the steps of charity for me.

1323 She did as I asked, but with some reluctance,
saying: 'I hope it doesn't cost me as dear
as the Moroccan girl who put me on the spot.
But a loyal friend is prepared for good and evil.'

1324 She went to plead my suit and strove on my behalf.
She pretended to sell jewellery, as was the custom.
She went into the house but got no answer –
the old woman was seen by neither man, nor cat, nor dog.

1325 Dixol por que yva e diole aquestos verssos:
     'Señora,' diz, 'conprad traueseros e aviesos.'
     dixo la buena dueña: 'tus desires trauiesos
     entyende los, vrraca, todos esos y esos.'

1326 'fija,' dixo la vieja, '¿osar vos he fablar?'
     dixo la dueña: 'vrraca ¿por que lo has de dexar?'
     'Señora, pues yo digo de casamiento far.'
     '¡ca! mas val suelta estar la viuda que mal casar.'

1327 'Mas val tener algun cobro mucho ençelado,
     ca mas val buen amigo que mal marido velado,
     fija qual vos yo daria que vos serie mandado,
     muy loçano E cortes, Sobre todos esmerado.'

1328 Sy Recabdo o non la buena menssajera,
     vyno me muy alegre, dixo me de la primera:
     'el que al lobo enbia ¡a la fe! carne espera.'
     estos fueron los versos que leuo mi trotera:

1329 ffablo la tortolilla en el rregno de rrodas,
     diz: '¿non avedes pauor, vos, las mugeres todas,
     de mudar vuestro amor por aver nueuas bodas?'
     por ende casa la duena con cauallero apodas.

1330 E desque ffue la dueña con otro ya casada,
     escusose de mi e de mi fue escusada,
     por non faser pecado, o por non ser osada,
     toda muger por esto non es de ome vsada.

1331 Desque me vy señero e syn fulana solo
     enbie por mi vieja; ella dixo: '¿adolo?'
     vino a mi rreyendo, diz: 'omillome, don polo,
     fe a que buen amor qual buen amiga buscolo.'

DE COMO TROTA CONVENTOS CONSSEJO AL ARÇIPRESTE
QUE AMASE ALGUNA MONJA E DE LO QUE LE CONTESÇIO
CON ELLA
1332 Ella dixo: 'amigo, oyd me vn poquiello,
     amad alguna monja, creed me de conssejo,
     non se casara luego, nin saldra a conçejo,
     andares en amor de grand dura sobejo.

1325   She told the woman why she'd come, and gave her these
                                                verses:
      'Madam,' she said, 'buy my pillows and bedclothes.'
      The good lady replied: 'I understand your naughty
      comments, Urraca, every one of them.'

1326   'My dear,' said the old woman, 'dare I speak?'
      She replied: 'Why would you not speak, Urraca?'
      'Madam, in that case, I am talking of marriage.
      It's better for a widow to be free, than make a bad marriage.

1327   It's worth more to have hidden solace,
      a good lover is better than a bad husband.
      My dear, I could find you a man who'd be obedient,
      vigorous, polite and above all careful.'

1328   Whether she succeeded or not, the good messenger
      came back in a happy mood and said straight off:
      'He who sends the wolf – by heavens! – should expect meat.'
      These were the verses my convent-trotter took:

1329   The little turtle-dove sang in the kingdom of Rodas:
      'Aren't all you women afraid to change
      your love for a new relationship?
      Is this why a lady marries a gentleman, I wonder?'

1330   And when the lady had married someone else,
      she shunned me and was shunned by me
      so as not to sin, or because she didn't dare.
      All women cease to have dealings with me for this reason.

1331   I was again alone, without a woman, solo,
      so I sent for the old dame, who said: 'Where next?'
      She came laughing and said: 'I bow, Sir Polo,*
      as "good love" who found you a good woman friend.'

HOW TROTACONVENTOS ADVISED THE ARCHPRIEST TO LOVE A NUN AND WHAT HAPPENED AS A RESULT

1332   She said: 'My friend, listen to me a moment,
      why not love a nun, it's good advice.
      She won't go and get married, or make things public,
      and your love should last a very long time.

1333　yo la serui vn tienpo, more y byen dies años.
　　　tienen a sus amigos viçiosos syn sosaños;
　　　¡quien dirie los manjares, los presentes tamaños,
　　　los muchos letuarios nobles e tan estraños!

1334　Muchos de leutarios les dan muchas de veses,
　　　diaçitron, codonate, letuario de nueses,
　　　otros de mas quantia de çahanorias rraheses
　　　enbyan e otras cada dia arreueses.

1335　Cominada alixandria, con el buen dia-gargante,
　　　el diaçitron abatys, con el fino gengibrante,
　　　miel rrosado, diaçiminio, diantioso va delante,
　　　e la rroseta nouela que deuiera desir ante.

1336　adraguea e alfenique con el estomatricon.
　　　e la garriofilota con dia margariton,
　　　tria sandalix muy fyno con diasanturion,
　　　que es, para doñear, preçiado e noble don.

1337　ssabed que de todo açucar ally anda bolando,
　　　poluo, terron e candy e mucho del rrosado,
　　　açucar de confites e açucar violado,
　　　E de muchas otras guisas que yo he oluidado.

1338　Monpesler, alexandria, la nonbrada valencia,
　　　non tyenen de letuarios tantos nin tanta espeçia;
　　　los mas nobles presenta la dueña ques mas preçia,
　　　en noblesas de amor ponen toda su femençia.

1339　E avn vos dire mas de quanto aprendi:
　　　do an vino de toro non enbian valadi.
　　　desque me parti dellas todo este viçio perdy;
　　　quien a monjas non ama non vale vn marauedy.

1340　ssyn todas estas noblesas han muy buenas maneras,
　　　Son mucho encobiertas, donosas, plasenteras,
　　　mas saben e mas valen sus moças cosineras,
　　　para el amor todo, que dueñas de sueras.

1341　Commo ymajenes pyntadas de toda fermosura,
　　　fijas dalgo muy largas e francas de natura,

1333 I was their servant for a while, for a good ten years.
      They keep their men-friends happy and carefree.
      You'd never guess at the food, the size of their gifts,
      the number of electuaries, rich and strange!

1334 They often give their lovers electuaries –
      preserved lemon rind, sweet quinces, some with nuts,
      others in larger quantities made from cheap carrots.
      They send them every day, alternately.

1335 Candy with cumin seed from Alexandria, and gum
                                                    tragacanth,
      a monk's special recipe for citrus rind, with finest ginger,
      honey of roses, cumin-seed sweets, sweets made of flowers,
      and the new pink one, I should have mentioned before.

1336 Sugar-coated sweets and almond paste, with cures for
                                                    stomach-
      ache, and electuaries with gillyflower and those with
                                                    powdered
      pearls, very fine sandalwood mixed with *Satyrium trifolium,*
      which is for love-making, a valued and noble gift.

1337 I tell you, all kinds of sugar brim over there,
      powdered or in lumps or candy or rose sugar,
      confectionery sugar and violet sugar,
      and lots of other kinds I have forgotten.

1338 Montpellier, Alexandria and renowned Valencia
      don't have such a variety of electuaries.
      The lady with most self-esteem offers the best ones.
      They put all their energy into the refinements of love.

1339 I'll tell you more of what I learned:
      where there is Toro wine, they don't drink the cheap stuff.
      When I left them, I lost all this luxury.
      You're not worth a farthing if you don't have a nun.

1340 Even without all this subtlety, they are well-mannered,
      very discreet, witty and glad to give pleasure.
      Their kitchen girls know more and are better at
      love than any aristocratic lady.

1341 They are like a painted statue of beauty,
      noblewomen with open, generous natures,

grandes demandaderas, amor sienpre les dura,
con medidas conplidas e con toda mesura.

1342 Todo plaser del mundo e todo buen donear,
ssolas de mucho Sabor e el falaguero jugar,
todo es en las monjas mas que en otro lugar;
prouad lo esta vegada e quered ya sossegar.'

1343 yo le dixe: 'trota conventos, escucha me vn poquillo;
¿yo entrar como puedo, ado non se tal portillo?'
ella diz: 'yo lo andare en pequeño rratillo,
quien fase la canasta, fara el canestillo.'

1344 ffuese a vna monja que avia Seruida,
dixo me quel preguntara: '¿qual fue la tu venida?
¿como te va mi vieja? ¿como pasas tu vida?'
'Señora,' dixo la vieja, 'asy comunal vyda.

1345 Desque me party de vos a vn açipreste siruo,
mançebo byen andante, de su ayuda biuo,
para que a vos sirua cadal dia lo abyuo.
Señora, del convento non lo fagades esquiuo.'

1346 Dixol doña garoça: '¿enbio te el a mi?'
dixele: 'non Señora, mas yo melo comedi.
por el byen que me fesistes en quanto vos serui,
para vos lo querria, tal que mejor non vy.'

1347 aquesta buena dueña avie seso bien Sano,
era de buena vida, non de fecho lyuiano.
diz: 'asy me contesçeria con tu consssejo vano,
como con la culebra contesçio al ortolano.

ENXIENPLO DEL ORTOLANO E DE LA CULUEBRA
1348 Era vn ortolano byen sinpre e syn mal;
en el mes de enero con fuerte tenporal,
andando por su huerta, vido so vn peral
vna culebra chica, medio muerta atal.

1349 Con la nieue E con el viento e con la elada fria,
estaua la culebra medio amodorrida;
el omne piadoso que la vido aterida,
doliose mucho della, quisole dar la vida.

and very flirtatious. Love always lasts with them,
for they are courteous, accomplished and moderate.

1342 All the pleasure in the world and courtship too,
delight that is savoured, flattering playfulness,
all these things are better with nuns than with anyone else.
Try it this time and you'll be quite content.'

1343 I replied: 'Trotaconventos, listen to me,
how can I get in, when I don't know the entrance?'
She said: 'I can get there in a short time;
whoever can make a large basket can make a little one too.'

1344 She went to see a nun she used to work for
and told me the nun asked her: 'Why have you come?
How are you, old mother? How is life with you?'
'Madam,' she replied, 'it is reasonable, not too bad.

1345 Since I left you I have worked for an archpriest,
a prosperous young man, and I live with his help.
I urge him to serve you, every day I do.
Madam, don't send him away from the convent.'

1346 The nun Garoza* said: 'Did he send you to me?'
The reply was: 'No, it was my idea,
for the good you did me when I worked here.
I would like him to be yours, as I've never seen a better.'

1347 That good lady was full of wisdom and common sense,
and lived a pure life, without frivolity.
She said: 'Your vain advice reminds me
of what the snake told the gardener.

THE FABLE OF THE GARDENER AND THE SNAKE
1348 There was a simple, honest gardener
who was walking through his garden
in January, in a bad storm. Under a pear tree
he spied a small snake which looked half-dead.

1349 The snake was very sluggish
because of the snow and wind and ice.
When the kind man saw it stiff with cold
he felt very sorry for it and tried to revive it.

1350   Tomola en la falda e leuola a su casa,
        pusola çerca del fuego, çerca de buena blasa,
        abiuo la culebra ante que la el asa,
        entro en vn forado desa cosina rrasa.

1351   aqueste ome bueno dauale cada dia
        del pan E de la leche e de quanto el comia;
        creçio con el grand vyçio e con el grand bien que tenia,
        tanto que sierpe grande a todos paresçia.

1352   venido es el estio, la siesta affyncada,
        que ya non avia miedo de viento nin de elada,
        salyo de aquel forado sañuda E ayrada;
        començo de enponçoñar con venino la posada.

1353   dixole el ortolano: "¡vete de aqueste lugar,
        non fagas aqui dapño!" elle fuese en-sañar,
        ablaçolo tan fuerte que lo querria afogar,
        apretandolo mucho, cruel mente, syn vagar.

1354   alegrase el malo en dar por miel venino,
        E por fructo dar pena al amigo e al vesino,
        por piedat engaño donde bien le avino,
        ansi derecha mente a mi de ty me vino.

1355   tu estauas coytada, poble, ssyn buena fama,
        onde ovieses cobro non tenias adama,
        ayudete con algo, fuy grand tyenpo tu ama,
        conssejas me agora que pierda la mi alma.'

1356   'sseñora,' dixo la vieja, '¿por que so baldonada?
        quando trayo presente so mucho falagada,
        vine manos vasias, finco mal escultada;
        conteçe me como al galgo viejo que non caça nada.

ENXIENPLO DEL GALGO E DEL SEÑOR

1357   El buen galgo ligero, corredor e valyente,
        avia, quando era jouen, pies ligeros, corriente,
        avia buenos colmillos, buena boca e diente;
        quantas liebres veya prendialas ligeramente.

1358   al su Señor el sienpre algo le presentaua,
        nunca de la corrida vasio le tornaua,
        el su Señor por esto mucho le falagaua,
        a todos sus vesinos del galgo se loaua.

1350   He wrapped it in his clothes and carried it to his house;
        he put it near the fire, near the warmth of the blaze.
        The snake perked up, and before it was roasted,
        it went and found a hole in the smooth kitchen floor.

1351   Every day the good man gave it
        bread and milk, and some of his own food.
        The snake grew because it was happy and well cared for,
        until it looked like an enormous serpent to everyone.

1352   When the summer came, with the heat well established,
        and no longer a threat from the wind and cold,
        it came out of its hole angry and irate,
        and began to poison the house with its venom.

1353   The gardener said to it: "Get out of here!
        Don't you harm this place!" and it grew enraged.
        It wrapped itself round him tightly as if to strangle him,
        squeezing him cruelly, hissing all the time.

1354   The bad person takes pleasure in giving venom for honey,
        and giving sorrow, not fruit, to friend and neighbour,
        deceit for compassion, when it has been received.
        This has come to me from you in the same way.

1355   You were poor and suffering, down on your luck;
        where you were successful, you had no affection.
        I helped you a little, I was your mistress a long time,
        and now you're advising me to lose my soul.'

1356   'Mistress,' said the old woman, 'why insult me?
        When I bring a present, you make a great fuss of me –
        today when my hands are empty, you scold me.
        It's like the story of the old greyhound who caught nothing.

THE FABLE OF THE GREYHOUND AND HIS MASTER

1357   The good hare-hunting greyhound, fast and brave,
        had swift feet when he was young.
        He had good fangs, a sound mouth and teeth,
        and when he saw a hare he caught it with agility.

1358   He always gave his master something,
        he never came back from the chase with nothing.
        His master made a great fuss of him because of this,
        and boasted about the greyhound to all his neighbours.

1359 Con el mucho laserio ffue muy ayna viejo,
perdio luego los dientes e corria poquiello,
fue su Señor a caça e Salio vn conejo,
prendiol e nol pudo tener, fuesele por el vallejo.

1360 El caçador al galgo firiolo con vn palo;
el galgo querellandose dixo: "¡que mundo malo!
quando era mançebo desian me: ¡halo, alo!
agora que so viejo disen que poco valo.

1361 En mi joventud caça por pies non sse me yua,
a mi Señor la daua quier muerta o quier byua,
estonçes me loaua, agora que so viejo me esquiua,
quando non le trayo nada non me falaga nin me sylua.

1362 los byenes E los loores muchos de mançebos,
defienden la fraquesa, culpa de la vejez;
por ser el omne viejo non pierde por ende prez,
el seso del buen viejo non se mueue de rrefez.

1363 En amar al mançebo e a la su loçania,
E des-echar al viejo e faser le peoria,
es torpedat e mengua e maldat e villania;
en el viejo se loa su buena mançebia.

1364 El mundo cobdiçioso es de aquesta natura:
sy el amor da fructo, dando mucho atura;
non dando nin seruiendo, el amor poco dura.
de amigo syn prouecho non ha el ome cura.

1365 byen quanto da el omne, en tanto es preçiado:
quando yo daua mucho era mucho loado,
agora que non do algo so vil e despreçiado;
non ay mençion nin grado de seruiçio ya pasado.

1366 Non sse nienbran algunos del mucho byen antyguo,
quien a mal ome sirue sienprel sera mendigo,
el malo a los suyos non les presta vn figo,
apenas quel pobre viejo falla ningud amigo."

1367 E, sseñora, convusco a mi atal acaesçe:
serui vos byen e syruo en lo que contesçe;

1359   Because of all his hard work, he soon grew old;
he lost his teeth and couldn't run very far.
His master went to hunt and out came a rabbit.
The dog picked it up but couldn't hold it; it escaped into the
valley.

1360   The hunter hit the greyhound with a stick.
The greyhound complained: "What an evil world!
When I was young, they said, 'Go on, halloo!'
and now I am old, they say I am worth nothing.

1361   In my youth the prey didn't get through my legs,
I took it to my master, dead or alive.
Then he praised me, now he scolds me
when I don't bring him anything, he doesn't praise me or
whistle.

1362   The good things and praise of youth
are hindered by weakness, the scourge of old age.
If a man is old, he doesn't lose his value;
good sense doesn't change easily with age.

1363   To love youth and strength
and cast old age aside is harmful,
it is foolish and a mistake, evil and villainy.
The youthfulness of the old is praised.

1364   The covetous world is like this.
If love bears fruit, it usually lasts through giving.
Love does not last without serving or giving.
A man ignores a friend who is of no benefit to him.

1365   Whatever a man gives, by that he is valued.
When I gave a lot, I was greatly praised.
Now when I give nothing, I am vile and despised;
there's no mention of, no thanks for past services.

1366   Some people forget what good there was.
If you serve a bad man you will always be a beggar.
The bad man does not give a toss for his own,
a man who is old and poor can scarcely find a friend."

1367   And, mistress, you are acting the same with me.
I served you well and serve you still in these circumstances,

por que vyn syn presente, la vuestra Saña cresçe,
e so mal denostada segud que ya paresçe.'

1368 'vieja,' dixo la dueña, 'çierto yo non menty,
por lo que me dixiste yo mucho me ssenti,
de lo que yo te dixe luego me arrepenty,
por que talente bueno entiendo yo en ty.

1369 Mas temome e Reçelo que mal engañada sea,
non querria que me fuese commo al mur del aldea,
con el mur de la villa yendo a faser enplea;
desir te he la fasaña e fynque la pelea.

ENSIENPLO DEL MUR DE MONFERRADO E DEL MUR DE
GUALFAJARA

1370 Mur de guadalajara vn lunes madrugara,
fuese a monferrado, a mercado andaua,
vn mur de franca barua rresçibiol en su caua,
conbidol a yantar e diole vna favaua.

1371 Estaua en mesa pobre buen gesto E buena cara,
con la poca vianda buena voluntad para,
a los pobres manjares el plaser los rrepara,
pagos del buen talente mur de guadalajara.

1372 la su yantar comida el manjar acabado,
conbido el de la villa al mur de mon ferrado,
que el martes quisiese yr ver el su mercado,
e como el fue suyo fuese el su conbidado.

1373 ffue con el a ssu casa E diol mucho de queso,
mucho tosino lardo que non era salpreso,
enxundias e pan cocho syn rraçion e syn peso,
con esto el aldeano touos por byen apreso.

1374 Manteles du buen lyenço, vna branca talega
byen llena de farina, el mur ally se allega;
mucha onrra le fiso e seruiçio quel plega,
alegria, buen Rostro con todo esto se llega.

1375 Esta en mesa rrica mucha buena vyanda,
vn manjar mejor que otro amenudo y anda,
E de mas buen talente, huesped esto demanda;
solas con yantar buena todos omes ablanda.

but because I came without a gift, you are very annoyed,
and I am maligned, it seems.'

1368 'Old lady,' said the nun, 'I didn't tell a lie.
I am greatly offended at what you have said.
I was immediately sorry for what I said to you,
because I think you mean well.

1369 But I greatly fear that I will be deceived.
I don't want to be like the country mouse
when he went shopping with the town mouse.
I'll tell you the story, then the argument must stop.

THE FABLE OF THE MOUSE FROM MOHERNANDO AND THE MOUSE FROM GUADALAJARA

1370 The mouse from Guadalajara got up at dawn one Monday
and went off to market at Mohernando.
A generous-hearted mouse welcomed him into his hole
and invited him to eat, giving him a bean.

1371 Good manners and friendship graced that poor table,
and goodwill accompanied the lack of victuals.
Pleasure made up for the poor meal.
The mouse from Guadalajara enjoyed the good company.

1372 When he'd eaten and the meal was over,
the town mouse invited the mouse from Mohernando
to go and visit him at his market next Tuesday,
when he would be the guest, in return.

1373 He took him back to his house and gave him a lot of cheese,
a lot of fatty bacon, which was unsalted,
animal fat and cooked bread, as much as he wished.
The country mouse thought he was in clover.

1374 Tablecloths of white linen, a white bag
full of flour, which the mouse took a fancy to,
he did him great honour and gave anything he pleased;
happiness, smiling faces were part and parcel.

1375 On the laden table was a lot of good food,
each course better than the one before,
along with the goodwill – a guest demands it.
Pleasure and a good meal relax anyone.

1376 Do comian e folgauan, en medio de su yantar,
la puerta del palaçio començo a ssonar,
abriala su Señora, dentro querria entrar;
los mures con el miedo fuxieron al andar.

1377 Mur de guadalajara entro en su forado,
el huesped aca e alla fuya des-errado,
non tenia lugar çierto do fuese anparado,
estouo a lo escuro, a la pared arrimado.

1378 Cerrada ya la puerta e pasado el temor.
estaua el aldeano con miedo e con tremor;
falagaual el otro desiendol: "amigo Señor,
alegrate E come de lo que as mas sabor;

1379 Este manjar es dulçe, sabe como la miel."
dixo el aldeano al otro: "venino jas en el;
el que teme la muerte, el panal le sabe fiel;
a ty solo es dulçe, tu solo come del.

1380 Al ome con el miedo no sabe dulçe cosa,
non tiene voluntad clara la vista temerosa;
con miedo de la muerte la miel non es sabrosa,
todas cosas amargan en vida peligrosa.

1381 Mas quiero rroer faua Seguro e en paz
que comer mill manjares corrido e syn solas;
las viandas preçiadas con miedo son agraz,
todo es amargura do mortal miedo yas.

1382 ¿Por que tanto me tardo? aqui todo me mato
del miedo que he avido; quando bien melo cato,
como estaua solo, sy viniera el gato,
ally me alcançara e me diera mal rrato.

1383 Tu tyenes grandes casas, mas ay mucha conpaña;
comes muchas viandas, aquesto te engaña.
buena mi poblesa en ssegura cabaña,
que mal pisa el omne, el gato mal Rascaña."

1384 con paz E segurança es buena la poblesa,
al rrico temeroso es poble la rriquesa,
syenpre tyene rreçelo e con miedo tristesa;
la pobredat alegre es Segura noblesa.

1376   As they were eating happily, in the middle of their meal
the door of the room made a sound;
the mistress opened it and was about to come in –
the mice fled in terror, as fast as they could.

1377   The mouse from Guadalajara went into his hole
but his guest ran here and there, quite lost.
He knew no safe place where he could shelter,
and kept in the dark, close up against the wall.

1378   When the door was closed and the terror had passed,
the country mouse was all feverish and trembling.
The other coaxed him saying: "My friend,
cheer up, come and eat whatever you fancy.

1379   This food is sweet, it tastes like honey."
The country mouse replied: "There is poison in it,
honeycomb tastes like gall to someone in fear of their life.
It is only sweet to you, so eat it on your own.

1380   Nothing tastes sweet to a man who is afraid,
his will is blurred, his sight is fearful.
Honey has no savour amid the terror of death.
All things are bitter when life is full of danger.

1381   I'd rather gnaw a bean, in safety and in peace,
than eat a thousand delicacies, pursued and helpless.
Rich food is like sour grapes when mixed with fear.
Everything is bitter where mortal fear lies.

1382   Because I'm still here, the more everything threatens me.
What a fight I've had, when I think about it.
When I was on my own, if a cat had come,
it could have got me and given me a bad time.

1383   You have a large house, but there are a lot of people,
you eat a lot of good food – but you are deceived.
My poverty in a safe shelter is better –
because man's footsteps are cruel and so is a cat's scratch."

1384   Poverty is a wealth amid peace and security;
the wealth of a rich and fearful man is poverty;
he is always suspicious, full of sadness and fear;
happy poverty is a sure nobility.

1385   Mas vale en convento las sardinas saladas,
       E faser a dios seruiçio con las dueñas onrradas,
       que perder la mi alma con perdises assadas
       E fyncar escarnida con otras des-erradas.'

1386   'Señora,' diz la vieja, 'desaguisado façedes,
       dexar plaser E viçio E laseria queredes.
       ansy commo el gallo, vos ansy escogedes;
       desir vos he la fabla e non vos enojedes.

EXIENPLO DEL GALLO QUE FALLO EL ÇAFIR EN EL
MULADAR

1387   andaua en el muladar el gallo ajeuio;
       estando escarbando mañana con el frio,
       fallo çafyr culpado, mejor ome non vido;
       espantose el gallo, dexol como sandio:

1388   "Mas querria de vuas o de trigo vn grano
       que a ty nin a ciento tales en la mi mano."
       el çafir diol Respuesta: "bien te digo, villano,
       que sy me conosçieses tu andarias loçano.

1389   Sy a mi oy fallase quien fallar me deuia,
       sy aver me podiese el que me conosçia,
       al que el estiercol cupbre mucho rresplandesçeria;
       non conosçes tu nin sabes quanto yo meresçria."

1390   Muchos leem el libro, touiendo lo en poder,
       que non saben que leem nin lo pueden entender;
       tyenen algunas cosas preçiadas e de querer,
       que non les ponen onrra la qual deuian aver.

1391   A quien da dios ventura e non la quiere tomar,
       non quiere valer algo, nin saber, nin pujar,
       aya mucha laseria e coyta e trabajar,
       contesçel commo al gallo que escarua en el muladar.

1392   byen asy acaesçe a vos, doña garoza;
       queredes en couento mas agua con la orça
       que con taças de plata e estar ala roça
       con este mançebillo que vos tornaria moça.

1385   Pickled sardines in the convent are better,
      and so is serving God with venerable nuns,
      than losing my soul with roast partridge,
      and being mocked along with other lost women.'

1386   'Mistress,' said the old woman, 'you are making a mistake,
      you want to renounce pleasure and solace, and embrace
                                               suffering.
      You are making the same choice as the cockerel.
      I'll tell you the story, and don't get cross.

THE FABLE OF THE COCKEREL WHO FOUND A SAPPHIRE IN A DUNG HEAP

1387   A daft cockerel was rummaging in a dung heap,
      scratching about on a cold morning.
      He found a fine sapphire, the best ever seen.
      The cockerel took fright and left it alone, like an idiot.

1388   "I'd rather have grapes or a grain of corn
      than you or a hundred like you in my hand."
      The sapphire replied: "I can tell you, peasant,
      that if you had known what I was, you'd have been very
                                               happy.

1389   If I were found by someone worthy of finding me,
      if someone who acknowledged my worth would own me,
      what the manure covers would truly sparkle.
      You don't know or understand what I am worth."

1390   Many read a book, and have it in their possession,
      who don't know what they read, nor can they understand it.
      Some people have a precious and desirable thing
      but they don't give it the respect it deserves.

1391   The person to whom God gives luck and who doesn't make
                                               use
      of it has no wish to improve, learn or prosper.
      He will have great sorrow, suffering and travail.
      He will be like the cockerel, scratching in the dung heap.

1392   The same will happen to you, Garoza.
      You ladies in the convent prefer an earthenware jug of water
      to silver cups, and acting like a Moorish bride
      with this young man, who would make you quite girlish.

1393 Comedes en convento Sardinas e camarones,
      verçuelas e laseria e los duros caçones,
      dexades del amigo perdizes E capones,
      perdedes vos coytadas mugeres syn varones.

1394 Con la mala vyanda, con las Saladas Sardinas,
      con sayas de estameñas comedes vos mesquinas,
      dexades del amigo las truchas, las gallynas,
      las camissas fronçidas, los paños de mellynas.'

1395 Dixol doña garoça: 'oy mas no te dire,
      en lo que tu me dises, en ello penssare.
      ven cras por la rrepuesta e yo tela dare;
      lo que mejor yo viere de grado lo fare.'

1396 otro dia la vieja fuese a la mongia
      E fallo a la dueña que en la misa seya:
      '¡yuy, yuy!' dixo, 'Señora ¡que negra ledania!
      en aqueste rroydo vos fallo cada via.

1397 o vos fallo cantando o vos fallo leyendo,
      o las vnas con las otras contendiendo, Reñiendo:
      nunca vos he fallado jugando nin Reyendo;
      verdat dise mi amo a como yo entiendo.

1398 Mayor Roydo fasen, mas bozes syn rrecabdo
      dies ansares en laguna que çient bueyes en prado;
      dexat eso Señora, dire vos vn mandado,
      pues la misa es dicha vayamos al estrado.'

1399 Alegre va la monja del coro al parlador,
      alegre va el frayle de terçia al rrefitor,
      quiere oyr la monja Nueuas del entendedor,
      quiere el frayle goloso entrar en el tajador.

1400 'sseñora,' dis la vieja, 'dire vos vn juguete,
      non me contesca commo al asno contesçio con el blanchete,
      que el vio con su Señora jugar en el tapete;
      dire vos la fablilla sy me dades vn Risete.

ENXIENPLO DEL ASNO E DEL BLANCHETE

1401 Vn perrillo blanchete con su Señora jugaua,
      con su lengua e boca las manos le besaua,
      ladrando e con la cola mucho la fallagaua,
      demonstraua en todo grand Amor que la Amaua.

1393   In the convent you eat sardines and shrimps,
little cabbages and misery with tough old dogfish.
You leave the partridges and capons left by your friend.
You will lose out, you poor, man-starved women.

1394   You make do, you wretched things, with salt sardines
and poor-quality food, and thick woolly clothes.
You turn away the trout, chickens,
the pleated blouses, the Flanders cloth from your friend.'

1395   Garoza said: 'I shall say nothing more today.
I will think about what you've said.
Come back tomorrow for my answer,
I will do what I think is best.'

1396   The next day the old woman went to the convent
and found the lady, who was at Mass:
'My! my!' she said, 'what a black litany, mistress!
Every day I find you listening to this racket.

1397   I either find you singing or reading,
or you are arguing with each other and fighting.
I've never found you playing or laughing.
My master speaks the truth, as I see it.

1398   Ten geese on the lake make more noise,
more pointless shouting, than a hundred oxen in a field.
Come away, mistress, and I'll give you a message.
As Mass is over, let's go to the visiting room.'

1399   Happily the nun goes from the choir to the parlour,
happily the friar goes from Terce to the refectory.
The nun wants to hear news of the lover,
the greedy friar wants to get to the trencher.

1400   'Mistress,' said the old woman, 'I'll tell you a joke.
Don't let us be like the ass with the little white lap-dog,
which he saw playing with his mistress on the mat.
I'll tell you the tale, if you give me a smile.

THE FABLE OF THE ASS AND THE LITTLE WHITE LAP-DOG

1401   A little white lap-dog was playing with its mistress.
It kissed her hands with its mouth and tongue,
it barked and wagged its tail to please her;
in this way it showed the great love it felt for her.

1402 Ante ella E sus conpañas en pino se tenia,
tomauan con el todos solas E plasenteria,
dauale cada vno de quanto que comia;
veya lo el asno esto de cada dia.

1403 El asno de mal Seso penso E touo mientes,
dixo el burro nesçio ansy entre sus dientes:
"yo a la mi Señora E a todas sus gentes
mas con prouecho syruo que mill tales blanchetes.

1404 yo en mi espinazo les tayo mucha leña,
trayoles la farina que comen del açeña,
pues tan bien torne pino e falagare la dueña
commo aquel blanchete que yaze so su peña."

1405 Salio bien rrebusnando de la su establia,
commo garanon loco, el nesçio tal venia,
rretoçando E fasiendo mucha de caçorria,
fuese para el estrado do la dueña seya.

1406 Puso en los sus onbros entranbos los sus braços;
ella dando Sus boses, vinieron los collaços,
dieron le muchos palos con piedras e con maços,
fasta que ya los palos se fasian pedaços.

1407 Non deue ser el omne a mal faser denodado,
nin desir nin cometer lo que non le es dado;
lo que dios e natura han vedado E negado
de lo faser el cuerdo non deue ser osado.

1408 quando coyda el bauieca que dis bien e derecho,
E coyda faser seruiçio e plaser con su fecho,
dise mal con neçedad, fase pesar E despecho;
callar a las de vegadas fase mucho prouecho.

1409 E por que ayer Señora vos tanto arrufastes,
por lo que yo desia por byen vos ensanastes,
por ende non me atreuo a preguntar que pensastes;
rruego vos que me digades en lo que acordastes.'

1410 la dueña dixo: 'vieja, mañana madrugeste
a desir me pastrañas de lo que ayer me fableste;

1402   It stood on its hind legs before her and her friends,
       and they all took pleasure and delighted in it.
       They each used to give it some of their own food
       and the ass saw all of this every day.

1403   The foolish ass thought about it for a while
       and said between his silly teeth:
       "I serve my mistress and all her folks
       much better than a thousand little white lap-dogs.

1404   I carry loads of wood for them on my back,
       and bring them flour for food from the water mill.
       I will also stand on my hind legs and please the lady,
       like that little white dog that lies under her cloak."

1405   He came out of his stable braying loudly,
       like a crazy stud jackass the idiot came out,
       frisking and gambolling and playing the fool.
       He headed for the lady's drawing room, where she was
                                                     sitting.

1406   He put his front feet on her shoulders,
       she began to scream; the farmhands came
       and beat him thoroughly with clubs and stones
       until the very clubs themselves broke into pieces.

1407   A man should not persist in doing wrong
       nor do or say what is not appropriate.
       What God and nature have forbidden,
       the wise man should never dare to do.

1408   When the fool thinks he is speaking well and correctly
       and thinks his deeds will serve and please,
       he is speaking badly, foolishly, causing trouble and
                                                     displeasure.
       Sometimes keeping silent is the best thing.

1409   So because yesterday you got so angry, mistress,
       at what I said for your own good, you were so cross,
       that I dare not ask what you thought,
       but I beg you to tell me what you have decided.'

1410   The lady replied: 'Old woman, you got up very early
       to come and tell me stories. What you spoke of yesterday

yo non lo consentria commo tu melo rrogueste,
que conssentyr non deuo tan mal juego como este.

1411 Sy dixo la comadre quando el çirugiano
el coraçon querria sacarle con su mano;
desir te he su enxienplo agora por de mano,
despues dar te he rrespuesta qual deuo e bien de llano.

ENXIENPLO DE LA RAPOSA QUE COME LAS GALLINAS EN
LA ALDEA

1412 Contesçio en vna aldea de muro byen çercada
que la presta gulhara ansi era vesada,
que entraua de noche, la puerta ya çerrada,
comia las gallinas de posada en posada.

1413 Tenian se los del pueblo della por mal chufados,
çerraron los portillos finiestras E forados;
desque se vido ençerrada diz: "los gallos furtados
desta creo que sean pagados E escotados."

1414 Tendiose a la puerta del aldea nonbrada,
fisose commo muerta, la boca rregañada,
las manos encogidas, yerta e des-figurada;
desian los que pasauan: "¡tente esa tras nochada!"

1415 passaua de mañana por y vn çapatero:
"¡o!" diz, "¡que buena cola! mas vale que vn dinero;
fare traynel della para calçar lygero."
cortola e estudo mas queda que vn cordero.

1416 El alfajeme pasaua, que venia de ssangrar,
diz: "el colmillo desta puede aprouechar
para quien dolor tiene en muela o en quexar."
Sacole e estudo queda syn se mas quexar.

1417 vna vieja passaua quel comio su gallina,
diz: "el ojo de aquesta es para melesina
a moças aojadas E que han la madrina."
Sacolo E estudo Sosegada la mesquina.

1418 El fisico passaua por aquella calleja,
diz: "¡ que buenas orejas son las de la gulpeja
para quien tiene venino o dolor en la oreja!"
cortolas E estudo queda mas que vn oveja.

I cannot consent to in the way you asked me,
as I must not agree to such a wicked game as this one.

1411   That is what the vixen answered when the quack doctor
wanted to take her heart out with his hand.
I will tell you the story now, at once,
then I will give you a clear, dutiful answer.

THE FABLE OF THE VIXEN WHO ATE THE VILLAGE CHICKENS

1412   It happened in a village encircled by a wall,
where the agile vixen was accustomed to go.
She went in at night, when the gate was shut,
and ate the chickens as she went from house to house.

1413   The villagers felt they were being severely mocked,
they closed all the entrances, windows and holes.
When the vixen realized she was trapped, she said:
"The stolen hens will be well and truly paid for this time."

1414   She stretched herself out at the gate of the village
and pretended to be dead, with her mouth contorted,
her paws drawn up, stiff and disfigured.
Passers-by said: "There's the fly-by-night, done in!"

1415   Early in the morning a shoemaker went by.
"Oh!" he said, "what a lovely tail! It's worth more than real
money; I'll make a shoehorn from it so shoes will go on
easily."
He cut it off, and the vixen stayed quiet as a lamb.

1416   The blood-letter went by, having bled a patient,
and said: "I could use this fang to help
someone with toothache or pain in the jaw."
He took it out and she stayed quiet, without complaint.

1417   An old woman passed by, whose hen she had eaten,
and said: "One of those eyes is a cure
for girls who are bewitched or who have period pains."
She took it out and the poor wretch lay still.

1418   A doctor went by along the little street
and said: "A fox's ears are very good
for earache or cases of poisoning."
He cut them off and she stayed as quiet as a ewe.

1419   Dixo este maestro: "el coraçon del rraposo
        para el tremor del coraçon es mucho prouechoso."
        ella diz: "¡al diablo catedes vos el polso!"
        leuantose corriendo E fuxo por el coso.

1420   Dixo: "todas las coytas puede ome sofrir,
        mas el coraçon sacar E muerte rresçebir,
        non lo puede ninguno nin deue consentyr;
        lo que emendar non se puede non presta arrepentyr."

1421   Deue catar el omne con seso E con medida
        lo que faser quisiere que aya del salyda;
        ante que façer cosa quel sea rretrayda
        quando teme ser preso ante busque guarida.

1422   Desque ya es la dueña de varon escarnida
        es del menos preçiada e en poco tenida,
        es de dios ayrada e del mundo aborrida,
        pierde toda su onrra la fama e la vida.

1423   E pues tu a mi dises Rason de perdimiento,
        del alma e del cuerpo e muerte e enfamamiento,
        yo non quiero fazer lo, vete syn tardamiento,
        sy non dar te he gualardon qual tu meresçimiento.'

1424   Mucho temio la vieja deste brauo desir.
        "Señora," diz, "mesura, non me querades ferir,
        puede vos por ventura de mi grand pro venir,
        commo al leon vino del mur en su dormir.

ENXIENPLO DEL LEON E DEL MUR
1425   Dormia el leon pardo en la frida montaña,
        en espesura tiene su cueua soterrana,
        ally juegan de mures vna presta conpaña,
        al leon despetaron con su burla tamaña.

1426   El leon tomo vno e querialo matar;
        el mur con el grand miedo començol a falgar;
        "Señor," diz, "non me mates, que non te podre fartar,
        en tu dar me la muerte, non te puedes onrrar.

1427   ¿Que onrra es al leon, al fuerte, al poderoso,
        matar vn pequeno, al pobre, al coytoso?

1419 This learned man said: "A fox's heart
is very beneficial in cases of heart tremors."
She said: "You can take the devil's pulse!"
She leapt up and fled down the street.

1420 She said: "A person can suffer anything
except being killed by having their heart plucked out."
No one could, nor would, allow it.
Repenting is worth nothing when a wrong cannot be righted.

1421 A man should think sensibly and moderately
about what he wants to do and whether there is a way out.
Before doing something which will be thrown back at him,
he must find a refuge if he fears being caught.

1422 When a woman is scorned by a man
and held in low esteem, belittled,
she is an object of God's anger and abhorred in the world.
She loses all honour, good repute and life itself.

1423 And since you are speaking in these terms,
when I might lose my soul and body, and gain only death
        and defamation,
I do not want to do it. Go, without delay,
or I'll give you the reward you deserve!'

1424 The old woman greatly feared these bold words:
'Mistress,' she said, 'moderation! don't hurt me!
I may be of great benefit to you,
like the mouse who brought good fortune to the lion while
        he slept.

THE FABLE OF THE LION AND THE MOUSE

1425 The tawny lion was sleeping on the cold mountain,
in his underground cave in the midst of a thicket.
A lively band of mice was playing nearby
and they woke the lion up with their jollity.

1426 The lion caught one and wanted to kill it,
so in great terror the mouse began to plead:
"Sir," he said, "don't kill me, I wouldn't fill you up,
you would gain no honour from my death.

1427 What honour is there in the strong and powerful lion
killing a poor, wretched little thing?

es desonrra E mengua e non vençer fermoso,
el que al amor vençe es loor vergonçoso.

1428 Por ende vençer es onrra a todo ome nasçido,
es maldad E pecado vençer al desfallydo;
el vençedor ha onrra del preçio del vençido,
su loor es atanto quanto es el debatido."

1429 El leon destos dichos touose por pagado;
solto al moresillo. el mur quando fue soltado,
diole muy muchas graçias e quel seria mandado,
en quanto el podiese, quel siruirie de grado.

1430 ffuese el mur al forado, el leon fue a caçar;
andando en el monte, ouo de entropeçar,
cayo en grandes rredes, non las podia Retaçar,
enbuelto pies e manos non se podia alçar.

1431 Començo a querellarse, oyolo el murisillo,
fue a el, dixol: "Señor, yo trayo buen cochillo,
con aquestos mis dientes Rodre poco a poquillo,
do estan vuestras manos fare vn grand portillo.

1432 los vuestros blasos fuertes por ally los sacaredes,
abriendo e tirando las rredes rresgaredes,
por mis chiquillos dientes vos oy escaparedes,
perdonastes mi vida e vos por mi byuiredes."

1433 Tu, rrico poderoso, non quieras des-echar
al pobre, al menguado non lo quieras de ti echar;
puede faser seruiçio quien non tyene que pechar;
el que non puede mas puede aprouechar.

1434 Puede pequeña cossa E de poca valya
faser mucho prouecho E dar grand mejoria,
el que poder non tyene oro nin fidalguia
tenga manera E seso, arte e Sabidoria.'

1435 ffue con esto la dueña ya quanto mas pagada:
'vieja,' dixo, 'non temas, esta byen Segurada,
non conviene a dueña de ser tan denodada,
mas rresçelo me mucho de ser mal engañada.

It is dishonourable and demeaning, not a worthy victory.
Beating someone smaller is shameful praise.

1428   Although to win is honourable for all men,
it is an evil sin to gain victory over the weak.
The winner's honour is proportionate to the value of the
                                                    conquest,
his praise depends on whom he conquers."

1429   The lion was pleased at these words.
He let the little mouse go, and when he was free,
he thanked the lion very much and said
that the lion's word was his command, to serve with
                                                    gratitude.

1430   The mouse went into its hole, the lion went to hunt.
As he walked on the mountain, he stumbled
and fell into a great net, which he couldn't tear in pieces.
He was bound hand and foot and couldn't stand up.

1431   He began to complain and the little mouse heard him
and went to him, saying: "I've brought a good knife,
I will gnaw with my teeth bit by bit.
I'll make a big opening near your front paws.

1432   If you push through with your strong front paws,
tugging and stretching, you will tear the net.
You shall escape today by my small teeth.
You pardoned my life and now you shall live because of me."

1433   You who are rich and powerful, don't cast aside
the poor and unfortunate.
They may not pay tribute but they can be of service.
When all is lost, it can be advantageous.

1434   A small thing of little value may
do much good and bring great benefit.
A person who has no power, nor gold nor noble birth
may have sense and cleverness, skill and wisdom.'

1435   The lady was rather pleased with this.
'Old woman,' she said, 'don't worry, rest assured,
it does not suit a lady to be so inflexible,
but I greatly fear that I'll be deceived.

1436   Estas buenas palablas, estos dulçes falagos,
       non querria que fuesen a mi fiel E amargos,
       commo fueron al cueruo los dichos, los encargos
       de la falsa rraposa con sus malos trasfagos.

ENXIENPLO DE LA RRAPOSA E DEL CUERUO

1437   la marfusa vn dia con la fanbre andaua,
       vido al cueruo negro en vn arbol do estaua,
       grand pedaço de queso en el pico leuaua,
       ella con su lijonga tan bien lo saludaua:

1438   "o cueruo tan apuesto, del çisne eres pariente,
       en blancura, en do-no, fermoso, rrelusiente,
       mas que todas las aves cantas muy dulçe mente,
       sy vn cantar dixieres dire yo por el veynte.

1439   Mejor que la calandria nin el papa gayo,
       mejor gritas que tordo, nin Ruy Señor nin gayo;
       sy agora cantasses, todo el pesar que trayo
       me tiraries en punto mas que otro ensayo."

1440   bien se coydo el cueruo que con el gorgear
       prasie a todo el mundo mas que con otro cantar;
       creye que la su lengua e el su mucho gadnar
       alegraua las gentes mas que otro juglar.

1441   Començo a cantar, la su boz a erçer,
       el queso de la boca ouosele a caer;
       la gulhara en punto selo fue a comer;
       el cueruo con el dapño ouo de entristeçer.

1442   falsa onrra E vana gloria y el Risete falso
       dan pessar e tristesa e dapno syn traspaso;
       muchos cuydan que guarda el viñadero e el paso,
       e es la magadaña que esta en el cada halso.

1443   Non es cosa Segura creer dulçe lyjonja
       de aqueste dulçor Suele venir amarga lonja,
       pecar en tal manera non conviene a monja,
       rreligiosa non casta es perdida toronja.'

1444   'Señora,' dis la vieja, 'esse miedo non tomedes,
       el omne que vos ama, nunca lo esquiuedes,
       todas las otras temen eso que vos temedes,
       el miedo de las liebres las monjas lo auedes.

1436   These good words, such sweet flattery,
        I wouldn't want them to be bitter gall,
        like the words and entreaties of the false vixen
        were to the crow, with her evil deceits.

THE FABLE OF THE VIXEN AND THE CROW

1437   One day the vixen was feeling hungry;
        she saw a black crow in a tree nearby.
        He had a large piece of cheese in his beak,
        and she greeted him with flattering words:

1438   "Oh, elegant crow, the swan's relation
        in whiteness and grace, beautiful and resplendent,
        you sing more sweetly than any other bird –
        if you sing one song, I would sing twenty for it.

1439   Better than a lark or a parrot,
        you sing better than a thrush or nightingale or jay.
        If you were to sing now, you would take away
        all my cares at once, better than anything else."

1440   The crow really thought that his cawing
        pleased everyone more than any other singing.
        He believed that his tongue and constant croaking
        cheered people more than any minstrel.

1441   He began to sing and raised his voice.
        The cheese fell out of his beak,
        and at once the vixen went to eat it.
        The crow was very sad because of the wrong done.

1442   False honour and vainglory and false smiles
        bring sorrow and sadness and endless harm.
        Many think the vineyard keeper guards the path,
        yet it's really the scarecrow standing on its stick.

1443   It is not safe to believe in sweet flattery,
        for a bitter slice of pie is usually made from such sweetness.
        It is not fitting for a nun to sin like that;
        an unchaste nun is a rotten grapefruit.'

1444   'Mistress,' said the old woman, 'you need not fear,
        don't avoid the man who loves you.
        All men fear what you fear,
        you nuns are all as nervous as hares.

ENXIENPLO DE LAS LIEBRES

1445   Andauan se las liebres, en las seluas llegadas;
Sono vn poco la selua e fueron espantadas,
fue sueno de laguna, ondas arrebatadas,
las liebres temerosas en vno son juntadas.

1446   Andauan a todas partes, non podian quedas ser,
desien con el grand miedo que se fuesen a esconder;
ellas esto fablando ovieron de ver
las rranas con su miedo so el agua meter.

1447   Dixo la vna liebre: "conviene que esperemos,
non somos nos señeras que miedo vano tenemos,
las rranas se escondem de balde ya lo veemos,
las liebres E las rranas vano miedo tenemos.

1448   a la buena esperança nos conviene atener,
fase tener grand miedo lo que non es de temer,
somos de coraçon fraco, ligeras en correr,
non deue temor vano en sy ome traer."

1449   acabada ya su fabla, començaron de foyr,
esto les puso miedo, e fiso a todos yr;
en tal manera tema el que bien quiere beuir
que non pierda el es-fuerço por miedo de morir.

1450   El miedo es muy malo syn esfuerço ardid,
esperança e esfuerço vencen en toda lid,
los couardes fuyendo mueren desiendo: ¡foyd!
biuen los esforçados desiendo: ¡daldes, ferid!

1451   Aquesto acaesçe a vos, Señora mia,
E a todas las monjas que tenedes freylia;
por vna syn ventura muger que ande rradia,
temedes vos que todas yres por esa via.

1452   Tened buena esperança, dexad vano temor,
amad al buen amigo, quered su buen amor,
sy mas ya non fablande como a chate pastor,
desilde: ¡dios vos salue!, dexemos el pauor.'

1453   'Tal eres,' diz la dueña, 'vieja, commo el diablo,
que dio a su amigo mal consejo e mal cabo;

THE FABLE OF THE HARES

1445 Some hares were running in the woods;
      they heard a noise in the trees and took fright.
      It was the sound of water, of strongly lapping waves in a
                                                          pond.
      The frightened hares drew close together.

1446 They looked all round, they couldn't keep still;
      in their great fright they thought they should hide.
      While they were saying this they happened to see
      some frogs go under the water in fear of them.

1447 One of the hares said: "We had better wait,
      we are not alone in being afraid for nothing,
      the frogs hid themselves for no reason, we've just seen them.
      Hares and frogs have groundless fears.

1448 We should be more hopeful of better things.
      We are very frightened of what is not to be feared.
      We are faint-hearted, quick to flee.
      You should not be fearful for nothing."

1449 When she had finished speaking, she began to run,
      which spooked the others and they all went too.
      A person who wants to live well dreads
      dissipating his energy for fear of death.

1450 Fear is an evil thing if you lack boldness and courage.
      Hope and courage can win any battle.
      The fleeing cowards shall die, saying: "Run!"
      The courageous live, saying: "Go for them, wound them!"

1451 This is what is happening to you, my lady,
      and to all the nuns who live in the convent.
      Because of one unlucky woman who goes astray,
      you all fear you will walk the same road.

1452 Keep hope alive, leave aside vain fear,
      love a good man, desire his good love,
      at least, speak to him like a simple shepherd,
      say: "May the Lord save you! and stop being afraid." '

1453 'Old woman,' said the lady, 'you are like the devil
      who gave his friend bad advice and a bad end.

puso lo en la forca, dexolo y en su cabo.
oye buena fabla, non quieras mi menoscabo.

ENXIENPLO DEL LADRON QUE FIZO CARTA AL DIABLO DE SU ANIMA

1454 En tierra syn justiçia eran muchos ladrones,
fueron al rrey las nuevas, querellas e pregones,
enbio alla su alcalde, merinos e Sayones,
al ladron enforcauan por quatro pepiones.

1455 Dixo el vn ladron dellos: "ya yo so desposado
con la forca, que por furto ando desorejado,
si mas yo so con furto del merino tomado
el me fara con la forca ser del todo casado."

1456 Ante que el desposado penitençia presiese
vino a el vn diablo por que non lo perrdiese;
dixol que de su alma la carta le feciese,
E furtase syn miedo quanto furtar podiese.

1457 otorgole su alma, fisole dende carta;
prometiole el diablo que del nunca se parta.
desta guisa el malo sus amigos enarta;
fue el ladron a vn canbio, furto de oro grand sarta.

1458 El ladron fue tomado, en la cadena puesto,
llamo a su amigo quel conssejo aquesto;
vino el mal amigo, dis: "fe me aqui presto.
non temas, ten es-fuerço que non moras por esto.

1459 quando a ty sacaren a judgar oy o cras,
aparta al alcalde E con el fablaras;
pon mano en tu Seno E dalo que fallaras;
amigo con aquesto en saluo escaparas."

1460 ssacaron otro dia los presos a judgar;
el llamo al alcalde, apartol e fue fablar;
metio mano en el seno E fue dende sacar
vna copa de oro muy noble, de preçiar.

1461 diogela en presente, callando, al alcalde.
diz luego el judgador: "amigos, el Ribalde

He put him on the gallows and left him there alone.
Listen to the tale, and you will not want me harmed or
                                                    scorned.

THE FABLE OF THE ROBBER WHO SOLD THE DEVIL HIS SOUL IN A LETTER

1454   In a lawless land there were many robbers.
        All news, complaints and proclamations reached the king,
        who sent his judge, governor and guards there.
        They hung robbers then for very little indeed.

1455   One of the robbers said: "Now I am betrothed
        to the gallows, as I have lost my ears for thieving.*
        If I am caught for robbery by the governor,
        I shall have to marry them, without doubt."

1456   Before the betrothed repented
        the devil came, so as not to lose him.
        He told him to give him his soul in writing,
        then the robber could steal whatever he wanted.

1457   He handed over his soul and wrote a letter.
        He promised the devil permanent allegiance.
        In this way the Evil One deceives his friends.
        The robber went to a bank and stole a large amount of gold.

1458   The robber was caught and put in chains.
        He called on his friend, who gave him some advice.
        The evil friend came and said: "Here I am at once,
        don't be afraid, be strong, you will not die for this.

1459   When they take you to be judged today or tomorrow,
        take the judge aside and speak to him.
        Put your hand in your breast pocket, give him what you find
                                                              there,
        and then, my friend, you shall stay free."

1460   The next day the prisoners were taken to be tried.
        The robber called the judge and spoke to him.
        He put his hand on his heart and produced
        a gold goblet, very fine and of great value.

1461   He gave it as a present to the judge in silence,
        then the judge said: "Friends, I can't find

non fallo por que muera, prendistes le de balde;
yo le do por quito suelto; vos, merino, soltalde.'

1462 salio el ladron suelto, sin pena de presion,
vso su mal ofiçio grand tienpo e grand sason,
muchas veses fue preso, escapaua por don,
enojose el diablo, fue preso su ladron.

1463 llamo su mal amigo asy commo solia,
vino el malo E dixo: "¿que me llamas cada dia?
faz ansi como sueles, non temas, en mi fia,
daras cras el presente, saldras con arte mia."

1464 Aparto al alcalde el ladron Segud lo avia vsado,
puso mano a su Seno e fallo negro fallado;
saco vna grand soga, diola al adelantado.
el alcalde diz: "mando que sea enforcado."

1465 leuando lo a la forca, vido en altas torres
estar su mal amigo, diz: "¿por que non me acorres?"
rrespondio el diablo: "¿E tu? ¿por que non corres?
andando E fablando, amigo, non te engorres.

1466 luego sere contigo desque ponga vn frayle
con vna freyla suya que me dize: '¡trayle, trayle!'
engaña a quien te engaña, a quien te fay fayle.
entre tanto, amigo, vete con ese bayle."

1467 Cerca el pie de la forca començo de llamar:
"Amigo, ¡valme, valme! ¡que me quieren enforcar!"
vino el malo e dixo: "ya te viese colgar,
que yo te ayudare commo lo suelo far.

1468 Suban te, non temas, cuelgate a osadas,
E pon tus pies entranbos sobre las mis espaldas,
que yo te soterne Segund que otras vegadas
sotoue a mis amigos en tales caualgadas."

1469 Entonçes los sayones al ladron enforcaron,
coydando que era muerto, todos dende derramaron,
a los malos amigos en mal lugar dexaron;
los amigos entranbos en vno rrasonaron.

any reason for him to die, you seized him in vain.
I decree he should be freed – you, guard, let him go."

1462   The robber went free, with no fear of prison.
He used his evil-doing frequently.
He was often imprisoned and escaped using a "gift".
The devil got tired and his robber was imprisoned.

1463   He called his evil friend, as he usually did.
The Bad One came and said: "Why do you call me every day?
Do as you usually do, trust me, do not fear,
give the present tomorrow, you'll soon be out with my
                                                        astuteness."

1464   The robber took the judge aside, as was his habit,
put his hand on his heart and made a terrible discovery.
He drew out a great rope and gave it to the judge,
who answered: "I order you to be hung."

1465   As he was taken to the gallows he saw his evil friend
at the top of a high tower and he said: "Why don't you help
                                                        me?"
The devil replied: "And you? Why don't you run?
By walking and talking, my friend, you're wasting time.

1466   I'll be with you in a minute, after I've taken a monk
to his nun, who is calling: 'Bring him to me! Bring him!'
Deceive who you can, do as you're done by;
meanwhile, go with that bailiff, my friend."

1467   At the foot of the gallows he began to cry out:
"Friend, save me! save me! they're going to hang me."
The Evil One came and said: "If only I could see that!
I will help you as I always do.

1468   Let them put you up, don't fear, let them hang you, don't be
afraid, and put both feet on my shoulders.
I will support you, as on other occasions
I've supported my friends in these situations."

1469   Then the executioners hung up the robber.
Thinking he was dead, they all dispersed.
They left the evil friends in an evil place,
and they spoke to each other.

1470   El diablo quexose, diz: "¡ay! ¡que mucho pesas!
       ¡tan caros que me cuestan tus furtos e tus presas!"
       dixo el enforcado: "tus obras mal apresas
       me troxieron a esto por que tu me sopesas."

1471   fablo luego el diablo, diz: "amigo, otea
       e di melo que vieres, toda cosa que sea."
       el ladron paro mientes, diz: "veo cosa fea,
       tus pies descalabrados e al non se que vea.

1472   beo vn monte grande de muchos viejos çapatos,
       suelas rrotas e paños Rotos e viejos hatos,
       e veo las tus manos llenas de garauatos,
       dellos estan colgados muchas gatas e gatos."

1473   Respondio el diablo: "todo esto que dixiste
       E mucho mas dos tanto, que ver non lo podiste,
       he Roto yo andando en pos ty Segund viste;
       non pudo mas sofrirte, tenlo que mereçiste.

1474   Aquellos garauatos son las mis arterias,
       los gatos E las gatas son muchas almas mias,
       que yo tengo travadas: mis pies tienen sangrias
       en pos ellas andando las noches E los dias."

1475   Su Rason acabada, tirose, dyo vn salto,
       dexo a su amigo en la forca tan alto;
       quien al diablo cree, traual su garavato,
       el le da mala çima E grand mal en chico Rato.

1476   El que con el diablo fase la su criança,
       quien con amigo malo pone su amistança,
       por mucho que se tarde mal galardon alçanca,
       es en amigo falso toda la mal andança.

1477   El mundo es texido de malos arigotes,
       en buena andança el omne tyene muchos galeotes,
       parientes apostisos, amigos pauiotes;
       desque le veen en coyta non dan por el dotes motes.

1478   De los malos amigos vienen malos escotes,
       non viene dellos ayuda mas que de vnos alrrotes,
       sinon falssas escusas, lysonjas, amargotes;
       ¡guarde vos dios, amigos, de tales amigotes!

1470   The devil complained: "Oh! how heavy you are!
        Your robberies and thieving cost me dear!"
        The hung man said: "Your confounded deeds
        have brought this about, so you have to support me."

1471   Then the devil said: "My friend, have a look
        and tell me what you see, anything at all."
        The robber considered, then said: "I see something awful,
        your misshapen feet, and something else I'm not sure of.

1472   I can see a great mountain of old shoes,
        broken soles and rags and old clothes,
        and I see your hands, laden with hooks,
        from which are hanging lots of male and female cats."

1473   The devil replied: "All you said,
        and twice as much, which you couldn't see,
        I have worn out in running after you, as you've seen.
        I cannot bear it any more, take what you deserve.

1474   These hooks are my cunning wiles,
        the male and female cats are many of my souls,
        which I have in fetters. My feet are bleeding
        running after them day and night."

1475   When he finished speaking, he moved away, gave a great
                                                         leap,
        and left his friend on the high gallows.
        If you believe in the devil, his hook will seize you.
        You will have a bad end and suffer great evil in a short time.

1476   He who lives side by side with the devil,
        who gives his friendship to an evil friend,
        will get an evil reward, sooner or later.
        All misfortune lies in a false friend.

1477   The world is woven with evil rags.
        A man with good fortune has many oarsmen,
        sham relatives, false friends;
        when they see him in trouble they don't give a toss.

1478   Bad friends give bad returns,
        they don't help any more than a rogue.
        They make false excuses, flatter, pretend to help –
        may God protect you from such fine pals.

1479 Non es dicho amigo el que da mal conssejo,
ante es enemigo E mal queriente sobejo;
al que te dexa en coyta nol quieras en trebejo,
al que te mata so capa nol salues en conçejo.'

1480 'Señora,' diz la vieja, 'muchas fablas sabedes,
mas yo non vos conssejo eso que vos creedes,
si non tan sola mente ya vos que lo fabledes;
abenid vos entre anbos desque en vno estedes.'

1481 'farias,' dixo la dueña, 'Segund que ya te digo,
que fiso el diablo al ladron su amigo:
dexar mias con el sola, çerrarias el postigo;
seria mal escarnida fyncando el con-migo.'

1482 Diz la vieja: 'Señora, ¡que coraçon tan duro!
de eso que vos rresçelades ya vos yo asseguro,
E que de vos non me parta en vuestras manos juro;
si de vos me partiere, a mi caya el perjuro.'

1483 la dueña dixo: 'vieja, non lo manda el fuero
que la muger comiençe fablar de amor primero;
cunple otear firme que es çierto menssajero.'
'Señora, el aue muda,' diz, 'non fase aguero.'

1484 dixol doña garoça: 'que ayas buena ventura,
que de ese arçipreste me digas su figura;
bien atal qual sea, dime toda su fechura,
non Respondas en escarnio do te preguntan cordura.'

DE LAS FIGURAS DEL ARÇIPRESTE
1485 'Señora,' diz la vieja, 'yol veo amenudo.
el cuerpo ha bien largo, mienbros grandes e trifudo,
la cabeça non chica, velloso, pescoçudo,
el cuello non muy luengo, cabos prieto, orejudo.

1486 las çejas apartadas, prietas como cabron,
el su andar enfiesto bien como de pauon,
su paso ssosegado e de buena Rason,
la su nariz es luenga, esto le desconpon.

1487 las ençiuas bermejas E la fabla tunbal,
la boca non pequena, labros al comunal,

1479   It is not a friend who gives bad advice,
       but an enemy and supreme wrong-doer.
       You don't want to have fun with a friend who leaves you in
                                                    the lurch,
       or greet him publicly when he privately has it in for you.'

1480   'Lady,' said the old woman, 'you know a lot of stories,
       but I'm not advising what you think,
       only asking you to speak to him.
       Come to an agreement when you are together.'

1481   'You would do what I said,' replied the lady,
       'as the devil did to his friend the robber.
       You'll leave me alone with him and shut the door.
       I will be badly dishonoured, left on my own with him.'

1482   The old woman said: 'Mistress, you are so hard-hearted!
       I can reassure you about what you fear,
       and I swear on both your hands I will not leave you alone.
       If you are separated from me, I shall suffer perjury.'

1483   The lady said: 'Old woman, the law doesn't state
       that the woman has to speak of love first.
       Glances send the firmest, surest messages.'
       'Lady, a dumb bird gives no augury,' she replied.

1484   Garoza said: 'So, I wish you good luck.
       Tell me what this archpriest looks like.
       Whatever he's like, tell me about him,
       don't answer in mockery when asked in earnest.'

WHAT THE ARCHPRIEST LOOKED LIKE
1485   'Mistress,' said the old girl, 'I see him often.
       He has a broad frame and long limbs, he's robust and
                                                    muscular.
       His head is not small, he is hairy and has a thick neck,
       but not too long, and he has dark hair with large ears.

1486   His brows are wide apart, as black as coal,
       he walks proudly, like a peacock,
       with a calm and measured step.
       His nose is long, which rather spoils him.

1487   His gums are red, his voice is deep,
       his mouth's not small, his lips are average,

mas gordos que delgados, bermejos como coral,
las espaldas byen grandes, las muñecas atal.

1488   los ojos ha pequeños, es vn poquillo baço,
los pechos delanteros, bien trifudo el braco,
bien conplidas las piernas, del pie chico pedaço;
Señora, del non vy mas, por su amor vos abraço.

1489   Es ligero, valiente, byen mançebo de dias,
sabe los jnstrumentos e todas juglerias,
doñeador alegre ¡para las çapatas mias!
tal omne como este, non es en todas erias.'

1490   A la dueña mi vieja tan byen que la enduxo
'sseñora,' diz, 'la fabla del que de feria fuxo,
la merca de tu vço dios que la aduxo,
¡amad, dueñas, amalde tal omne qual debuxo!

1491   ssodes las monjas guarrdadas, deseosas, loçanas,
los clerigos cobdiçiosas desean las vfanas,
todos nadar quieren, los peçes e las rranas,
a pan de quinçe dias fanbre de tres selmanas.'

1492   Dixol doña garoça: 'verme he, da my espaçio.'
'¡alahe!' dixo la vieja, 'amor non sea laçio,
quiero yr a desir gelo; ¡yuy! ¡como me engraçio!
yol fare cras que venga aqui, a este palaçio.'

1493   la dueña dixo: 'vieja, ¡guarde me dios de tus mañas!
ve, dil que venga cras ante buenas conpañas,
fablar me ha buena fabla, non burla nin picañas,
e dil que non me diga de aquestas tus fasanas.'

1494   vino la mi leal vieja, alegre, plasentera,
ante del 'dios vos salue' dixo la mensajera:
'se que el que al lobo enbia ¡a la fe! carne espera,
que la buena corredera ansy fase carrera.

1495   Amigo, dios vos salue, folgad, sed plasentero.
cras dise que vayades, fabladla non señero,

on the thick side, as red as coral,
with broad shoulders and wrists likewise.

1488   His eyes are small, he's slightly swarthy,
his chest is prominent, his arms muscular,
his legs are shapely, his feet small,
but, madam, I've seen no more than this, and embrace you
in the name of his love.

1489   He is agile, brave, youthful,
he knows all the instruments and minstrelsy,
he's a cheerful suitor, by my shoes!*
You won't find a man like him everywhere.'

1490   My old woman really managed to attract her:
'Mistress, like the saying about the man who fled from the
fair,
"God brought this merchandise to your door."
Love, ladies, love a man like the one I've described!

1491   You nuns are hidden, desiring, lively,
covetous priests desire the proud ones.
They all want to swim, the fish and the frogs,
two-week-old bread for three-week-old hunger.'

1492   Garoza said: 'I'll think about it, give me time.'
'Truly,' said the old woman, 'love must not be slow.
I want to go and tell him – oooh, I'm so pleased,
tomorrow I'll get him to come here, to this room.'

1493   The lady said: 'Old woman, God protect me from your wiles!
Go on, tell him to come tomorrow, in the presence of
company.
He can talk to me sensibly, no jokes or tricks,
and tell him not to relate any of your stories.'

1494   My loyal old lady came back happy and content,
and before I could greet her, the messenger said:
'I know that if you send a wolf – by heaven! – you should
expect meat.
A good go-between covers the distance.

1495   My friend, the Lord save you, rejoice! be happy.
She says tomorrow go and talk to her, not alone,

mas catad non le digades chufas de pitoflero,
que las monjas non se pagan del abbad fasañero.

1496 De lo que cunple al fecho, aquesto le desit,
lo que cras le fablardes, vos oy lo comedit,
a la misa de mañana vos en buena ora yd,
enamorad a la monja e luego vos venid.'

1497 yol dixe: 'trota conventos, Ruego te, mi amiga,
que lieues esta carta ante que gelo yo diga,
e si en la rrespuesta non te dixiere enemiga,
puede ser que de la fabla otro fecho se ssyga.'

1498 leuol vna mi carta a la missa de prima,
troxo me buena rrepuesta de la fermosa Ryma;
guardas tenie la moja mas que la mi esgrima,
pero de buena fabla vino la buena çima.

1499 En el nonbre de dios fuy a misa de mañana,
vy estar a la monja en oraçion loçana,
alto cuello de garça, color fresco de grana;
des-aguisado fiso quien le mando vestir lana.

1500 ¡val me santa maria, mis manos aprieto,
quien dyo a blanca rrosa abito, velo prieto!
mal valdrie a la fermosa tener fijos e nieto,
que atal velo prieto, nin que abitos çiento.

1501 Pero que sea errança contra nuestro Señor
el pecado de monja a omne doñeador,
¡ay dios! ¡E yo lo fuese aqueste pecador
que fesiese penitençia desto fecho error!

1502 oteome de vnos ojos que paresçian candela,
yo sospire por ellos, diz mi coraçon: ¡hela!
fuy me para la dueña, fablome e fablela,
enamorome la monja e yo enamorela.

1503 Resçibio me la dueña por su buen Seruidor,
ssyenprel fuy mandado e leal amador,
mucho de bien me fiso con dios en lynpio amor,
en quanto ella fue byua, dios fue mi guiador.

1504 Con mucha oraçion a dios por mi Rogaua,
con la su abstinençia mucho me ayudaua,

and watch you don't tell her any jokes in bad taste,
for nuns don't take to swanky abbots.

1496　Say what is appropriate,
think over what you will talk about.
Go to Mass tomorrow early,
make the nun fall in love and then come back.'

1497　I said: 'Trotaconventos, I beg you, my friend,
to take this letter before I speak to her,
and if the reply is not unfavourable,
perhaps something more than talk will take place.'

1498　She took my letter at Prime Mass
and brought me a good answer to my skilful rhyme.
The nun had a better sheath than my sword,
but a successful outcome came from good conversation.

1499　In the name of God I went to morning Mass,
and saw the nun at prayer – lovely,
a long heron's neck, fresh pink colouring.
Whoever made her wear wool did wrong.

1500　Help me, Virgin Mary! I clasp my hands.
Who gave the white rose a black veil and habit?
She would be better off with sons and grandchild
than a hundred habits and black veils.

1501　Though it may be an error in the eyes of God
for a suitor to sin with a nun,
dear Lord! if only I were that sinner –
I'd do penance after the sin!

1502　She raised eyes to me that blazed like flames,
and I sighed for them. My heart said: 'Behold.'
I went to her, spoke to her, she spoke to me;
I fell in love with the nun and she with me.

1503　The lady accepted me as her good servant;
I was always a loyal and obedient lover.
She did me great good in God's pure love;
as long as she lived, God was my guide,

1504　She interceded for me through prayer to God.
Her abstinence was a great help to me,

la su vida muy lynpia en dios se deleytaua,
en locura del mundo nunca se trabajaua.

1505 Para tales amores son las rreligiosas,
para rrogar a dios con obras piadosas,
que para amor del mundo mucho son peligrosas,
E Son las escuseras peresosas, mentirosas.

1506 Atal fue mi ventura que dos messes pasados,
murio la buena duena, oue menos cuydados,
a morir han los onbres, que son o seran nados,
dios perdone su alma e los nuestros pecados.

1507 Con el mucho quebranto ffiz aquesta endecha,
con pesar e tristesa non fue tan sotil fecha;
emiende la todo omne e quien buen amor pecha,
que yerro E mal fecho emienda non desecha.

DE COMO TROTA CONVENTOS FABLO CON LA MORA DE
PARTE DE ARÇIPRESTE E DE LA RESPUESTA QUE LE DIO
1508 Por oluidar la coyta tristesa E pessar
rrogue a la mi vieja que me quisiese casar;
fablo con vna mora, non la quiso escuchar,
ella fiso buen seso, yo fiz mucho cantar.

1509 Dixo trota conventos a la mora por mi:
'¡ya amiga, ya amiga, quanto ha que non vos vy!
non es quien ver vos pueda, y ¿como sodes ansy?
saluda vos amor nueuo.' dixo la mora: 'yznedri.'

1510 'fija, mucho vos Saluda vno que es de alcala,
enbia vos vna çodra con aqueste aluala,
el criador es con vusco, que desto tal mucho ha,
tomaldo, fija Señora.' dixo la mora: 'le ala.'

1511 'fija, ¡si el criador vos de paz con Salud!
que non gelo desdeñedes, pues que mas traher non pud;
aducho bueno vos adugo, fablad me alaud,
non vaya de vos tan muda.' dixo la mora: 'ascut.'

1512 Desque vido la vieja que non Recabdaua y,
diz: 'quanto vos he dicho, bien tanto me perdi;

and her pure life delighted in God.
She never strove for the madness of the world.

1505 Nuns are made for that kind of love,
to beseech God through pious works,
but they are very dangerous in worldly love,
they are lying, lazy and hypocritical.

1506 My lot was such that after two months
the good lady died and I had new troubles.
All people born and to be born must die.
God forgive her soul and our sins!

1507 In my great sorrow I wrote this dirge;*
it was not very subtle, because of my grief and sadness.
Anyone can amend it who pays tribute to good love,
since error and wrong-doing do not preclude amendment.

HOW TROTACONVENTOS SPOKE TO THE MOORISH GIRL ON BEHALF OF THE ARCHPRIEST AND THE ANSWER SHE GAVE

1508 To forget my cares, sadness and sorrow,
I implored my old woman to find me a lover.
She spoke to a Moorish girl, but she wouldn't listen.
She acted wisely, I wrote a lot of songs.

1509 Trotaconventos spoke to the Moorish girl on my behalf:
'Hey, girl, hey, my friend, it's a long time since I've seen you!
No one can manage to see you nowadays, why are you like
this?
A new love greets you.' The girl said: 'I don't understand.'

1510 'Young lady, someone from Alcala sends greetings;
he sends you a blouse with this letter of love.
The Creator is with you, for this man has a lot like this.
Take it, girl.' The girl said: 'No, by Allah!'

1511 'Lady, may the Creator give you health and pleasure,
don't disdain this, as it's the best I can do!
I bring a valuable gift, so speak to me kindly.
Don't leave me unanswered.' The Moorish girl said: 'Be
quiet!'

1512 When the old woman saw she was getting nowhere,
she said: 'All my words have been in vain.

pues que al non me desides, quiero me yr de aqui.'
cabeçeo la mora, dixole: 'amxy axmy.'

EN QUALES INSTRUMENTOS NON CONVIENEN LOS
CANTARES DE ARAUIGO

1513 Despues fise muchas cantigas de dança e troteras,
      para judias E moras e para entenderas,
      para en jnstrumentos de comunales maneras;
      el cantar que non sabes, oylo a cantaderas.

1514 Cantares fiz algunos de los que disen los siegos
      E para escolares que andan nocheriniegos,
      e para muchos otros por puertas andariegos,
      caçurros E de bulrras, non cabrian en dyez priegos.

1515 Para los jnstrumentos estar byen acordados,
      a cantigas algunas son mas apropiados;
      de los que he prouado aqui son Señalados
      en quales quier jnstrumentos vienen mas assonados.

1516 arauigo non quiere la viuela de arco,
      çinfonia, guitarra non son de aqueste marco,
      çitola, odreçillo non amar caguyl hallaço,
      mas aman la tauerna e sotar con vellaco.

1517 albogues e mandurria, caramillo e çanpolla,
      non se pagan de arauigo quanto dellos boloña,
      commo quier que por fuerça disenlo con vergoña,
      quien gelo desir fesiere pechar deue caloña.

1518 Dize vn filosofo, en su libro Se nota,
      que pesar e tristeza el engenio en-bota,
      E yo con pessar grande non puedo desir gota,
      por que trota conventos ya non anda nin trota.

1519 assy fue ¡mal pecado! que mi vieja es muerta,
      murio a mi seruiendo, lo que me desconuerta;
      non se como lo diga: que mucha buena puerta
      me fue despues çerrada que antes me era abierta.

I shall go, since you will say nothing to me.'
The Moorish girl nodded and said: 'Go away, go!'

INSTRUMENTS NOT SUITABLE FOR ARABIC SONGS

1513   After this I wrote a lot of songs for dancing and travelling,
for Jewesses and Moorish girls, and for lovers too,
with beautiful melodic phrasing for the instruments.
If you don't know these songs, listen to the women who
                                                  sing them.

1514   I wrote some songs for blind men
and for scholars who are up and about at night,
and for many others who beg from door to door,
burlesque songs and mocking songs, well over ten sheets'
                                                  worth.

1515   Some instruments are more appropriate
for certain songs in terms of their harmony.
Here is a list of those I've tried
which sound best with the songs.

1516   Arabic song does not favour the viol and bow,
the hurdy-gurdy and guitar are not in this category,
the zither and bagpipes don't go with Arabic song,
they are better in the tavern and for peasant dancing.

1517   Pastoral recorders and mandora, the reed pipe and the
                                                  syrinx
don't suit Arab song, nor does Bologna like them.
If they are obliged to play, they do so shamefully.
Anyone who makes them sound should pay a fine.

1518   As a philosopher says in his book,
sorrow and sadness dull the mind.
I am so overcome with grief I cannot say a word,
for now Trotaconventos no longer walks or trots.

1519   It happened – how sad! – that my old lady has died.
She died serving me, which grieves me too.
I cannot express it. Many promising doors
were then closed to me, which before had been open.

DE COMMO MORIO TROTA CONVENTOS E DE COMMO
EL ARÇIPRESTE FAZE SU PLANTO DENOSTANDO E MAL-
DIZIENDO LA MUERTE

1520 ¡ay muerte! ¡muerta sseas, muerta e mal andante!
mataste a mi vieja, matasses a mi ante.
enemiga del mundo que non as semejante,
de tu memoria amarga non es que non se espante.

1521 Muerte, al que tu fieres, lieuas telo de belmez,
al bueno e al malo, al Rico E al rrefez,
a todos los egualas e los lieuas por vn prez,
por papas E por Reyes non das vn vil nues.

1522 Non catas Señorio debdo nin amistad,
con todo el mundo tyenes continua en-amistat,
non ay en ty mesura, amor nin piedad,
sy non dolor, tristesa, pena e grand crueldad.

1523 Non puede foyr omne de ty nin se asconder,
nunca fue quien contigo podiese bien contender,
la tu venida triste non se puede entender,
desque vienes non quieres a ome atender.

1524 Dexas el cuerpo yermo a gusanos en fuesa,
al alma que lo puebra lieuas tela de priesa.
non es omne çierto de tu carrera aviesa,
de fablar en ti, muerte, espanto me atrauiesa.

1525 Eres en tal manera del mundo aborrida,
que por bien que lo amen al omne en la vida,
en punto que tu vienes con tu mala venida,
todos fuyen del luego como de rred podrida.

1526 los quel aman E quieren e quien ha avido su conpaña
aborresçen lo muerto como a cosa estraña,
parientes E amigos todos le tyenen Saña,
todos fuyen del luego como si fuese araña.

1527 De padres E de madres los fijos tan queridos,
amigos e amigas deseados E Seruidos,
de mugeres leales los sus buenos maridos,
desque tu vienes, muerte, luego son aborridos.

1528 ffases al mucho Rico yaser en grand poblesa,
non tyene vna meaja de toda su Riquesa,

THE DEATH OF TROTACONVENTOS AND HOW THE
ARCHPRIEST LAMENTS, REVILING AND CURSING DEATH

1520 Oh death! May you die, be dead and wretched!
You killed my old lady! Better to have killed me first!
Enemy of the world, you have no equal,
no one fails to take fright at your bitter memory.

1521 Death, those you wound you take without mercy,
both good and bad, noble and lowly,
you make all folks equal and they have the same price.
You care not a jot for popes or kings.

1522 You do not take account of lordship, kinship or friendship,
you are the daily enemy of everyone.
You show no moderation, love nor pity,
only pain, sadness, sorrow and great cruelty.

1523 No man can flee from you, or hide;
there has never been anyone who can contend with you.
No one understands your sad arrival;
when you come, you will not wait.

1524 You leave the uninhabited body to the worms and the grave,
and take the soul that lived in it as fast as you can.
No man is certain of your crooked path.
When I speak of you, Death, terror passes through me.

1525 You are so loathed by the world,
that however much a man is loved in life,
as soon as your evil presence is felt,
all flee from him as from rotten cattle.

1526 Those who love and desire his company in life
abhor it when he is dead, like an alien thing.
Relatives and friends all feel aversion to him,
they flee from him as if he were a spider.

1527 The beloved children of fathers and mothers,
the men desired and served by women friends,
the good husbands of loyal wives,
are all abhorred when you come, Death.

1528 You make the very rich lie in great poverty,
without a farthing of all their wealth.

el que byuo es bueno e con mucha noblesa,
vyl, fediondo es muerto, aborrida villesa.

1529 Non ha en el mundo libro nin escrito nin carta,
ome sabio nin neçio que de ty byen de-parta;
en el mundo non ha cosa que con byen de ti se parte,
saluo el cueruo negro que de ty, muerte, se farta.

1530 Cada dia le dises que tu le fartaras,
el omne non es çierto quando E qual mataras;
el que byen faser podiese, oy le valdria mas
que non atender a ty nin a tu amigo cras, cras.

1531 Señores non querades ser amigos del cueruo,
temed sus amenasas, non fagades su Ruego;
el byen que faser podierdes, fased lo oy luego,
tened que cras morredes ca la vida es juego.

1532 la Salud E la vida muy ayna se muda,
en vn punto se pierde quando omne non coyda,
el byen que faras cras, palabla es desnuda,
vestid la con la obra ante que muerte acuda.

1533 quien en mal juego porfia mas pierde que non cobra,
coyda echar su ssuerte echa mala çocobra;
amigos aperçebid vos e fased buena obra,
que desque viene la muerte a toda cosa sonbra.

1534 Muchos cuydan ganar, quando disen: '¡a todo!'
viene vn mal azar trae dados en Rodo;
llega el omne thesoros por lograr los apodo,
viene la muerte luego, e dexalo con lodo.

1535 Pierde luego la fabla e el entendimiento,
de sus muchos thesoros e de su allegamiento
non puede leuar nada nin faser testamento,
los averes llegados derrama los mal viento.

1536 Desque los sus parientes la su muerte varruntan,
por lo heredar todo amenudo se ayuntan;
quando al fisico por su dolençia preguntan,
si disen que sanara todos gelo rrepuntan.

He who lives is good and noble,
but a vile and stinking, loathsome thing when dead.

1529   There is no book, writing or letter in the world
nor wise man or fool who speaks any good of you.
Nothing in the world departs from you to their benefit,
except the black crow, who has his fill from you, Death.

1530   Every day you say you will give the crow his fill.
No man is sure when and who you will kill.
It is best to do good today while you can,
rather than wait for you and your cawing friend tomorrow.

1531   Gentlemen, don't be the crow's friends;
fear his threats, don't do as he asks.
The good you can do, do it now, at once;
think that tomorrow you may die, for life is a game.

1532   Life and health can change so quickly,
it is lost all of a sudden, when a person least expects it.
The good you will do tomorrow is a naked word.
Dress it with the deed before death arrives.

1533   If you persist in playing a bad game, you lose more than you
gain.
You think your throw will be lucky, but the cast of the dice
brings misfortune.
Friends, take heed and do good deeds,
for when death comes, it overcomes all else.

1534   Many think they will win when they say: Out!
A bad throw comes and moves the dice.
The man gains treasure to enjoy it, I suppose,
then death comes and leaves him in the dirt.

1535   Then he loses his power of speech and understanding;
he can do nothing with his great treasure
and hoarded wealth, nor even make a will.
An evil wind scatters the possessions acquired.

1536   As soon as his relatives sniff out his impending death,
they often cleave together so they can inherit everything.
When they ask the physician about his pain,
if he says he will be cured, they all disapprove.

1537   los que son mas propyncos, hermanos E hermanas,
non coydan ver la ora que tangan las canpanas;
mas preçian la erençia çercanos e çercanas
que non el parentesco nin a las baruas canas.

1538   Desque sal el alma al rrico pecador
dexan lo so la tierra solo, todos han pauor,
rroban todos el algo, primero lo mejor,
el que lieua lo menos tyene se por peor.

1539   Mucho fasen que luego lo vayan a soterrar,
temense que las arcas les han de des-ferrar,
por oyr luenga misa non lo quieren errar,
de todos sus thesoros dan le poco axuar.

1540   Non dan por dios a pobres nin cantan sacrifiçios,
nin disen oraçiones, nin cunplen los ofiçios;
lo mas que sienpre fasen los herederos nouiçios
es dar boses al sordo mas non otros seruiçios.

1541   Entieran lo de grado, E desque a graçias van
amidos, tarde o nunca en misa por el estar,
por lo que ellos andauan ya fallado lo han,
ellos lieuan el algo, el alma lyeua satan.

1542   Sy dexa muger moça, Rica o paresçiente
ante de misa dichas otros la han en miente,
que casara con mas rrico o con moço valiente,
muda el trentanario, del duelo poco se syente.

1543   Allego el mesquino E non ssopo para quien,
E maguer que cada esto ansi avien,
non ha omne que faga su testamento byen
fasta que ya por ojo la muerte vee que vien.

1544   Muerte por mas desir te a mi coraço fuerço,
nunca das a los omes conorte nin esfuerço,
sy non de que es muerto quel come coguerço;
en ty tienes la tacha que tiene el mestuerço.

1545   faze doler la cabeça al que lo mucho coma,
otrosi tu mal moço en punto que assoma,
en la cabeça fiere, a todo fuerte doma,
non le valen mengias des-que tu rrauia le toma.

1537   The closest family, brothers and sisters,
can't wait for the time when the bells toll.
Next of kin, both male and female, value the inheritance
                                                more
than their blood ties or a grey beard.

1538   As soon as the soul leaves a wealthy sinner,
they leave him alone in the ground. All fear him;
they steal his property, the best first.
The one who takes least considers himself worst off.

1539   They try hard to get him buried as soon as they can;
they fear that the coffers will be broken open;
they don't want to be diverted and hear a long Mass;
they give him a small tribute out of all their wealth.

1540   They do not give to the poor in God's name,
nor do they pray or fulfil religious duties.
What new inheritors usually do is
lament the deceased, but nothing else.

1541   They bury him gladly, and after thanks have been given,
they hardly ever go to Mass for him, or do so unwillingly.
They have got what they wanted,
they have got the money, Satan can take the soul.

1542   If he leaves a young wife, rich or pretty,
before Mass has been said other men have their eye on her.
She marries either a richer or bolder youth;
they forget the Gregorian Mass* and the month's mourning.

1543   The poor wretch gathered wealth but didn't know for whom,
and although it happens every day,
no man makes a good will unless
he clearly knows that death is coming.

1544   Death, I wring my heart to say more to you.
You never give a man consolation or strength;
instead, as soon as he's dead, the worms get him.
You have the same natural defect as watercress.

1545   It makes your head ache if you eat too much.
Your evil club, as soon as it is raised
injures our heads and tames the strongest.
Once your madness strikes, no medicine is any good.

1546 los ojos tan fermosos pones los en el techo
çiegas los en vn punto, non han en so prouecho,
en-mudeçes la fabla, fases en-rroqueser el pecho,
en ty es todo mal, rrencura E despencho.

1547 El oyr E el olor, el tañer, el gustar,
todos los çinco sesos tu los vienes tomar;
non ay omne que te sepa del todo denostar,
quando eres denostada do te vienes acostar.

1548 Tyras toda verguença, desfeas fermosura,
des-adonas la graçia, denuestas la mesura,
en-flaquesçes la fuerça, en-loquesçes cordura,
lo dulçe fases fiel con tu much amargura.

1549 Despreçias loçania, el oro escureçes,
desfases la fechura, alegria entristeses,
mansillas la lynpiesa, cortesia envileçes;
muerte, matas la vida, al mundo aborresçes.

1550 Non plases a ninguno, a ty con muchos plase,
con quien mata e muere e con qual quier que mal fase;
toda cosa bien fecha tu maço las desfase,
non ha cosa que nasca que tu rred non en-lase.

1551 Enemiga del bien en el mal amador,
Natura as de gota, del mal e de dolor;
al lugar do mas sigues aquel va muy peor,
do tu tarde rrequieres, aquel esta mejor.

1552 Tu morada por sienpre es jnfierrno profundo,
tu eres mal primero, tu eres mal Segundo,
pueblas mala morada e despueblas el mundo,
dises a cada vno: yo sola a todos mudo.

1553 Muerte, por ti es fecho el lugar jn-fernal,
ca beuiendo omne sienpre e mundo terrenal,
non aurien de ti miedo nin de tu mal hostal,
non temerie tu venida la carne vmagnal.

1554 Tu yermas los pobrados, puebras los çiminterios,
rrefases lo fosarios, destruyes los jnperios,
por tu miedo los santos fisieron los salterrios;
sy non dios todos temen tus penas e tus laserios.

1546 The most beautiful eyes you direct at the ceiling,
you blind them at once, they are no use;
you take away speech, you bedevil the chest;
all evil, rancour and unpleasantness lie in you.

1547 Hearing and smell, touch and taste,
you destroy the five senses.
No man knows how to revile you enough –
but how greatly you are reviled when you come near.

1548 You take away all shame, make the beautiful ugly,
you take away all grace, you insult moderation,
you weaken strength, make the wise go crazy,
you turn sweetness into gall with your great bitterness.

1549 You despise vigour, you darken gold,
you destroy the created, you sadden joy,
you stain cleanliness and vilify courtesy.
Death, you kill life and abhor love.

1550 You please no one but get pleasure from everyone,
from the killer and the dead, from the evil-doer.
Your club destroys everything well made.
Nothing has been born that your net does not ensnare.

1551 Enemy of good and lover of evil,
you are like gout, like evil and pain,
things go badly in the places you frequent.
When you call late, people feel better.

1552 Your domain is deepest hell for ever;
you are the first evil, and it is the second.
You live in an evil place and deprive the world of people.
You say to each person: 'I can destroy everyone single-
handed.'

1553 Death, the infernal regions were made for you,
for if man lived always in the earthly world,
he would not fear you or your evil dwelling,
and human flesh would not fear your coming.

1554 You desolate populations and people the cemeteries,
you renew the graveyards and destroy empires.
The saints wrote the psalters in fear of you.
All fear your sorrow and suffering, except God.

1555 Tu despoblaste, muerte, al çielo e sus svllas,
los que eran lynpieça fesiste los mansillas,
feçiste de los angeles diablos e rrensillas,
escotan tu manjar adobladas e sensillas.

1556 El Señor que te fiso, tu a este matas,
jhesu xpisto dios E ome tu aqueste penaste,
al que tiene el çielo e la tierra, a este
tu le posiste miedo e tu lo demudeste.

1557 El jnfierno lo teme e tu non lo temiste,
temio te la su carne, grand miedo le posiste,
la su humanidat por tu miedo fue triste,
la deydat non te temio, entonçe non la viste.

1558 Nol cataste nil viste, vyo te el, byen te cato,
la su muerte muy cruel a el mucho espanto,
al jnfierno E a los suyos E a ty mal quebranto,
tul mataste vna ora, el por sienpre te mato.

1559 quando te quebranto, entonçe lo conoçiste,
sy ante lo espantaste, mill tanto pena oviste,
dionos vida moriendo al que tu muerte diste,
saco nos de cabptiuo la cruz en quel posiste.

1560 A santos que tenias en tu mala morada
por la muerte de xpistos les fue la vida dada,
ffue por su santa muerte tu casa despoblada,
quieres la poblar matandol, por su muerte fue yermada.

1561 Saco de las tus penas a nuestro padre adan,
a eua nuestra madre, a sus fijos sed e can,
a jafet, a patriarcas, al bueno de abrahan,
a ysac e a ysayas tomolos, non te dexo dan.

1562 A ssant johan el bautista con muchos patriarcas
que los tenies en las penas, en las tus malas arcas,
al cabdillo de moysen que tenias en tus baraças,
profectas E otros santos muchos que tu abarcas.

1563 yo desir non ssabria quales eran tenidos,
quantos en tu jnfierno estauan apremidos,

1555   You desolated heaven and its mansions, Death,
those who were pure you stained;
you made contentious devils out of the angels.
They pay for your sustenance in lavish coinage.

1556   The Almighty who made you, you also killed,
Jesus Christ, God and man, you made him suffer too.
You brought terror to the One feared by Heaven
and Earth, and you made him turn pale.

1557   Hell fears Him but you did not fear Him;
His flesh feared you, you filled Him with terror.
His humanity was saddened by fear of you;
the godhead did not fear you, but you didn't see Him.

1558   You did not look nor see Him, but He saw you quite clearly.
His cruel death filled you with great horror,
for He rent Hell asunder with you and its occupants.
You killed Him for an hour, He killed you for ever.

1559   When He crushed you, then you recognized Him.
If you terrified Him before, now you were to fear more
                              greatly.
If you caused Him sorrow, He caused you to sorrow a
                          thousand times more.
You killed Him, but in dying He gave us life.

1560   The saints you held in your evil realm
were given life through the death of Christ.
Your dwelling was diminished by His holy death,
though you hoped to people it, but His death made it
                              barren.

1561   He freed our father Adam from your sorrows,
like Eve our mother, and Ham and Seth, their sons,*
and Japheth too, the patriarchs, good Abraham,
Isaac and Jacob, not even Dan was left.

1562   You held St John the Baptist, many other patriarchs
as captives in your evil coffers,
and the leader Moses in your jail,
and prophets and many other saints, imprisoned.

1563   I couldn't say which ones were taken,
how many lay oppressed in your inferno.

a todos los saco como santos escogidos,
mas con-tigo dexo los tus malos perdidos.

1564 A los suyos leuolos con el a parayso,
do an vida veyendo mas gloria quien mas quiso;
el nos lieue consigo que por nos muerte priso,
guarde nos de tu casa, non fagas de nos rriso.

1565 a los perdidos malos que dexo en tu poder
en fuego jnfernal los fases tu arder,
en penas jnfernales los fases ençender,
para sienpre jamas non los has de prender.

1566 Dios quiera defender nos de la tu çalagarda,
aquel nos guarde de ty que de ty non se guarda,
ca por mucho que vyuamos, por mucho que se tarda,
a venir es a tu rrauia que a todo el mundo escarda.

1567 Tanto eres, muerte, syn byen E atal,
que desir non se puede el diezmo de tu mal;
a dios me acomiendo, que yo non fallo al
que defender me quiera de tu venida mortal.

1568 Muerte desmesurada, ¡matases a ty sola!
¡que oviste con-migo? ¿mi leal vieja dola?
que me la mataste, muerte, ihesu xpisto conplola
por su santa sangre e por ella perdonola.

1569 ¡ay! ¡mi trota conventos! ¡mi leal verdadera!
muchos te siguian biua, muerta yases Señera;
¿ado te me han leuado? non cosa çertera;
nunca torna con nuevas quien anda esta carrera.

1570 Cyerto en parayso estas tu assentada,
con dos martyres deues estar aconpañada,
Sienpre en este mundo fuste por dos maridada;
¿quien te me rrebato, vieja, por mi sienpre lasrada?

1571 a dios merçed le pido que te de la su gloria,
que mas leal trotera nunca ffue en memoria;
faset te he vn pitafio escripto con estoria,
pues que a ty non viere, vere tu triste estoria.

All chosen saints were released by Him,
and the lost and wicked He left with you.

1564　He took His own to paradise with Him,
where those who loved most behold the greatest glory.
He takes us with Him, who was put to death for us.
Keep us from your dwelling place, don't mock us.

1565　The wicked and lost now left in your power
you burn in the fires of Hell.
You set light to them in lasting torment,
they shall never be lost to you, for evermore.

1566　May God protect us from your sudden attack;
He guards us from you, who needs no guard Himself.
For however long we live, and however late it may be,
your fury must come to weed the world.

1567　You are so devoid of goodness or anything like,
I cannot describe a tenth of your evil.
I commend myself to God, as I find nothing
which can defend me from your mortal coming.

1568　Immoderate death, if only you were to slay yourself!
What did you want with me? Where is my loyal old lady?
Death, you have killed her. Jesus Christ redeemed her
by His holy blood and pardoned her.

1569　Oh! my Trotaconventos, my true and loyal friend!
Many followed you while you lived, in death you lie alone.
Where have they taken you? I know nothing for certain;
no one ever brings back news who walks that path.

1570　For certain you are seated in paradise,
in the company of all the martyrs.
You were always martyred for God in the world.
Who snatched you away from me, old lady I made to
suffer?

1571　I ask God's mercy that He might give you His glory,
for there has never been a more loyal go-between in living
memory.
I shall compose an epitaph describing your life,
then, since I cannot see you, I shall see your sad story.

1572 Dare por ty lymosna e fare oraçion,
    fare cantar misas e dare oblaçion;
    la mi trota conventos, ¡dios te de rredepnçion!
    el que saluo el mundo ¡el te de saluaçion!

1573 Dueñas, non me rretebdes nin me digades moçuelo,
    que si a vos syruiera vos avriades della duelo;
    llorariedes por ella, por su Sotil ansuelo,
    que quantas siguia todas yuan por el suelo.

1574 alta muger nin baxa, ençerrada nin ascondida,
    non sele detenia do fasia debatida;
    non se omne nin dueña que tal oviese perdida
    que non tomase tristesa e pesar syn medida.

1575 ffizele vn pitafio pequeño, con dolor,
    la tristesa me fiso ser rrudo trobador;
    todos los que lo oyeren, por dios nuestro Señor,
    la oraçion fagades por la vieja de amor.

EL PETAFIO DE LA SSEPULTURA DE VRRACA
1576 'vrraca so que yago so esta Sepultura,
    en quanto fuy al mundo oue vyçio e soltura,
    con buena rrazon muchos case, non quise locura,
    cay en vna ora so tierra del altura.

1577 Prendiome syn sospecha la muerte en sus Redes,
    parientes E Amigos aqui non me acorredes,
    obrad bien en la vida, a dios non lo erredes,
    que byen como yo mori asy todos morredes.

1578 El que aqui llegare, si dios le bendiga,
    e sil de dios buen amor E plaser de amiga,
    que por mi pecador vn pater noster diga;
    Si dezir non lo quisiere, a muerta non maldiga.'

DE QUALES ARMAS SE DEUE ARMAR TODO XRISTIANO
PARA VENÇER EL DIABLO, EL MUNDO E LA CARNE
1579 Señores, acordad vos de bien, si vos lo digo,
    non fiedes en tregua de vuestro enemigo,
    ca non vee la ora que vos lyeue consigo;
    Si vedes que vos miento, non me preçiedes vn figo.

1572 I will give alms for you and pray,
      I will have Masses sung and will give oblation.
      My Trotaconventos, may God give you redemption!
      He saved the world, may He give you salvation!

1573 Ladies, don't chide me or say I am like a baby,
      for if she had served you, you too would have mourned her.
      You would have cried for her, for her subtle baiting;
      all she followed were run to ground.

1574 No woman tall or short, locked up or hidden,
      could stop her where she made a raid.
      I know no man or woman, if they had lost one like her,
      who would not feel infinitely sad and sorrowful.

1575 I composed a short epitaph, with grief.
      My sadness made me a poor versifier.
      All those who hear it, through God our Lord,
      please pray for love's old servant.

THE EPITAPH ON URRACA'S TOMB

1576 'I, Urraca, who lie beneath this tomb,
      lived in the world at ease and free.
      I joined many lovers with good reason. I did not want
                                              foolish love.
      I fell to the ground from the heights in just an hour.

1577 Death trapped me unsuspecting in its net.
      Relations and friends, here you cannot help me.
      Do good works in life, and do not offend God,
      for as I died, so all shall die.

1578 May God bless him who comes here!
      Give him good love and a fine woman!
      And say the Lord's prayer for me and my sins.
      If you'd rather not, then do not curse the dead.'

HOW A CHRISTIAN SHOULD ARM HIMSELF AGAINST THE DEVIL, THE WORLD AND THE FLESH

1579 Sirs, I urge you, remember goodness.
      Don't rely on a truce from your enemy, the devil,
      for you do not know when he may take you with him.
      If you think I am lying, you won't value my words one bit.

1580   Deuemos estar çiertos, non Seguros de muerte,
       ca nuestra enemiga es natural E fuerte,
       por ende cada vno de nos sus armas puerte,
       non podemos, amigos, della fuyr por suerte.

1581   Sy qual quier de nos otros oviese cras de lydiar,
       con algun enemigo en el canpo entrar,
       cada qual buscaria armas para se armar,
       Syn armas non querria en tal peligro entrar.

1582   Pues si esto fariamos por omes como nos byuos,
       muy mas deuemos faserlo por tantos e tan esquiuos
       enemigos que nos quieren faser sieruos captiuos,
       E para sienpre jamas disen: ¡al jnfierno yd vos!

1583   los mortales pecados ya los avedes oydos,
       aquestos de cada dia nos trahen muy conbatidos,
       las almas quieren matar pues los cuerpos han feridos,
       por aquesto deuemos estar de armas byen guarnidos.

1584   lydyan otrosi con estos otros tres mas prinçipales:
       la carne, el diablo, el mundo, destos nasçen los mortales,
       destos tres vienen aquellos, tomemos armas atales
       que vençamos nos a ellos; quiero vos desir quales:

1585   obras de missericordia E de mucho bien obrar,
       dones de spiritu santo que nos quiera alunbrar,
       las obras de piedat, de virtudes nos menbrar,
       con siete sacramentos estos enemigos sobrar.

1586   Contra la grand cobdiçia el bautismo porfia,
       dono de spiritu santo, de buena Sabidoria,
       saber nos guardar de lo ajeno, non desir 'esto querria'
       la virtud de la justiçia judgando nuestra follia.

1587   vestir los pobles desnudos, con santa esperança
       que dios por quien lo faremos nos dara buena andança;
       con tal loriga podremos con cobdiçia que nos trança,
       E dios guardar nos ha de cobdiçia mal andança.

1588   Sobrar a la grand soberuia, desir mucha omildat;
       debdo es temer a dios e a la su magestad;

1580   We must be certain of, not safe from, death,
for our enemy is both natural and strong.
My friends, we cannot flee from it by chance,
so each of us must carry his arms.

1581   If any of us were to fight tomorrow
against some enemy on the battlefield,
we would each search for arms to protect us.
You would not enter danger without them.

1582   If we would do this against living men like us,
we should do so all the more against worse, more harmful
enemies, who want us for their servants and captives,
to say for evermore: 'Get to Hell with you!'

1583   The mortal sins you have already heard of
battle with us constantly daily.
They try to kill the soul, since they have wounded the body,
and so we need to be well protected with arms.

1584   Three greater enemies also fight alongside:
the flesh, the devil, the world – from these the mortal sins
                                       are born,
they come out of these three, so let us take up arms
to conquer them, and I shall tell you which.

1585   Works of mercy and many good deeds,
gifts of the Holy Spirit, who wants to light our way,
deeds of piety and remembrance of virtue,
overcoming the enemy with the seven sacraments.

1586   Great covetousness is contended against by baptism,
a gift of the Holy Spirit, of great wisdom.
We must know how to shun others' possessions and not to
                                         say:
'I want that!' with the virtue of justice judging our folly.

1587   We must clothe the naked poor, in the holy hope
that God, for whom we do it, will give us good fortune.
With this armour we can fight the covetousness which
                                         assails us,
and God will keep us from coveting and from error.

1588   To conquer great pride, speak humble words.
It is our duty to fear God and His majesty.

vyrtud de tenperamiento, de mesura e onestad,
con esta espada fuerte Segura mente golpad.

1589 Con mucha misericordia dar a los pobres posada,
tener fe que santa cosa es de dios gualardonada,
non rrobar cosas ajenas, non forçar muger nin nada,
con esta confirmaçion la soberuia es arrancada.

1590 ayamos contra avariçia spiritu de pyedat,
dando lymosna a pobles, dolyendo nos de su mal;
virtud de natural justiçia judgando con omildal,
con tal mata al avarisia bien larga mente dad.

1591 El santo Sacramento de orden saçerdotal
con fe santa escogida, mas clara que cristal,
casando huerfanas pobres; e nos con esto tal
vençeremos a avariçia con la graçia spiritual.

1592 ligera mente podremos a la loxuria Refrenar
con castidat E con conçiençia podernos emos escusar,
spiritu de fortalesa que nos quiera ayudar,
con estas brafuneras la podremos bien matar.

1593 quixotes E canilleras de santo Sacramento,
que dios fiso en parayso matrimonio E casamiento,
cassar los pobres menguados, dar a beuer al sediento,
ansi contra luxuria avremos vençimiento.

1594 yra, que es enemiga e mata muchos ayna,
con don de entendimiento e con caridad dyna,
entendiendo su grand dapno, fasiendo blanda farina,
con paçiençia bien podremos lydiar con tal capelina.

1595 Con vertud de esperança E con mucha paçiençia,
visitando los dolientes e fasiendo penitençia,
aborresçer los denuestos e amar buena abenençia,
con esto vençeremos yra E avremos de dios querençia.

1596 grand pecado es gula, puede a muchos matar,
abstinençia E ayuno puede lo de nos quitar,
con spiritu de çiençia, sabiendo mesura catar,
comer tanto que podamos para pobres apartar.

1597 otrosi rrogar a dios con santo Sacrifiçio,
que es de cuerpo de dios sacramento e ofiçio,

The virtues of temperance, moderation and honesty
make a powerful sword with which to strike.

1589 Give the poor shelter with great mercy,
have faith that holy works are rewarded by God.
Rob nothing you do not own, nor force any woman or
anything else.
With such confirmation, pride is uprooted.

1590 We need a spirit of piety against avarice,
giving alms to the poor, lamenting their plight.
It is the virtue of natural justice to judge with humility.
Beat avarice insistently with this kind of club.

1591 The holy sacrament of the priestly order
chosen with holy faith, clearer than crystal.
Marrying off poor orphan girls – through this
we will conquer avarice by spiritual grace.

1592 We should easily restrain lechery.
With chastity and our conscience we can avoid it;
the spirit of fortitude wishes to help us.
With this kind of arm protection we can kill lechery dead.

1593 Armour for the thighs and shins is the holy sacrament,
which God made in paradise, marriage or matrimony;
marriage of the wretched poor, giving the thirsty a drink,
this is how we shall conquer lechery.

1594 Anger is an enemy which kills many.
With the gift of understanding and divine charity,
understanding its great harm, making white flour
patiently, we can fight wearing this helmet.

1595 With the virtue of hope and with a lot of patience,
visiting the suffering and doing penance,
abhorring insults and loving concord,
we shall conquer anger and gain the love of God.

1596 Gluttony is a great sin, which can kill many;
abstinence and fasting can cure us of it.
We must seek moderation in the spirit of knowledge,
and eat what we can and leave some for the poor.

1597 We must also implore God with holy sacrifice
for the body of God is sacrament and office,

con fe en su memoria lidiando por su seruiçio,
con tal graçia podremos vençer gula que es viçio.

1598 la enbidia mato muchos de los profectass;
contra esta enemiga que nos fiere con saetas,
tomemos escudo fuerte pyntado con tabletas,
spiritu de buen conssejo encordado destas letras.

1599 Sacramento de vnçion meternos e soterremos,
auiendo por dios conpasion con caridat non erremos,
non fasiendo mal a los sinplex, pobres non denostemos,
con estas armas de dios a enbidia desterraremos.

1600 armados estemos mucho contra acidia mala cosa,
esta es de los siete pecados mas sotil e engañosa,
esta cada dia pare do quier quel diablo posa,
mas fijos malos tyene que la alana rrauiosa.

1601 Contra esta e sus fijos que ansy nos de-vallen
nos andemos rromerias e las oras non se callen,
E penssemos pensamientos que de buenas obras salen,
ansy que con santas obras a dios baldios non fallen.

1602 De todos buenos desseos e de todo bien obrar
fagamos asta de lança, e non queramos canssar
con fierro de buenas obras los pecados amatar;
con estas armas lydiando podemos los amanssar.

1603 Contra los tres prinçipales que non se ayunten de consuno,
al mundo con caridad, a la carne con ayuno,
con coraçon al diablo, todos tres yran de yuso,
nin de padres nin de fijos con esto non fynca vno.

1604 Todos los otro pecados mortales E veniales
destos nasçen commo Ryos de las fuentes perhenales,
estos dichos son comienço e suma de todos males;
de padres, fijos, nietos, dios nos guarde de sus males.

1605 denos dios atal esfuerço, tal ayuda E tal ardid
que vençamos los pecados e arranquemos la lid,
por que el dia del juysio sea fecho a nos conbyd,
que nos diga jhesu xpisto: ¡benditos, a mi venid!

with faith in His memory, fighting for His service.
With this grace we can beat the sin of gluttony.

1598 Envy killed many of the prophets,
so against this enemy which wounds with arrows,
let us take a strong shield decorated with heraldic lozenges
and bearing the letters 'the spirit of good advice'.

1599 Let us take the sacrament of extreme unction and bury the
dead.
Have compassion through God, with charity we will not err.
Do no evil to the simple, nor insult the poor.
With these God-given arms we will banish envy.

1600 Let us arm ourselves against sloth and its evils,
the most subtle and deceitful of the seven sins.
It gives birth daily where the devil appears,
and has more bad children than a mad female mastiff.

1601 To fight against her, and her sons, who bring us down,
we must make pilgrimages, continue to pray the canonical
hours,
we must think thoughts that lead to good deeds,
so that holy works show God we are not lazy.

1602 From all good desires and good deeds
let us make the shaft of a lance and not tire
of killing sins with the iron of good works.
If we fight with these arms, such sins can be tamed.

1603 Against the three greatest dangers, so they don't unite,
fight the world with charity, the flesh with fasting,
the devil with our hearts – we will defeat all three,
not one of the parent sins or offspring will remain.

1604 All other venial, mortal sins
are born of these like rivers from perennial fountains.
They are the start and summit of all evils.
May God keep us from bad fathers, sons and grandsons.

1605 May God give us enough strength, help and bravery
to conquer sin and win the battle,
so that on Judgement Day we are invited
so that Jesus can say: 'Blessed ones, come unto me!'

DE LAS PROPIEDADES QUE LAS DUEÑAS CHICAS HAN

1606 quiero vos abreuiar la predicaçion,
que sienpre me pague de pequeno sermon
e de dueña pequena E de breue Rason,
Ca poco E bien dicho afyncase el coraçon.

1607 Del que mucho fabla Ryen; quien mucho rrie es loco;
es en la dueña chica amor E non poco.
dueñas ay muy grandes que por chicas non troco,
mas las chicas e las grandes se rrepienden del troco.

1608 De las chicas que byen diga el amor me fiso Ruego,
que diga de sus noblesas, yo quiero las dezir luego,
desir vos he de dueñas chicas que lo avredes por juego,
son frias como la nieue e arden commo el fuego.

1609 Son frias de fuera, con el amor ardientes,
en la cama solas, trebejo, plasenteras, Ryentes,
en casa cuerdas, donosas, sosegadas, byen fasientes,
mucho al y fallaredes ado byen pararedes mientes.

1610 En pequena girgonça yase grand rresplandor,
en açucar muy poco yase mucho dulçor,
en la dueña pequeña yase muy grand amor;
pocas palabras cunplen al buen entendedor.

1611 Es pequeño el grano de la buena pemienta,
pero mas que la nues conorta E calyenta,
asi dueña pequena, sy todo amor consyenta,
non ha plaser del mundo que en ella non sienta.

1612 Commo en chica rrosa esta mucha color,
en oro muy poco grand preçio E grand valor,
commo en poco blasmo yase grand buen olor,
ansy en dueña chica yase muy grad sabor.

1613 Como Roby pequeño tyene mucha bondat,
color, virtud e preçio e noble claridad,
ansi dueña pequena tiene mucha beldat,
fermosura, donayre, amor E lealtad.

THE QUALITIES OF SMALL WOMEN

1606   I am going to cut short my preaching to you,
        as I have always preferred a short sermon,
        a small woman and a brief discussion,
        for what is short and well stated is well remembered.

1607   People laugh if someone talks a lot, and laughing too much
                                        suggests madness.
        The small woman gives great love, not little.
        I exchanged big women for small, but small I will not change,
        and neither small nor large regret the exchange.

1608   Love asked me to speak of the good qualities
        in the small women he talks of – I shall speak now,
        and tell you about small women – take it as a joke.
        They are cold as snow yet they burn like fire.

1609   They are cold on the outside, yet they are burning with love.
        In bed they give pleasure and sport, they are pleasing and
                                        smiling,
        in the house they are wise, witty, calm and dependable,
        much more besides, if you think about it.

1610   A small hyacinth stone* shines very brightly;
        great sweetness lies in just a little sugar.
        In small women lies great love;
        the good suitor needs only a few words.

1611   A grain of good pepper is small,
        but it comforts and warms more than a nut,
        like the small woman, when she gives all her love.
        There is no pleasure in the world which cannot be found in
                                        her.

1612   As a small rose has a lot of colour,
        and a little gold is high in price and value,
        as a little balsam smells very strongly,
        so great delight lies in the small woman.

1613   A small ruby contains great goodness,
        colour, virtue, price and noble clarity;
        the small woman has great beauty,
        loveliness, grace, love and loyalty.

1614	Sycha es la calandria E chico el rruyseñor,
	pero mas dulçe canta que otra ave mayor;
	la muger que es chica por eso es mejor,
	con doñeo es mas dulçe que açucar nin flor.

1615	sson aves pequenas papagayo e orior,
	pero qual quier dellas es dulçe gritador,
	ado-nada, fermosa, preçida cantador;
	bien atal es la dueña pequena con amor.

1616	De la muger pequeña non ay conparaçion,
	terrenal parayso es e grand consso-laçion,
	solas E alegria, plaser E bendiçion
	mejor es en la prueua que en la salutaçion.

1617	ssyenpre quis muger chica mas que grande nin mayor,
	non es desaguisado del grand mal ser foydor,
	del mal tomar lo menos, diselo el sabidor,
	por ende de las mugeres la mejor es la menor.

DE DON FFURON MOÇO DEL ARÇIPRESTE
1618	ssalida de febrero, entrada de março,
	el pecado que sienpre de todo mal es maço,
	traya abbades lleno el su rregaço,
	otrosi de mugeres fasie mucho rretaço.

1619	Pues que ya non tenia menssajera fiel,
	tome por mandadero vn Rapas traynel,
	huron avia por nonbre, apostado donçel,
	sy non por quatorse cosas nunca vy mejor que el.

1620	Era mintroso, bebdo, ladron e mesturero,
	thafur, peleador, goloso, Refertero,
	rreñidor E adeuino, susio E agorero,
	nesçio, pereçoso; tal es mi escudero.

1621	Dos dias en la selmana era grand ayunador,
	quando non tenia que comer ayunaua el pecador,
	sienpre aquestos dos dias ayunaua mi andador,
	quando non podia al faser, ayunaua con dolor.

1622	Pero sy diz la fabla que suelen Retraher,
	que mas val con mal asno el omne contender,
	que solo e cargado fas acuestas traer,
	pus lo por menssajero con el grand menester.

1614   The calendar lark and the nightingale are small,
       but they sing more sweetly than larger birds.
       The woman who is small is all the better for it;
       she is sweeter in courtship than sugar or flowers.

1615   The parrot and oriole are tiny birds,
       but each of them can sing sweetly,
       as a beautiful, gifted, valued songster,
       like the small woman in the case of love.

1616   Nothing can compare with the small woman.
       She is an earthly paradise and consolation,
       pleasure and happiness, joy and blessing.
       Intimate proof is better than the first greeting.

1617   I have always loved a woman who is small, not large or tall.
       It is not foolish to flee the larger evil,
       and take the lesser, as the wise man says,
       so therefore in women, the least is the best.

ABOUT FERRET, THE ARCHPRIEST'S BOY*

1618   February was over, it was now early March,
       and the devil, the cudgel of all evil,
       had a whole lapful of abbots in tow,
       and had wreaked devastation upon many women.

1619   As I no longer had my loyal messenger,
       I took a young pimp as my go-between,
       by the name of Ferret, an elegant youth,
       I never saw better, except in at least a dozen ways.

1620   He was a liar, a drunkard, a thief and a trouble-maker,
       a card-sharp, a brawler, a glutton and quarrelsome too,
       a wrangler, a fortune-teller, dirty and superstitious,
       stupid and lazy – that was my squire.

1621   For two days a week he was one for fasting.
       When he had nothing to eat, the sinner went on a fast;
       when he could do nothing else, he fasted and suffered.
       My messenger always fasted for two days.

1622   But the old saying they often quote is true,
       that 'a man is better coping with a bad donkey
       than carrying a burden uphill on his back alone'.
       I took him as my messenger in my great need.

1623   Dixele: 'huron, amigo, buscame nueua funda.'
       'a la fe,' diz, 'buscare avn que el mundo se funda,
       e yo vos la trahere syn mucha varahunda,
       que a las veses mal perro rroye buena coyunda.'

1624   El ssabia leer tarde, poco e por mal cabo;
       dixo: 'dad me vn cantar E veredes que Recabdo;
       e, Señor, vos veredes, maguer que non me alabo,
       que sy lo comienço que le dare buen cabo.'

1625   Dil aquestos cantares al que de dios mal fado,
       yua se los desiendo por todo el mercado;
       dixol doña fulana: '¡tyra te alla, pecado!
       que a mi non te enbia, nin quiero tu mandado.'

DE COMMO DIZE EL ARCIPRESTE QUE SE HA DE ENTENDER ESTE SU LIBRO

1626   Por que santa maria, Segund que dicho he,
       es comienco E fyn del bien, tal es mi fe,
       fiz le quatro cantares E con tanto fare
       punto a mi librete, mas non lo çerrare.

1627   buena propiedat ha do quier que sea,
       que si lo oye alguno que tenga muger fea,
       o sy muger lo oye que su marido vil sea,
       faser a dios seruiçio En punto lo desea.

1628   Desea oyr misas E faser oblaçones,
       desea dar a pobres bodigos E rrasiones,
       faser mucha lymonsna E desir oraciones.
       dios con esto se sirue, bien lo vedes varones.

1629   qual quier omne que lo oya, sy byen trobar sopiere,
       mas ay añadir E emendar si quisiere,
       ande de mano en mano a quien quier quel pydiere,
       como pella a las dueñas, tomelo quien podiere.

1630   Pues es de buen amor, enprestadlo de grado,
       non des-mintades su nonbre nin dedes rrefertado,
       non le dedes por dineros vendido nin alquilado,
       ca non ha grado nin graçias nin buen amor conplado.

1631   ffiz vos pequeno libro de testo, mas la glosa
       non creo que es chica ante es byen grad prosa,

1623 I said to him: 'Ferret, my friend, find me a new tart.'
      'By faith,' he said, 'I shall search to the world's end
      and bring her to you with very little trouble.
      At times a bad dog gnaws a good leather rope.'

1624 He could read slowly, little and badly.
      He said: 'Give me a song and you'll see what I can achieve.
      You will see, sir, that I am not boasting.
      What I start, I will finish successfully.'

1625 I gave him those songs, may God bring him misfortune;
      he went all over the market singing them.
      Miss So-and-So said: 'Get out of here, you devil!
      No one is sending you to me, I don't want your message.'

THE ARCHPRIEST TELLS US HOW WE SHOULD UNDERSTAND HIS BOOK

1626 Because the Virgin Mary, as I have said,
      is the start and end of all good, as I believe,
      I wrote her four songs, with which I will
      put a full stop to my book, but will not end it.

1627 It has great value, wherever it may lie,
      and if someone hears it who has an ugly woman,
      or if a woman hears it who has a useless man,
      they will at once long to serve God.

1628 They will long to hear Mass and make oblation,
      and give holy bread and alms to the poor,
      to give alms freely and say their prayers.
      God will be pleased, as you will see, lads.

1629 Any man who hears the book and knows how to write verse
      may add to it or amend it, if he wishes.
      May it pass from hand to hand, to whoever asks for it,
      like a ball in a women's game, take it who will.

1630 Since it is about good love, lend it gladly.
      Don't deny its name nor criticize it,
      don't sell it for money or rent it out,
      for there is no pleasure or thanks in good love bought.

1631 I have written you a short text, but the gloss
      is anything but, I think; it is substantial holy verse,

que sobre cada fabla se entyende otra cosa,
syn la que se a-lega en la Rason fermosa.

1632 De la santidat mucha es byen grand lyçionario,
mas de juego E de burla es chico breuiario,
por ende fago punto E çierro mi almario,
Sea vos chica fabla, solas E letuario.

1633 Señores, he vos seruido con poca sabidoria,
por vos dar solas a todos fable vos en jugleria.
yo vn gualardon vos pido: que por dios en rromeria
digades vn pater noster por mi E ave maria.

1634 Era de mill E tresientos E ochenta E vn años
fue conpuesto el rromançe, por muchos males e daños
que fasen muchos e muchas a otras con sus engaños,
E por mostrar a los synplex fablas e versos estraños.

GOZOS DE SANTA MARIA
1635 Madre de dios gloriosa,
virgen santa marya,
fija E leal esposa
del tu fijo mexia,
tu, Señora, da me agora
la tu graçia toda ora,
que te sirua toda via.

1636 por que seruir te cobdiçio
yo percador, por tanto
te ofresco, en seruiçio,
los tus gosos que canto.
el primero,
fue terçero angel a ty menssajero
del spiritu santo.

1637 Conçebiste a tu padre,
fue tu goço segundo;
quando lo pariste, madre,
syn dolor salio al mundo,

where every story has another meaning
in addition to the one affirmed by elegant discourse.

1632 It is a book full of advice on holiness,
but also a brief breviary of play and jest.
I will now punctuate it with a full stop and close my
bookcase.
May it be short, entertaining and like an electuary to you.

1633 Sirs, I have served you with scant wisdom,
and spoken to you as a minstrel to please you all.
I ask a reward of you, that, for God, on pilgrimage,
you say the Lord's prayer for me and a 'Hail Mary'.

1634 In the era year of Caesar, thirteen hundred and eighty one,*
the poem was composed because of many evils and harm
that men and women bring upon each other with their
deceit, and to show extraordinary verse and tales to
ordinary folk.

THE JOYS OF THE VIRGIN MARY
1635 Glorious Mother of God,
Holy Virgin Mary,
daughter and loyal wife,
through your son the Messiah,
my lady,
now give me
your grace always,
that I may serve you always.

1636 Because I desire to serve you,
I, a sinner, do
offer in service to you
your joys, which I sing;
the first
was truly when
the messenger angel came to you
from the Holy Spirit.

1637 You conceived by the Father
and your second joy was
when you gave birth to Him, Mother;
He came into the world without pain

qual nasçite
bien atal rremaneçiste,
virge del santo mundo.

1638   El terçero, la estrella
guio los Reyes poro
venieron a la lus della,
con su noble thesoro,
e laudaron,
E adoraron,
al tu fijo presentaron
ençienso, mirra, oro.

1639   fue tu alegria quarta
quando ovyste mandado
del hermano de marta,
que era rresuçitado
tu fijo dus,
del mundo lus,
que viste morir en crus,
que era leuantado.

1640   quando a los çielos sobio,
quanto plaser tomaste;
el sesto quando enbio
espiritu santo goseste;
el septeno
fue mas bueno
quando tu fijo por ti veno
el çielo pujaste.

1641   Pydo te merçed gloriosa;
sienpre, toda vegada,
que me seades piadosa,
alegre e pagada;
quando a judgar,
juysio dar
jhesu vinier, quiere me ayudar
E ser mi abogada.

[line missing]
as you were born,
so you remained
Virgin of the Holy World.

1638   The third, the star
which led the kings, as
they came in its light
with their noble treasure
and gave praise
and adoration;
they presented your Son
with incense, myrrh, gold.

1639   Your fourth joy was
when you were told
by Martha's sister
that He was risen from death.
Your sweet son,
light of the world,
whom you saw die on the cross,
was risen again.

1640   When He ascended into heaven,
this was your fifth joy;
the sixth when He sent
the Holy Spirit, such pleasure;
the seventh
was the best:
when your Son came for you
and you ascended into Heaven.

1641   I ask you for mercy, Glorious One,
always, every time,
be merciful to me,
happy and contented;
when in judgement
Jesus comes
to pass sentence, help me
and be my advocate.

GOZOS DE SANTA MARIA

1642 Todos bendigamos
a la virgen santa,
sus gozos digamos,
E su vida quanta
fue, segund fallamos
que la estoria canta
vida tanta.

1643 El año doseno
a esta donsella,
angel de dios bueno,
saludo a ella
[salta el texto]
virgen bella.

1644 pario ssu fijuelo,
¡que goso tan maño!
a este moçuelo
el treseno año.
rreyes venieron lluego,
con presente estraño
dar, adorallo.

1645 Años treynta e tres
con xpristos estudo:
quando rresuçitado es
quarto goço fue conplido;
quinto, quando jhesus es
al cielo sobido,
E lo vido.

1646 Sesta alegria
ovo ella quando,
en su conpañia
los dicipulos estando,
dios ally enbya
spiritu santo
alunbrando.

1647 la vida conplida
del fijo mexia,
nueue años de vida

THE JOYS OF THE VIRGIN MARY

1642   We all bless
       the Holy Virgin,
       we speak of her joys
       and her life, such a
       life, as we find
       the story tells,
       such a fine life.

1643   In her twelfth year,
       this young lady
       was greeted by
       an angel of God
       [text missing]
       Beautiful Virgin.

1644   She gave birth to her infant Son,
       such Great Joy!
       to this little boy
       in her thirteenth year;
       and then came kings
       with exotic gifts
       to adore Him.

1645   For thirty-three years
       she was with Christ;
       when He was raised from death,
       the fourth joy was complete,
       and the fifth when Jesus
       ascended into Heaven,
       and she saw it take place.

1646   The sixth joy
       she felt when,
       in company
       of the disciples,
       God sent the
       Holy Spirit there,
       bringing light.

1647   When the life of
       her son Messiah was over,
       the Virgin Mary lived on

byuio santa maria;
al çielo fue subida,
¡que grand alegria,
este dia!

1648 gosos fueron siete,
años çinquaenta
e quatro çierta mente
ovo ella por cuenta.
¡defiende nos sienpre
de mal E de afruenta,
virgen genta!

1649 Todos los xpistianos
aved alegria
en aquel dia,
que nasçio por saluar nos
de la virgen maria
en nuestra valia.

DE COMMO LOS SCOLARES DEMANDAN POR DIOS

1650 Señores, dat al escolar
que vos vien demandar.

1651 dat lymosna o rraçio,
fare por vos oraçion
que dios vos de saluaçion,
quered por dios a mi dar.

1652 El byen que por dios feçierdes,
la lymosna que por el dierdes,
quando deste mundo salierdes
esto vos avra de ayudar.

1653 quando a dios dierdes cuenta
de los algos E de la Renta,
escusar vos ha de afruenta
la lymosna por el far.

1654 Por vna Rasion que dedes,
vos çiento de dios tomedes,
E en parayso entredes,
¡ansi lo quiera el mandar!

for nine more years,
then ascended into Heaven.
What great happiness
on that day!

1648   There were seven joys
and of years
fifty-four, on
her account.
Protect us always
from evil and affront,
gracious Virgin!

1649   May all Christians
be joyous
[text missing]
on this day.
He was born to save us,
of the Virgin Mary,
to help us all.

HOW SCHOLARS BEG IN THE NAME OF GOD

1650   Sirs, give to the scholar
who comes to beg.

1651   Give alms, give alms:
I will say a prayer for you,
may God give you salvation;
please give me something for the grace of God.

1652   The good you do in the name of God,
the alms that you give to me,
when you pass from this world
will be bound to help you.

1653   When you give God an account
of the capital and the income,
He will exempt you from judgement
because of the alms you gave for Him.

1654   For every bit of alms you give,
God will repay you a hundred times
and you shall enter Paradise.
This is how He ordains it!

1655 Catad que el byen faser
nunca se ha de perder;
poder vos ha estorçer
del jnfierno mal lugar.

1656 señores, vos dat a nos
esculares pobres dos.

1657 El Señor de parayso,
xpistos, tanto que nos quiso
que por nos muerte priso;
mataron lo jodios.

1658 Murio nuestro Señor
nor ser nuestro saluador;
dad nos por el su amor,
¡Si el salue a todos nos!

1659 Acordat vos de su estoria,
dad por dios en su memoria,
¡Sy el vos de la su gloria,
dad lymosna por dios!

1660 agora en quanto byuierdes,
por su amor sienpre dedes,
E con esto escaparedes
del jnfierno e de su tos.

DEL AUE MARIA DE SANTA MARIA

1661 Aue maria gloriosa,
virgen santa preçiosa,
¡commo eres piadosa
toda via!

1662 graçia plena, syn mansilla,
abogada,
por la tu merçed, Señora,
faz esta marauilla
Señalada.
por la tu bondad agora
guardame toda ora
de muerte vergoñosa,
por que loe a ty, fermosa,
noche e dya.

1655 Take careful note that good done
is never lost:
it can have the power to save you
from the evils of Hell.

1656 Sirs, give to us
two poor scholars.

1657 The Lord of paradise,
Christ, so loved us
that He died for us:
the Jews killed Him.

1658 Thus Our Lord died
to be our Saviour;
give in the name of His love
and He will surely save us all!

1659 Remember His story;
give for God in His memory
and He will surely give you His glory.
Give us alms for the sake of God!

1660 Now, while you live,
always give through His love,
and by this you shall escape
from Hell and its cough.

THE VIRGIN MARY'S 'AVE MARIA'

1661 Ave Maria, glorious One,
precious Holy Virgin,
how merciful you are
always!

1662 *Gratia plena* (Full of grace), without stain,
intercessor,
through your mercy, Lady,
create this miracle
so rare:
through your goodness now
keep me always
from shameful death,
so that I might praise you, O Beauty,
night and day.

1663 Dominus tecum,
estrella Resplandeçiente,
melesina de coydados,
catadura muy bella,
rrelusiente,
syn mansilla de pecados,
por los tus gosos preciados
te pido, virtuosa,
qu me guardes, lynpia rrosa,
de ffollya.

1664 benedita tu,
onrrada syn egualança
syendo virgen conçebiste,
de los angeles loada
en altesa;
por el fijo que pariste,
por la graçia que oviste,
¡o bendicha fror e Rosa!,
tu me guarda piadosa
E me guia.

1665 in mulyeribus
escogida, santa madre,
de xpistianos anparança,
de los santos bien seruida.
E tu padre
es tu fijo syn dubdança,
¡o virgen, mi fiança!
de gente maliçiosa
cruel, mala, soberuiosa
me desuia.

1666 E benedictus fructus,
folgura E saluaçion
del lynaje vmanal,
que tiraste la tristura
e perdimiento
que, por nuestro esquiuo mal,
el diablo, susio tal,
con su obla engañosa,

1663   *Dominus tecum* (The Lord is with Thee), resplendent
       star,
       medicine for suffering,
       so lovely in appearance,
       shining,
       with no stain of sin,
       through your priceless joys,
       I ask you, Virtuous one,
       pure rose, to keep me
       from folly.

1664   *Benedita tu* (Blessed art Thou), honoured one,
       without equal,
       who conceived as a virgin,
       and is praised by the angels
       on high;
       through the Son you bore,
       through the grace you had,
       oh, blessed flower and rose!
       guard me, merciful one,
       and guide me.

1665   *In mulyeribus* (Among women) chosen,
       Holy Mother,
       the shelter of Christians,
       well served by the saints;
       Your Father
       is your Son without doubt:
       oh Virgin, my surety!
       from malicious people,
       those who are cruel, evil, proud,
       turn me away.

1666   *benedictus fructus* (Blessed fruit), consolation
       and salvation
       of human kind,
       who cast away sadness
       and loss,
       which for our harm
       the foul devil
       and his deceitful works

en carcel peligrosa
ya ponia.

1667 Ventris tuy,
      ssanta flor non tanida,
      por la tu grand santidad
      tu me guarda de errar,
      que my vida sienpre sigua
      en bondad;
      que meresca egualdad
      con los santos, muy graçiosa,
      en dulçor marauillosa,
      ¡o maria!

CANTICA DE LOORES DE SANTA MARIA
1668 Miraglos muchos fase virgen sienpre pura,
      aguardando los coytados de dolor E de tristura;
      El que loa tu figura non lo dexes oluidado,
      non catando su pecado, saluas lo de amargura.

1669 Ayudas al ynoçente con amor muy verdadero,
      al que es tu seruidor bien lo libras de lygero,
      non le es falleçedero tu acorro syn dudança,
      guardalo de mal andança el tu bien grande, llenero.

1670 Reyna virgen, mi esfuerço, yo so puesto en tal espanto,
      por lo qual a ty bendigo, que me guardes de quebranto;
      pues a ty, Señora, canto, tu me guarda de lisyon,
      de muerte E de ocasion por tu fijo jhesu santo.

had already prepared
in a dangerous prison.

1667   *Ventris tuy* (Of thy womb), holy flower
unsullied;
through your great sanctity
keep me from error,
that my life
may always imitate your goodness
to equal the saints, most Gracious One,
of marvellous sweetness,
Oh, Mary!

SONG OF PRAISE TO THE VIRGIN MARY

1668   The Virgin, ever undefiled
performs many miracles,
protecting the suffering
from pain and sadness;
do not forget
the one who praises your countenance
and disregard his sins,
saving him from bitterness.

1669   You help the innocent
with truest love
and easily free the one who is
your servant:
your succour is
undoubted and infallible;
keep him from ill fortune
with your great and perfect goodness.

1670   Queen, Virgin, my strength,
I am in such terrible fear,
for which I bless you,
and ask you to keep me from destruction;
since I sing, my Lady, to you;
guard me from harm,
from death and from accident,
through your Son, Holy Jesus.

1671 Yo so mucho agrauiado en esta çibdad seyendo,
      tu acorro E guarda fuerte a mi libre defendiendo;
      pues a ty me encomiendo, non me seas desdeñosa,
      tu bondad marauillosa loare sienpre seruiendo.

1672 A ty me encomiendo, virgen santa maria;
      la mi coyta tu la parte, tu me salua E me guia,
      E me guarda toda via, piadosa virgen santa,
      por la tu merçed que es tanta que desir non la podria.

CANTICA DE LOORES DE SANTA MARIA
1673 Santa virgen escogida,
      de dios madre muy amada,
      en los çielos ensalçada,
      del mundo salud E vida.

1674 Del mundo salud E vida,
      de muerte destruymiento,
      de graçia llena conplyda,
      de coytados saluamiento;
      de aqueste dolor que siento
      en presion syn meresçer,
      tu me deña estorçer,
      con el tu deffendimiento.

1675 Con el tu deffendimiento,
      non catando mi maldad.
      nin el mi meresçemiento,
      mas la tu propia bondad,
      que conffieso en verdat
      que so pecador errado;
      de ty sea ayudado
      por la tu virginidad.

1671   I have been greatly wronged
         while in this city dwelling;
         may your succour and great protection
         free me through defence;
         so I commend myself to you,
         do not disdain me;
         I shall always praise
         your marvellous goodness by serving you.

1672   I commend myself to you,
         Holy Virgin Mary.
         Take away my torment,
         save and guide me
         and keep me still,
         merciful Holy Virgin,
         through your Grace, which is so great
         I could never express it.

SONG OF PRAISE TO THE VIRGIN MARY

1673   Holy Virgin elect,
         beloved Mother of God,
         praised in heaven,
         health and life of the world.

1674   Health and life of the world,
         destruction of death,
         full of perfect grace,
         salvation of the suffering:
         deign to save me
         from this pain I feel
         in prison undeservedly,
         with your protection.

1675   With your protection,
         not looking upon my iniquity
         nor my worthiness,
         but your own goodness;
         I confess truthfully
         that I am an errant sinner;
         may I receive your help
         through your virginity.

1676   Por la tu virginidad
que non ha conparaçion,
nin oviste egualtad
en obra e entençion,
conplida de bendiçion;
pero non so meresçiente
venga a ti, Señora, en miente
de conplir mi petiçion.

1677   De conplir mi petiçion,
como a otros ya conpliste,
de tan fuerte tentaçion
en que so coytado triste,
pues poder as E oviste,
tu me guarda en tu mano;
bien acorres muy de llano
Al que quieres E quisiste.

CANTICA DE LOORES DE SANTA MARIA
1678   quiero Seguir a ty, flor de las flores,
sienpre desir cantar de tus loores,
non me partir de te seruir,
mejor de las mejores.

1679   grand fyança he yo en ty, Señora.
la mi esperança en ty es toda ora,
de tribulaçion syn tardança
ven me librar agora.

1680   virgen muy santa, yo paso atribulado
pena atanta con dolor atormentado,
en tu esperança coyta atanta
que veo ¡mal pecado!

1676 Through your virginity
which cannot be compared,
you have no equal
in works and intention,
perfect in blessing;
though I am not worthy,
please remember, Lady,
to answer my plea.

1677 To answer my plea,
as you answered others,
in such great temptation;
I am tormented, sad,
but you had and have power,
keep me in your hand;
simply protect
the one you love and loved.

SONG OF PRAISE TO THE VIRGIN MARY

1678 I want to follow
you, flower of flowers,
always speak
and sing your praises,
never stop
serving you,
best among the best.

1679 Great trust
I have in you, Lady;
my hope
is always in you:
from tribulation,
without delay,
come and free me now.

1680 Most Holy Virgin,
I spend in tribulation
such punishment
with pain tormented
and I fear
such anguish,
as I see, oh, pity!

1681 Estrella del mar, puerto de folgura,
de dolor conplido E de tristura,
ven me librar E conortar,
Señora del altura.

1682 Nunca falleçe la tu merçed conplida,
syenpre guaresçes de coytas E das vida;
nunca peresçe nin entristeçe
quien a ty non oluida.

1683 sufro grand mal syn meresçer, a tuerto,
esquiuo tal por que pienso ser muerto;
mas tu me val, que non veo al
que me saque a puerto.

CANTICA DE LOORES DE SANTA MARIA

1684 En ty es mi sperança,
virgen santa maria;
en Señor de tal valia
es rrason de aver fiança.

1685 ventura astrosa,
cruel, enojosa,
captiua, mesquina,
¿por que eres sañosa,
contra mi tan dapñosa
E falsa vesina?

1686 Non se escreuir,
nin puedo desir,
la coyta estraña
que me fases sofrir,
con deseo beuir
en tormenta tamaña.

1681   Star of the sea
         and safe haven,
         from my great sorrow
         and sadness
         come, release
         and comfort me,
         Lady on high.

1682   Your perfect mercy
         never fails,
         you always protect
         from suffering and give life;
         he shall never perish
         nor be saddened
         who never forgets you.

1683   I suffer great ill
         unjustly, wrongly,
         such harm
         that I think of death;
         but you will aid me.
         I see no other
         to lead me to a safe port.

SONG OF PRAISE TO THE VIRGIN MARY

1684   My hope is in you,
         Holy Virgin Mary.
         It is right to place trust
         in a lady of such worth.

1685   Ill-fated fortune,
         cruel, angry,
         wretched, mean,
         why are you enraged,
         so damaging to me,
         such a false neighbour?

1686   I cannot write
         I cannot speak
         the extraordinary torment
         you make me suffer.
         I do not want to live
         in such great anguish.

1687   ffasta oy toda via,
       mantouiste porfia
       en me mal traher;
       faz ya cortesia
       e dame alegria
       gasado E praser.

1688   E si tu me tyrares
       coyta e pesares,
       E mi grand tribulaçion
       en goço tornares,
       E bien ayudares,
       faras buena estança.

1689   Mas si tu porfias
       E non te desvias
       de mis penas cresçer,
       ya las coytas mias
       en muy pocos dias
       podran fenesçer.

CANTICA DE LOS CLERIGOS DE TALAUERA

1690   Alla en talavera, en las calendas de abril,
       llegadas son las cartas del arçobispo don gil,
       en las quales venia el mandado non vil
       tal que si plugo a vno peso mas que a dos mill.

1691   aqueste açipreste que traya el mandado,
       bien creo que lo fiso mas con midos que de grado;
       mando juntar cabildo, aprisa fue juntado,
       coydando que traya otro mejor mandado.

1692   ffablo este açipreste E dixo bien ansy:
       'Sy pesa a vos otros, bien tanto pesa a mi;
       ¡ay, viejo mezquino! ¿en que envegeçi?
       en ver lo que veo E en ver lo que vy.'

1693   llorando de sus ojos, començo esta rraçon,
       diz: 'el papa nos enbia esta constituçion,
       he vos lo a desir, que quiera o que non,
       maguer que vos lo digo con rrauia de mi coraçon.'

1687   Until today, still
you persisted
in ill-treating me.
Now be kind
and bring me happiness,
joy and pleasure.

1688   And if you take away
torment and sorrows,
and great tribulation,
turn it into joy
and help me,
then your deed will be good.

1689   But if you are stubborn
and do not cease
to make my sorrows grow,
then my anguish
in just a few days
may end in death.

THE POEM OF THE TALAVERA CLERGY

1690   It was early in April over in Talavera,
letters arrived from Archbishop Gil,*
in which appeared a worthy decree.
If it pleased one man, it displeased at least two thousand.

1691   The archpriest who had brought the decree –
well, I think he brought it with a bad grace, not gladly.
He ordered a meeting of the ecclesiastical assembly,
soon arranged, for they thought he brought another, better
                                        mandate.

1692   This archpriest spoke as follows:
'If it grieves you, it grieves me just as much;
oh, wretched old man! I have grown old through this!
seeing the things I see and have seen.'

1693   Eyes filled with tears, he began to speak:
'The Pope has sent us this decree.
I have to impart it, whether I wish to or not,
but I am telling you with rage in my heart.'

1694 Cartas eran venidas que disen en esta manera:
que clerigo nin cassado de toda talauera
que non touiese mançeba cassada nin soltera,
qual quier que la touiese descomulgado era.

1695 Con aquestas rrasones que la carta desia
fynco muy queblantada toda la clerisia;
algunos de los legos tomaron asedia,
para aver su acuerdo juntaron se otro dia.

1696 Ado estauan juntados todos en la capilla,
leuanto se el dean a mostrar su mansilla,
dis: 'amigos, yo querria que toda esta quadrilla
apellasemos del papa antel Rey de castilla.

1697 que maguer que somos clerigos, Somos sus naturales,
seruimos le muy byen, fuemos le sienpre leales,
demas que sabe el rrey que todos somos carnales;
quered se ha adolesçer de aquestos nuestros males.

1698 ¿que yo dexe a ora-buena, la que cobre antaño?
en dexar yo ella rresçibierya yo grand dapño;
dile luego de mano dose varas de pano
E avn, ¡para la mi corona! anoche fue al baño.

1699 Ante Renunçiaria toda la mi prebenda,
E desi la dignidad E toda la mi Renta,
que la mi ora-buena, tal escatima prenda;
creo que otros muchos syguiran por esta senda.

1700 Demando los apostolos E todo lo que mas vale,
con grand afyncamiento, ansi como dios Sabe,
E con llorosos ojos E con dolor grande:
'vobis enim dimitere quam suaue.'

1701 ffablo en pos de aqueste luego el thesorero,
que era desta orden confrade derechero,
diz: 'amigos, si este Son a de ser verdadero,
si malo lo esperades, yo peor lo espero.

1702 E del mal de vos otros a mi mucho me pesa,
otrosi de lo mio E del mal de teresa;
pero dexare a talauera E yr me a oropesa
ante que la partyr de toda la mi mesa.

1694   Letters arrived, which said that
no married man or priest in all of Talavera
should have a mistress, married or single.
Anyone who does shall be excommunicated.

1695   Hearing the words contained in the letter,
all the clergy were greatly afflicted.
Some of the lay brothers were disgusted;
they met the next day to come to agreement.

1696   When they were all gathered in the chapel
the dean arose to express his sorrow,
saying: 'Friends, I would like this whole group
to appeal to the Pope before the King of Castile.

1697   For although we are priests, we are his subjects.
We always serve him well, have always been loyal.
Moreover, the king knows we are flesh and blood.
He will want to commiserate with our bad news.

1698   Must I leave Good Time, the woman I had before?
If I left her I would be harming myself.
I gave her twelve yards of cloth straightaway,
and last night she even had a bath, upon my tonsure!*

1699   I would first renounce all my prebend
as well as the honour, all my income,
than let Good Time suffer such harm.
I think many others would do the same.'

1700   He invoked the Apostles and all most esteemed,
with great importunity, as God knows,
with tearful eyes and considerable pain:
'*vobis enim dimitere quam suave*' (We must send soft
                                                 pussy away).

1701   After him, the treasurer spoke,
who was a full brother of the Order:
'Friends, if this news turns out to be true,
and if you expect something bad, then I expect worse.

1702   Your misfortune weighs heavily on me,
as does my own, and Teresa's misfortune.
I shall leave Talavera and go to Oropesa
rather than be separated from her,

1703   Ca nunca fue tan leal blanca flor a frores
     nin es agora tristan con todos sus amores;
     que fase muchas veses rrematar los ardores,
     E sy de mi la parto nunca me dexaran dolores.

1704   Por que suelen desir que el can con grand angosto
     E con rrauia de la muerte a su dueño traua al rrostro,
     ¡Sy yo touiese al arçobispo en otro tal angosto,
     yo le daria tal buelta que nunca viese al agosto!'

1705   ffablo en post aqueste el chantre Sancho muñoz,
     diz: 'aqueste arçobispo non se que se ha con nos,
     el quiere acalañar nos lo que perdono dios,
     por ende yo apello en este escripto, abiuad vos.

1706   que sy yo tengo o toue en casa vna seruienta,
     non ha el arçobispo desto por que se sienta,
     que non es mi comadre nin es mi parienta,
     huefana la crie, esto por que non mienta.

1707   En mantener omne huerfana obra es de piedad,
     otro si a las vibdas, esto es cosa con verdat;
     por que si el arçobispo tiene que es cosa que es maldad,
     dexemos a las buenas E a las malas vos tornad.

1708   Don gonçalo canonigo, Segud que vo entendiendo,
     es este que va de sus alfajas prendiendo,
     E van se las vesinas por el barrio desiendo
     que la acoje de noche en casa avn que gelo defiendo.'

1709   Pero non alonguemos atanto las rrazones:
     appellaron los clerigos, otrosy los clerizones,
     ffesieron luego de mano buenas approllaçones
     E dende en adelante çiertas procuraçones.

Este es el libro del arçipreste de hita, el qual conpuso seyendo preso
por mandado del cardenal don gil arçobispo de toledo. Laus tibi
xpriste quem liber explicit iste.
Alffonus paratinen.

1703   for Blanchefleur was never so loyal to Fleur
nor is Tristan now with all his loves,*
for she often calms my ardour,
but if I leave her, pain will never leave me.

1704   It is often said that a dog in dire straits
and in a mortal frenzy will claw his master's face.
If I had the archbishop in such a narrow pass,
I'd give him such a going over, he'd never see the August
                                     harvest!'

1705   Next spoke the preceptor, Sancho Nuñoz,
who said: 'I don't know what the archbishop has against us.
He wants to blame us for what God has pardoned,
so therefore I appeal against this document. Rouse yourselves,

1706   for if I keep or have kept a maidservant in my house,
the archbishop has no need to complain.
She is not a god-parent, nor my relative,
I brought her up as an orphan. I cross myself because it's
                                        true.

1707   It is an act of piety to support an orphan,
as it is with widows, the truth is clear;
and if the archbishop thinks it is bad,
let's turn aside from good women and turn to bad ones.

1708   It's Gonzalo, the canon, as I understand it,
who is forking out his jewels,
while the neighbours go around the district saying
that he sees his girl at home at night, though I don't believe
                                        it.'

1709   But we mustn't prolong these speeches.
The priests appealed and higher clergy too;
they drew up these appeals straightaway
and thereafter certain powers of attorney.

This book was written by the Archpriest of Hita during his imprisonment at the order of Cardinal Gil, Archbishop of Toledo. *Laus tibi, xpriste quem liber explicit iste* (Praise to Thee, Christ, for this book is ended).
Alfonso of Paradinas.

CANTAR DE CIEGOS

1710   Varones buenos e onrrados queret nos ya ayudar,
        A estos çiegos lasrados la uuestra limosna dar,
        somos pobres menguados, avemos lo a demandar.

1711   de los bienes deste siglo non tenemos nos pasada,
        beuimos en gran peligro en vida mucho penada,
        çiegos bien commo vestiglo del mundo non vemos nada.

1712   Señora santa maria tu le da la bendeçion
        al que oy en este dia nos d[ie]re primero rraçion,
        dal al cuerpo alegria e al alma saluaçion.

1713   santa maria madalena, rruega a dios verdadero
        de quien nos diere buena estrena de meaja o de dinero,
        para mejorar la çena a nos e a nuestro conpanero.

1714   el que oy nos estrenare con meja o con pan,
        dele en quanto començare buena estrena santa julian,
        quanto a dios demandare otorge gelo de plan.

1715   sus fiios e su conpana dios padre espritual
        De çegedat atamaña guarde e de coyta atal,
        s[u]s ganados e su cabaña santo anton lo guarde de mal.

BLIND BEGGARS' SONG*

1710   Good and honourable men,
please give us your help,
give your alms
to us wretched blind men.
We are poor and unfortunate,
we have to ask you for it.

1711   Of the wealth of this world
we have no resources;
we live in great affliction,
live a life of great torment;
we are blind, deformed monsters,
we see nothing of the world.

1712   Our Lady Holy Mary,
give your blessing
to the man who gives us
our first alms today.
Bring happiness to his body
and salvation to his soul.

1713   Holy Mary Magdalene,
pray to the true God
for whoever gives us something first,
a mite or some money
to buy a better dinner
for myself and my companion.

1714   He who gives us first today
some scraps or some bread
will have good fortune
in all he undertakes, through St Julian;
whatever he asks of God,
it will fully be granted.

1715   May God, spiritual father,
keep his children
and family
from this blindness
and similar suffering,
and may St Anthony
keep his flocks and herds from evil.

1716 a quien nos dio su meaja por amor del saluador,
señor, dal tu gloria, tu graçia e tu amor,
guarda lo de la baraxa del pecado en-ganador.

1717 Ca con bien aventurado angel señor san miguel
tu seas su abogado de aquella e de aquel
que del su pan nos a dado, ofrecemos telo por el.

1718 quando las almas pasares estos ten con la tu diestra
que dan çenas e yantares a nos e a quien nos adiestra.
Sus pecados e sus males echa los a la siniestra.

1719 señor, merçet te clamamos con nuestras manos amas,
la limosna que te damos que las tomes en tus palmas,
a quien nos dio que comamos de parayso a sus almas.

CANTAR DE CIEGOS
1720 xristianos de dios amigos, a estos çiegos mendigos
con meajas o con bodigos queret nos acorrer,
e queret por dios faser.

1721 si de vos non lo auemos, otro algo non tenemos
con que nos desayunar, non lo podemos ganar
con estos cuerpos lasrados, çiegos, pobres e cuytados.

1722 dat nos de uuestra caridat e guarde uos dios la claridat
de los uestros ojos dios, por quien lo fasedes uos;
goso e plaser veades de los fijos que mucho amades.

1716   Whoever gives us his mite
        for love of the Saviour,
        Lord, give him your grace,
        your glory and your love;
        keep him from the snares
        of the deceiving devil.

1717   For, with the blessed
        angel St Michael,
        you shall be the advocate
        of whichever man or woman
        has given us of their bread.
        We offer it to you for them.

1718   When you judge souls,
        keep these on your right hand,
        for they give meals and dinners
        to us and our guide;
        cast their sins and wrongdoings
        into oblivion.

1719   Lord, we call for mercy
        with both our hands.
        The alms we give you
        take in both your palms,
        and whoever gives us food,
        give paradise to their souls.

BLIND BEGGARS' SONG

1720   Christians, friends of God,
        please give succour
        to us blind beggars
        with some scraps and pieces of bread,
        and give for the sake of God.

1721   If we get nothing from you,
        we shall have nothing else
        with which to break our fast:
        we cannot earn it
        with our wretched bodies.

1722   Give us your charity,
        and may God preserve
        the clarity of your eyes,

1723   nunca veades pesar, dexe uos los dios criar,
          o ser arçidianos, sean rricos e sean sanos,
          non les de dios çegedat, guarde los de pobredat.

1724   deles mucho pan e vino que de al pobre mesquino,
          deles algos e dineros que de a pobres rromeros,
          de les paños e vestidos que de a çiegos tollidos.

1725   las vuestras fiias amadas veades las bien casadas
          con maridos caualleros e con onrrados pecheros,
          Con mercadores corteses e con rricos burgeses.

1726   los vuestros suegros e suegras,
          los vuestros yernos e nueras,
          los biuos e los finados de dios sean perdonados.

1727   a vos de buen garlardon e de los pecados perdon;
          El angel esta ofr[e]nda en las sus manos la prenda;
          Señor, oy a pecadores por los nuestros bien fechores.

1728   tu rresçibe esta qançion e oye esta nuestra oraçion,
          que nos pobres te rrogamos por quien nos dio que comamos
          e por el que dar lo quiso, dios por nos muerte p[ri]so, vos de
                                         santo parayso.
     Amen.

as you do this for Him;
may you see the joy and pleasure
of the children you love so much.

1723 May you never see trouble,
may God let them grow
and become archdeacons,
be rich and healthy;
God keep them from blindness,
and preserve them from poverty.

1724 God, give them plenty of bread and wine,
give to the poor and lowly,
give them property and money,
to give to poor pilgrims,
give them apparel and clothes
to give to the crippled blind.

1725 May you see your beloved
daughters married well
to gentlemanly husbands
and honourable tax-payers,
well-mannered merchants
and wealthy townsmen.

1726 Your fathers-in-law and mothers-in-law,
your sons-in-law and daughters-in-law,
the living and the dead
shall be pardoned by God;
may He give you a good reward
and pardon your sins.

1727 May the angel take this
offering in his hands.
Lord, hear us sinners,
on behalf of our benefactors,
receive this song
and hear our prayer,

1728 for we, the poor, plead to you
for whoever has given us food
and for whoever wanted to give;
God, who died for us,
give you Holy Paradise.
Amen.

NOTES

Line 24 of the prose prologue: This quotation is not in the Book of Wisdom, though it is an idea often expressed in the Scriptures.

Line 80 of the prose prologue: These were Gratian's *Decretals*, written about 1140. It was a compilation which served as a basis for the teaching of canon law.

Line 80a: There has been much critical debate about this and subsequent textual references to songs and poems which do not in fact appear in the manuscripts. One view is that these were not added by copyists working from an archetypal manuscript, while it has also been suggested that the Archpriest was merely using an empty formula in this case. Possibly Juan Ruiz intended to add these songs but failed to do so.

Line 112d: The verb used in the original, *cruizar*, meaning 'to suffer', is clearly a pun on the Archpriest's name of Ruiz, as well as alluding to the name of the baker's wife, Cruz, and to Christ's suffering on the cross.

Line 114a: The poet uses the term *troba caçura* to describe the verse form of the next story about his messenger Ferrand García. This was the verse form used by the lowest category of minstrel, and Juan Ruiz probably uses it here because of the burlesque tone and subject matter of his poetry rather than its metrical form.

Line 116a: The meaning of this line, '*Cruz cruzada panadera*', is not totally clear in the original and once again has sparked off critical controversy. There seems to be an obvious allusion to a crusade in *cruzada*, though Michalski (*Romance Notes* XI, 1969) suggested a meaning of 'to impale' for *cruciar* here, which easily translates into sexual terms. The *panadera* or baker's wife was a traditional racy character in Castilian lyric poetry.

Line 116d: Joset points to the common idea of Andalusians as both daydreamers and typical crafty picaresque characters in vol. 1 of his edition of the *Libro de buen amor* (Espasa-Calpe, Madrid, 1974).

Line 119c: Though a rabbit was a valued foodstuff, Ferrand García's gift here has undoubtedly erotic undertones, both in the suggestiveness of the word itself and because of the rabbit's well-known capacity to reproduce freely.

Line 170b: Joset, *op.cit.*, has a useful note here about the possible autobiographical reference to the River Henares, as the river passes through the areas within the Archpriest's jurisdiction. However, he also points to an underlying suggestion that *avena* (oats) are symbols of lechery.

Line 171d: More songs referred to, but not extant in the manuscripts. See note to line 80a.

Line 281b: The name 'Mongibel' used in the Spanish was the medieval name for Mount Etna, symbol of Hell. The volcano erupted in 1183, killing 15,000 people.

Line 295a: The reference to gluttony in the desert relates to Psalm 78, verses 24–31, when the children of Ephraim were given a feast in the wilderness by God, at which they ate heavily. God slayed them as they ate.

Line 334a: Legal exception was the legal title or grounds which a defendant could plead to render the action of the plaintiff ineffective. It was a kind of demurrer.

Line 337d: Vilforado is the present-day Belorado in the province of Burgos. There is also a pun here on the words 'vil' and 'forado' meaning 'dirty hole'.

Stanzas 374–87: A great deal has been written on this parody of the canonical hours. See in particular Otis Green, 'On Juan Ruiz's Parody of the Canonical Hours' in *Hispanic Review* XXIV, 1958, pages 12–34. The Latin texts cited are all taken from the Psalms.

Line 381d: The Latin has been amended in this line, as the S manuscript has a scribal error.

Stanzas 436–51: These stanzas are missing from both the S and T manuscripts, existing only in Gayoso.

Line 438d: The meaning of the original *lagrimas de moysen* (literally 'Moses' tears') is obscure. The most likely explanation is that this refers to some kind of glass or sequinned embroidery decoration, or a kind of bead considered to have magical properties.

Line 441a: The word *pecas* at the end of this line in Gayoso has been amended by various editors to correct the line length, giving, among others, the term *pegatas*, or 'tricks'. *Pecas* has a perfectly valid meaning of 'freckles' both in modern and medieval Castilian, which has been used in the translation.

Line 470d: The tambourine has a double meaning, particularly in southern Spain, also denoting the female sexual organs.

Stanza 489: The person referred to in this stanza is ambiguous, as there is nothing to indicate whether the recipient of the gift is the potential lover, or her friend referred to in stanza 488.

Stanzas 548–63: These stanzas are missing from the S and T manuscripts, existing only in G.

Line 554c: This kind of usury was authentic, as described in one of Alfonso XI's royal ordinances drawn up in Burgos in 1315.

Line 556a: Master Roland was the author of a book on the subject of dice, which must have been quite well known.

Line 570d: The Spanish *dicha* here may be a pun on its meanings of 'luck' and 'something spoken'.

Stanzas 580–96: These stanzas are extant only in the G manuscript.

Line 596a: The name Endrina, which means 'sloe' in English, is possibly meant to indicate something of her character to the audience or reader. It may have some humour in it, since the sloe is bitter-sweet, or it may suggest the colour or texture of her skin.

Stanzas 665–8: These stanzas are extant only in the G manuscript.

Line 738a: Trotaconventos is used here for the first time as the name of the bawd herself and literally means 'convent-trotter'.

Stanzas 756–66: These stanzas are extant only in the G manuscript.

Line 763: Frieze was a rough, heavy woollen cloth and it was worn when people were in mourning.

Stanzas 765–6: There are six stanzas missing between 765 and 766 in all manuscripts, which in all likelihood narrated the start of the tale of the wolf deceived by a sneeze, which he took to be a good omen, from the Aesopic tradition, and which continues in stanza 766.

Line 812c: There appears to be a pun on 'branch' with its literal meaning, its association with good and bad luck (see lines 101c and 936c) and the name of Endrina's mother first used in stanza 824.

Line 869c: In spite of various attempts to decode the meaning of the word *tenico*, it remains obscure. All that can really be said is that it has a negative, pejorative sense, hence its translation here as 'wimp'.

Stanzas 877–8: There is a lacuna of approximately thirty-two stanzas in all three manuscripts between 877 and 878, which must have related Endrina's seduction and her reproach of Trotaconventos. Perhaps they were removed by a prudish scribe.

Line 919c: Urraca means 'magpie' in English, and may be a jibe at the talkativeness of the go-between. It had been used as a first name since at least the early twelfth century, as evidenced by Queen Urraca of Castile and León (1109–26).

Line 951a: St Emeterius's Day is 3 March.

Line 972cd: These two lines remain a mystery, as there is no serpent, Rando nor Moya which can be logically related to this passage. The Archpriest may be referring to a local tradition no longer known. For a fuller analysis see Joset, *op.cit*.

Line 980a: 'Ferruzo' refers presumably to the girl's husband or companion.

Line 1073d: Castro Urdiales was an important fishing port.

Line 1085c: Some editors have interpreted *fresuelos* in G as *quesuelos* or 'cheese', which seems an illogical introduction into the troops which are meats. Joset suggests a derivation from Vulgar Latin, *frixura*, and Old French *froissure*, meaning offal, which fits the context and has been used in the translation.

Line 1115d: Velinchón is in the province of Cuenca, where there are salt mines.

Line 1118a: Laredo was also a fishing port on the Cantabrian coast, from which conger eels came.

Line 1131a: At this point in the text the narrator changes from the friar confessing Carnal to the author addressing his audience or reader.

Line 1143a: King Hezekiah was condemned to death and reprieved by God, as described in Kings XX, 1ff.

Line 1146b: Requena is a small city in the province of Valencia.

Stanza 1152: In line a, the Speculum referred to is the *Speculum Judiciale* and the Repertorium the *Repertorium aureum juris,* both by Guillermo Durand (1230–96). Line b refers to the Cardinal of Ostia's having written a number of books, in particular the *Summa Hostiensis,* in the second half of the thirteenth century. With reference to line c, Innocent IV was Pope from 1243 to 1254 and was known for his legal works, while line d refers to the body of legal doctrine written by the Bolognese Guido de Baisio, notably his *Rosarium Decreti.*

Line 1184a: Medellín was a sheep-raising centre in Extremadura.

Lines 1187ab: The geographical references in these lines confirm their importance as sheep paths, as well as Juan Ruiz's accuracy of documentation.

Line 1205c: Pilgrims' staffs were decorated with carvings of a pious nature. The palm is the symbol of pilgrims in general and specifically of those returning from Jerusalem.

Line 1209d: Ronceveaux, or Roncesvalles, is a pass in the Pyrenees which formed part of the pilgrim way. It was also the scene of the famous battle of epic tradition, in 778, when the Christians were defeated by the Moors.

Line 1229b: This line remains obscure in the original, but appears to refer to a well-known Arabic song.

Line 1229c: Current thinking is that '*la mota*' refers to the famous La Mota castle in Medina del Campo.

Line 1235d: Much attention has been given to this line and to the identification of the Abbot of Borbones. It is likely to be another of the Archpriest's references to topical matters no longer apparent. For detail, see Joset, *op. cit.*

Line 1239d: There is a pun here on the word 'Amen' with its standard meaning of 'So let it be' and its other, Spanish use as an imperative of the verb *amar,* 'to love'.

Line 1251a: Friars traditionally dressed in wool.

Line 1278d: Paula may represent woman in general. The reference is obscure.

Line 1282d: A pun on oats as a cereal crop and on its symbolic meaning of 'pubic hair'.

Line 1312b: The Spanish for 'St Quitit', which is *Santa Quiteria*, contains a clear pun on the meaning of the verb *quitar*, 'to leave' or 'to quit'.

Line 1331c: The explanations given for the name of Sir Polo are rather far-fetched. See D. C. Clarke, 'Juan Ruiz as Don Polo', *Hispanic Review* XI, 1972, pages 245–59. It could perhaps be attributed to the need to create a suitable rhyme to fit in with the rest of the stanza.

Line 1346a: The name Garoza is Arabic in origin and can mean either 'girlfriend', 'fiancée', or 'bride'.

Line 1455b: Minor thieving offences were punished by cutting off the robber's ears or nose, or branding him.

Line 1489c: 'By my shoes!' was the characteristic exclamation of the go-between, as 'by my tonsure!' was for monks.

Line 1507a: See note to line 80a. Once again, the Archpriest describes a song which does not appear in the text.

Line 1542d: The Gregorian Mass was said for the redemption of the souls of the dead.

Line 1561b: There is some confusion in this line over the names of the children of Adam and Eve. Ham and Japheth were the sons of Noah, while Seth was Adam's son and Sem the son of Noah.

Line 1610a: A hyacinth was a semi-precious blue stone prized by people of ancient times. It may have been what we now know as an aquamarine.

Stanzas 1618ff: The name Furón used in the original has been translated because the figurative force of 'Ferret' seemed preferable to the exoticism of leaving the Spanish, of low rhythmic or musical value in this particular case.

Line 1634a: The era year 1381 was AD 1343.

Line 1690b: The Archbishop Gil referred to here was the powerful figure of Cardinal Gil de Albornoz, Archbishop of Toledo between 1337 and 1350, who allegedly had Juan Ruiz imprisoned at his orders.

Line 1698d: A bath was a great luxury in the Middle Ages.

Line 1703ab: Blanchefleur, Fleur and Tristan were three great heroes of

French epic narrative, evidently well known to the Castilian public of the time.

Line 1710ff: These blind beggars' songs appear only in the G manuscript.

RUIZ AND HIS CRITICS

In his Introduction to Elisha Kane's translation of the *Book of Good Love*, John Keller states that 'probably no other book written in Spanish, possibly not even *Don Quijote*, has raised such a harvest of criticism, theory and study of sources and influences as this one' (page xxxiv). That still holds true, for there are now approaching two thousand books, articles and reviews available for consultation, and clearly any survey of this critical material can give only a broad idea of areas of significance and interest. The following selection of brief extracts from critical writings on the text charts the general development of criticism from the nineteenth century to the present. Details of references written in English will be found in the Suggestions for Further Reading.

The first printed text of the *Book of Good Love* was published with a commentary by Tomás Antonio Sánchez in 1790. The earliest critical attitude, expressed by José Amador de los Ríos over fifty years later, was to view the work as fundamentally satirical and didactic. He considered Juan Ruiz to be an exemplary priest hoping to expiate his wickedness and show repentance and virtue through satire:

> His satirical genius, the irony which sprang constantly from his lips, and above all the nature of the ideas he developed infused his verse with that roguish vividness and freshness which contrasts with the implied seriousness of the social condition and the national character and constitutes the clearest feature of his poetic work.
>
> *Historia Crítica de la Literatura Española* (Madrid, 1863), vol. IV, page 199.

No significant critical work on the text appeared after this until the early twentieth century, when Julio Puyol produced a critical study of the Archpriest's work in 1906. In it he stressed both the originality of the subject matter and of the satire, and suggested that Juan Ruiz believed man should wrest as much joy from life as possible in a sad world:

> ... he loved life, and yet he was powerfully affected by what men think and do, their desires, their virtues and their squalor, a feeling he transformed into the inner pleasure of solitary meditation upon it all, with perhaps sympathy for poor mankind, subjected to the horrendous disproportion between the constant longing inherent in the common daily task, and the meagre victories over suffering. Perhaps in order not to add to its sum, he hid his tears with Democritus' smile. He was the first since Classical times to have this perception of the world, hence his facility as both a realistic writer and a satirical one, because realism and particularly satire, were the two great innovations of the Archpriest within the sphere of Castilian letters.
>
> *El Arcipreste de Hita, Estudio Crítico* (Madrid, 1906), pages 131-2.

Nearly twenty years later the great Spanish scholar Ramón Menéndez Pidal saw the *Book of Good Love* as ending the period of thirteenth-century didacticism and heralding the era of social, religious and personal rebellion. He found no didactic intention in the work, which he believed was firmly rooted in the European tradition, emphasizing its troubadour aspect, and the potential of the text to be performed or sung:

> So the Archpriest made the bold innovation of exerting his powerful poetic genius upon the minstrel poetry of the streets and squares, and turned a deaf ear to palace fashion. In this popular quality lies his most intimate originality, because the *Book of Good Love* owes its distinctive features in large part to the compositions of the Castilian minstrels, namely its jovial frankness, its sceptical, roguish humour, and the tendency to lists of words, as well as that charming and utter lack of order so characteristic of the lowest form of minstrelsy in the fifteenth century.
>
> *Poesía Juglaresca y Juglares* (Madrid, 1924), page 267.

In his 1931 edition of *Book of Good Love*, Julio Cejador y Frauca once more took up the idea of didactic purpose, claiming that Juan Ruiz used the first-person narrative to gain audience sympathy. He felt the entire work was a satire on fourteenth-century manners, bearing the message that man will overcome his weakness and renounce sin:

The essential idea of the book lies consequently in the portrayal of the man of the world, in particular the Christian priest, who knows the evil he does and repents, falls again into the trap of love and passion and finally conquers it. The unity of the idea could not be clearer, nor could the intention to satirize foolish clergy, naturally for their own benefit and that of others. In the same way that Cervantes' powerful genius converted all the society of his time into satire, and the humankind in books of chivalry into all humanity, the Archpriest's genius, perhaps as great as that of Cervantes, if less classical and measured, more primitive and untamed, converted the satire of the clergy into the satire of fourteenth-century society and of humanity down the ages.

> *Juan Ruiz, Arcipreste de Hita, Libro de Buen Amor* (Madrid, 1931), page xxi.

One of the most indispensable early studies of the *Book of Good Love* was made by Félix Lecoy. He situated the many themes and forms of the work within their particular traditions, examining sources as individual literary units. Lecoy claimed that the Archpriest had assembled fragments in one book, without doctrinal or moral unity, but that these are given shape by the 'autobiographical' narrative and the art of love:

The real meaning of this work lies in that short phrase in the prologue itself, where the author declares that after all, if his verses are of no benefit to those who are walking the path of spiritual health, they will at least serve as a guide for those undertaking a career in foolish passion.

> *Recherches sur le Libro de Buen Amor* (Paris, 1938, reprinted with new prologue and additional bibliography compiled by Alan Deyermond, Farnborough, 1974), page 361.

In his book *España en su historia* of 1948, Américo Castro approached the *Book of Good Love* in a completely new way which has had a lasting influence on later criticism. He believed the work had no true moral intention and that its vital, fluctuating reality was characteristic of Arabic models, in particular *The Dove's Neck-Ring* by Ibn Hazm:

The attention oscillates between prosaic simplicity and poetic tension, between what is known or learned and what is imagined. Ultimately, the essential theme of the *Book* is the oscillation between ambiguities of words, between morality and fantasy, between good and foolish love, between vulgar coarseness and artistic refinement. Juan Ruiz knew Islamic art wonderfully well.

España en su Historia (Buenos Aires, 1948), page 395.

María Rosa Lida de Malkiel took this idea even further, suggesting that the *Book of Good Love* was a *mudéjar* work, in other words the work of a Christian living under Moorish rule and immersed in Moorish and Jewish culture. She initially felt it was an artistic work with a solely didactic purpose, a view which she retracted latterly:

In short, the *Book of Good Love*, a work of *mudéjar* art, fits its Christian motifs into the structure of the Hispano-Hebraic maqamat. As a result, it is an artistic composition with a didactic purpose, which above all proposes to inculcate precepts of moral behaviour, and to that end utilizes the autobiography of the author, who acts as protagonist and teacher, repeatedly heaping ridicule on himself so as to warn the public against his own moral conduct.

Two Spanish Masterpieces (Urbana, 1961), page 32.

Although contemporary with Lida de Malkiel, Otis Green took a different view, that the *Book of Good Love* was a book of favourite poetry, a work of literary art based on sustained parody and not on didacticism. He saw it as a satire of the art of love:

I submit as a reasonable hypothesis – perhaps more illuminating than any other for the understanding of this complex work of art – that the doctrinal parts appear to a modern reader as subordinate to the overall spirit of fun-making, as payers-of-the-freight, regarded by the Archpriest as possessing merit, as worthy of him, indeed as inseparable from the work of art. Had not Geoffroi de Vinsauf said: 'The beautiful surface of the words, unless it be ennobled by sane and recommendable doctrine, is like a basely conceived picture, which pleases the observer standing at a distance, but is displeasing to him who looks at it from a closer vantage point.' Robert of Basevorn permitted the inclusion in sermons of jests, picaresque sallies, a certain amount of humour, and even shocking allusions which he places under the heading *iocatio opportuna*; but these should not be more than three to a sermon; and of course impossible fables or dirty stories are excluded (ibid. pages 70–1). This, or a similar concept of the preacher's art and duty, must have been known to Juan Ruiz; but in the *Libro de buen amor* he is much less concerned to preach –

according to my hypothesis – than to realize himself as an artist. His work, he has told us, surpasses that of other poets by a ratio of a thousand to one.

Spain and the Western Tradition (University of Wisconsin, 1963), vol. 1, page 70.

Just two years later, Anthony Zahareas's book *The Art of Juan Ruiz, Archpriest of Hita* picked up on Green's hypothesis and broke new ground in escaping from the established critical polarity between didacticism and entertainment, European origins and Arabic and Hebrew origins. He examined the book first and foremost as a work of art and suggested that the poetic function took precedence over any others:

It is Juan Ruiz's artistic sensibility, evident in the narrator's ironic manner, that records the nuances of the entire *Libro*. This self-styled moralist uses many sources, changes them and exaggerates them in a spirit of pure, rollicking fun designed to challenge and amuse the reader. He burlesques sermons, plays upon words and ideas, teases the dogmatist, suggests contraries and finally perhaps has a laugh even at the expense of the didactic scheme of his own moral commentary. To see the author – lover, narrator, commentator, craftsman – as anyone other than a marvellously alert master of every situation he borrows or creates is to miss the artistic aspect of the *Libro*. For historical purposes, we know next to nothing about Juan Ruiz the man, but for all practical purposes, we know a great deal about Juan Ruiz the author: he acts as the central narrative personality; he always confronts his readers with judgements on his poems' meaning or art; he assumes a diverting character of his own; he presents his moral discourses in an ironic or comic vein; he infuses playfulness with telling hints about the human condition; he pretends to guide the reader's understanding but leads him to ambiguities and contradictions; he often shatters splendidly the illusion of traditional authorities, the better to point up humour and vital preoccupations; and he is a proud personality, always conscious of his literary skills. To sum up: the argument which I have proposed is that the 'I' of the *Libro de buen amor* is not only Juan Ruiz the man or priest, not only the minstrel or goliard, not merely the satirical-didactic 'I' of the sinner and moralist, but also – and above all – Juan Ruiz the poet.

The Art of Juan Ruiz, Archpriest of Hita (Madrid, 1965), pages 216–17.

The constant and profuse dedication to the study of the *Book of Good Love* continues. Since Zahareas's seminal study of 1965, the critical tendency has been to see the work as ambiguous and intentionally conveying multiple meanings, resulting in a more nuanced view of its didacticism (Brownlee, 1985; Burke, 1982). Contemporary theory has left the *Libro* largely untouched other than in a few isolated studies (e.g. Fleischman, 1990). Areas of current critical interest include: the audience of the work; intertextuality and the author's attitude to the sources and genres he uses; humour, parody and the grotesque according to Bahktin's methodological orientations; linguistic aspects relating to the history of the language and poetic characterization; the structure of the work; its underlying ideology. No dominant theory has emerged, although there are exciting new ideas on social background (Zahareas, 1977; Kelly, 1984) and on the bawdy nature of the text (Vasvari, 1991). The largely unpublished work by John Walsh has brought to life the view of the poem as an oral and performance text, full of song and gesture, and is a complement to by far the most major recent development in criticism of Ruiz's writing, *The Ethics of Reading in Manuscript Culture: Glossing the Libro de buen amor* (Princeton University Press, 1994), in which John Dagenais proposes a change of focus, 'a reorientation of the way we approach medieval literature', from privileging the author and/or text to privileging the individual reader and all the medieval activities, such as commentary, translation and copying, that mirror reading. This view gives central position to the reader and arose from Dagenais's attempts to understand the literary ideas of the *Book of Good Love* through their sources in Latin culture as transmitted to thirteenth- and fourteenth-century Castile. It is a stimulating new way of interpreting the work, which recognizes the power of incoherence in the text, rather than seeking to impose coherence upon it.

There is an excellent bibliography available for those who are interested in delving deeper into the mysteries of the text: *Bibliografía sobre Juan Ruiz y su Libro de buen amor*, by José Jurado (Madrid, 1993).

SUGGESTIONS FOR FURTHER READING

General Background
O'Callaghan, J. F., *A History of Medieval Spain* (Ithaca, 1975).
Reilly, B. F., *The Medieval Spains* (Cambridge University Press, 1993).

Critical Books and Articles
Bloomfield, Morton W., *The Seven Deadly Sins, an introduction to the history of a religious concept* (Michigan State University, 1952).
Brenan, Gerald, *The Literature of the Spanish People* (Cambridge University Press, 1951), pages 69–87.
Brownlee, Marina Scordilis, *The Status of the Reading Subject in the 'Libro de buen amor'* (Chapel Hill, University of North Carolina, 1985), Studies in Romance Languages and Literatures, no. 224.
Burke, James F., 'A New Critical Approach to the Interpretation of Medieval Spanish literature', *La Corónica* 11 (1982–3), pages 273–9.
Castro, Américo (trans. by E. L. King), *The Structure of Spanish History* (Princeton, 1954).
Dagenais, John, *The Ethics of Reading in Manuscript Culture: Glossing the Libro de buen amor* (Princeton University Press, 1994).
Fleischman, Suzanne, 'Philology, Linguistics and the Discourse of the Medieval Text', *Speculum* 65 (1990), pages 19–37.
Gericke, Philip O., 'On the Structure of the Libro de buen amor: A Question of Method', *Kentucky Romance Quarterly* 28 (1981), pages 13–21.
Green, Otis, *Spain and the Western Tradition* (Madison and Milwaukee, 1936–66), vol. 1 chapter II, pages 22–71.
Gybbon-Monypenny, G., ed., *'Libro de buen amor' Studies* (London, 1970).
Gybbon-Monypenny, G., ed., 'Autobiography in the *Libro de buen amor* in the light of some literary comparisons', *Bulletin of Hispanic Studies* XXXIV (1957), pages 63–78.
Hernández, Francisco J., 'The Venerable Juan Ruiz, Archpriest of Hita', *La Corónica* 13 (1984), pages 10–22.

Kelly, Henry A., *Canon Law and the Archpriest of Hita* (New York, 1984).

Lida de Malkiel, M. R., *Two Spanish Masterpieces: The Book of Good Love and the Celestina* (Urbana, 1961).

Michael, Ian, 'The Function of the Popular Tale in the *Libro de buen amor*', *'Libro de buen amor' Studies*, ed. G. B. Gybbon-Monypenny (London, Tamesis, 1970), pages 177–218.

Sturm, Sara, 'The Greeks and the Romans: the Archpriest's warning to his reader', *Romance Notes* X (1968–9), pages 404–12.

Vasvari, Louise O., 'The battle of Flesh and Lent in the Libro del Arcipreste: Gastro-genital Rites of Reversal', *La Corónica* 20 (1991–2), no. 1, pages 1–15.

Walker, Roger M., 'Towards an interpretation of the *Libro de buen amor*', *Bulletin of Hispanic Studies* 43 (1966), pages 1–10.

Zahareas, A., *The Art of Juan Ruiz* (Madrid, 1965).

Zahareas, A., 'Celibacy in History and Fiction: the case of the *Libro de buen amor*', in *Ideologies and Literature* 1, no. 2 (1977), pages 77–82.

Zahareas, A., 'Structure and ideology in the *Libro de buen amor*', *La Corónica* 7 (1978–9), pages 92–104.

Comparative Works

The following works may be of comparative interest:

Boccaccio, *The Decameron*, translated in the Penguin series (Harmondsworth, 1995).

Brewer, D. S., *Medieval Comic Tales* (Cambridge, 1973).

Chaucer, G., *The Canterbury Tales*, modern English version by Neville Coghill (Harmondsworth, Middlesex, 1951).

Bibliographical Details of Earlier English Translations

Kane, Elisha K., ed., *The Book of Good Love of the Archpriest of Hita*, translated into English verse (New York, 1933).

Mignani, Rigo, and Di Cesare, M. A., *Book of Good Love*, prose translation (State University of New York Press, 1970).

Willis, Raymond, ed., *Libro de buen amor*, with an introduction and English paraphrase (Princeton University Press, 1972).

Zahareas, A., and Daly, S., *The Book of True Love: A Bilingual Edition*, translation in verse and introduction by Saralyn R. Daly (Pennsylvania State University Press, 1978).

TEXT SUMMARY

The *Book of Good Love* is the great literary masterpiece of the Spanish Middle Ages. It is a text of baffling complexity, a collection of apparently disparate elements presented amid dazzling metrical virtuosity, a text rich in meaning and ambiguity, and sustained by an underlying core of lasting artistic value. The book has aroused enduring critical interest and there are innumerable monographs and general studies on virtually every aspect of this outstanding and enigmatic poem. It consists of 1,728 stanzas of verse written in a remarkable variety of metrical forms, plus a prose prologue. As its title suggests, the predominant theme is love, and specifically the apparent conflict between the spiritual love of God and carnal love. The book has the appearance of an autobiography, but of dubious authenticity, and in spite of constant encouragement to the reader or listener to understand its meaning correctly, our efforts to do so are sabotaged by humour and ambiguity.

The *Book of Good Love* begins with an invocation to God and the Virgin Mary, asking for help in the author's time of trouble. This is followed by the only part of the work which is written in prose, a prologue in the form of a learned sermon of the kind which would have been addressed to the clergy. In this the Archpriest sets out his didactic, recreative and artistic aims, but confuses his listeners or readers by stating a wish to warn against worldly love, while giving advice in how to indulge in it. The first narrative consists of a comic tale about the dispute over sign-language between the Greeks and the Romans, after which we are exhorted to interpret both the tale and the book correctly.

Next comes the first 'autobiographical' adventure, in which the protagonist falls in love. He sends a woman go-between to the lady concerned, who refuses to listen. His second love affair ends in humiliation when he realizes that his go-between, this time a young man called Ferrand García, gets Cross the baker's wife for himself. He then has a third unsuccessful attempt at an affair, which is followed by an allegorical vision of Love, who appears before him in person. The protagonist berates Love over these disastrous failures, using the opportunity to develop a treatise on the seven deadly sins, each illustrated by a fable or story and all originating, according to the Archpriest, in Love and his evil ways. Love responds by giving him advice on how to succeed in future amorous ventures. At Love's suggestion the protagonist consults Venus herself and, now named Lord Melon of the Kitchen Garden, he embarks upon a successful affair with a young widow called Endrina, a name which means 'sloe' in English. His famous go-between, an old crone named Trotaconventos, literally meaning 'convent-trotter', persuades Endrina to visit her house by means of a debate in which they exchange *exempla*, or short, moralizing tales. Here Endrina is seduced and afterwards severely chastizes Trotaconventos, who arranges for the lovers to marry. The Archpriest concludes this story by warning women against the wiles of men.

After another dalliance with a lady who dies, the Archpriest takes to the mountains of the sierra, partly to assuage his grief and partly in search of new experiences. He finds these in the form of four *serranas* or mountain women, all of whom are strong, hideous and frightening. Freezing cold, lost and hungry in the winter mountains, the Archpriest is forced by these women to pay with sex for the food and warmth they provide.

These racy episodes are succeeded by some contrite religious lyrics to the Virgin Mary, which lead on to one of the central episodes in the *Book of Good Love*, the wonderful mock epic battle between Carnal and Lent, where the soldiers in their armies are meat, fish and other foodstuffs. The Archpriest develops the strong European tradition of Carnival and Lent poems in a unique and humorous way. Initially Carnal's army is defeated by Lent and he is captured and forced to do penance. This allows the author to develop a more serious subject, the nature of confession and the question of priestly authority and jurisdiction in relation to it. Carnal is unabashed and escapes by means of a ruse to join forces with Love and overcome Lent, who flees as the victors ride triumphantly through the town amid a glorious welcome from religious orders and laymen and women alike.

Although the Archpriest as narrator is involved in a minor way in these events, he plays a principal role in the next story, when Trotaconventos persuades him that he would be wise to love a nun. She approaches a nun she knows, called Garoza, and their ensuing argument is the basis for another series of exemplary tales, plus a description of the protagonist's appearance. Eventually Garoza is persuaded to see the Archpriest and they enjoy a relationship which is entirely ambiguous in terms of its sexual dimension. Whether or not the nun is physically seduced, she dies within two months, and is shortly followed by

Trotaconventos, for whom the Archpriest composes an epitaph and lament. This leads to a powerful denunciation of death and a treatise on the arms available to the Christian in his fight against worldly sin. But laughter is never far away and the author cuts short his lesson to digress on the virtues of small women.

The text ends with various religious lyrics, songs of beggars and scholars and a highly ambiguous statement about the meaning and purpose of the book, plus a witty exposé of the very real problem of clerical concubinage and its conflict with papal legislation in the concluding poem of the clergy of Talavera.